D1001362

# FROM TREATY PEOPLES
# TO TREATY NATION

GREG POELZER AND KEN S. COATES

# from treaty peoples to treaty nation

## A ROAD MAP FOR ALL CANADIANS

**UBC**Press · Vancouver · Toronto

23 22 21 20 19 18 17 16 15    5 4 3 2 1

Printed in Canada on FSC-certified ancient-forest-free paper
(100% post-consumer recycled) that is processed chlorine- and acid-free.

LIBRARY AND ARCHIVES CANADA CATALOGUING IN PUBLICATION

Poelzer, Greg, author
From treaty peoples to treaty nation : a road map for
all Canadians / Greg Poelzer and Ken S. Coates.

Includes bibliographical references and index.
Issued in print and electronic formats.
ISBN 978-0-7748-3087-4 (bound : trade edition). –
ISBN 978-0-7748-2755-3 (pdf). – ISBN 978-0-7748-2756-0 (epub)

1. Native peoples – Government policy – Canada. 2. Native peoples –
Legal status, laws, etc. – Canada. 3. Native peoples – Canada – Economic
conditions. 4. Native peoples – Canada – Social conditions. 5. Canada –
Ethnic relations. I. Coates, Kenneth, author II. Title.

E92.P56 2015          971.004'97          C2015-901826-9
                                          C2015-901827-7

Canadä

UBC Press gratefully acknowledges the financial support for our publishing
program of the Government of Canada (through the Canada Book Fund),
the Canada Council for the Arts, and the British Columbia Arts Council.

This book has been published with help from the University of
Saskatchewan Publications Fund and from the International Centre
for Northern Governance and Development.

UBC Press
The University of British Columbia
2029 West Mall
Vancouver, BC V6T 1Z2
www.ubcpress.ca

# contents

# PREFACE: TOWARDS EQUALITY
# OF OPPORTUNITY

IN 2012, WE PUBLISHED a series of opinion pieces in Canada's national newspapers expressing our outlook on the future of Aboriginal affairs in Canada. At the time, the papers were full of stories about the dreadful housing conditions and infrastructure crisis at the Attawapiskat First Nation in northern Ontario, complete with overheated rhetoric and finger pointing. On February 17, in the *Globe and Mail,* we outlined the two camps of public opinion in "We Are All Responsible for the Plight of Canada's First Nations": there were those who believed that responsibility lay with the Government of Canada and those who claimed it lay with First Nations themselves.

The first camp, composed of a number of First Nations leaders and many non-Aboriginal Canadians, argued (then as now) that Ottawa should take primary responsibility for the mess. It had, after all, created the Indian Act in 1876 (the federal statute dealing with status, local government, and the management of reserve lands and communal monies), the reserve system, and residential schools. The federal government needed to move quickly to address the dependency and despair that characterized First Nations communities. It needed to provide equality of result to remove what many considered a black mark on the nation.

The opposing camp argued that Aboriginal people needed to clean their own house. They needed to root out corrupt politicians, abandon uneconomical reserves for towns and cities, reject further reliance on government handouts, and free themselves and the country from their unsustainable dependence on the Government of Canada. Some writers, such as the provocative University of Calgary political scientist Tom Flanagan, recommended that "special" status for Indians be eliminated. Flanagan's work on Louis Riel, Aboriginal rights, and Indigenous government has generated strong and critical responses from Aboriginal leaders for over a quarter of a century and received substantial support from critics of Aboriginal rights.

We argued then, and we argue now, that both camps have it wrong.

Canadians as a whole must take ownership of the challenges facing Aboriginal communities: substance abuse and suicide, poverty and deplorable housing and living conditions, high dropout rates and unemployment. But we as a people, or peoples, need to stop looking for a single, sweeping solution, whether it be constitutional change, a government program, or a radical overhaul of Aboriginal governance. Meaningful change will require not just policy makers but millions of Canadians to step forward to create the Canada they want. As we wrote in the *Globe and Mail,* we must invite Aboriginal people "fully into the fold as neighbours, friends, and full partners in Confederation. It is about time all Canadians began to live as treaty peoples."

After our opinion pieces ran in the papers, prominent political and business leaders, Aboriginal *and* non-Aboriginal, contacted us personally to make positive comments. We were taken aback, though, by the vitriolic comments posted online. Here are a few samples from the *Globe*:

> > If I was allowed to live tax free, have a panoply of services, and funds available to me, and ignore a variety of laws (like hunting seasons), etc., etc. Yeah, I would feel disadvantaged . . . uhuh . . .

> > The authors of this piece have come to the wrong conclusion and any remedies they prescribe are therefore wrong. The native people are mostly responsible for their present condition and future remedies. There are a few native bands who have developed a new economy for their members. But most have developed a culture of reliance on government for their well being. I see very little desire to take responsibility for their current position. Many reserves are located far from places of

employment, and yet the band members insist on their rights to live on their reserve. Any reasonable person would recognize the unsustainable position they are in and pick up and move to where employment could be found. But not these natives. There is absolutely no reason for the taxpayers to continue to support these people, when they are unwilling to help themselves.

> I am NOT responsible for the plight of the First Nations people. Until they decide to take responsibility for themselves and become aware that THEY are responsible for their own lives, they will NEVER escape from the poverty, rampant alcoholism, substance abuse, crime, and unemployment that is so prevalent on reserves.

Seventy-five percent of the comments were negative, and close to half fell along the lines of "Get a job," "Stop whining," and "Clean up your act – then we'll talk."

No one who spends any time working in Aboriginal affairs is immune from the expression of such sharp opinions, and the response to our opinion pieces served as a reminder that the path ahead will not be easy. Yet we remain optimistic, and it is in that spirit that we have written this book. We recognize that many Canadians have had their fill of Aboriginal affairs over the past forty years, but supportive comments from some Canadians and our conversations with community leaders have made it clear that we stand not at a breaking point but at a break*through* point. Everyone agrees on the need for change – we simply lack agreement on how best to move forward.

This consensus – which can more pessimistically be viewed as the fundamental contradiction in Canada's current Aboriginal policy – became clear in the aftermath of the much-debated Kelowna Accord, an intergovernmental agreement signed in 2005 by Prime Minister Paul Martin and leaders of the main national Aboriginal organizations and the provincial and territorial governments. Ever since Confederation, Conservative and Liberal governments had followed a cautious, piecemeal approach. Now, the accord's negotiators were promising a fundamentally new approach to Aboriginal affairs in Canada and laying the groundwork for sweeping commitments. Aboriginal leaders enjoyed unprecedented control over the substance of the negotiations and used it to set the main priorities: housing, education, economic development, health, and accountability. Ottawa's financial commitment was unprecedented – $5.1 billion over five years, an amount unheard of in Canadian history, with a promise of a second five-year commitment to be negotiated after the accord expired.

The main commitments focused on practical matters: improved housing, education, health care, and water and sewage; the encouragement of private homeownership; and increased support for Aboriginal governments. Critics, particularly in the Conservative Party, warned that the accord was expensive, not carefully thought out, and constituted an expansion of "government knows best" approaches. Clearly, the Tories were not on board – a key consideration as the country headed into an election.

Yet it was clear that a new and unprecedented consensus existed among federal and provincial leaders – the status quo was no longer tenable. During the Trudeau years, roughly from 1968 to 1984, it was the provincial premiers who had routinely led the opposition to Aboriginal demands. At Kelowna, by contrast, Gordon Campbell, premier of British Columbia, insisted that Canada, if it wanted to be a truly compassionate nation, needed an agreement like the one now being crafted. The meeting ended with the recognition that short-term infusions of money would not meet Aboriginal people's needs and aspirations, with a promise of further sessions, and with a highly public affirmation of the status and authority of Aboriginal governments. Long-term observers of Aboriginal–government relations in Canada believed that something profoundly important had happened at Kelowna and that, at least conceptually, the country had set out down a new path. That there was growing recognition that Aboriginal communities had the right to self-government amounted to a step towards the acceptance of a third order of government (not only federal and provincial/territorial but also Aboriginal). The discussions themselves made it clear that no one expected quick solutions to the challenges facing Aboriginal people, which had been several hundred years in the making. Critically, the meetings signalled that equality of opportunity for Aboriginal people had become a national priority for Canada. The agreement held the promise of real and sustainable partnerships – the only conceivable foundation for a long-term solution to the challenges facing Canada's Indigenous peoples.

The Kelowna Accord did not survive the next few months. During the 2006 election, Aboriginal issues got some attention but did not take centre stage. Stephen Harper's Conservatives went public with their opposition to the accord; many Aboriginal leaders spoke out against the Conservative position and clearly supported the Liberals. Paul Martin tried to use uncertainty about the accord's future, along with other policy positions, to demonize the Conservatives, suggesting that his opponents had a hidden agenda. To some degree, though, all of the contending parties recognized a simple truth about electoral politics in Canada: Aboriginal issues, however urgent, simply do not matter much to non-Aboriginal Canadians.

When Canadians elected the Conservatives to a minority government, Prime Minister Harper and his newly appointed Indian affairs minister, Jim Prentice, declared themselves and their party to be committed to the principles and goals of the accord. Yet their first budget stepped back from the commitments that had been negotiated at Kelowna. The news that the accord would not go forward was met more with resignation than with anger. There was no public outcry, and Aboriginal leaders turned to developing good relations with the new administration. In retrospect, many Canadians had misgivings about making major financial commitments to Aboriginal communities.

But there was an unexpected twist to all this. Although he did not support the accord, Harper adopted a conciliatory stance on Aboriginal issues once in office, and Prentice was one of the most qualified people ever to hold the Indian Affairs portfolio. The Conservatives picked up on the work begun by the Liberals and concluded three land claims with BC First Nations in 2006. When a cabinet shuffle loomed in early 2007, Aboriginal politicians urged Harper to leave Prentice at his post. Harper listened to them, even though he needed Prentice elsewhere. After a cabinet shuffle later in the year, Prentice's replacement, Chuck Strahl, maintained the conciliatory line, as would Strahl's successor, John Duncan. The Conservatives might have disagreed with the accord's details, but clearly they understood that much more was needed to address Aboriginal issues and aspirations. Provincial and federal politicians across the political spectrum had come to realize that change had to happen.

In light of all this, *From Treaty Peoples to Treaty Nation* is an optimistic book. Issues of profound importance continue to challenge Canada's Aboriginal peoples – First Nations, Métis, and Inuit. But at the same time, much has been changing for the better, major improvements are under way, and significant opportunities lie ahead. Indeed, we argue that negative commentary and unrelenting stories of poverty and despair, in the media and on message boards, have actually limited Aboriginal people's options and had a negative impact on how non-Aboriginal Canadians view their obligations. There is too much focus on failure, and not enough on success. There are ways forward, and they do not necessarily require a remaking of Confederation or radical changes in Aboriginal people's aspirations. This book offers all Canadians practical, viable steps forward.

In an effort to define (or redefine) Aboriginal–newcomer relations in Canada, Aboriginal leaders and scholars have taken up metaphors such as the Two Row Wampum and have long referenced concepts such as the honour of the Crown, nation-to-nation negotiation, and the power imbalance between the colonized and the colonizer. In this book, we examine all of these views, but we also argue that there is a simple and direct concept – one steeped in law and history and embedded in the Constitution – that points the way to the future. This concept – that Canadians are treaty peoples – is deeply meaningful to Aboriginal peoples, yet it has largely been forgotten by other Canadians. The Prairie First Nations who signed the Numbered Treaties with the Crown between 1871 and 1921 talk openly about being treaty peoples. The concept expresses their belief in the promises made at the time of treaty and their dreams for a better relationship with non-Aboriginal people and governments.

Canada has a tradition of treaty making dating back to the eighteenth century, when the British Crown signed "peace and friendship" treaties in the Maritimes. Throughout Canada's history, Aboriginal people have generally understood these treaties as the foundation for a living and sustained partnership. Leaders often speak of the "spirit of the treaties," which to them is more significant than the specific terms and technical language contained in the documents. These treaties were often ignored by later British and Canadian governments, and while this robbed them of much of their practical vitality, it did nothing to diminish their social and symbolic importance.

Scholars such as Peter Russell and Sákéj Henderson have reintro-
duced the concept of treaty peoples to national debates, highlighting
the prospect for more positive and constructive partnerships. Prairie
First Nations understand that treaties are expressions of hope and primarily about relationships. They are not dry, ossified documents but
starting points for friendship, collaboration, and respectful coexistence. Non-Aboriginal Canadians "get" the legal and technical aspects
of treaties but have largely missed the boat on the point that treaties
bind Aboriginal and non-Aboriginal Canadians together in a permanent and mutually beneficial partnership.

Many Canadians have forgotten that in a hundred ways we are all
treaty peoples, that two groups of people came to the original bar-
gaining table, and that hundreds of agreements have been signed
since the eighteenth century: constitutional agreements, self-government agreements, and agreements to devolve federal and provincial
responsibilities to Aboriginal governments. Aboriginal people have
participated in the Canadian military and in the country's ceremonial
life; they have forged intellectual partnerships at universities and colleges; they have sought and accepted apologies for the harms done to
them in residential schools. And this is only a partial list. The core
treaty between First Nations and other Canadians is not one document or a hundred. Rather, the centrepiece of this relationship is the
realization that First Nations and other Canadians agreed from the
early days of New France, and later British settlement, to coexist in
friendship, to work to find the best solutions for the country as a
whole, and to build relationships that will endure and allow all parties
to flourish culturally, socially, economically, and politically. That the
history of Aboriginal–newcomer relations is marked by so little violence and so few confrontations illustrates that Aboriginal peoples
have respected their part of the bargain.

Some will argue that our proposal is too radical and that honouring
the treaties and taking up our responsibilities as treaty peoples will
entail abrogation of authority and power to Aboriginal peoples. We
ask them to consider this: although we never apply the term to the relationship that has evolved between Quebec and the rest of Canada
(or, for that matter, between Canada and every province in the nation),
this relationship can be characterized as an informal treaty. The arrangement has never been fully defined and is clearly a work in progress;

nonetheless, it serves as a comprehensive accord between two or more cultures. Many Aboriginal scholars, as we discuss, share the view that the treaties are alive, vital, and important documents that should shape the future, as they defined the past, and that reconciliation based on equality is possible. Non-Aboriginal writers such as Michael Asch, in *On Being Here to Stay: Treaties and Aboriginal Rights in Canada* (2014), question the legitimacy of the Crown's assertion of sovereignty and urge Canadians to rethink, at the most fundamental level, their relationship with Aboriginal peoples. In *The Comeback* (2014), John Ralston Saul argues that "if we start down a road of shared reconciliation and restitution, we will have taken a crucial step in building a sense of ourselves and the country. It is a matter of being true to where we are, to what is fair and possible here. That consciousness, that sense of ourselves, will solidify our ability to live together and to do so in an atmosphere of justice." Clearly, Canadians continue to debate and review the fundamental elements of Aboriginal-newcomer relations.

As we will show, other countries have done much better than us at bringing the treaty concept into the core of their existence. New Zealand has a foundational accord – the Treaty of Waitangi of 1840. That treaty, ignored for more than a century, has been reborn as the central pillar of New Zealand society, redefining Māori–Pākehā (newcomer) relations and, in ways that have proven complicated, controversial, and constructive, the very nature of what it means to be a New Zealander. In the United States, treaties with American Indians remain influential, primarily in the level of autonomy asserted by tribal authorities and recognized by the US government. In many instances, the political re-empowerment of American Indian communities has also resulted in substantial socioeconomic transformation.

In our hearts, we believe that Canadians are already on the path to becoming a treaty nation. During the opening ceremonies of the Vancouver Winter Olympics in 2010, cheers engulfed the stadium when the chiefs of the four First Nations on whose lands the games were taking place were afforded head-of-state status by the organizers. The applause spoke volumes to the emergence of a new, revitalized understanding of Canada. You can see it, too, in the ceremonial life that now surrounds other high-profile events, in the art in our embassies and major galleries, and in the slowly growing realization that

First Nations are not rivals, enemies, or constitutional children but true partners in the grand Canadian experiment. The practice of non-Aboriginal people acknowledging that they stand on the traditional territories of First Nations – unheard of even a decade ago – is now expected protocol.

Canadians need to get serious about being treaty peoples and realize that the responsibility for doing so lies with everyone, not just with governments and the courts. Beyond legal and contractual requirements, beyond the complex negotiation of land claims and self-government agreements, Canadians must treat Aboriginal people with respect and understanding. The treaty system in Canada is first and foremost a pact between cultures and peoples and only secondarily a set of legal documents defining relationships between governments and First Nations. In the spirit of moving Canada along a new path, we offer Canadians a road map for change. This book is our attempt to break the logjam, to move beyond rhetoric and finger pointing, and to delve into the art of the possible. Canada can and must do better. Aboriginal governments and peoples can and must do better, even if the weight of history falls disproportionately on their shoulders. Canada needs new ideas and a new level of commitment.

In *From Treaty Peoples to Treaty Nation,* we begin by reviewing the barriers – historical and contemporary – to productive and mutually beneficial relations between Aboriginal peoples and other Canadians. We then review the key ideas and metaphors brought forward by Aboriginal and non-Aboriginal scholars and commentators to explain long-festering problems in Canada. We consider the intellectual elements of the arguments and their practical application in the twenty-first century. In a shift from the standard approach to the study of Aboriginal affairs in Canada, we also focus on the many positive, constructive, and beneficial developments that have occurred in Aboriginal communities and organizations over the past two decades. It is easy to get lost in the bad news, to be rendered catatonic by stories of hardship and despair, and to get drawn into highly emotional battles between advocates of Aboriginal sovereignty and those who would eliminate Aboriginal rights. These arguments are part of the Canadian political landscape, but they are wholly inadequate for dealing with contemporary realities and finding common ground.

The story of Aboriginal success and achievement is well hidden in this country and must be shared. Remarkable stories about acts of reconciliation – deliberate and positive steps taken by Aboriginal and non-Aboriginal groups – provide reasons for considerable optimism. Developments in Yukon, Northwest Territories, and Saskatchewan provide solid reasons to believe that viable solutions will be found. The crises in Aboriginal communities are real, but it's important to recognize that the First Nations, Métis, Inuit, and non-Aboriginal people of this country have made great strides in developing more positive and constructive relationships.

In this book, we offer practical, realistic, and affordable solutions to the challenges facing Aboriginal peoples and Canadians seeking a path towards reconciliation. Some are radical and, if implemented, will be unique to Canada; others already exist, either in one part of Canada or in another country. We hope our recommendations will reach governments (Aboriginal, federal, provincial, and municipal), corporations, and Canadians at large. We are realistic enough to accept that some of our ideas may not work and that many will not be attempted. But we act in the full realization that Aboriginal people have carried far too much of the burden for this country's inadequate and lethargic policy making. Aboriginal people understand the full meaning of the concept of being treaty peoples and have been waiting for non-Aboriginal Canadians to catch on. It is time.

But here is the greatest irony – and the greatest challenge. In the final decades of the twentieth century, national guilt and the Canadian social conscience intersected, leading to an outpouring of support for intervention in Aboriginal affairs and a commitment to government-led programs and support. The rapid empowerment of Aboriginal peoples through the courts and political processes that followed, however, upset what appeared to be a Canadian consensus about the urgency of addressing Aboriginal needs and aspirations. Generosity of spirit also ran up against anger and deep frustration among Aboriginal people. A generation of Aboriginal leaders launched bitter critiques of Canada and its policies, reflecting the politicization of Aboriginal issues and growing despair at the community level. Aboriginal and other Canadians, having seemingly found a middle ground of government-led problem solving, started to head in opposite directions.

It would be a mistake to underestimate the current of anger and animosity that exists towards Aboriginal peoples and affairs in our country. Frustration mounts with each Aboriginal legal victory or new political agreement, and Canadians are generally uneasy about the emergence of wealthy and powerful Aboriginal leaders and communities. Many new Canadians, in particular, have had trouble recognizing the logic of massive financial transfers, Aboriginal self-government, and legal entitlements. As the political power of this group grows, the national consensus is further eroding. Many Canadians reject Aboriginal aspirations. They resent modern treaties, the duty to consult on resource development, and federal transfers to Aboriginal communities; they resent what they perceive as a culture of dependency on reserves and radicalism in the Assembly of First Nations and other Indigenous organizations. There were strong negative reactions when the Assembly of First Nations rejected a deal with the Government of Canada to add $1.5 billion per year to First Nations educational funding. The Supreme Court of Canada's decision to recognize Aboriginal title on non-treaty lands in the William (Tsilhqot'in) court case in 2014 disturbed many non-Aboriginal people. Where we see people working together to achieve a common ground, they see the failure of decades of government intervention to do anything to solve the deep crises in First Nations, Métis, and Inuit communities.

It would be a mistake to simply write off these critics' concerns. The overwhelming majority of them are not racists, and they are not uncaring people. Most simply believe that self-reliance trumps reliance on government. But their point of view is based on a number of misunderstandings: "Aboriginal Canadians get everything for free"; "None of them pay taxes"; "all the chiefs are crooks"; "band governments are incompetent"; and so on. There is a strong undercurrent of opposition to special status and to the growing legal authority of Aboriginal communities. Many people want to shut down isolated reserves and move those residents to towns and cities. When Aboriginal people stop or slow down a development project of potential value to society as a whole, frustrations come to the surface. When these folks speak up, supporters of Aboriginal aspirations can be too quick to judge them as bigots and hatemongers – terms that apply to only a tiny percentage of opponents.

There is nothing inherently wrong with opposing new plans or initiatives. Criticizing self-government or other ways of empowering Aboriginal people is not automatically racist – and people profoundly resent being labelled as racists simply because they disagree with the legal, academic, and political consensus that has emerged around Aboriginal rights in Canada. The problem, ultimately, is not that the status quo does not work to the satisfaction of all Canadians but that we are on the verge of things getting much worse. Canadians face the return of Aboriginal radicalism.

Canadians have been troubled by the conditions that have faced Aboriginal people for generations, but we as a nation have tended to take a paternalistic approach to the search for solutions. After the 1990 Oka Crisis, the first well-publicized violent conflict between First Nations and the federal government in the late twentieth century, Prime Minister Brian Mulroney established the Royal Commission on Aboriginal Peoples and tasked it with examining the root causes of Aboriginal difficulties and recommending changes. This proved to be a controversial exercise. In its first year, the commissioners focused more on identifying problems than on articulating solutions, and non-Aboriginal interest declined throughout the multi-year inquiry. The final report, issued in 1996, offered sweeping recommendations for a renewed relationship based on four principles: recognition, respect, sharing, and responsibility. The principle of recognition called on all Canadians to recognize that "Aboriginal people are the original inhabitants and caretakers of this land and have distinctive rights and responsibilities flowing from that status" and that "non-Aboriginal people are also of this land now, by birth and by adoption, with strong ties of love and loyalty." The third principle recognized that sharing "is the basis on which Canada was founded, for if Aboriginal peoples had been unwilling to share what they had and what they knew about the land, many of the newcomers would not have lived to prosper. The principle of sharing is central to the treaties and central to the possibility of real equality among the peoples of Canada in the future."

These principles were clear and simple. And beyond them, the final report articulated seven general and hundreds of specific recommendations to address the challenges facing Aboriginal Canadians. The seven general recommendations called for a radical restructuring of Aboriginal–non-Aboriginal relations in Canada, including a new

Royal Proclamation, an Aboriginal Treaties Implementation Act, an Aboriginal Lands and Treaties Tribunal Act, and an Aboriginal Nations Recognition and Government Act. The report provided this country with a toolbox full of ideas and suggestions about how Canada could reconfigure its relations with Aboriginal peoples. But the very comprehensiveness (and cost) of the recommendations spooked Canadians, so they did not receive widespread public support.

The report was more effective at articulating the challenges than in proposing broadly acceptable solutions. Again, everyone recognized there was a problem, but there was nothing approaching a nationwide consensus about how to solve it. Then as now, Aboriginal radicalism had little support outside Aboriginal communities and only a sliver of support in academia. At the same time, opponents of Aboriginal empowerment generated real fury among Aboriginal Canadians. Decades after the commission, Canadians' long-held affection and compassion has eroded even further, and not just as it relates to Aboriginal peoples. Belief in the benign intervention of the nation-state in the affairs of citizens has given way to fear and anger. Non-Aboriginal people reject the idea that more money will solve problems even as Aboriginal leaders, facing ongoing crises in their communities, demand greater funding. More and more non-Aboriginal Canadians oppose the legal and constitutional empowerment of Aboriginal governments, just as those governments are gaining the levers of power and the ability to manage them more effectively.

*From Treaty Peoples to Treaty Nation* offers solutions and suggestions that fit with the core values of most Canadians, Aboriginal and non-Aboriginal. Most Canadians believe fundamentally in *equality of opportunity*. They embrace the idea that government *and* society should level the playing field for both individuals and communities. These ideas run deep in our country and are reflected in everything from equalization arrangements among Canada's provinces to student loan programs. As a nation, we cherish individual rights and freedoms as enshrined in our Charter of Rights and Freedoms, and we defend the rights of individuals *and* communities. But we also recognize that all Canadians have a measure of responsibility for their own well-being. The level of volunteerism in Aboriginal and non-Aboriginal communities across Canada speaks to that sense of responsibility; so does the willingness of individuals to serve on band and municipal councils. Canadians as a whole are pragmatic about creating institutions that enable their values and ideals to thrive. They embrace the idea of Canada as a community of communities, and they define their country in large measure by the quality and availability of social assistance, medical care, and other support programs.

In this book we argue that there are three keys to creating a country in which all Canadians can enjoy and accept their rights and responsibilities as treaty peoples. First, Aboriginal people must be accorded status and honour in both state and society. Second, Aboriginal political communities must be empowered within our political systems, possibly through a Commonwealth of Aboriginal Peoples, which would replace the Department of Aboriginal Affairs. Such a body would create more space for Aboriginal self-government and more acceptance of the idea of a third order of government. It would also open a space for redefining Aboriginal citizenship, addressing questions of accountability, and accommodating the political needs of urban Aboriginal populations. Third, Aboriginal people must be put on an equal footing with other Canadians through expanded economic opportunities.

If we don't do these things, we will never evolve into a treaty nation. We have taken some pragmatic steps in this direction, but we need to take more – steps that will demonstrate a commitment to compromise, mutual understanding, and innovation. It is hard to overstate the importance of Prime Minister Harper's 2008 apology for residential schools as a means of addressing the status and honour of Aboriginal peoples in Canada. Other steps could include a parliamentary review of the royal commission, exchanges between Aboriginal and non-Aboriginal students, and accommodations for Aboriginal culture in schools and workplaces. In the economic realm, stereotypes and national mythology notwithstanding, Aboriginal people and communities are anxious, indeed sometimes desperate, for economic opportunity. Indigenous leaders often speak out against the welfare culture that pervades many of their communities. Indeed, Aboriginal people acknowledge that decades of welfare dependency, or what Ellis Ross calls "managing poverty," have not served their communities well.

We are optimistic about the opportunities for success. Improvements in Aboriginal peoples' economic performances will enhance their status and increase their political power; enhanced political authority will strengthen the hand of Aboriginal businesses and workers. For their part, Aboriginal Canadians will have to recognize the limits of Canada's generosity and flexibility. They will, to secure the necessary compromises, need to realize that concessions will be required on their part, especially as they relate to public accountability and exemptions from comparable levels of taxation. For their part, non-Aboriginal Canadians will have to recognize that they must take important and enduring steps and that the time is now.

Many able and insightful commentators have written at length about the future of Aboriginal people within Canada. In this book we will be acknowledging and outlining their ideas and contributions with knowledge and respect. Many of the most compelling and passionate arguments, however, have one fatal flaw: they are disconnected from Canadian practicalities. However strong the passions and commitment of Aboriginal leaders, Canada is not going to recognize Aboriginal people's demands for full sovereignty, although it might – and should – support more than limited self-government. Arguments advanced by non-Aboriginal Canadians in favour of eliminating Aboriginal legal status and closing reserves are likewise completely unworkable. The rejection of the extreme positions on both sides of the debate still leaves an enormous amount of space for innovation, creativity, and new ideas. It is on this common ground – part of the long-standing tradition in this country of finding accommodations between Aboriginal peoples and newcomers – that the future of our country rests. So long as our future strategies stay true to the core principles that define Canada, including equality of opportunity and the idea that Canada is a community of communities, we have reason to hope.

# ACKNOWLEDGMENTS

This book was inspired by the hundreds of Aboriginal students who Greg taught in postsecondary programs in northern Alberta and northern BC in the 1990s and in Saskatchewan in the 2000s and 2010s. These students spoke frankly about the real challenges their communities faced. However, they were also committed to building self-reliant communities within Canada and were proud to be both First Nations or Métis *and* Canadian. Métis students in Grouard held tremendous pride in the achievements of the 1990 Métis Settlement Act, the first and only legislation of its kind in Canada, while Nisga'a students in Gitlaxt'aamiks (then New Aiyansh) took pride in the fact that their First Nation had made Canadian history by pioneering a third order of government.

At that time, however, most books and academic research focused on the problems facing Aboriginal peoples in Canada. Students were perplexed. Even in the midst of difficult social problems and economic challenges, Aboriginal students saw resilient cultures and vibrant communities. Just as importantly, they rightly saw that Aboriginal people had made, and continue to make, significant contributions to the development of Canada as a nation. They often asked, "Why doesn't anyone talk about the positives of Aboriginal peoples? Why does everyone only focus on the problems?"

*From Treaty Peoples to Treaty Nation* also originated over lunch with the Honourable Ron Irwin, then minister of Indian affairs and northern development. Ken was living in Hamilton, New Zealand, and teaching at the University of Waikato. Irwin was on a fact-finding trip to meet with the Government of New Zealand and Māori leaders. In the midst of a robust and constructive conversation, the minister let slip his frustration with academics. To paraphrase his comments, for this happened in the mid-1990s, he stated: "You academics are great at identifying problems, but you are short on providing solutions." It was a fair challenge.

So, some twenty years ago, we started working on the book that eventually became *From Treaty Peoples to Treaty Nation*. Our students inspired us tell the very real and vitally important and positive story of Aboriginal peoples in Canada. We were also challenged by elected officials to spell out practical and realistic solutions to building Canada as a treaty nation.

Over the last two decades, we have accumulated numerous personal and professional debts. Our work has been greatly enriched by conversations – and debates – with Aboriginal leaders and academics, non-Aboriginal scholars, government officials, and many people across the country. We have been in meetings where much-maligned government officials worked hard to find viable and affordable policies to address and meet Aboriginal people's needs. We have been in meetings with Aboriginal leaders and administrators (people who work under daunting pressure and with a complex set of files of crucial importance) as they struggled to find the resources to provide the most basic services to their members while simultaneously negotiating complicated legal and political agreements with provincial, territorial, and federal governments. We extend great thanks to these people for sharing their thoughts, ideas, and commitment to finding an honourable and prosperous path for Aboriginal communities in Canada, one based on values shared by all Canadians.

While it is not possible to thank, by name, everyone who has helped us, we would particularly like to extend our gratitude to individuals, Aboriginal and non-Aboriginal alike, who have helped us over the years, including our Aboriginal friends and colleagues Chief Perry Bellegarde, Ovide Mercredi, Jodi Wilson-Raybould, Denelle Spencer, Justin Ferby, Herb George, Don Ryan, Georgina Martin, Chris Thomas, Rena Zatorski, Sean Atleo, Guy Lonechild, Ed John, Deanna Nyce, Justa Monk, Roger Augustine, Kim Recalma-Clutesi, Chief

Tammy Cook-Searson, Elijah Harper, Valerie Galley, Robert Joseph, Rebecca Jamieson, Milton Tootoosis, Don Deranger, Guy Larivière, Peter Beatty, John Paul, Danette Starblanket, Candace Wasacase-Lafferty, Ron Michel, Kelley Lendsay, Gary Merasty, Else-Grete Broderstad, Sean Willy, George Lafond, Mary Ellen Trupel-Lafond (whose comments on an early draft had a major influence on our thinking), Dwayne Lasas, Yvonne Boyer, Wayne Semagamis, Zane Hansen, George Henry, and Ken Kane. We have benefitted, too, from the insights and ideas of such important non-Aboriginal policy thinkers as Michael Wernick, Jim Prentice, Chuck Strahl, Harald Finkler, Rob Norris, Shirley Bond, George Paul, Brian Lee Crowley, Tom Mann, Brenda Boucher, Tony Penikett, Peter Vician, and many senior civil servants in the federal, territorial, and provincial governments. We want to draw special attention to the assistance provided by Tom Molloy, Saskatoon lawyer, former University of Saskatchewan chancellor, and the best land claims negotiator in Canadian history. That a man of his stature and accomplishment took the time to read the entire manuscript, making many excellent suggestions for corrections, is a testament to his commitment to Indigenous peoples and being a mentor and friend, qualities we treasure greatly.

We have been fortunate to work with wonderful colleagues at several universities. We first met at the University of Northern British Columbia, where Ken was the founding vice-president (academic) and Greg was one of the famous "First Forty" faculty members. We were blessed with many excellent colleagues whose work and dedication to Aboriginal issues influenced our thinking, including Robin Fisher, W.R. Morrison, Gary Wilson, John Young, Tracy Summerville, Gail Fondahl, Mary-Ellen Kelm, Margaret Anderson, James McDonald, Antonia Mills, and Perry Shawana.

Prior to our meeting, Ken had worked at the University of Victoria, where he benefitted greatly from the professional friendships of Eric Sager, Peter Baskerville, Ian McPherson, John Lutz, and Victoria Wyatt. He then moved to the University of Waikato and the University of New Brunswick at Saint John, where he learned a great deal from John McLaughlin and Rick Miner, as well as from Wade MacLauchlin. Ken also spent six years at the University of Waterloo, where he capitalized on discussions with such impressive colleagues as Alan Cairns, Whitney Lackenbauer, John English, Graham Brown, and (six blocks down the road at Wilfrid Laurier University) Susan Neylan, Terry Mitchell, and Chris Alcantara.

Greg had also taught in Aboriginal social work programs in northern Alberta, where he gained tremendously from colleagues William Pelech and Reginald Smith. He is especially grateful to the students he met in Aboriginal social work programs in Grouard, High Level, and Slave Lake. While at the University of Saskatchewan, Greg served as founding dean of undergraduate studies, University of the Arctic, a consortium of more than 150 universities, colleges, Indigenous organizations, and NGOs across the eight Arctic states committed to program delivery and research in and with northern and Indigenous communities. He is particularly grateful for discussions with Sven Roald-Nystø, Vasilly Robbek, Lars Kullerud, Cindy Dickson, Margaret Imrie, Bård Berg, Bjørn Sagdahl, Glenys Plunz, Anatoly Sleptsov, Rune Fjellheim, Sally Weber, Outi Snellman, Mary Simon, Audrey McLaughlin, Mac Clendenning, Richard Boone, Richard Caulfield, Rune Ryden, Olav Hesjedal, Peter Sköld, and Scott Forrest. However, his most important insights into scholarship and teaching have come from his parents, Frances and Herold Poelzer.

Ken and Greg connected again at the University of Saskatchewan, a campus with many scholars devoted to the study of Aboriginal policy and to improving the life conditions of Indigenous peoples. These colleagues include such eminent scholars as J.R. Miller, Bill Waiser, Trish Monture, Sákéj Henderson, Marie Battiste, Winona Stevenson, Dwight Newman, Keith Carlson, Lee Swanson, David Zhang, Maureen Reed, Bram Noble, Doug Clark, and our special friends and colleagues Bonita Beatty and Bob Bone.

We have had rich academic lives, made very much the better by the willingness of so many colleagues to share ideas, offer constructive criticism, and tolerate our long commentaries on Aboriginal issues in Canada. Beyond these institutional colleagues, we have capitalized over the years on the talents and ideas of such diverse scholars, all of whose work we admire greatly, as Frances Abel, Kiera Ladner, Graham White, David Robinson, Terry Rodon, Roger Epp, Kerry Abel, Peter Kulchyski, David Robinson, Frances Widdowson, Tom Pocklington (who supervised Greg's PhD thesis), Gurston Dacks, Tom Flanagan, Harold Finkler, A.J Ray, David Breen (Ken's PhD supervisor), Colin Coates, and Steven Patterson.

Greg was the founding director of the International Centre for Northern Governance and Development at the University of Saskatchewan. With the generous support of the Government of Saskatchewan and Cameco, he built the centre into perhaps the leading Subarctic research and service unit in Canada, with a particular commitment to northern Saskatchewan. Ken took over as director in 2013. The ICNGD team played a significant role in the preparation of this book, and special thanks are due to Audra Krueger, Mark Korthuis, Wilna Masuskapoe, D'Lee Johnson, Paola Chistie, Kathy Walker, Tessa Mannix, Cathy Wheaton, Heather Exner-Pirot, Colleen Cameron, Emmy Neuls, Joelena Leader, Stan Yu, Greg Finnegan, Ryan Gibson, and Heather Hall. Collectively, they comprise the most effective northern research team in the country. A special note of thanks is due to Sherilee Diebold-Cooze, Ken's executive assistant, who has been an enormous help with this project for almost a decade – that she joined ICNGD in 2014 was an enormous relief to Ken. Ken and Greg are also associated with the Johnson-Shoyama Graduate School of Public Policy at the University of Saskatchewan and have enjoyed its collegial and supportive environment. In particular, they wish to acknowledge the many contributions of their friends and colleagues Michael Atkinson, Murray Fulton, and Dionne Pohler and the endless help provided by Tracey Howell-Perrett and Erica Schindel.

That this book has finally emerged in print is due in large measure to the support and tenacity of our friends at UBC Press. Darcy Cullen has shepherded this book through the complex maze of university press approval processes and has made countless suggestions for improvement to the manuscript. We learned early on to bow to her advice. Nadine Pedersen has been great to work with on promotional aspects. Lesley Erickson has been wonderful to work with on the editing and production side of the house, and our manuscript benefitted greatly from the careful ministrations of Matthew Kudelka. We can say, without a moment's hesitation, that this book is much stronger for the contributions, attention, and commitment of UBC Press staff.

Special thanks, as well, to the anonymous readers who examined the manuscript on several occasions. Their careful and detailed reading saved us from significant errors. Even more importantly, they challenged us to refine our arguments and explanations, resulting in a significantly better work. Anonymous peer reviewing is the lifeblood of the academic publishing enterprise, but we wish, at this final stage of the process, that we could find out the readers' names so that we could thank them, profusely, for their major contributions to this book.

A project that took some twenty years to complete required, finally, enormous commitment from our families. When we started this project, Greg had two boys (Gregory and Max), and Ken had two sons (Bradley and Mark) and a daughter (Laura). Ken has added a daughter (Hana) and a son (Marlon) in the interim. Greg got a dog. Greg added a daughter-in-law (Darci); Ken gained two (Nikki and Gillian) and a son-in-law (Josh). Greg now has his first granddaughter, Emma. Ken has almost seven: Katie, Christopher, Hazel, William, Spencer, and Victoria, plus one whose birthdate coincides with the publication date of this book. There is a reason twenty years seems like a long time!

Our wives, Anna Poelzer and Carin Holroyd, have been gracious and forgiving beyond belief. The sacrifices that they made so that this book could be completed have not gone unnoticed, and they certainly are appreciated. Indeed, the support they have provided has been the fuel that pushed us to complete a project that worried, perplexed, and frustrated us for many years. For these practical reasons, and for the love and encouragement they provided, we are pleased to dedicate this book to them.

# FROM TREATY PEOPLES TO TREATY NATION

# introduction

THE STRUGGLE to find common ground is nothing new. Indigenous peoples and newcomers in the northern half of North America have been seeking workable accommodations for several hundred years. From the arrival of the first Europeans to the present, these very different peoples have sought – and typically found – ways to coexist in relative peace and to considerable mutual benefit. From the days of the first European explorers through the fur trade and various military alliances, Indigenous peoples and newcomers generally managed to avoid the battles and massacres that have plagued most other frontiers in history. Treaties, partnerships, friendships, intermarriage, cultural sharing, cooperation: these were the hallmarks of early contact.

The passage of time soon told a bleaker story. Imported diseases ravaged Indigenous peoples. Aboriginal groups found themselves drawn into the Europeans' brutal wars. Aboriginal peoples suffered through the peaceful occupation of their lands and experienced a jolting transition from being economic and military partners to wards of empire and nation. As with so many historical transformations, the impacts of these changes were rarely immediately evident. Canadians in the first decades of the twenty-first century are generally unaware of the mistaken assumptions that have shaped the contemporary world; in much the same way, our ancestors were oblivious to the long-term impact of their values and actions.

Despite their ignorance, non-Aboriginal Canadians set about solving the "Indian problem." After generations of conflict, cooperation, trade, and partnership ended with the Indigenous population being shunted onto reserves and to the margins of society, the country's political leaders began worrying about how to deal with their Aboriginal subjects. The point here is that the debate that now bedevils Canadian officials, angers Indigenous supporters, and frustrates Aboriginal leaders is nothing new. The list of ideas for meeting the needs of Aboriginal Canadians grows longer with each passing decade, yet Canadians seem to have forgotten that we have been travelling down crisscrossing paths for many generations. The history of Indigenous–newcomer contact resists easy categories. Even so, some broad themes can serve a useful guide.

## INDIGENOUS PEOPLES AS PARTNERS

For most of Canadian history, European settlers counted on strong partnerships and alliances with Indigenous peoples. The fur trade – the dominant economic force in Canada's mid- and Far North from the 1600s until well into the twentieth century – required close cooperation between the fur companies and Aboriginal peoples. There were certainly inequities in this trading relationship, but First Nations were tough bargainers and generally extracted a fair return. For a time in the late eighteenth century, the Hudson's Bay Company (established in 1670) and its Montreal-based rivals fought bitterly; intense competition caught Aboriginal traders in a vicious tug-of-war. The fur trading companies relied on Aboriginal people and struggled to maintain cordial relations with them, and both sides often got a good deal. More to the point, the fur trade was the first, longest-lasting, and most successful example in Canadian history of our ability to find common ground.

Canada's governments built the Indigenous–newcomer relationship around partnerships. The authorities in New France routinely made political and military alliances with First Nations in the region. The French relationship with the Mi'kmaq survived for many decades, often in the face of determined efforts by the British to break the alliance. Only after the French left the region in the 1750s did the Mi'kmaq negotiate peace and friendship treaties with the British. According to some historians – and the Supreme Court of Canada would concur two centuries later in the *Marshall* decision – the Mi'kmaq believed that their accords with the British guaranteed an ongoing partnership with them. So it was that around the Great Lakes and the St. Lawrence, the First Nations developed a complex web of alliances with the French and later the British that would continue up to the War of 1812 between the latter and the newly founded United States. Both the British and the First Nations saw these arrangements as nation-to-nation alliances. And those alliances were solidified through gift exchanges and by the healthy respect the British authorities extended to First Nations leaders and warriors. The British government's Royal Proclamation of 1763, which committed it to signing treaties with Indigenous peoples before occupying their lands, arose from this collaborative spirit – and from the realization that conflict with First Nations would wreak havoc on Britain's plans to settle and develop the colonies. The idea of working in partnership, or at least in cooperation, with Aboriginal people was central to Britain's strategy for governing its colonies. The proclamation established, in law and practice, the centrality of this commitment to working with First Nations.

Even before the War of 1812, Britain had depended on its Aboriginal allies. During the American Revolution, the British relied heavily on support from the Iroquois. In recognition of this contribution, the government assigned the Iroquois a large piece of what is now southern Ontario – the Haldimand Tract along the Grand River. (That tract would shrink dramatically over subsequent decades. The Six Nations are still battling that loss in the courts.) First Nations in what is now central Canada expected the good relationship they had developed with the British to serve as the foundation for their place in the rapidly evolving British North American society. Alliances made sense. The First Nations knew that European immigrants were coming and would be eager to carve farms out of the forests and to build industries along the lakes and rivers. In a rapidly changing world, a partnership with the British would protect them from the excesses of immigrant men, who were known to be heavy drinkers and lecherous towards Aboriginal women. Alliances would make it possible for Aboriginal people to adjust to the new order, mainly through education and training. A now little-known treaty – the Robinson–Superior Accords of the 1850s – established formal and legal relationships between the British and the First Nations. To the parties involved, this arrangement promised to ensure the First Nations' long-term engagement with British North American society.

But when hostilities ended on the continent, the idea that Aboriginal peoples would be full partners, or allies, disappeared. During the decades of war, the First Nations had been vital allies; then peace came, and they were forgotten. The Mi'kmaq in the Maritimes were the first to experience this profound marginalization. Their treaties were ignored, and they were pushed to the social and economic fringes of the rapidly industrializing region. Much the same thing happened around the Great Lakes. After the War of 1812, for all their fine words and solemn pledges, the British no longer saw Aboriginal peoples as important long-term allies. Instead, they were viewed as child-like and as unsuited for the modern industrial world. Indeed, with endemic diseases such as tuberculosis rapidly depleting their numbers, it was no sure thing that Aboriginal people would even survive as distinctive societies. So the British developed a new policy towards the Aboriginal population: they were to be assimilated gradually into the British North American mainstream, except in the sparsely populated northern and remote regions, where they would likely continue as hunters, trappers, and gatherers. The British Colonial Office found support for this new approach among Christian missionaries, who hoped that the Bible and British civilization would sweep away what was left of Indigenous barbarism and paganism. In an ironic twist, missionaries and government officials worried, and rightly so, about the impact that less savoury elements of British North American society – traders, soldiers, miners, other frontiersmen – would have on the New World's Indigenous peoples. Church and state agreed that the First Nations had to be protected from alcohol and frontier debauchery until such time as they were ready to take their place, shoulder to shoulder and plough to plough, with the non-Aboriginal industrial workers and farmers who were the backbone of the new society.

## THE DISAPPEARANCE OF ABORIGINAL PEOPLES

One of the strongest assumptions governing Aboriginal affairs in Canada (and the United States and Australia) was that Indigenous people would disappear. The logic seemed unassailable. From the time the first Europeans arrived until the early twentieth century, Aboriginal populations dropped steadily, sometimes precipitously. They had lived for centuries without exposure to European diseases. Then the newcomers arrived carrying "virgin soil epidemics," and by the late nineteenth century, Aboriginal societies across the continent had been ravaged by diseases for which traditional medicines and healing practices provided little relief. Smallpox, the most virulent of all imported illnesses, killed millions of Indigenous people the world over and destroyed whole communities in British North America. Some groups, such as the Beothuk in Newfoundland and a small Inuit population in Hudson Bay, disappeared entirely. In many other cases, like the Huron, catastrophic population losses forced groups to combine for survival. Across the continent, dozens of Aboriginal groups lost between 50 and 90 percent of their people to epidemics. Government agents and missionaries urged the survivors to settle in agricultural communities, where they could be educated, trained, Christianized, and protected. Once Indigenous peoples adapted to more sedentary lifestyles, they faced a new scourge, tuberculosis, which continued the killing. All of this convinced many government officials that Aboriginal peoples would vanish sooner or later. Meanwhile, for a generation or two, government policy focused on protecting and assisting the "noble savages," who were doomed by God and Empire to be dominated and eventually replaced by Europeans.

Early in the twentieth century, the process slowly reversed itself. Better health care, a national campaign against tuberculosis, and strengthening immunity to introduced diseases halted the population decline. By the 1930s, the country's Aboriginal population had begun to grow again. The Aboriginal birth rate increased dramatically, sometimes approaching Third World levels. Ottawa could no longer assume that Aboriginal people would one day vanish. Visions of their physical extinction were now replaced by assumptions that they would one day lose their social and cultural distinctiveness.

## ABORIGINAL POLICY IN THE AGE OF EXPANSION

In the latter half of the nineteenth century – decades that saw the founding of the Dominion of Canada in 1867 and the expansion of the new nation to the east, west, and north – British and Canadian authorities implemented a new strategy for Aboriginal peoples, developed with little input from the affected communities. Under the terms of union (outlined in the British North America Act of 1867; after 1982 called the Constitution Act), the new Government of Canada gave itself responsibility for Indian people, continuing the pattern begun in the colonial era. The government codified its relationship with Aboriginal people in the Indian Act of 1876, one of the most fundamental documents in Canadian legal and political history. The Indian Act assigned ward-like status to First Nations, giving the government extensive control over many aspects of their lives and ensuring that First Nations people on reserves did not enjoy full citizenship rights, such as voting, the right to own land, and the ability to run a business.

Although the concept attracted little attention at the time, the Indian Act also defined who qualified as an "Indian" in the eyes of the federal government. Those with status (full rights as an Indian under the Indian Act) were marked as distinct from non-Status Indians (i.e., those with a non-Aboriginal father) or Métis, neither of which enjoyed Aboriginal rights. Inuit were not mentioned in the Indian Act, and seventy years passed before a legal challenge defined Canada's ongoing responsibility for the Inuit. The legal rights of the Métis (people of mixed ancestry, typically children of Aboriginal women and non-Aboriginal men and their descendants) remained in limbo much longer (a court case due to be heard in 2015 could provide some measure of finality on this important question). Canadian policy makers expected some groups, especially the Métis, to achieve full participation in the Canadian mainstream. But when the Métis took umbrage at this and pushed back against the European westward expansion, the government changed course. After suppressing Métis resistance in Manitoba in 1869–70 and a full-scale rebellion in Saskatchewan in 1885, Ottawa gave very little thought to their needs and aspirations. It provided them with scrip, whereby each eligible Métis would be entitled to claim land for his own use; they assumed that this would result in them eventually taking their place as able participants in the new economy.

Regarding the Inuit and First Nations in the Far North, officials hoped that hunting and the fur trade would continue to keep them off government rolls. Governments at this time avoided expensive commitments to their citizens and lacked both the funds and the inclination to launch support programs. Federal policy in the northern reaches of the country consisted of selectively enforcing Canadian law, providing rudimentary health care where possible, and offering small relief payments (usually allocations of food) to the small number of Aboriginal people who were truly incapable of looking after themselves.

For the rest, the government was more ambivalent. The authorities' goal was to assimilate Aboriginal people to European ways. It was believed they weren't ready for it, so they were segregated from the rest of the Canadian population. This was not intended to be a permanent state of affairs, but rather a holding position until the educational and spiritual efforts of the state and its Christian partners could take full effect. Crucially, the Department of Indian Affairs was not an important government department. It attracted little national attention, save for occasional criticism for spending too much money. No federal government would assign a high priority to the department until after the Second World War. With little funding, few employees, and a mandate that centred on ensuring that no further crises erupted in the field, the department was far from being an activist or interventionist agency.

To achieve its limited goals, the federal government sought ways to encourage assimilation while continuing to protect Aboriginal people. It negotiated treaties with First Nations starting in 1870, which removed them from the best agricultural land (earmarked for European settlement) and drew them into the farm economy (which they themselves wanted). To the government's surprise, several of the western First Nations took well to farming. Confronted with strong evidence of successful adaptation, the government reduced the expenditures it had promised in the 1870s treaties, undermining progress in this area. The cutbacks were made before First Nations had a chance to adapt fully to commercial farming, which effectively cut them out of this burgeoning economic sector. The government managed Aboriginal reserves poorly; it focused mainly on minimizing costs, maximizing opportunities for non-Aboriginal people, and attending to the political and patronage interests of the governing party. Led by officials such as Duncan Campbell Scott, the department sought to eradicate "Indianness," in the belief that Aboriginal language, culture, and spiritual and economic traditions were preventing Aboriginal people from participating fully in Canadian society. As the First Nations became economically and socially integrated with mainstream society, reserves and Indian status would disappear – or so Ottawa thought.

Physical separation provided an opportunity for Indian Agents, schoolteachers, and missionaries – often one and the same, or closely connected in mission and mindset – to "civilize" Aboriginal people. The government believed that by keeping First Nations away from non-Aboriginal Canadians, it could slowly raise their wards to the standards of the rest of the country. When basic, reserve-based education proved ineffective, department officials launched an extensive program of industrial and boarding schools. The industrial schools provided First Nations students with an opportunity to learn marketable skills, the better to ease their transition to paid work. These and other boarding schools required children to be removed from their parents and communities, thus giving teachers a chance to transform the values, customs, habits, and aspirations of their students. The use of Aboriginal languages was discouraged at these institutions, when not actively suppressed. Traditional skills received short shrift. Long periods away from families ensured that students were exposed, uninterrupted, to a Christian, Western, industrial social environment. The schools did not work as intended. As Canadians now well know, they would become the focus of enormous controversy in the decades that followed, generating thousands of legal challenges, largely on the basis of physical, sexual, or cultural abuse that the students suffered while attending them.

The federal government surmised that Aboriginal people were clinging to their culture too tenaciously. While the churches applauded from the sidelines, Ottawa passed a series of amendments to the Indian Act that outlawed crucial Aboriginal cultural practices. The West Coast potlatch, a cornerstone of regional economic and social relations, was decried as anti-capitalist and non-Christian. Efforts to destroy the tradition pushed it underground as communities refused to give up a practice that was so central to their culture. The government imprisoned Aboriginal leaders for refusing to obey the regulations. The tight controls now being instituted included a pass law that required First

Nations individuals heading off reserve to first secure permission from the Indian Agent; also, First Nations people could no longer sell livestock or produce without the agent's permission. These initiatives were meant to establish government control and stifle Aboriginal independence. In 1927, the federal government went so far as to bar Indian groups from hiring lawyers for the purpose of challenging the Crown. This undermined efforts by church groups and other supporters to press for greater recognition of Aboriginal rights.

Aboriginal individuals and communities resented the regulations and chafed under federal control. Some groups, especially in BC and southern Ontario, sought relief in the courts; when that failed, they resorted to direct petitions to the British Crown or, famously, the League of Nations in the case of the Mohawk. First Nations across the country complained about Ottawa's failure to honour treaties, to protect Indigenous hunting and fishing rights, and to keep the commitment the British had made to sign treaties before occupying traditional lands. Aboriginal communities began banding together to press their case – residential schools, ironically, developed common cause among many students – but found governments largely unmovable and the general public uninterested in their plight. Indigenous peoples protested when and as they could. They ignored regulations, such as the prohibition on drinking alcohol, which they found ridiculous. Passive resistance to government officials became commonplace. Separation from the rest of Canadian society, intended to prepare Aboriginal people for integration, provided a buffer from the government's rules and allowed language and culture to survive systematic attacks.

By the 1920s, policy makers realized that the country's Indian "problem" was not going away. There was little enthusiasm in Ottawa for spending large sums on Aboriginal initiatives, and outside a few Christian denominations, there was little public concern about the state of Aboriginal communities. Efforts at assimilation had largely failed, and Aboriginal people remained far outside the social and economic mainstream. Most of them lived far from cities, on reserves and in isolated northern regions where gathering, hunting, and fishing remained important to survival well into the 1950s. Residential and industrial schools had not prepared a generation of young people for entry into Canadian society – although the teachers kept trying, and the children continued to pass through the classrooms and dormitories.

Successive governments knew that something had to be done, for there was clear evidence that Indigenous people remained socially and economically marginalized. But public interest was low. Then as now, there was no consensus on what could or should be done.

## THE POSTWAR SOCIAL WELFARE AGENDA

Towards the end of the war, Western nations recoiled in horror as they uncovered evidence of Nazi efforts to exterminate European Jews. Around the same time, North Americans realized that they too had been guilty of racism, especially towards Japanese Canadians and Americans. The casual acceptance of racial distinctions had caused enormous suffering and diminished everyone in society. The postwar response to all of this included the founding of the UN in 1945, international pledges to respect the collective rights of ethnic minorities, and strong efforts to prevent further genocides and to respect the human rights of all people. In this climate, Western countries found themselves forced to address their history of racial discrimination. When Canada and the United States criticized other countries for ignoring basic human rights, they found themselves being attacked as hypocrites because of their treatment of Aboriginal populations.

Canada's renewed interest in the plight of Aboriginal people also reflected a growing sense that the state could and should address major social problems. During and shortly after the war, the government begin laying the foundations for the Canadian welfare state. Mother's Allowance, Unemployment Insurance, postwar housing projects, and the like established a new pattern of government activism. Wealthier Canadians paid through their taxes for programs designed to alleviate economic suffering and to build a sense of optimism and opportunity for all. As the country engaged in a crucial exercise of introspection, the condition of Aboriginal people stood out as a glaring example of Canada's failures. Farley Mowat's exposé of conditions among the Inuit in his best-selling *People of the Deer* (1952) was a loud call to action but not the only one; demands by Aboriginal war veterans for greater equality also drove the country to act. Other criticisms of Canadian Indian policy followed, including Harold Cardinal's best-selling *The Unjust Society* (1969) and Heather Robertson's *Reservations Are for Indians* (1970). The government set about providing economic and social opportunities for Indigenous peoples.

An activist state, middle-class liberal guilt, and growing national and international attention to human rights generated a surge in Aboriginal programs. The belief that education was the foundation for social and economic change resulted in the expansion of day schools, the incorporation of First Nations students into provincial and territorial schools where appropriate, and the rapid expansion of residential schools, despite their uneven impact. The government also became more insistent that Aboriginal parents keep their children in school, using the Mother's Allowance and other federal payments to compel compliance. At the start, federal Indian schools had been run largely by the churches; by the 1960s, education was becoming much more secular.

Public awareness of conditions in the residential school has been shaped strongly by the horrifying testimony in court cases brought by former students. There is no question that some teachers and other school staff were brutal pedophiles who abused their authority over vulnerable children. In 2000, when the Christian churches offered an apology to the Innu for past actions, the Innu rejected it, stating bluntly that the image that stuck in their minds about the churches' work was of a child being sexually abused by a priest. Many survivors of the schools spoke bitterly about the teachers' efforts to prevent them from speaking their language and about how they disparaged Aboriginal cultures and restricted contact with parents and families. Yet the national experience of residential schools was more mixed than the current highly charged debate suggests. Some schools – Kuper Island in BC stands out – seem to have been almost uniformly loathed by former students. At the other extreme, schools such as Grandin College in Fort Smith, NWT, have been described by graduates as encouraging personal growth and providing a supportive environment.

For students who suffered sexual or physical abuse at the hands of school personnel, there is no middle ground. For them, those schools were simply evil. Some who did not suffer direct assaults during their school years would reflect later that criticism of their culture and separation from family and community had deprived them of vitally important cultural, parenting, and social skills, to say nothing of bonds with parents, grandparents, and their traditional lands. Still others, whose lives had been hard before they were removed to the schools, argued that friendly teachers, a warm bed, and decent food were improvements over their previous existence. And some graduates – a much smaller number – remember their residential school fondly and remember their old teachers with affection. There is a terrible irony in the residential school experience. The schools were presented as a panacea – a powerful means of bringing Aboriginal children to full equality with non-Aboriginal people and ensuring their participation in Canadian society. They are now portrayed as the root cause of much of the current social despair and community distress. The schools were never the solution they were initially intended to be, but neither are they solely responsible for the severe social problems facing Aboriginal communities today.

There was much more to the government's package of programs than education, although schools were the fulcrum for many of the efforts made on Aboriginal people's behalf. The overarching goal of government initiatives was to bring the standard of living of Aboriginal people up to national levels. This meant moving Aboriginal people to more accessible reserves. It also meant careful oversight by an Indian Agent; a variety of financial support programs (Mother's Allowance, the Old Age Pension, and welfare benefits); health services, targeted especially at tuberculosis but also including inoculations and proper nutrition; and economic development initiatives. The government built homes for the many of the now sedentary residents. Most Aboriginal people in the North had moved across the land as hunters, trappers, and gatherers until the collapse of the fur trade and the surge of government intervention in the 1950s. They now moved onto new reserves and into government-supplied housing.

The programs sounded useful in the halls of Parliament and reassured Canadians that the country was looking after its poorest citizens. Canadians felt good when annual reports listed sizable expenditures on programs intended to integrate Inuit and First Nations people into the mainstream. There was, in fact, considerable self-satisfaction across the country, based largely on the proliferation of programs and the rapid growth of the department's budgets. But the reality differed greatly from the political rhetoric. Most of the postwar homes were poorly constructed, better suited for southern Canada than for the deep cold of the mid- and Far North. Also, they were designed with non-Aboriginal families and customs in mind and did not suit the people's cultural needs. Reserve schools had difficulty attracting and keeping good teachers and were known mainly for their authoritarian policies and distaste for Aboriginal cultures. Parents resented sending their children off to residential school and disliked having to stay year-round on a government-run reserve. Indian Agents and other civil servants dominated the communities. Some ruled gently and with compassion; others abused their authority.

Government intervention brought uneven benefits. Health care improved, and so did the life expectancy of Indigenous people. Tuberculosis was brought under control. However harsh the residential schools were, Aboriginal students developed skills there, and a small number went on to university or college. Government cultural programs made it possible for musical, dance, and sports groups to participate in regional and even national festivals and competitions.

The sharp decline in the fur trade after the war coincided with the postwar support programs, which sustained Aboriginal communities during lean economic times. There was little long-term economic development at this time, and as a result, welfare dependency emerged as the core economic feature of Aboriginal communities. The resource boom on Indigenous territories in the 1950s and 1960s generated few jobs for Aboriginal workers, leaving them on the outside looking in at an increasingly prosperous economy. Reserve communities looked and felt like ghettos; typically, they were separate from non-Aboriginal towns, ill-kempt and poorly built zones of poverty and despair. (In many parts of the provincial North, official reserve communities were separate from Métis and non-Status settlements. The latter tended to be more poorly served than official reserves.) Most band governments weren't ready to take over management of their reserves. This left the Indian Agents in *de facto* control; it also stuck Aboriginal organizations with a reputation as poor administrators.

Money was not the solution. In the 1950s and 1960s the Canadian government spent a great deal of it on programs for Aboriginal people at a time when the nation was creating a welfare state for all. But optimism and good intentions produced few results. In fact, this postwar version of paternalistic colonialism was as disruptive – often even more so – than the policies of the nineteenth century had been. The government had come forward with housing and support payments for Native people at precisely the moment when Aboriginal Canadians were losing the alternative of surviving through hunting, gathering, and fur trading. And the fur trade's decline coincided with an invasion of Canada's remote regions by prospectors, miners, loggers, construction workers (for roads and hydroelectric projects), and others who arrived to service the vast Canadian resource boom. Most Aboriginal Canadians lived on isolated reserves, far from Canadian urban centres. With the postwar boom, Aboriginal communities found themselves caught in the maelstrom of an expansionist and culturally insensitive new economic order.

## THE COLLAPSE OF IDEALISM AND THE SEARCH FOR NEW SOLUTIONS

By the mid-1960s, the federal government was beginning to question its approach to Aboriginal programs. The churches had long been active allies of the government when it came to education, civilization, and centralization. Now, in this decade of widespread social unrest and soul searching, those same churches were openly questioning their commitment to eradicating Aboriginal spirituality and culture. The walk down the long path towards reconciliation had begun. Meanwhile, the government had tried a series of grand solutions – assimilation, education, agricultural and industrial training, welfare support, government intervention – and found that none of them had worked: Aboriginal people's lives seemed to be getting worse, not better. Alcoholism was becoming a serious problem on many reserves and in towns and cities. Indigenous people were showing up in courts and prisons in shocking numbers. Unemployment remained distressingly high, because of limited skills, the lack of jobs in remote communities, and the supplanting of hunting and fishing by government welfare cheques. Those who stayed in remote communities had few opportunities to earn a regular income. Those who moved to major cities and towns found hostility, discrimination, and deep poverty.

Changes in Indian policy came slowly. Revisions to the Indian Act removed some of the restrictive policies and blatant attacks on Indigenous cultures. In 1960, Status Indians received the right to vote in federal elections, and after a major court decision, they were also granted the right to buy and drink alcohol. But still the government floundered in search of a clear policy.

In 1966, the federal government received a report, one of many to come, on the future of Aboriginal people in Canada. Completed under the direction of Harry Hawthorn of the University of British Columbia, *A Survey of the Contemporary Indians of Canada* (the Hawthorn Report) called for more money to be spent on improving First Nations living conditions, for funds to be directed to First Nations wishing to leave reserves, and for health, education, and social services to be provided by the provinces. The same report concluded that First Nations people were "citizens plus," deserving of both special status and extensive government assistance to address the social and economic ills afflicting their communities. The report dropped the rhetoric of assimilation, but it also urged the government to encourage Aboriginal people to abandon isolated reserves and to find places for themselves in the broader Canadian economy.

The Hawthorn Report and the government's response to it – which was to spend more money without altering administrative arrangements – revealed the fundamental flaw in government policy. Canadian officials assumed that Aboriginal people *wanted* to be like other Canadians, that they sought similar jobs and living arrangements, and that they placed priority on acquiring material goods. They thought this, in large measure, because liberal economic assumptions ran deep in the country, especially the one that held that all people were much the same under their skin. The notion that Aboriginal people might be different and that governments should listen to what they said they wanted had not yet jarred the paternalistic and egalitarian mindset of politicians and bureaucrats. To be sure, Aboriginal people wanted an end to poverty, and they wanted more wealth and comfort, but more than these things, they wanted social and cultural strength and the right to choose their future. In the new welfare state, in which the government assumed it knew best for all Canadians, especially the poorest of them, ideas like these rarely reached the corridors of the Department of Indian Affairs.

Pierre Trudeau was elected prime minister of Canada in 1968 and quickly added a sharp-edged philosophical element to the growing debate about the future of Aboriginal Canadians. Trudeau despised nationalism, in Quebec and everywhere else, and he believed that separatism was inherently destructive. He did not believe in special status, and indeed, he came to power fully intending to end the threat of Quebec separatism and to eliminate other pleas for special rights and status. This was the era during which various minorities and special interest groups were demanding immediate government attention. Trudeau, a civil libertarian at his core, opposed these demands and sought instead to build a society based on individual freedom and reduced social inequality. He rejected ethnic separatism and espoused a vision of civic nationalism in which the ties that bound Canadians would be built on principles of individual rights and social justice, not language or culture. This perspective reflected the values of those pursuing social justice in the 1960s; it was also consistent with the civil rights movement in the United States led by Martin Luther King Jr.

The federal government raised the idea of making dramatic changes in Indian policy. In 1969, Jean Chrétien, Trudeau's minister of Indian affairs and northern development, presented a White Paper on Indian Affairs. The document, prepared after a series of meetings with Aboriginal leaders, rejected much of their advice and proposed instead that Indigenous people be incorporated with the rest of Canada. It called for the dismantling of the Department of Indian Affairs, the transfer of administrative responsibilities to the provinces, and the closing of reserves. Aboriginal people were to have the same rights as all other Canadians – no more, no less. The government seemed to believe that Aboriginal groups would favour such an approach, which promised real equality and full participation in Canadian society.

Ottawa could not have been more wrong. Aboriginal leaders across the country lambasted the government for pretending to consult them and demanded that the policy be retracted. They were appalled that the government believed it could walk away from generations-old treaties and legal obligations. They were horrified that Indigenous peoples' status as the first peoples of Canada could be swept aside and their situation equated with that of recent immigrants to the country – as if they were no more deserving than people with only a few years' commitment to Canada. Aboriginal organizations throughout the country had long done a poor job of coordinating their activities, but not now – they banded together in an effective national campaign to battle the federal proposals with one voice. First Nations, Inuit, and Métis leaders made it clear that Ottawa's plans were unacceptable to them and that Canada could not simply abandon its historical and legal commitments to them. The Liberals backed down, shelved the

White Paper, looked for ways to mollify angry Aboriginal leaders, and sought new approaches to the "Indian problem" in Canada.

As it turned out, that White Paper was the last comprehensive "solution" Ottawa ever brought to the Aboriginal crisis in Canada. Having tried assimilation and integration, and having considered the radical step of eliminating special status, and now buffeted by ferocious attacks from Aboriginal peoples and their growing band of non-Aboriginal supporters, the federal government turned away from sweeping visions and began trying to manage the growing crisis. Government policy quickly became conciliatory, with the focus on small measures and baby steps. Policy makers no longer believed that sweeping changes in Aboriginal conditions were possible. The search for new ideas would now be carried out by Indigenous leaders and organizations themselves.

## POWER SHIFT: ABORIGINAL PEOPLE IN THE DRIVER'S SEAT

The White Paper of 1969 was the last time the federal government offered an administrative plan for managing Aboriginal affairs in Canada. That document had generated a powerful Aboriginal voice that could not be ignored. Native people had been mobilized, indeed radicalized. The national initiative shifted from the Department of Indian Affairs and the Prime Minister's Office to the still loosely connected First Nations, Métis, and Inuit organizations. Aboriginal people across the country quickly pressed the agenda. The Yukon Native Brotherhood tabled the first modern comprehensive land claim proposal in 1973. That same year, the Nisga'a court case before the Supreme Court of Canada (the *Calder* case) forced the federal government to rethink its approach to Aboriginal land claims and begin negotiating treaties. First Nations pressed for more rights and assurances, on everything from support for postsecondary education to constitutional protection for Indigenous rights. (Importantly, the government's position remains, to this day, that Aboriginal people who do not have treaties do not have a *right* to their traditional territories. They do have a right to *claim* their territories. The latter is what land claims negotiations are about.) More importantly, the public at large seemed either disturbed by federal high-handedness or convinced that Aboriginal claims were legitimate. Support for First Nations positions ran strong and deep in the country.

Ottawa had lost control of the pace and direction of the policy agenda and found itself responding to Aboriginal demands. Various new approaches came out of the Department of Indian Affairs and Northern Development, from Minister Keith Penner's 1983 report on the recognition of the inherent right to self-government to Minister Jane Stewart's 1998 *Gathering Strength,* which included something of an apology for past injustices. But these were not viewed as bold new initiatives. What happened instead was that Aboriginal political leaders and organizations placed demands on the table, and governments then tried to convert those demands into politically acceptable packages. The government ignored the more excessive ones, such as the Dene Declaration, which made a sweeping assertion of Aboriginal autonomy. It also attempted to make more palatable the moderate positions supported by the majority of First Nations, Inuit, and Métis leaders and communities.

The debate in the early 1990s about the inherent right of Aboriginal self-government reveals a great deal about the new pattern of federal–Aboriginal relations. The demand that Aboriginal communities recover the right to manage their affairs emerged from Indigenous communities as a political issue in the 1970s and 1980s. The concept was debated extensively at First Ministers' Conferences on Aboriginal Affairs, with provincial premiers angered and frustrated by the growing Indigenous invasion of the government's own turf. At the insistence of the Assembly of First Nations, and over the objections of many Indigenous women's groups, a call for Aboriginal self-government was added to the 1992 Charlottetown Accord. In the referendum that followed, Aboriginal self-government figured prominently in public debates, especially in BC and the northern regions of the provinces. When the referendum was defeated, many pundits attributed the loss at least in part to public opposition to the concept of Aboriginal self-government.

What is often missed in the analysis is that many Aboriginal voters also rejected self-government as defined in the accord. Many felt that the autonomy provisions did not go far enough and wanted stronger recognition of Aboriginal sovereignty. Others were uncertain about how self-government could be implemented in communities that had yet to address serious internal issues, or lacked a strong economic base, or did not have the administrative skills to govern effectively.

Still others were concerned about the implications of self-government for Aboriginal women in communities dominated by all-male band councils. The referendum foreshadowed later political debates and future misunderstandings between Aboriginal and non-Aboriginal people. Many First Nations expected far more than the federal government was prepared to offer. A sizable number of non-Aboriginal people, represented by the increasingly influential Reform Party of Canada, appeared to believe that the Charlottetown proposals had gone much too far. Efforts over the previous decade to draw the two sides together had failed. The political battle had created a formidable cultural and political chasm.

The federal government realized it had to do something to meet the aspirations of Aboriginal people, and the provision it had just offered had been voted down in a national referendum. A solution was found. The Canadian Constitution recognized "existing Aboriginal and treaty rights." So, if Ottawa signed self-government treaties with First Nations, the logic went, these treaties would immediately gain constitutional protection. The government had been thwarted when the option required public input, open debate, and voting. Now it found a different route to the same objective, one that required only legal interpretation and a willingness to ignore the clear wishes of most Canadians. The government declared the self-government agreements to be treaties, thus ensuring that the self-government provisions would enjoy full constitutional protection. Moreover, future self-government agreements would require the involvement of provincial governments.

The approach to Aboriginal affairs that emerged from the 1980s to the early twenty-first century had this central characteristic: it was driven by Aboriginal peoples, not the government. Ottawa clearly viewed itself as an intermediary between Indigenous peoples and other Canadians. Also, its actions during those decades showed what it had the capacity to do administratively, legally, and constitutionally. With regard to self-government, while it sometimes sacrificed public input and ratification in order to meet pressing Aboriginal demands, far more often it backed away from the Indigenous position to avoid the wrath of non-Aboriginal Canadians. This was evident, for example, in its approach to the Burnt Church controversy over Mi'kmaq fishing rights in 1999–2001; the government tried to bend the rules (such as they were) to suit First Nations demands without alienating non-Indigenous people in the Maritimes. The consequences left nobody happy.

For over forty years, then, federal Aboriginal policy has been react-
ive rather than proactive. Ideas have emerged from Aboriginal communities, not as a single, unified voice but rather as a complicated and
sometimes contradictory series of assertions, expectations, and ambitions. The lack of Aboriginal consensus is hardly surprising. There
are huge cultural differences between Indigenous groups in Canada,
and they have rarely shared a common vision, any more than non-
Aboriginal Canadians have achieved a consensus about downstream
plans and priorities. The federal government placed itself between
Aboriginal and other Canadians, from which position it served as a
buffer between the growing assertiveness of one side and the rising
unease of the other. As a result, it has satisfied neither proponents nor
critics of Aboriginal rights and indeed has angered both. Government
programs have not gone as far, as fast, or as comprehensively as
Aboriginal peoples demand, but they have gone faster, spent more,
and provided more legal and constitutional benefits to Indigenous
people than many Canadians feel comfortable with. It is an odd situation and one that is out of step with past federal actions: the federal
government is accustomed to feeling it knows what is best for
Aboriginal people and acting accordingly. It no longer does, or can.
No one really understands any more where Canada's Aboriginal
policy is going. In classic Canadian fashion, the present arrangement
seems designed to upset many while infuriating as few as possible.

Federal policy on Aboriginal affairs operates in a conceptual and
ideological vacuum. At the political level, Ottawa has learned simple
lessons over the past few decades. Especially in rural and western
Canada, there are some votes to be gained by taking an aggressive
stance against Aboriginal peoples. There are almost no non-Aboriginal
votes to be gained by being overly generous with Indigenous
groups. Southern Canadians have turned their attention to other
issues. There is no assurance that expensive or expansive federal offers
will result in either Aboriginal support or, importantly, significant
improvements in Aboriginal living conditions. The country at large
demanded and expected changes in the 1960s; the nation's record in
dealing with Indigenous people was embarrassing, and conditions on
reserves were disgraceful. Massive expansion in federal support programs took the sting out of domestic and international criticism – and
resulted in more attention being focused on the difficulties faced by

Indigenous groups in responding to change. There is no consensus or shared vision anywhere in the country – as there once was around education, Christianization, and assimilation – about what can be done for First Nations. This is hardly surprising, in that past panaceas did not serve Indigenous peoples or the country well. Truth be told, most Canadians simply wish the issue would go away, that massive federal spending would slow or stop, that Aboriginal people would assume responsibility for their lives and communities, and that the claims to special status would disappear. They also hope – and this is rather contradictory – that First Nations' economic and social conditions will improve and that the difficulties of the past will be eliminated through greater integration with the broader Canadian society. Aboriginal Canadians desire the same results – who would not? – but they want to control the process.

## FAILED AND COMPETING VISIONS

Aboriginal peoples and the Canadian government have been struggling for a long time to determine the future for the Indigenous peoples of this country. For generations, the government worked independently from Aboriginal organizations and developed paternalistic programs designed to segregate, educate, and assimilate Indigenous people. The results of a long history of broken promises, racial discrimination, and marginalization are now clear. Over the past forty years, Aboriginal proposals have driven the debate, generating some movement and an increasing amount of critical comment. There is no single Indigenous response, nor should there be or will there ever be. Individual communities have different needs, aspirations, styles of leadership, and social conditions. They will gravitate towards one of a variety of options and will, as many have already done, change their tactics over time. The federal government and the country at large have no competing alternative on offer. Non-Aboriginal Canadians tend to react to Indigenous proposals (overreact, more often than not) and have had little to suggest in return. Until the 1990s, even the critics tended to keep their ideas to themselves – a situation that changed during the public debate surrounding the Charlottetown Accord. Today, opponents of Indigenous rights are louder and more emphatic than the non-Aboriginal proponents of those rights.

Although intellectuals and political leaders have put forward new ideas to reframe the debate (we explore their visions in the next two sections), the lessons of the past provide clear warnings. In the past, Indigenous peoples have been offered panaceas — always that *one* program that will solve all community ills and meet all needs. None of those solutions have delivered. Ethnic relations in Canada are complicated, and racism runs deep in Canadian history, entrenching problems and preventing quick solutions. On top of that, Indigenous communities must cope with a variety of issues and concerns, and practical matters and local tragedies often distract them from the sweeping and complicated work of political reform and reorientation. Although discussions about sovereignty and self-government have been progressing and recent court decisions have alerted governments and non-Aboriginal Canadians that changes in Aboriginal authority must be recognized, the country does not feel the urgency as strongly as Indigenous peoples do. Government responses and efforts by non-Aboriginal Canadians to accommodate Aboriginal aspirations have been inadequate for generations. They continue to be so, and the search for solutions continues to flounder in the waters of Canadian indifference. Also missing from this debate is a focus on pragmatic solutions and ones based on core Canadian values.

The debate about Aboriginal living conditions and futures is all too familiar: always, there is an emotive sense of the Aboriginal reality, disquiet about politicians' inaction, a lack of clear or plausible solutions, an almost desperate desire to rid Canada of the embarrassment of Aboriginal poverty and suffering, and a nod towards the requirement for Aboriginal peoples to help themselves. The desire to do right by Aboriginal people goes way back in Canada's past, but only recently has the discourse broken with the paternalistic "government knows best" mindset that has long dominated Indigenous affairs in Canada. Canadians clearly want solutions. They simply do not know how to find them.

## WHO ARE THE ABORIGINAL PEOPLE IN CANADA?

A brief word is in order about one of the more perplexing facets of the debate about Aboriginal peoples in Canada. In recent years, the answer to the question "Who are the Aboriginal people in Canada?" has changed significantly. For several generations, an Indian woman who married a non-Indian man immediately lost her Indian status, as did her children. Then in 1985, with the passage of Bill C-31, women who lost their status in this way got it back, albeit with conditions. So did their children, if they wanted it, but not necessarily their grandchildren, for the continuation of official status depended on whom, in turn, they married. Ovide Mercredi regained his Indian status through Bill C-31, but because he had a non-Aboriginal partner, his children do not and will not have Indian status. There are large groups of non-Status Indians – individuals with clear Aboriginal ancestry but without legal status under the Indian Act – who are now demanding Aboriginal rights and government services. In 1982, the Métis, a long-standing and well-known cultural group in many parts of Canada, were recognized as Aboriginal in the Constitution Act. But their legal status, their right to hunt and fish like First Nations people, and the legal obligations of the Government of Canada towards them remain unclear. They have gained limited hunting and fishing rights in recent years, and in 2013, they won a major legal case in which the Supreme Court ruled that the Métis and non-Status Indians were "Indians" for the purposes of government policy and legislation. The Government of Canada has appealed that decision. The Inuit present an equally interesting case. In the distant past, the Government of Canada argued that they were not Indians and therefore that it had no specific obligations to provide them with services and programs. They lost that case in the courts in 1939. The Inuit are now considered the responsibility of the federal government.

The national situation is confusing, however. There are Status Indians on duly constituted Indian reserves who hold the full range of rights under the Indian Act. To complicate matters, there are Status Indians living on lands *like* reserves, particularly in northern Canada, who may have the same rights. There are beneficiaries under modern land claims agreements, such as the Nisga'a in northern BC and Yukon First Nations people, who are no longer covered by the Indian Act and who live on settlement lands. Unlike many other groups, the beneficiaries of modern treaties have, as communities, substantial powers of self-government and strong claims on government resources. Importantly, the Indian Act no longer applies to them. In addition, close to half the Status Indians in Canada no longer live on reserves. Until recently, off-reserve Indians were barred from participating in band elections and often did not have full access to band services and programs. In the territorial North, in contrast, Aboriginal people play a prominent role in territorial affairs (dominant in the case of Nunavut, roughly equal in Northwest Territories, and significant in Yukon). This strong influence on regional governments supplements the power recently gained by Aboriginal authorities. Native women's groups have become prominent in recent decades, exerting considerable informal influence and serving as a counterbalance to male-dominated regional and national organizations, such as the chiefs-only Assembly of First Nations. Métis groups lack the formal, government-sanctioned membership of the First Nations and Inuit, but they now have their own citizenship procedures, especially on the Prairies. They also have uneven claims on the government's purse. Non-Status groups, particularly in the Maritimes, struggle for recognition and acknowledgment and are often ignored by Aboriginal organizations and governments.

A brief comment on Aboriginal population figures is also in order. According to the 2011 National Household survey – the first national enumeration completed after the traditional census was dropped – there were 1.4 million Aboriginal people in Canada, representing 4.3 percent of the national total. Of this overall number, 59,445 were Inuit, 451,795 were Métis, and 851,560 were First Nations. Of the First Nations people, one quarter were not Registered (or Status) Indians. Of course, the number of Canadians with partial Aboriginal ancestry is much larger – easily double the "official" total for First Nations, Métis, and Inuit. Indigenous people are a majority of the population only in Nunavut and Northwest Territories. They represent a sizable percentage (above 20 percent) in Manitoba, Saskatchewan, and Yukon. Although the percentage in Ontario is very small, Aboriginal Canadians account for over half the population in the northern third of the province. These population figures, incidentally, represent a 20.1 percent increase over the 2006 census – a growth rate four times higher than the national one. Ontario, Manitoba, Saskatchewan, Alberta, and British Columbia had the largest numbers of Aboriginal people.

We address later on the vexing question of membership and Aboriginal citizenship. For now, it is important to grasp the complexity of the Aboriginal population in Canada. The diversity of

Aboriginal voices complicates matters for the courts and for governments besides generally confusing the population at large. There are substantial tensions *within* Canada's Aboriginal community, including long-standing conflicts between the Inuit and northern Athapaskans (now somewhat muted) and often tense relations between First Nations and Métis on the Prairies. In the Maritimes, First Nations organizations have been strongly critical of non-Status groups, and relations are tense between Aboriginal women's groups and mainline political organizations. For non-Aboriginal observers, including national politicians and government officials, Aboriginal diversity has often been a hornet's nest. (It must be added, for balance, that Aboriginal politicians have likewise found national and provincial governments to be ideologically confusing and frustratingly inconsistent.)

All of this diversity has generated a patchwork of ideas, demands, and negotiation positions on various public issues. The lack of consensus among Indigenous organizations and communities has made it easier for governments and politicians to justify inaction and delay. Too often, the public at large can't tell Métis from Status Indians from non-Status Indians (although they grasp that the Inuit are a unique group). This situation is at best confusing and at worst impenetrable. The high rate of intermarriage between Aboriginal people, especially between Indigenous women and non-Indigenous men, promises to cloud Canada's political demography even more in the coming years. The absence of a clear and easy answer to the simple question "Just who are the Aboriginal peoples in Canada?" foreshadows some of the challenges ahead. The issues surrounding the present and future place of Aboriginal peoples within Canada are extremely complex. No one can reasonably suggest that there are clear, simple, and easy solutions to problems that have taken more than two centuries to develop. It will take time to set things right in Canada. But that is no excuse to delay any longer one of the most important challenges facing Canadian society.

aboriginal leaders and
scholars point the way

# 1

# the traditionalists

THE ABSENCE of a clear Canadian policy for Aboriginal peoples is not for lack of thinking hard. At no time in our history have so many people devoted so much time to trying to solve the greatest conundrum in Canadian public life. The collapse in the 1960s and 1970s of the long-held non-Aboriginal understanding of Aboriginal peoples' place in Canadian society left the country without a clear national Indigenous policy. In the late 1960s, in the wake of the federal White Paper on Indian Affairs, Aboriginal people seemed to rally around the concept of citizens plus, a proposal advanced in the Hawthorn Report. Aboriginal people seemed willing to accept the idea of being distinct peoples *within* the Canadian system. But the subsequent search for a new model has not produced anything like a consensus. Aboriginal and non-Aboriginal thinkers have generated many ideas about how Aboriginal people and other Canadians might coexist. The sheer volume of these ideas exposes the broadening gap between Indigenous and non-Indigenous conceptions of Canada. The two sides are far from agreement on political, economic, and administrative strategies.

If the possibility existed for a meeting of political minds in the late 1960s and early 1970s, it collapsed as a result of government inattentiveness to Aboriginal concerns, non-Aboriginal resistance to enhanced "special status," and growing Aboriginal interest in expanded Aboriginal political and legal rights. Subsequent legal battles and constitutional conflicts broadened the gulf between Indigenous and other Canadians, empowering Aboriginal peoples through the courts and resulting in dozens of proposals for resolving the continuing uncertainty about the position of Aboriginal communities within Confederation. Although the ideas initially emanated largely from non-Aboriginal writers, an influential group of university-based Aboriginal intellectuals has greatly enriched the debate in recent years.

The men and women whose ideas we examine in this chapter and the next two aim at high-level concepts and understandings. Most of them address broad moral, historical, and cultural questions and posit ideal worlds. So their ideas are not always rooted in practice and experience; instead, they offer visions of what might or should be. In each case, their ideas flow from long experience in contemporary Canadian or Aboriginal politics and reflect specific cultural or ideological perspectives. Most Aboriginal writers – much more than their non-Aboriginal counterparts – bring a wealth of lived experience to their work, drawing on personal, family, and community histories to fill out their conceptual understandings and to fuel their passion for rapid and meaningful change. There is no consensus among Aboriginal thinkers on premises or approaches; the debate remains highly emotional, largely because the participants have had intensely personal encounters with the reality of Aboriginal peoples' experiences in Canada. Their ideas are not necessarily wrong or misguided, although they often differ dramatically from the proposals we put forward. In each case, they stem from a heartfelt desire to create a better future for Aboriginal people in Canada and to heal the bruised relationship between Indigenous and other Canadians.

There is much anger among Aboriginal scholars, as there is among Indigenous leaders generally. There are good reasons for this. Each of them must cope routinely with personal and collective challenges that few non-Aboriginal people deal with. One Indigenous scholar, a friend for many years, was regularly drawn into intense community crises. Her extended family experienced the full range of medical, legal, and financial disasters. Rarely a month went by when she was not helping out a family member financially. Herself a victim of abuse when she was younger, she worked with Aboriginal women in distress, devoting hundreds of hours a year to one-on-one support for teenagers and young adults in despair. Relatives, even those of great accomplishment, struggled with the pressures that engulfed their communities and their lives. She felt more heartache in a year than most Canadians experience in a lifetime, yet she managed to raise her own children with an intense Aboriginal pride, a strong sense of injustice, and a commitment to their First Nation. Non-Aboriginal scholars working in the field, like us, typically experience these challenges second- and third-hand. They (and we) feel them strongly and agonize about our country's inability to address Aboriginal needs. But there is a qualitative difference between non-Aboriginal and Indigenous life experiences, and it shows.

There is no single Aboriginal perspective on the future of Indigenous–non-Indigenous relations, nor will there ever be one. The Aboriginal peoples of Canada are culturally, socially, and economically diverse. Their experiences, needs, and aspirations differ. Their pre-European political structures vary dramatically, and so do their present-day political, economic, and social conditions. Add to this the different educational and life experiences of individual Aboriginal people and it becomes self-evident that academics of Aboriginal ancestry will approach future political and legal relationships from a variety of perspectives. The emergence over the past two decades of a group of Aboriginal legal and political scholars has greatly broadened and improved the debate about the future of Indigenous peoples in Canada. Views previously articulated by elders and political leaders in non-academic settings have begun to appear in articles, books, and conference papers. These ideas have changed the discussion profoundly, shifting the debate away from non-Indigenous perceptions of what is necessary, possible, and appropriate towards a complex cross-cultural analysis of how competing visions of history, politics, law, and culture can be reconciled within the Canadian political and administrative system.

The political thinkers we've chosen to discuss in this section illustrate the diversity of Aboriginal thought on the issues at hand. They do not represent the full range, and, as with non-Aboriginal academic writers, they tend not to focus on the nuances of public administration. The perspectives offered by Patricia Monture-Angus and John Borrows are vitally important, for they reveal the very different assumptions and underlying passions that fuel Aboriginal approaches to

Canadian political issues. These two perspectives combine cultural/ spiritual understandings with direct experience of contemporary social and economic realities as well as a qualitatively different sense of urgency (sometimes expressed as anger, understandably so) about the slow and often weak progress of the Canadian political and legal system in the field of Aboriginal rights.

For many Aboriginal political thinkers, the search for solutions to Indigenous political and social challenges requires respect for the past. These scholars argue that existing structures pay too little heed to Aboriginal cultures and values and are therefore, by definition, institutions of colonialism. By this view, empowering Aboriginal peoples requires an understanding by Aboriginal *and* non-Aboriginal people alike of long-standing Indigenous political structures, as well as official recognition of the moral and political authority of traditional Indigenous values.

Over the past generation, Canadian politics and constitutional debates have been focused on, some would say obsessed about, the "two solitudes" of national life – the division between English- and French-speaking Canadians. **Taiaiake Alfred**, one of the most provocative of today's Aboriginal thinkers, argues that an even deeper divide separates Indigenous from non-Indigenous Canadians. A political scientist and Mohawk activist, he challenges current government structures and initiatives designed to bring about an accommodation between Aboriginal peoples and the Canadian state and society. He has articulated his passionate views in two books, *Heeding the Voices of Our Ancestors* (1995), a scholarly analysis of Mohawk politics and Native nationalism, and *Peace, Power, Righteousness* (1999; 2nd ed., 2009), a strongly worded statement on Aboriginal–state relations in Canada.

Alfred is fundamentally a traditionalist, one who sees the revival of Aboriginal political communities as essential to cultural survival. And to sustain those communities will require a return to traditional values and governing principles. In *Peace, Power, Righteousness,* he makes his separatist views clear: "If we are to emerge from this crisis with our nations intact, we must turn away from the values of the mainstream of North American society and begin to act as self-determining peoples" (xii). He suggests that it is not politically useful to condemn different cultures or to "ascribe a greedy, dominating nature to white people," but he does so anyway: "European states and their colonial offspring still embody the same destructive and disrespectful impulses that they did 500 years ago. For this reason, questions of justice – social, political, and environmental – are best considered outside the framework of classical European thought and legal traditions" (21). Many Canadians would be offended by this assertion; it is the kind of rhetoric that, however sincere, stops productive discussions in their tracks.

For Alfred – and he is not alone in this – there is a fundamental difference between Indigenous and non-Indigenous (here, Canadian) societies. European and colonial states and societies are, at root, hierarchical and coercive. They are propelled by possessive individualism, an ideological commitment to individual rights and freedoms that dominates all political and administrative systems. By contrast, Indigenous communities reflect egalitarian values and a strong commitment to sharing, respect for others, spiritual and ecological balance, and decision making based on consensus rather than majority rule. Aboriginal peoples must reject non-Aboriginal concepts of rights, citizenship, and sovereignty, for these spring from a commitment to individual rights, freehold property, and materialism – things that are intrinsically at odds with Indigenous understandings of governance and social organization.

Many Aboriginal leaders and academics support current efforts to re-establish Aboriginal self-government. Alfred, however, offers strong warnings about the dangers of that approach for Aboriginal cultures. For him, self-government – limited, constitutionally constrained, and ultimately defined by national and provincial governments – would be a step towards assimilation into colonial legal frameworks as well as an implicit acceptance of oppressive political structures. Those structures are, after all, premised on non-Aboriginal notions of sovereignty – sovereignty that in turn is based on a hierarchy of political power, with national and provincial governments remaining at the apex of the political system. They also entail coercion by the nation-state, exemplified by the federal insistence that Aboriginal governments adhere to nationally imposed formats, accountability provisions, and political structures. As he summarizes it in *Peace, Power, Righteousness,* "Native communities have a choice between two radically different kinds of social organization: one based on conscience and the authority of the good [Indigenous], the other on coercion and authoritarianism [Euro-Canadian]" (25).

Alfred conflates liberalism with colonialism, yet the two are not synonymous. Also, his critique of Euro-Canadian liberal values is based on a caricature; few Canadians would identify with the assumptions he makes. That the Canadian state dominated Aboriginal peoples and communities is indisputable. But non-liberal states – Marxist ones, for example – have been just as destructive towards Indigenous cultures as capitalist ones. Even if the larger Euro-Canadian political community possessed different values than liberalism and organized its politics around ideas closer to those espoused by Alfred, it is likely that he would still "want out" of Canada.

Alfred's conceptions are clearly radical. He argues that Aboriginal self-determination is incompatible with recognizing the sovereignty of the Canadian state. By accepting the definitions of Aboriginal rights as outlined in Canadian law and policy, Aboriginal people would be buying into a colonial system and limiting their ability to determine the future of their communities. Alfred is harshly critical of the treaty process in British Columbia on the grounds that it is assimilationist and inherently colonial. For that reason, treaty-making processes hold out false promise for Indigenous peoples – they will do little more than perpetuate colonial relationships under another name.

There is, Alfred argues, an alternative. Aboriginal people can and must resist the current approach of Ottawa and the provinces and seize control of the agenda. They can do so, he asserts, by adhering to key principles. To start, they must balance a commitment to community values with respect for individual differences. This will require a high level of group solidarity but also a tolerance of difference with regard to matters that are not central to the community's identity. They must also remember that culture is fundamental to political survival. Community members need to know their traditions, norms, and values and demand that they be adhered to by their political leaders. Furthermore, there must be open and extensive communication among community members. Suspicion and distrust can only be heightened when this is missing. Aboriginal communities must be based on respect and trust. Members of a community must care about and cooperate with one another and must support its Indigenous government.

Members of the group must also dedicate themselves to its survival. People have to take pride in their community and collectively establish clear cultural boundaries and membership criteria, which, in turn, will define their society. And Aboriginal governments themselves must be respectful of Indigenous traditions. Governments, in part, must be participatory and consensus-based. Community leaders cannot act according to the dictates and standards of the colonial society. Instead, they must be responsive and accountable to their members, consult widely, and secure decisions based on community consensus.

Because the viability of Aboriginal communities depends on the next generation, they must ensure that youth are mentored, educated, and empowered. This will happen only if the community is committed to the task. And finally, individual communities need to foster strong and productive links with the outside world, especially other Indigenous communities. Positive social, economic and political relations with other Indigenous peoples and cultures, both within Canada and internationally, are crucial to solidarity and cultural persistence.

So Alfred tells us. And he offers other ideas. He supports the idea of using blood quantum (the percentage of a person's ancestry that is Indigenous and community-based) as a means of ensuring the maintenance of the group. This approach, which has been implemented by the Mohawk, has generated considerable debate. For many, the thought of linking culture and identity to biological ancestry is unacceptable. Ironically, this notion parallels the racialist aspects of the Indian Act and colonialist approaches to defining who is legally an Indian. The Royal Commission on Aboriginal Peoples was aware of this problem and rejected that approach as the basis for future membership codes both on moral grounds and because it was unlikely to survive a Charter challenge. Instead, the commission argued that cultural definitions of membership should be adopted.

Like other Aboriginal thinkers, Alfred references the Two Row Wampum, but he does not see this Aboriginal idea as leading to treaty federalism. In fact, he rejects that notion and views agreements such as those signed by the Sechelt and Nisga'a as sellouts to the colonial system. His understanding of Two Row Wampum is close to that of sovereignty-association (albeit without accepting the European concept of sovereignty) in that it highlights the right of Aboriginal people to determine their own future and define their political relationship with other political communities. He knows that his ideas go further than those of Aboriginal organizations and are at variance with federal and provincial policy. He also knows that the Mohawk are among the more politically radical First Nations in Canada; indeed, they are one of the few Aboriginal groups willing to push for a dramatic realignment of political relations with provincial and federal governments, and they are willing to endure the displeasure, even the wrath, of non-Aboriginal governments and people and the criticism of other Aboriginal people in pushing this agenda.

Many of Alfred's ideas are outside the mainstream of Canadian political thought. They are clearly at variance with official Canadian policy and with moderate non-Aboriginal positions. They occupy the opposite end of the political spectrum from the concepts advanced by those non-Aboriginal thinkers who wish to abolish Indigenous rights, special status, and constitutional protections. His ideas are politically impractical, especially on a national scale. They certainly do not mesh with current legal judgments, national or provincial priorities, or what passes for a consensus on Aboriginal rights among non-Indigenous Canadians. At the same time, his ideas represent more than a critique of the colonial power relations embedded in Canadian Aboriginal policy. A significant number of Aboriginal leaders and thinkers share many of his central concerns and many of his political suggestions, even if they do not go quite as far as Alfred. His arguments are explicitly separatist, passionately Indigenous, deeply cultural, and highly polemical; they also represent a significant and strongly held line of thought among Aboriginal people in Canada, even if a minority one.

Unlike Alfred, **Glen Coulthard**, a Yellowknife Dene and professor of First Nations studies at the University of British Columbia, focuses his work on the links between self-determination and reconciliation with non-Aboriginal people and political systems. He works in a theoretically informed manner, drawing on Frantz Fanon, a seminal thinker on anticolonialism, and others to explore Indigenous–newcomer relations. He offers an especially important analysis of the patterns of official "recognition" of Indigenous rights, treaties, and governments. In "Subjects of Empire" (2007), he challenges "the idea that the colonial relationship between Indigenous peoples and the Canadian state can be significantly transformed via a politics of recognition" (438). He argues that, rather than ushering in a new era of Aboriginal power and autonomy, Canada's policies of identifying and

recognizing Indigenous peoples and governments "promises to repro-
duce the very configurations of colonial power that Indigenous
peoples' demands for recognition have historically sought to tran-
scend" (437). Coulthard argues that, far from delivering peaceful coexistence based on the recognition of Aboriginal rights and authority,
the emphasis on recognition could reinforce the structures and authority of earlier colonial systems – the very institutions and processes
that brought Aboriginal people such sustained grief and hardship.

According to Coulthard, modern-day efforts to address political,
legal, and economic imbalances are not addressing the fundamental
problems facing Indigenous people. The colonial system remains intact. He is not impressed with formal apologies, like the one offered to
residential school survivors, or with the recognition of Aboriginal self-
government because, like Alfred, he believes that the underlying con-
test between values and world views continues to privilege
non-Aboriginal people and political institutions. And he is not convinced that the new processes for consultation, collaboration, and "deliberative democracy" will address the challenges embedded in racism
and the profound oppression of Aboriginal societies in Canada.

Coulthard perceives a false promise in today's Aboriginal politics.
He contends that current political processes will not address the real
needs of Aboriginal people, who cannot but be suspicious of short-
term half-measures to address their aspirations. Specifically, in
"Placing #IdleNoMore in Historical Context" (2013) he argues that

> if you want those in power to respond swiftly to Indigenous
> peoples' political struggles, start by placing Indigenous bodies
> (with a few logs and tires thrown in for good measure) between
> settlers and their money, which in colonial contexts is generated
> by the ongoing theft and exploitation of our land and resource
> base. If this is true, then the long term efficacy of the
> #IdleNoMore movement would appear to hinge on its protest
> actions being distributed more evenly between the shopping
> malls and front lawns of legislatures on the one hand, and the
> logging roads, thoroughfares, and railways that are central to the
> accumulation of colonial capital on the other. For better and for
> worse, it was our peoples' challenge to these two pillars of col-
> onial sovereignty that led to the recommendations of RCAP: the

Canadian state's claim to hold a legitimate monopoly on use of violence and the conditions required for the ongoing accumulation of capital.

Coulthard's work is politically charged, and like Alfred, he is more than a little angry about the false promises made by the status quo. Drawing on the writings of Fanon, he situates the struggle and aspirations of Aboriginal people in Canada in the context of global struggles against colonial political and economic systems.

Also in the traditionalist camp is **Joyce Green**, a political scientist at the University of Regina, who is of English, Ktunaxa, and Cree-Scots Métis descent. Green brings a critical feminist and anticolonialist approach to Indigenous–newcomer relations. Her work focuses on the politics of exclusion and on efforts by Aboriginal peoples and organizations to break through barriers – for example, by indigenizing the Canadian university system. She argues that the rise of identity politics in Canada over the past forty years has yet to embrace Indigenous identity and Aboriginal nationalism, even though Aboriginal groups have been working hard to challenge colonial systems and to change the Canadian status quo. She shares with Taiaiake Alfred and Patricia Monture-Angus an anti-colonial perspective, arguing that colonial-era institutions and processes persist in Canada and still wreak havoc on Indigenous cultures and political systems. That, in her view, is the issue facing Aboriginal peoples.

Green's writings, which cover a broad spectrum of issues with a gender studies perspective interwoven into the analysis, demonstrate the passion that Aboriginal scholars bring to their study of systemic inequalities in economic, political, and gender relations. Feminism has made few inroads into Indigenous political communities, and in that regard, she has engaged with Aboriginal activists in Canada and abroad, in the belief that there is an undercurrent of Aboriginal feminism that could strongly influence the Indigenous agenda. She argues that limited Indigenous self-government, while it may sound "empowering," has consigned many Aboriginal women to ongoing political marginalization. She also argues that many male-dominated band governments have limited the rights of women to full citizenship and participation, thereby perpetuating a broadly acknowledged abuse of the Indian Act and federal government policy.

Green's contributions have been principally twofold: she strongly articulates the marginalized position of Aboriginal women in Canada, and she places contemporary Indigenous policy in the broad context of colonialism, racism, and sexism. Her writings emphasize the special challenges facing Aboriginal women and the failure (so far) of Indigenous leaders and the federal government to fully embrace their issues and concerns. Her strongly worded analysis is a useful counterpoint to the perspective advanced by Thomas King (in *The Inconvenient Indian*), among others, for it highlights the systemic barriers to sweeping change that run through the Indigenous–newcomer relationship in Canada. Many Canadians still believe that Canada is not a racist or discriminatory nation and are uncomfortable with the intensity and anger in the work of Green and others, anger that exposes crucial elements in the historical and contemporary reality of Aboriginal women, and of Indigenous peoples generally.

**Patricia Monture-Angus**, a Mohawk (Kanien'kehá:ka) woman, trained lawyer, and academic at the University of Saskatchewan who passed away in 2010, folded a sharp critique of Canadian law into her understanding of Aboriginal futures. Historical studies and community experiences revealed to her the heavy weight of colonialism on Aboriginal peoples. She rejected the teaching of law because, as she writes in *Journeying Forward* (1999), she felt she was "cooperating too fully in my own oppression" (199). She concluded that the law, as an instrument of the state, was a powerful element in the maintenance of the status quo and was not, therefore, a route to Indigenous peoples' liberation. Her analysis of the political options advanced by Aboriginal leaders and Canadian officials' responses to them convinced her that the language and processes of self-government were too elitist and not properly connected to people and their communities. Solutions rooted in colonial authority were unlikely to address Aboriginal needs.

She offered a passionate and powerful analysis of the shortcomings of both Canadian law and Aboriginal politicians. She criticized the ongoing influence of the Indian Act and the power exercised by "Indian Act Chiefs," political leaders who hold power by virtue of their participation in colonial structures. She worried that the prevailing arguments and models were largely male-centred and did not recognize the historical role of women in Aboriginal communities and the political structures that incorporated Aboriginal women into decision making.

(In Monture-Angus's Kanien'kehá:ka cultural tradition, women exercise strong political authority.) While she found the current Aboriginal approaches wanting, she was especially angry about the slow response of non-Aboriginal governments and peoples to Aboriginal needs and aspirations. In *Journeying Forward* she states, "My goal, my dream for my children is that they may have freedom and independence" (11). In sharp contrast to political scientist Alan Cairns (see Chapter 4), who contends that Aboriginal and non-Aboriginal people need to develop a common citizenship, she wrote that "I do not think of myself as a Canadian as all of those state relations have been forced on Haudenosaunee people. I recognize that not all Aboriginal people share this belief. Consent is the central issue that requires resolution before I could consider myself to be both Kanien'kehaka and Canadian" (49). Cumulatively, her analysis illustrates the intensely personal values and experience-based emotions that underlie Aboriginal efforts to secure control of their futures.

Monture-Angus argued that freedom and independence rest with Aboriginal people and families, not formal institutions and constitutional provisions. She called for a reinvigoration of Aboriginal communities and reserve-centred life – a difficult argument to advance because of the many problems and harsh experiences a great number of Aboriginal people associate with reserves. More directly, she argued in *Journeying Forward* that "the solution lies with the people. Change will come not from institutions but from the people. It is just that simple. Being self-determining is simply about the way you choose to live your life every day. And from the people, comes my hope" (158). Her appeal to Aboriginal people, individually and collectively, to reassert control over their personal lives sprang from her deep understanding of the lingering impact of colonialism and from a realization that current political structures merely represent fresh forms of domination.

Monture-Angus situated the responsibility for the social, economic, and cultural plight of Aboriginal people clearly on the shoulders of non-Aboriginal Canadians, but she also made it clear that to expect substantial change from that quarter would be to hold out false hope. She wrote in *Journeying Forward,*

> Colonialism is about, among other things, controlling the lives of the individuals who comprise the people. When, for generations, a

people have been controlled, their ability to make decisions and advance change is impaired. In order to shake up our communities and get them thinking as communities again, relying on themselves instead of bureaucracies, all that needs to be done is to shift the pieces so the "common" answer, depending on the colonizer, is no longer available. It is out of this chaos that the change will come. I am quite certain that this is a gift brought to the people with the return or continued presence of the trickster. (159)

Monture-Angus's conception of Aboriginal peoples within Canada offered a bold assertion that it was important for Aboriginal people to take responsibility for their own circumstances. This view reflected her profound dissatisfaction with the law, the Canadian government, and Aboriginal governments. Her analysis was based on an understanding of historical processes and a profound lack of faith in existing institutions and political negotiations. The hope she placed in assertiveness and self-control came from her realization that Aboriginal people who could attend to themselves, their families, and their communities would no longer have to rely on the money and political will of the non-Aboriginal majority. She argued as well that the strength of Aboriginal values, customs, and beliefs could be extended and would eventually overcome the damage done by colonialism and its modern-day successors.

To suggest that Monture-Angus's arguments mesh with those of non-Aboriginal Canadians who argue for individual rights and personal responsibility would be to seriously misrepresent her position, although the two approaches do share a lack of confidence in political and administrative structures. For her, the re-establishment of First Nations control over personal lives and communities was a precursor to much more revolutionary change, which would happen when Aboriginal communities asserted the pre-eminence of traditional political structures and belief systems and demonstrated their contemporary relevance (contrary to the expectations of non-Aboriginal observers). That the Haudenosaunee (Iroquois) have created their own passports is, for example, precisely the kind of independent action that Monture-Angus would have supported. But she also argued that, at present, the onus lay with Indigenous people to step away from the endless dialogue with non-Aboriginal governments and seek instead to ensure Indigenous control of Indigenous lives.

**Kiera Ladner,** the Canada Research Chair in Indigenous Politics and Governance at the University of Manitoba, studies the long-term impact of colonization on Aboriginal peoples in Canada and examines efforts to reconcile Indigenous and non-Indigenous constitutional understandings. She focuses on the ecological foundations of Indigenous governance, the special challenges facing Aboriginal women, and the shortcomings of the Canadian state in responding to Indigenous aspirations. She seeks new ways of promoting reconciliation and decolonization among Aboriginal peoples. Aware of the lingering effects of historical relationships, she explores how community aspirations for self-determination might be squared with the Canadian state's overarching and often aggressively implemented constitutional assumptions.

Ladner is a harsh critic of many of the proposals that have circulated for transforming Aboriginal governance. For example, she has referred to the Royal Commission on Aboriginal People's recommendations on governance as negotiated inferiority, arguing that they failed to match the commission's stated vision of creating greater political equality for Indigenous Canadians. Early in the twenty-first century, when various proposals were circulating for renewed relationships, she found them wanting and argued that any discussion on the future of Aboriginal governance had to start with recognition of Indigenous peoples as partners in Confederation. In an important article provocatively titled "Out of the Fires of Hell," co-authored with Caroline Dick, she argues that debates about Aboriginal governance have hit a state of paradigm paralysis, marked by Ottawa's refusal to budge from a colonialist constitutional perspective. Because Ottawa has refused to question its own primacy and has rejected the nation-to-nation model preferred by Aboriginal peoples, discussion of possibilities has been truncated. Ladner and Dick suggest that global transformation – including trade liberalization, intellectual property rights regimes, and Indigenous engagement – provides mechanisms for improving Aboriginal rights, powers, and opportunities.

Ladner's passionately presented ideas illustrate the persistence of intellectual and political frustration with the present state of relations between the state and Aboriginal peoples. The political turmoil of the 1970s and 1980s, combined with real advances on the political, legal, and constitutional fronts, led many Indigenous leaders and intellectuals to believe that Aboriginal sovereignty would come in time. But since the 1990s, national attention has shifted so that there is greater emphasis on practical and local developments and much less on broad transformative visions of Indigenous affairs. Ladner's work illustrates the growing interest in international venues for Aboriginal activism as well as frustrations over stalled political progress in Canada, as if the Canadian imagination has been closed on matters of governance and reconciliation. Ladner continues to work for real reconciliation, grasping that Aboriginal communities bear by far the largest share of the cost for the shortcomings of the Canadian system and for the failure to develop sustainable models of Aboriginal governance and partnership with other Canadians.

Alfred, Coulthard, Green, Monture-Angus, and Ladner all offer biting critiques of the Canadian state and society and argue for a return to traditional values and political and social systems. They also argue that Aboriginal communities ought to "opt out of Canada." Alfred's solutions would lead to fundamental structural change within Canada. Monture-Angus called for Aboriginal communities to focus on their own responsibilities (she did not direct her attention to structural political change). These views do not represent mainstream Aboriginal political thinking in Canada; indeed, Alfred recognizes that his approach may reflect the aspirations of only 5 percent of Aboriginal communities. They are important positions nonetheless, as is evidenced in the politics of Mohawk communities in central Canada.

All five writers emphasize a critique of the status quo, but none of them suggest how Aboriginal autonomy would work in practice. Nor do they address questions about economic development within a global capitalist system. Although what they propose – a cultural exit from Canada and a return to traditional values – resembles what other social groups have succeeded in doing (the Amish, for example, and the Hutterites), there is little chance that their project will lead to solutions acceptable to either Aboriginal or non-Aboriginal Canadians, who would likely argue strongly that the focus must be on the self-determination of Aboriginal communities and not on relationships with provincial and federal governments.

# 2

# treaty federalism

**ABORIGINAL CANADIANS** attach enormous significance to the moral, legal, and political authority of the treaties they signed with the Crown. As many observers have pointed out, non-Aboriginal people view treaties as historical curiosities and minor legal irritants, not solemn commitments. By misunderstanding the centrepiece of Aboriginal understandings of nation-to-nation relationships, Canada has made a huge error. Aboriginal Canadians also argue that political accommodation between Indigenous and newcomer populations must rest on a comprehensive commitment to a partnership of peoples within Canada. A significant number of Aboriginal intellectual leaders emphasize the need to rebuild these federal relationships and to develop political structures that respect Indigenous autonomy and Aboriginal political systems and that bind Aboriginal and non-Aboriginal Canadians in a system built on mutual respect. As will become evident later in this book, the idea of becoming true treaty peoples is central to our view of how Indigenous–newcomer relations should unfold in the coming years.

The most consistent argument advanced by Aboriginal leaders and thinkers is summarized by the Two Row Wampum (in Mohawk, *guswen-qah*). **Ovide Mercredi**, then grand chief of the Assembly of First

Nations, and **Mary Ellen Turpel-Lafond**, a legal scholar and the representative for children and youth in British Columbia, summarized this concept in *In the Rapids* (1993):

> The two-row wampum, which signifies "One River, Two Vessels," committed the newcomers to travel in their vessel and not attempt to interfere with our voyage. The two vessels would travel down the river of life in parallel courses and would never interfere with each other. It was a co-living agreement. The two-row wampum captures the original values that governed our relationship – equality, respect, dignity and a sharing of the river we travel on. This is how the First Nations still understand our relationship with Canadians. (35)

The concept is simple: First Nations are nations in the broad, international understanding of that term, and as such they should enjoy sovereignty and self-government.

Political scientists understand this argument as a call for a form of parallelism – in other words, Indigenous and non-Indigenous Canadians would agree to live separate lives on a common land mass. In accepting the Canadian government's apology for residential schools, Phil Fontaine, grand chief of the Assembly of First Nations, said:

> It took some courage on the part of the Minister and government to take this historic step, to break with the past, and to apologize for the historic wrongs and injustices committed against our peoples. It is therefore a great honour for me, on behalf of the First Nations, to accept the apology of the Government and people of Canada. Let this moment mark the end of paternalism in our relations, and the beginning of the empowerment of First Peoples; the end of assimilationist policies, and the beginning of mutual respect and cooperation. This, after all, was the intention of our forefathers who agreed in the historic wampum treaty to paddle their canoes in separate but parallel paths.

For those who adhere to this view – and that would include many if not most Aboriginal political leaders in the country – the goal of constitutional negotiations, legal struggles, and political negotiations is to secure recognition of Aboriginal distinctiveness and to lay the foundation for peaceful but separate coexistence.

The most detailed statement of this philosophy is found in the *Report of the Royal Commission on Aboriginal Peoples*. That document pays little heed to the perspectives of non-Indigenous Canadians – a critical group to understand, for any government that hopes to formulate a "parallel" strategy. It does, though, make a strong and coherent case for separate institutions. Clearly, Aboriginal people would have to secure considerable political authority for this system to work. The country would have to acknowledge that Indigenous peoples are distinct political communities with an ongoing political relationship with the Canadian state.

Political scientist Alan Cairns (whose own perspective is discussed later) provides an excellent summation of the commission's argument in *Citizens Plus* (2000):

> The RCAP Report has a clear and consistent constitutional message. Its primary focus is on sixty to eighty Aboriginal nations, with separate treaty relations with Canada, whose governments are to be constitutionally entrenched in a third order of Aboriginal government. These governments are to occupy the maximum constitutional space possible within what are called core and peripheral areas of jurisdiction. The Aboriginal nation is to be the primary membership community for its citizens. It is a closed community in that the criteria for and admission to membership are controlled by the Aboriginal government. The Aboriginal nation or people is the appropriate unit for representation in an Aboriginal parliament, and, after constitutional amendment, in a House of First Peoples, with the primary goal of representing Aboriginal interest . . . What is clear is that the Commission has little enthusiasm for a direct individual citizen link with federal or provincial authorities. In general, the nation, through its government or its representatives, is to be the intermediary between the nation-based Aboriginal individual and the other two orders of government. For example, the vehicle for "negotiation adaptations in mainstream institutions that serve Aboriginal citizens" is neither Parliament nor provincial legislatures responding to voters and legislators, but self-

government, which is the "reinstatement of a nation-to-nation relationship." (153)

As Mercredi and Turpel-Lafond explain, Aboriginal peoples believe that their communities constitute "nations" much like Canada itself does. Historical processes resulted in Indigenous nations losing their authority, their ability to govern, and their land and resources. Today, however, politics and the law provide the opportunity to reinstate what has been lost. This view is based on a positive cultural understanding of Aboriginal governance systems and on the belief that those structures and values are suitable for contemporary Aboriginal realities. At the heart of this is the assumption that stripping away Indigenous political independence is what led to the current social and cultural malaise in Aboriginal communities. Regaining control – and the respect and cooperation of Ottawa and Canadians at large that would accompany being recognized as "sovereign" – would allow Aboriginal peoples to re-establish customary practices and rebuild damaged lives and communities.

Parallelism has its practical side. As Mercredi and Turpel-Lafond make clear, Aboriginal leaders do not truly believe that small, isolated reserve communities will become independent nations in the international sense of that term. (Critics of self-government describe this as the likely outcome, arguing that it would lead to hundreds of "fiefdoms" across the country.) They assume an ongoing financial and political relationship with the Government of Canada, and they would prefer that First Nations be minimally involved with provincial governments. They would prefer, as well, the concept of a third order of government, one that would recognize their effective independence over cultural, social, and local matters (which would not entail province-like status, however). They also recognize that economic and other relationships would continue; indeed, they argue that non-Aboriginal people would show more respect to self-governing and somewhat independent First Nations.

Forty years after Aboriginal political aspirations re-emerged in the public arena in Canada, parallelism has emerged as the standard Aboriginal position across Canada. Not all hold this view, as will be seen, but the idea has a strong following among Indigenous political leaders. Many Aboriginal people assume that self-governing Aboriginal communities with autonomy, assured resources, and a significant political presence are inevitable. For them, the more important discussion revolves around the practicalities of implementing this widely shared vision of Aboriginal–non-Aboriginal relations in Canada.

In this broader context of parallelism, some analysts are anxious for the Canadian federal system to expand to incorporate Aboriginal needs and ambitions. For scholars such as **James (Sákéj) Youngblood Henderson**, the appropriate goal for Aboriginal peoples is neither separation nor sovereignty-association (to borrow a Quebec nationalist term). Rather, Aboriginal peoples want *into* the Canadian federal system and seek a full and meaningful political partnership with it.

Henderson argues that the basis for treaty federalism can be traced back to the first treaties signed between Britain and Aboriginal peoples (and carried forward subsequently by the Dominion of Canada) and that those agreements were founded on nation-to-nation relationships. These initial treaties in central and western Canada attended to matters of land and resource rights and were generally silent when it came to administration and governance. At no point, Henderson argues, did Aboriginal peoples explicitly surrender their internal sovereignty (the capacity to govern their own affairs); it follows that they preserved the inherent right to self-government. As modern treaties unfold, advocates assert, Aboriginal peoples start with the rights of internal sovereignty and can cede certain areas of jurisdiction to the federal or provincial governments as part of a treaty agreement. The right of self-government, therefore, rests with Aboriginal peoples. It is not something for the Ottawa or the provinces to *grant* to Aboriginal communities.

Henderson's vision bears little resemblance to the James Bay Cree–Naskapi and Sechelt models of self-government. Those accords (the James Bay and Northern Quebec Agreement was signed in 1975; the Cree-Naskapi (of Quebec) Act, in 1984; the Sechelt Indian Band Self-Government Act, in 1986) rest on authority delegated by the federal and provincial governments to specific First Nations. This delegated self-government model clearly does not flow from the idea that internal sovereignty rests with Aboriginal communities. Furthermore, under the self-government agreements, delegated authority remains subject to future changes or manipulation by national or regional governments. Delegated self-government does not respect or acknowledge the assertion that these rights rest with the Aboriginal peoples.

Some observers see treaty federalism as a sharp departure from existing practice. Its advocates, however, argue that it does little more that formalize existing arrangements in a respectful manner. Bands and tribal councils already exercise many of the responsibilities sought under the treaty federalism model. The concept's primary importance is that it would, if implemented, acknowledge that administrative powers rest with the Aboriginal peoples as a matter of internal sovereignty and not as an act of generosity or benevolence by other levels of government. Properly acknowledged and implemented, treaty federalism would establish structures for the long-term peaceful coexistence of Aboriginal peoples and other Canadians, working under the common structures, processes, and protections of Canadian federalism. In this way, Aboriginal communities would be operating within, not outside, the Canadian federal system.

The mechanisms for implementing treaty federalism are fairly straightforward. Large Aboriginal communities, offering economies of administrative scale, could negotiate with the federal government as single nations. Smaller Aboriginal communities, struggling with limited resources and tiny populations, could enter into regional agreements with federal and provincial governments.

For Henderson, treaty federalism represents a critical symbolic and practical advance. Under this system, Aboriginal sovereignty would be recognized as a critical element of the Canadian federal system. Three sovereignties – Aboriginal, federal, and provincial – would be acknowledged and would be deemed to be equivalent in legal and constitutional terms. This would not, he cautions, mean that Aboriginal authority would match or supersede federal or provincial authority, save for the internal operations of the Aboriginal communities. Implementation would not be overly complicated, for it could be concluded by negotiating modern treaties or through a general measure of constitutional recognition. The Nisga'a treaty in British Columbia, finalized in 2000, comes very close to embodying the principles of treaty federalism, in that the Nisga'a have formally opted into the Canadian system while retaining (as opposed to being *granted*) control of their internal affairs.

Proponents of treaty federalism point out that the roots of this concept are in established legal concepts and American experience; treaty federalism would not, as critics suggest, put Canada's political system at risk. The Royal Proclamation of 1763, for example, declares that "the several Nations or Tribes of Indians with whom We are connected, and who live under our Protection, should not be molested or disturbed," which suggests British government support for the idea of continuing self-administration. Chief Justice Marshall of the US Supreme Court gave North American expression to this concept in the nineteenth century when he declared that Indians were "domestic dependent nations." As a result of this ruling, and continuing through to the present, the US federal and state governments have formally recognized American Indians as possessing internal sovereignty; this protects their legal right to attend to their affairs separate from non-Indian administrations. To Canadian critics who argue that treaty federalism would lead to a patchwork of tribal states and the erosion of provincial and federal authority, advocates need only point to the United States. Accepting the sovereignty of American Indians has clearly not undermined national or regional governance in that country.

Treaty federalism represents an important constitutional and administrative option for Canada and could be the centrepiece of future efforts towards political reconciliation. The key to the concept is that Aboriginal peoples would be *consenting* to join Canada as full and respected partners in national federalism, as many are doing through the modern treaty process. Treaty federalism does not turn Aboriginal political communities into new, full-blown federal/provincial governments. Rather, each level of government is recognized as retaining sovereignty and responsibility within clearly defined areas. This can be put differently. At present, Canadian federalism holds relatively little status or credibility with Aboriginal peoples, in that the Canadian political system was imposed on them, not selected by them. Advocates argue that the adoption of treaty federalism would give Canadian federalism greater legitimacy among Aboriginal people and provide a foundation for the effective administration of Aboriginal affairs as well as a basis for long-term relations between Indigenous and other Canadians.

Lest Canadians see Henderson's proposal as a radical or dramatic departure from existing practice, the concept actually speaks to the essence of federalism. As defined by scholars such as Canadian political scientist Thomas Hueglin and the German legal theorist Carl Schmitt, federalism is a treaty among constituent parts. So, Canadian federalism is a compact or agreement by which distinct communities joined a collectivity. The founding provinces of Canada (Nova Scotia, New Brunswick, Quebec, and Ontario) negotiated terms of Confederation that met, to a greater or lesser extent, the needs of their constituents. British Columbia, Prince Edward Island, Manitoba, and Newfoundland negotiated their way into Confederation by making treaty-like agreements. By contrast, Alberta, Saskatchewan, and the territories were created by federal fiat and struggled against their inferior constitutional and political status. The Nisga'a Final Agreement is a similar partnership with Canada and British Columbia. Clearly, the authority and legitimacy of regional partnerships in Canada rest on negotiated agreements with constitutional partners.

For Aboriginal political communities, Henderson is asking for what other political jurisdictions have secured in the past – the right to choose entry into Canadian federalism. Doing so would recognize Aboriginal communities' historical and traditional rights to control their own affairs; it would also signal an acceptance of the division of powers within the Canadian state. Treaty federalism would require an act of union through an individual or collective treaty; it would also imply a commitment by Aboriginal peoples to the political structures of Canada. By recognizing that internal sovereignty rests with Aboriginal political communities, it would empower Aboriginal peoples to attend to local administration without the potentially patronizing inference that self-government has been delegated or granted by federal and provincial governments (which would retain the right to revoke the delegated authority). Given the proposal's fit with the broad contours of Canadian federalism and with existing American practice, treaty federalism has the added advantage of being easily understood and monitored.

**Dan Russell**, an Aboriginal lawyer, offers a thorough but practical critique of Canadian Indian policy and makes a very strong case for Aboriginal self-government. Drawing on and challenging traditional political theory, he tackles the proposition that self-government is not viable. He writes that Aboriginal self-government is no panacea and will face significant short-term difficulties as Aboriginal people attempt to establish viable governing systems. There are, he points out, major issues to be resolved: the status of Aboriginal collective rights, the relationship between Aboriginal self-government and the Charter of Rights and Freedoms, and the possibility of implementing self-government inappropriately. Russell is not a strong supporter of the *Report of the Royal Commission on Aboriginal Peoples,* arguing that its recommendations would limit the effective sovereignty of Aboriginal governments and make it harder for Aboriginal people to address the issues of greatest concern to them.

For Russell, self-government is necessary to address the social, economic, and political challenges facing Aboriginal communities. But by itself, he adds, it will not resolve the many problems those communities face. The solutions to those problems must be rooted in the tried-and-true traditions and values of Aboriginal communities. He quotes the English conservative philosopher, Edmund Burke: "The rules best suited to promote the welfare of a community will emerge only from the experience of that community, so that more trust must be put in established social culture than in the social engineering of utilitarians who suppose they know better than history." This emphasis on tradition is consistent with the arguments of Alfred and Monture-Angus. It is also consistent with principles of Canadian conservative Toryism, which place great value on time-tested social institutions.

Russell's approach does not share the utopian perspective of some Aboriginal political philosophers. It is founded on what he describes as a realistic and pragmatic appraisal of the situation. He notes, for example, that in Canadian political debate, Aboriginal self-government is a relatively new concept, one that originated in the patriation debate of 1982 and the 1983 Penner Report on Native Self-Governance. He observes as well that in the referendum of 1992, the Canadian public rejected the Charlottetown Accord, which would have extended self-government to Aboriginal people. Government policy has since then recognized and supported Aboriginal self-government; however, the concept does not have legal or constitutional protection, although some government and Aboriginal leaders talk as if it does.

Russell's approach to Indigenous governance and Aboriginal rights in Canada leans heavily on lessons drawn from the United States. As he points out, Indian tribes in the United States enjoy considerable legal sovereignty, including the right to operate their own police forces and court systems. In other words, US practice already includes a variety of political powers and rights that Canadian critics view as unworkable and as a threat to the Canadian political fabric. In the United States, this recognition goes back to the nineteenth century, particularly the famous *Cherokee Nation v. Georgia* case of 1831, in which the US Supreme Court defined Indian nations as "dependent domestic nations." This meant they had and could continue to have under US law a high degree of sovereignty and self-government. That self-government is not a panacea for the ills facing Aboriginal communities is suggested by the fact that self-governing Indian nations in the United States face poverty, crime, and domestic problems comparable to those of Aboriginal communities in Canada.

Within the Canadian system, Ottawa's limited recognition of Aboriginal self-government has permitted some local administration. Russell argues that much more should be done in this regard. He suggests in *A People's Dream* (2000) that "local governments may know how best to utilize resources within their communities in resolving such problems" (35). Focusing again on practical questions, he suggests that greater attention should be paid to tribal rather than band governance so as to capitalize on economies of scale and broader perspectives. Groups, he argues, should be based on self-identification and not on an externally imposed structure, which has caused problems in the past.

In arguing for the importance of self-identification as the key to future governance, Russell draws from Western political thinkers as diverse as Rousseau and John Rawls to advance a contract argument of political legitimacy. A governing authority and its laws, he suggests, are legitimate only to the degree that individuals in the affected community consent to them. Since this concept applies to the Canadian government, why should it not also apply to Aboriginal governments? He cites the Nisga'a Lisims government, which is based on the principle of Aboriginal people choosing the style and structure of administration that best reflects community needs and aspirations.

Russell differs dramatically from many other Aboriginal political thinkers in his emphasis on pragmatic solutions. In particular, he differs from most by agreeing that Aboriginal governments have to negotiate with provincial governments, since many of their self-governing powers will overlap or compete with those of the provinces. "This requirement may be unpalatable for certain Aboriginal communities,"

he writes, but they will have to overcome their reluctance and negotiate with provincial governments. He questions whether treaty negotiations are the best means for achieving self-government for Aboriginal
communities. Referring again to the Nisga'a, he asks in *A People's
Dream,* "If the Nisga'a people, with all the advantages of their bar-
gaining position, could only achieve meagre municipal-like authority,
then what lies in store for those Aboriginal people who do not share
these strengths?" (55).

According to Russell, the best means to establish self-government is
the principled approach, which will require entrenching self-government formally in the Constitution. A constitutionally entrenched right
to self-government would be limited to domestic matters; currency,
international treaties, armies, external affairs, and the like would be
excluded from the range of powers. On domestic issues, including
criminal and civil law, Aboriginal authority would be substantial, just
as US law permits, to a limited extent. If there is conflict between
Aboriginal and provincial or federal law, Russell argues, Aboriginal
law should prevail, but only within Aboriginal communities. These
laws would extend beyond the boundaries of duly constituted First
Nations. This arrangement would go further than the Nisga'a agreement. However, given the difficulties of amending the Constitution
over the past forty years, it is hard to see how this particular proposal
has any prospects.

In advancing his argument, Russell makes an interesting case related to Aboriginal collective rights. Aboriginal communities, he
points out, typically do not possess the concept of personal rights –
the emphasis is more on personal *duties* than individual rights. He
uses the example of the Navajo court system, which uses regular
Western-style courts, as well as the Peacemaker Court system, which
draws on traditional principles of conflict resolution. For Aboriginal
communities, the balance between rights and duties is critical to the
success of any government and legal system.

Unlike many critics of Aboriginal governance plans, Russell argues
that the collective approach found in Aboriginal governing systems is
compatible with democratic practices, largely because that approach
has its own checks and balances. Furthermore, any tensions between
the Charter of Rights and Freedoms and Aboriginal self-government
need not be fatal. (This was a matter of considerable concern for

Aboriginal people, especially women, and was largely resolved in 2011 when the Canadian government passed legislation ensuring that the Charter applied on reserves.) Many fear that traditional collectivist customs and values will impinge on individual rights. Aboriginal communities, Russell asserts, must be able to place limits on the application of the Charter. Failure to do so would undercut the very concept of culturally based Aboriginal self-government. He proposes going beyond current Canadian and US practice by creating Aboriginal charters that would recognize both individual and collective rights and that would commit communities and their governments to identifying and observing an appropriate balance between the two value systems.

Russell's vision is both bold and technically refined. He proposes the recognition of Aboriginal sovereignty at a very broad level, and he supports the extension of self-government rights beyond those recommended by the royal commission. At the same time, he is a pragmatist, noting that new governance systems represent at best a partial solution to the challenges facing Aboriginal peoples in Canada. He also accepts that the tribal rather than band approach to governance is important and that steps must be taken to recognize the potential conflict between collective and individual rights. And he acknowledges that Aboriginal governments have to work closely with provincial and federal authorities and accept that improvements in local conditions will come with time and effort, not immediately after new political structures have been established.

For Russell, the answer lies in creative and comprehensive approaches to Aboriginal self-government and sovereignty and in greater cooperation with other levels of government. He cautions against the vilification of federal and provincial governments: "Blame is seldom a very constructive instinct" (199). He points out that governments are sensitive to the blemish that many decades of Aboriginal poverty and suffering have left on Canada's international image. Violent outbreaks at Oka, Ipperwash, Gustafson Lake, Caledonia, and Rexton (Elsipogtog First Nation, in New Brunswick) have spurred the national desire to resolve the endlessly perplexing challenges facing Indigenous peoples in Canada. In calling for aggressive steps, he notes that all of these variables support the federal reconciliation of Aboriginal issues and that self-government would be a significant step forward. He believes that recent Supreme Court of Canada decisions (specifically *Sparrow* and *Van der Peet*) have strengthened the Aboriginal case and made it more likely that self-government will be approved by the courts.

Russell does not push his arguments to their logical conclusion, and he does not indicate how self-government would change the daily lives of Aboriginal people. He does make it clear that initiatives beyond those offered by the *Report of the Royal Commission on Aboriginal Peoples* are needed and that Aboriginal self-government is a first and critical step along that path. By introducing the comparative/ American perspective to the Canadian debate, he addresses some of the major concerns of critics of Aboriginal empowerment, demonstrating that respect for Indigenous sovereignty and self-government need not result in the dismantling of the Canadian federal system. His is a pragmatic, legalistic approach to the question of Aboriginal rights, one founded on the realization that Aboriginal people face a long and difficult challenge as they seek to regain control of their communities and, ultimately, their lives.

Mercredi and Turpel-Lafond, Henderson, and Russell all offer visions for the accommodation of Aboriginal peoples *within* Canada. Some critics see this as a form of parallelism that fragments citizenship within Canada. But as a general principle, treaty federalism is an extension of already-existing Canadian political practice.

# 3

# bridging the solitudes

**WHILE STILL** emphasizing the rebuilding of relationships and the re-structuring of political accommodation between Indigenous and non-Indigenous peoples, several Aboriginal scholars argue that the fundamental problem is not political institutions. Instead, they see an urgent need to create mutual understanding and to ensure respectful interaction between cultures in Canada. They look forward to a Canada that has moved beyond the obsession with contemporary political labels and differences and that has found the means to understand and accommodate Aboriginal people within society.

**John Borrows**, an Anishnabe lawyer, formerly based at the University of Victoria and now at the University of Minnesota, frames his analysis with a deep understanding of the Aboriginal world view and spirituality. His recent works, *Recovering Canada* (2002), *Canada's Indigenous Constitution* (2010), and *Drawing Out Law* (2010), are notable for bridging formal legal traditions with Indigenous cultures. Stepping away from the concept of Two Row Wampum, Borrows argues for a strong, Aboriginally-based interconnectedness with non-Indigenous Canada. He examines the long-standing preoccupation with the Constitution and legal rights and suggests that Aboriginal people have much more to offer Canada than a constant battle over narrow definitions of Aboriginal rights. In *Recovering Canada,* he advocates a broad approach to Aboriginal legal and constitutional rights and insists that rights, and their legal interpretation, must respond to contemporary realities:

> Aboriginal peoples are entitled to expect legal protection for their existence as communities and nations within North America. Otherwise, what is the value of entrenching aboriginal rights in the Constitution if the societies these rights were meant to protect cannot survive? Canadian courts have not yet come to terms with the fact that, like others, Aboriginal people are traditional, modern and post-modern. Physical and cultural survival depends as much on attracting legal protection for contemporary activities, as it does on gaining recognition for traditional practices. The courts need to recognize that Aboriginal rights attach to Aboriginal activities, whether making moccasins or marketing computers . . . The rights exist first and foremost to protect the group, and are only incidentally concerned with the protection of specific practices. (75)

To achieve this goal, non-Aboriginal courts must, he argues, be alert to the teachings and insights of Indigenous societies, and Aboriginal peoples must consider the benefits of operating within the non-Aboriginal legal system. Instead of focusing on separation and distinctiveness, both groups should learn to draw from each other. Self-government could use ideas, structures, and governing principles from the Aboriginal *and* non-Aboriginal experience; merging values with practice would not deny the indigeneity of the self-governing community. Borrows worries that the emphasis on colonialism and the shortcomings of the Canadian state are raising high barriers to mutual respect, thus impeding rather than strengthening the possibilities for cooperation.

For Borrows, the answer lies in greater mutual respect and the crossfertilization of models and approaches. Non-Aboriginal people have to accept the reality of Aboriginal self-government, for such structures are essential to cultural vitality and the effective management of Aboriginal communities. In rejecting the suggestion that Aboriginal peoples have to choose between traditional and contemporary government structures – one Indigenous, the other colonial – he argues that self-government

> [has to] incorporate the connections which life together on the same continent demanded. Therefore, the argument as to whether to accept or reject Western institutions in the exercise of self-government is misleading. While the exercise of power may have its source in the inherent right of self-government, the exercise of power transpires in a fashion that is completely new to the people employing it. The exercise of authority is neither adopted nor traditional, but is an amalgamation of the two perspectives. (311)

But for Aboriginal concepts of law and justice to be accepted by non-Aboriginals, they must first be applied in Indigenous communities: "In fact, the chances of Canadian law accepting Aboriginal legal principles would be substantially weakened if the First Nations did not continue to practice their own laws within their own systems . . . Aboriginal systems of law can and do operate with or without the reception of their principles in Canadian courtrooms" (27).

The central theme in Borrows's work is that it is possible to remain Aboriginal, exercise self-government, and participate actively with non-Indigenous Canadians to create a broader nation and more inclusive society. The country thus constituted would not be based on rivalries and tensions between Indigenous and non-Indigenous Canadians; instead, the two would draw inspiration and ideas from each other. In this way, Aboriginal models would circulate far outside the Aboriginal world (sentencing circles already do, for example), and would solidify relations between the groups. Borrows's world is not one where Aboriginal people are subsumed by other Canadians but one that recognizes and honours distinctiveness.

Borrows's optimism and commitment to mutual respect have not blinded him to the problems in the current system. He worries that governments and the courts tend to "freeze" Aboriginal rights by limiting legal authority to traditional and historical practices. He insists that Aboriginal rights must be made current and must be viewed as tools for ensuring Indigenous cultural survival. He is not comfortable with recent developments: "Canada continually uses its legislatures to modify, infringe, or extinguish Aboriginal and treaty rights. Courts have continued to develop, support, and implement this framework. The domestication of Aboriginal and treaty rights in this way represents another stage in the development of colonialism for Indigenous peoples" (11). Without greater flexibility, he argues, Aboriginal people will be unable to pursue the political and economic development necessary for their cultural survival.

What is particularly important about Borrows's analysis is his argument that the two systems can coexist and even strengthen each other. But this will only happen when the Canadian government and its court system adopt a more expansive view of Aboriginal and treaty rights and find ways to apply historic agreements to contemporary situations. Although Borrows is among the more integrationist of Aboriginal scholars, his emphasis on broadening the legal definitions of Aboriginal and treaty rights runs counter to prevailing sentiment in Canada. Many Aboriginal thinkers insist that sovereignty must be recognized and that Indigenous–newcomer relations must be dramatically rethought and constitutionally entrenched; and many non-Aboriginal lawyers and opponents of Indigenous rights favour a narrower, historically specific definition of Aboriginal legal entitlements. No doubt the battle will be waged in courtrooms across the country over the coming decades.

Aboriginal thinkers have devoted enormous energy to the future relationship between Aboriginal people and other Canadians. An early contribution to the debate about reconciliation comes from **Emma LaRocque**, a Métis from northern Alberta. LaRocque's important study *Defeathering the Indian* (1975) focuses on how the education system can help bring about cultural understanding. But her main goal is to chart a strategy for ensuring mutually respectful Aboriginal–non-Aboriginal relations in Canada.

For LaRocque, the greatest hurdle faced by Aboriginal peoples is stereotypes about them, which have become deeply entrenched. European images and assumptions have made it difficult for non-Indigenous peoples to conceive of First Nations and Métis fitting into the dominant society. She argues that the education system is key to bridging the gulf between cultures and societies. LaRocque, in a position with striking parallels to that of John Borrows, asserts that Aboriginal and other Canadians have to live together and therefore must learn to understand each other. It is not enough to teach

Indigenous peoples they should be proud of their heritage and culture, however essential this is for self-esteem and a positive self-image.
Educational systems have to adopt a more comprehensive agenda:

> Since a people cannot exist on an island, it is not enough for
> Native people to feel good about themselves; it is just as import-
> ant that others share this feeling with them. Authentic, consistent
> exposure of the past and present of the Indian and Métis in the
> provincial curriculums of this country would contribute greatly
> toward bridging the startling, emotional separation between
> Native and non-Native Canadians. (2)

For LaRocque, reconciliation must begin at a fundamental level, by
dispelling negative and irrelevant stereotypes about Indigenous
peoples. Consider the basic question, Who is an Aboriginal person?
Does an Aboriginal person who stops trapping in northern Alberta
and moves to Edmonton cease to be Native? The standard assumption
about Aboriginal Canadians would suggest that the answer is yes. For
LaRocque, it is a firm and declarative "no!" Aboriginal Canadians are,
she points out, constantly being asked whether they are still in touch
with their culture and traditional values. Within the existing Canadian
educational system, to be Aboriginal is to wear feathers and beads and
follow a harvesting lifestyle. For Aboriginal people but not other
Canadians, the separate categories of heritage and culture have been
conflated. In all societies, cultures change. Yet the dominant society
treats "Indian" history as if it were frozen at a fixed point in time – as
if Indians cannot change and adapt with the rest of humanity. This
does not take into account that all peoples are always changing – and
certainly Indians do.

Cultural double standards are nothing new. Change, LaRocque observes, does not boil down to a choice between staying on a reserve
and being Indian and leaving and being white. On reserve or off, an
Indian is still an Indian. She asks rhetorically, "How about the missionaries who learned the Indian languages? Did anyone call them
Indian? Did a Scot become a non-Scot when he no longer wore his kilt
or played the bagpipes?" (11). Educators face the challenge of over-
coming stereotypes and creating a reality-based image of Aboriginal
peoples. Without such a change, Aboriginal Canadians will continue

to be viewed as caricatures, wedded to the past and unable to adapt to the present. LaRocque suggests that the education system has to present a different view, one that sees Aboriginal people as hunters and trappers and also as farmers, ranchers, poets, and university graduates. The schools would have to tackle the difficult question of the treaties and the Indian Act, explaining both the origins of these critical legal documents and their relevance in contemporary Canada. The presentation would have to be sufficiently nuanced to underscore the difference between Status and non-Status Indians, First Nations, Inuit, and Métis. In other words, Aboriginal Canadians would be presented in all their diversity, as real and modern peoples and not as stick figures from the past. The portrait of Indigenous societies would have to be empathetic and realistic, but it would not obsess about negative characteristics.

The key to LaRocque's view of Aboriginal peoples, and of Canada generally, is that the country needs to better understand the complexity of the Aboriginal experience. She points out that Aboriginal religious activity blends Indigenous spiritual beliefs with Christianity, including in high-profile events such as the popular pilgrimages to Lac Ste. Anne, Alberta. Many Aboriginal people are comfortable on the land and with traditional lifestyles. But there are also other "native people who have very quickly and very comfortably adapted to traffic, noise, pollution, Chargex bills, gastritis, and other urban amenities" (22). Only when there is greater appreciation of the true nature and variety of Indigenous experiences, she asserts, will Canadians be able to move beyond hoary stereotypes, whether intended to be positive (the "noble red man," the "natural environmentalist") or negative ("dirty Indian," "lazy"). Eventually "there comes a time when we must recognize each person as an individual rather than as a carbon copy of what we suppose to be his culture" (74). It seems to her "that we are ever tempted to diverge into two extremes; we dwell upon our differences to the point of excluding our similarities, or we universalize everyone at the expense of identity and diversity" (76).

Compared to the other Aboriginal thinkers considered here, LaRocque devotes little time to law, constitutional change, and self-government. She offers instead an analysis of a fundamental weakness in Canadian society: the inability to remove the blinders of history and see Aboriginal people the way they are currently are and the way they intend to be. (She points out that the cultural myopia is not limited to Indigenous cultures, but extends to other groups outside the social mainstream.) She would have Canada place its emphasis on a systematic program of crosscultural education, in the belief that cultural understanding would form a permanent and sustainable foundation for reconciliation. By dismantling stereotypes and outdated cultural assumptions, non-Aboriginal Canadians would better appreciate the opportunities and promise of Indigenous peoples and would be more likely to create space for them in their social and economic world. The challenge is formidable; the work is of fundamental importance. She argues for a country where the barriers between Indigenous and non-Indigenous Canadians are replaced with mutual respect and understanding. Only then will the country really begin to repair its social, economic, and cultural rifts.

LaRocque's answer to the challenges facing Indigenous peoples in Canada is the one most Canadians would like to see work. It hasn't, at least not yet. For several decades, schools across Canada have offered much more Indigenous-friendly curricula. Some (the territories, Manitoba and Saskatchewan) have been comprehensive in their inclusion of Indigenous themes and perspectives. Across the country, education systems have adopted anti-racism agendas (which makes one ask whether the former systems were "pro-racism") and are strongly supportive of cultural understanding and inclusion. Faculties of education have been uniformly aggressive in adopting more favourable approaches to Aboriginal culture and Indigenous knowledge. But the years of educational inclusion have seen a significant rise in political and public opposition to Indigenous rights, which suggests that Indigenous-friendly education is no quick solution to the cultural gap between Canadian peoples.

Aboriginal leadership in Canada has been transformed, but not in a way most Canadians would recognize. The political rhetoric from the Assembly of First Nations, the Métis National Council, and regional and local Indigenous groups remains much the same: diverse, often angry, and focused on national policies and government funding. But in recent years, new leaders have been emerging, publicly quiet but often highly effective. Their emphasis is much different: economic development rather than constitutional change, effective governance rather than nation-to-nation negotiations, collaboration with the private sector rather than government departments. People such as Bernd Christmas of Membertou First Nation in Nova Scotia, Chief Clarence Louie of the Osoyoos First Nation in British Columbia, Paul Birckel of the Champagne-Aishihik First Nation in Yukon, Sophie Pierre of the St. Mary's Indian Band in British Columbia, Nellie Cournoyea of the Inuvialuit – all have reshaped their communities and changed the trajectory of Aboriginal affairs in Canada. What they have generally not done is enter the public debate about Aboriginal policy in Canada – at least until Calvin Helin came on the scene.

**Calvin Helin** has a commitment to business and job creation and effective governance, one that he shares with Canada's new wave of Aboriginal leaders. These people share with Helin a great deal of frustration and even anger about the past; they know about the legacy of discrimination and hostility that Indigenous people have faced and continue to endure, and they understand the depth of the social, cultural, and economic problems facing their communities. In this, they differ little from most Aboriginal commentators and thinkers we have profiled so far. But Helin and his contemporaries diverge from the Aboriginal mainstream with regard to their sense of what has to be done to address the problems. Helin is a Tsimshian lawyer with an impressive track record in organizations such as the Native Investment and Trade Association, the National Aboriginal Business Association, and the Canadian Council for Aboriginal Business. He has served on private and public sector boards and has actively promoted Aboriginal engagement with international trade, most recently by leading trade missions to New Zealand and China.

Helin has been lecturing, consulting, and organizing extensively, highlighting his belief that self-reliance, self-respect, and engagement with business are essential for Aboriginal adaptation and success in the twenty-first century. As he wrote on his blog in March 2007, announcing the publication of *Dances with Dependency* (2006):

> I have written this book with the simple interest of seeking to make the lives of ordinary indigenous people better. The toll that the current system is taking on indigenous people (particularly children and youth) is horrendous and unacceptable. There is something that can be done about the current situation now. That is what *Dances with Dependency* is all about. The bottom line for

Canada is that this is not an Aboriginal problem, it is a *Canadian* problem. The impending demographic tsunami will change the *status quo* – rather than a crisis, this can be the biggest opportunity ever presented to move indigenous people forward. It will, however, take constructive action from Aboriginal people, government, industry and labour now.

Helin has the same sense of urgency as other Aboriginal thinkers, the same passion for his community and for Indigenous people generally, and the same conviction that the current approach is not a workable foundation for the future. Where he differs – and differs dramatically – is in his call for action.

His approach is rooted in a long historical view and deep affection for Aboriginal cultures. He divides the history of Indigenous peoples into four waves. The first three comprise a long period of self-reliance and self-discipline in the centuries before the Europeans arrived; a disruptive and demoralizing period of colonization; and a wave of welfare dependency that, he argues, sapped the spirit and vitality of Aboriginal cultures and communities. Helin decries the destructive influence of the so-called welfare trap and argues that everything from economic marginalization and self-destructive behaviours to the shortcomings of the Aboriginal political processes can be traced to overreliance on government. He argues that Aboriginal Canadians have developed a culture of expectation and entitlement and allowed corruption and nepotism to dominate their governance system. They have, he asserts, squandered opportunities in the market economy, fostered a misery industry around their social pathologies, and lost the self-reliance and independence that long characterized their communities. This is a blunt and hard-hitting assessment, made all the more powerful by his long experience with Aboriginal societies. The fourth wave, which he describes as "a way out of the storm," focuses on economic development, effective use of land claims and other settlements, expanded and relevant education, strong attention to the needs and potential of urban Aboriginals, and the improvement of relations with other Canadians.

*Dances with Dependency* does not simply revisit old grievances or past battles with government and the dominant society. Instead, Helin argues that Aboriginal people need to rethink their confrontational status with government and Canadians at large, drop the culture of grievance, and battle their way out of welfare dependency:

> In order to take action that is likely to make a constructive difference, we must acknowledge the brutal reality regarding the place where the colonial storm has left us. We must acknowledge the welfare trap and the impact of "shaman economics" – how this has economically isolated communities and created the current complete reliance on transfer payments and welfare. We must concede the profound destruction the welfare trap has wreaked and the disturbing social and political pathologies created. We must be prepared to change the culture of expectancy and the dependency mindset preventing us from making our lives better. We must admit that the existing system requires enormous reform if indigenous people are to have any hope of moving forward. (259)

And he adds: "The staggering human and economic price that indigenous people are paying now for a few welfare dollars is simply far too high to justify continuing on this path – particularly when we know that a healthier and more fulfilling future is possible" (265).

In a provocative chapter titled "The Fourth Wave: A Way Out of the Storm," he offers advice on how to proceed. Among his many recommendations, the following stand out. First Nations must capitalize on their legal, location, and policy advantages to leverage additional spending and investment from government and the private sector. At the same time, they have to be provided with more control over land and resource management on reserves. They must make education a key priority, but at the same time, they need to raise their standards and expectations, rejecting the academic segregation of "cultural sensitivity" approaches. They need to focus their community activities on corporate development and local investments, taking their lead from successful models in the United States and Canada. And finally, besides strengthening the political voice of urban Aboriginal people, they need to promote economic integration through homeownership and personal responsibility.

Helin writes with anger and determination, pointing a fair amount of his condemnation at current Aboriginal policies, the culture of victimization, and overreliance on Ottawa and a guilt-ridden non-Aboriginal society. He provides a radically different view of present and future Indigenous affairs in Canada, one that is sharply focused on self-help rather than community grievances and the hornet's nest of Aboriginal politics. It is difficult to know how much support he has, just as it is hard to know if Alfred, Monture-Angus, or others have widespread backing in Indigenous communities. Non-Aboriginal business people and government officials, not surprisingly, are taken with Helin's approach. Given the rapid changes in Aboriginal society in Canada – higher levels of education, greater entrepreneurship, and local challenges to the political status quo – it is likely that his views have strong support and may well garner more in the coming years.

Then there is **Bonita Beatty,** an associate professor in Native Studies at the University of Saskatchewan, who brings more than twenty years' experience with the Peter Ballantyne Cree Nation, the Federation of Saskatchewan Indian Nations, and the Government of Saskatchewan to her academic work on Aboriginal–newcomer relations. She applies the so-called governance approach to her work, with the focus on decision making and stakeholders' engagement. She is especially interested in the balance in governance between the formal institutions (the state) and informal mechanisms of governance (community politics). Her work underscores the need for a deeper appreciation of how Indigenous affairs are managed, both at the band level and between Aboriginal groups and government, as part of any strategy for improving relations in Canada.

Beatty shows that the administrative devolution of recent decades (the transfer of power from the federal to Aboriginal governments) has had a positive influence on Aboriginal communities, improving their governance systems and administrative capacity in fields such as education, economic development, and health care. Bands are sharing power and responsibility with their communities, working to separate politics from administration, and are thereby producing more effective outcomes. Her case studies, drawn from northern Saskatchewan, stand in stark contrast to standard non-Aboriginal views of Indigenous self-government arrangements. With regard to health care, for example, Beatty has shown that local control has delivered stability, careful fiscal management, a sharp increase in Aboriginal capacity, localization of health care services, improved employment and, most importantly, significantly better health care services. She concludes that culturally reflective administration is helpful, provided that both managers and the policy makers (Aboriginal and governmental) adhere to them. She argues that community engagement is essential for the successful implementation of new approaches.

Beatty argues that "real life" governance is vital for Aboriginal programs and self-government. Her work draws from the experience of Indigenous governments and not from theoretical constructs or Western democratic models. She supports citizen engagement with decision making, arguing that Aboriginal people need to preserve and indeed emphasize their concepts of the land and spirituality. But at the same time, she emphasizes the importance of individual autonomy and responsibility, of strong families, and of public accountability enlightened by community consensus.

Beatty offers a valuable corrective to the debate about the future of Aboriginal–newcomer relations. She emphasizes practical and manageable approaches to improving governance at the local level and underscores how Aboriginal culture rests at the core of successful efforts to transform administration and political oversight. That she is examining arrangements currently in place – some of them of several decades' duration – speaks to an aspect of Aboriginal affairs that gets far too little coverage in Canada. Some of the major changes that Aboriginal activists and political leaders are advocating, from self-government to devolution, and from incorporating Indigenous values in administrative systems to building local capacity, are already in process in Aboriginal communities across the country. The revolutionary changes desired by many are not in place and are unlikely ever to be. But other important changes are occurring and are improving Indigenous lives and communities.

**Dale Turner** is an associate professor of government and Native American studies at Dartmouth College and a member of the Teme-Augama Anishnabai First Nation. A political philosopher, he has engaged with the work of Will Kymlicka and other scholars of contemporary liberalism, finding them wanting as the best means for explaining Indigenous Canada's current situation and future prospects. Like many Aboriginal thinkers, Turner argues that the Canadian debate is being fought almost exclusively in the language of the dominant society and dominated by the paradigms entrenched in the Western intellectual and governance tradition. Proposals for

Aboriginal self-government and shared authority are, at best, minor concessions that will not dramatically change Aboriginal independence. Non-Indigenous Canadians cannot move beyond the base assumptions of Western liberalism and have difficulty understanding, let alone accepting, Indigenous perspectives and aspirations.

Turner offers a clear critique of the 1969 White Paper, pointing out, as others have, that the system was designed to legislate Aboriginal people "into extinction," all the while claiming to be equitable and fair. Federal policy at the time represented the triumph of liberalism, with absolute primacy for individual rights. Although offered in a generous spirit, the White Paper was an affront to all Aboriginal peoples in the country. Rejecting this view of Canada, Turner argues for the recognition of Indigenous rights as a special case of rights, not simply a subset of the rights of minority peoples within Canada. Like others, he does not accept the status quo – or even the existence of the Canadian state – as a political fixity, suggesting that high priority should be assigned to incorporating Indigenous peoples constitutionally and politically, but on their own cultural and governmental terms.

Turner argues that any restructuring of the Canadian system will require intense engagement with Aboriginal peoples and cannot, as in the past, consist of minor gestures from the dominant society to Indigenous communities as poor and disadvantaged Canadians. This must be done because Aboriginal rights cannot be defined within the narrow confines of Western liberalism; instead, they require a substantial rethinking of the status quo. In his major work, *This Is Not a Peace Pipe* (2006), Turner tackles the arguments of Alan Cairns and Will Kymlicka, two prominent political scientists and major contributors to Canadian debates (their arguments are summarized in the next chapter.) He challenges Cairns on the question of the Two Row Wampum model. Cairns argues that it will not work. Turner counters that the concept is built on respect, peace, and friendship, all of which are required for true partnership. Turner challenges Kymlicka's assumption that Aboriginal rights are best understood as a subset of Canadian minority rights, asserting that Aboriginal people are not members of a single nation but rather a people of many parts seeking to negotiate true and sustainable partnerships.

For Turner, any realistic solution must spring from Indigenous principles, concepts, and cultural approaches. He argues for Indigenous people to engage with standard Canadian debates while continuing their work on separate, Aboriginally inspired approaches to governance and partnership with the dominant society. These people would be, in his conception, word warriors who would seek Indigenous solutions to the problems of reconciliation and engagement with other Canadians. Written without the anger that often slips into Aboriginal descriptions of political structures and relationships, Turner's work is no less passionate or engaged. He presents a formidable challenge to existing political structures and political relationships, suggesting that Indigenous thinkers and political leaders have to maintain their dialogue with the mainstream while developing Aboriginal models that will help their people and communities develop a true partnership in the future. Turner is vague as to what those structures might be – he is well aware of the diversity of Canada's Indigenous peoples – and is currently more concerned about processes than practical structures. Even so, his work provides a clear illustration of the ability of Aboriginal scholars to engage with academic scholarship while seeking to inspire and respect the cultural traditions of Indigenous communities.

## FINAL THOUGHTS

The ideas summarized in this section are only a small cross-section of complex and often controversial Aboriginal positions on legal, political, and constitutional entitlements. Aboriginal debate on these issues is intense, profound, and often diverse. It is important for Canadians, Aboriginal or not, to understand the complexity of this debate. The political manifestations of these ideas, and others, range from assertions that have no reasonable hope of succeeding, such as a cultural and political exit from Canada (Alfred, Monture-Angus), to those that support cooperation with the federal and provincial governments on the basis of renewed constitutional recognition of Aboriginal political communities (Mercredi and Turpel-Lafond, Henderson, Russell), to building mutual respect and sharing cultures and practices (Borrows, LaRocque, Turner), to competing and engaging with non-Aboriginal Canadians on their own terms (Helin, Beatty).

The political representations of these ideas range from assertions of sovereignty to support for cooperation with non-Aboriginal governments. Some Aboriginal people reluctantly support the Indian Act, others demand that the act be erased, along with the Department of Indian Affairs. Some Aboriginal people believe that the future rests with the currently constituted band governments and the chief and council system; others call for a reversion to hereditary leadership systems. Some Aboriginal leaders retain confidence in the goodwill and trustworthiness of non-Aboriginal peoples; others have all but given up on creating a meaningful working relationship with non-Indigenous governments. Some place their hopes on the Canadian courts; others believe that international law will provide Aboriginal peoples with the rights and authority they require. Critics have pointed out that the diversity of opinion on the Aboriginal side makes a meaningful resolution of Aboriginal demands impossible.

Individual Aboriginal political communities take a wide variety of political positions, and regional and national Aboriginal political organizations are coalitions, often without an overriding ideology. There is no national or even regional consensus on how to proceed politically, and even foundational questions such as the structure of government, the nature of the formal relationship with the federal government, and internal governance systems remain the subject of ongoing debate and negotiation. It is instructive, though, to consider some of the mission statements of the key Aboriginal organizations, for they indicate the degree to which the values, assumptions, and positions of Indigenous political philosophers are reflected in the actions of Aboriginal organizations and the positions of their leaders.

The logical place to start is with the Assembly of First Nations, Canada's most prominent Aboriginal association. The grand chief is elected by a vote of the chiefs, not by direct election of First Nations people, and typically is seen as the pre-eminent Aboriginal voice in the country. Leaders such as Phil Fontaine, Matthew Coon Come, Ovide Mercredi, and Shawn Atleo have held prominent positions in the national political debate and are better known than most provincial premiers. The assembly's vision statement (see Appendix A) clearly indicates the spiritual and cultural base of Aboriginal politics – no national political party in Canada would dare venture such a spiritually based founding document – and the broad and comprehensive sense of Aboriginal rights that animates the assembly's activities and pronouncements.

The Inuit Tapiriit Kanatami (ITK) provides a sharp contrast to the Assembly of First Nations. The Inuit have been among the most focused, coordinated, and successful Aboriginal organizations in the world over the past forty years, and they approached the negotiation of land claims and the creation of the new territory of Nunavut with pragmatism, determination, and a willingness to compromise. In the process, they have earned a reputation for being highly professional in their dealings with government, practical, and less prone to radical positions on matters of Indigenous rights. After land claims negotiations were completed, with self-government measures well in hand, the ITK recast its mission statement. Its current statement of aims and objectives (see Appendix B) reflects their practical approach and, even more, the fact that the ITK has achieved many of the objectives that other Aboriginal groups have identified as high priorities.

By contrast, the Union of British Columbia Indian Chiefs is among the more outspoken Aboriginal groups in the country, often harshly critical of government policy and aloof from current treaty negotiations in British Columbia. Its vision statement (see Appendix C), like that of the Assembly of First Nations, places a high priority on cultural survival, the protection of Aboriginal rights, and the determination to stand strong in the face of non-Aboriginal populations and governments.

There is a strong connection between the policy statements of Indigenous intellectuals and the positions taken by national, regional, and local Aboriginal groups. The key Indigenous commentators are typically well connected to their families, communities, and political organizations and find strength and inspiration in the words of their elders and leaders. Most of them spend a great deal of time and effort working directly with Aboriginal organizations and on the difficult behind-the-scenes negotiations with federal and provincial governments. Perhaps most importantly, their ideas and opinions spring from their understanding of and commitment to their traditional culture and values. As a consequence, the ideas reflect the passions, realities, and insights of Aboriginal politics. Conversely, Aboriginal political rhetoric, policy and public pronouncements also often reflect the ideas and writings of Aboriginal intellectuals.

Aboriginal people in Canada have strong beliefs about the best means of moving forward, of becoming real treaty peoples with other Canadians. Their intellectual and political leaders work in an intense and highly emotional environment, perhaps the toughest political situation in the country. To a degree that few Canadians realize, Aboriginal leaders are strongly committed to working within Canada. Despite their well-justified frustrations, they devote a remarkable amount of time and effort to finding viable and sustainable solutions to the issues facing Indigenous peoples in Canada.

non-aboriginal views
on the way forward

# 4

## legal rights, moral rights, and well-being

**NON-ABORIGINAL** people have had generations to speak their minds on Aboriginal issues, and they have done so. Beginning with the governors of New France and ever since, missionaries, military leaders, and government officials have offered their opinions on how to solve the "Indian problem." And they are still giving their opinions, although they are being somewhat drowned out by Aboriginal voices, besides being chastened by the realization that their solutions of the past have done lingering damage to Canada's original peoples. In the academic community, many committed and caring scholars believe that the current political logjam must be broken and that new approaches have to be developed. Many of them have worked closely with Aboriginal organizations and share some of the ideas and values circulating in Aboriginal politics. The political thinkers discussed in this chapter and the next have been selected to illustrate the range of opinion on basic issues and approaches. Just as there is no single Aboriginal position on the issues at hand, there is no single non-Aboriginal perspective or line of argument. We can, though, slot these approaches into four groups: legal rights, moral rights, well-being, and political or institutional arrangements. Here, we discuss the first three.

## THE LEGAL RIGHTS APPROACH

Canadians need to recognize existing Aboriginal authority. The struggle to meet Aboriginal aspirations is focusing more and more on legal and political issues. In the 1960s, governments emphasized economic and social development, hoping that reducing poverty would empower Aboriginal communities. But at the same time, Indigenous Canadians increasingly demanded attention to their specific legal and political rights, both their rights as Canadians and their distinct rights as Aboriginal people. More and more non-Aboriginal political thinkers have come to share their approach and its assumptions.

The basic assumption of the legal rights approach is that the Indigenous rights that exist under Canadian or international law must be recognized. This argument strips away the guilt that has long underpinned Canadian Indian policy, although not the passions and commitments that policy has inspired. Put simply, legal rights define what an individual is allowed or not allowed to do, and what others are allowed or not allowed to do to him or her. Basic rights include the right to vote in federal elections, the right to freedom from arbitrary detention, and the right to public education for children. Some rights, and the laws that have flowed from them, reflect specific moral principles, but not all of them do. Many Canadian legal rights have emerged over time from past political decisions or compromises and have gained considerable political force.

The intellectual and political questions raised by the legal rights approach are simple enough: Do Aboriginal rights exist in Canada? If they do, what is their legal basis, and how much sway do they have within the Canadian system? As you will soon see, the debates over these questions are formidably complicated. For some Canadian political thinkers, Aboriginal entitlements pose no moral or social questions and broach no historical guilt or responsibility – the debate is a legal one. If those rights exist – and there is considerable debate about *that* – then of course they must be honoured.

Adherents to the legal rights approach do not all line up behind Aboriginal claims and aspirations. Gordon Gibson, a media commentator and long-time BC politician, uses legal arguments to rebuff Aboriginal assertions. But it is **Mel Smith**, a one-time constitutional adviser to the BC government who died in 2000, who has provided the most detailed critique of Aboriginal policy in his book *Our Home or Native Land?* (1996). Smith believed that the 1969 White Paper, which called for an end to special status for Aboriginal people, was a positive step. The Trudeau government's later reversal of its position, especially after the *Calder* case, was for Smith a fundamental error: "The Calder case is no support whatsoever for a land claims policy that sees vast areas of public land transferred in fee simple to native people" (11). Smith argued that the Supreme Court had not ruled that Aboriginal title exists. In his view, and others agree, advocates of Aboriginal rights had cast the *Calder* decision as a sweeping victory and then embellished that decision by asserting far more than the court had actually found. For Smith, subsequent federal negotiations of outstanding Aboriginal claims were a legal fallacy, and an unjust one at that: "What was designed to redress historic wrongs, based on some colour of legal right, has now expanded to appease the insatiable demands of the native leadership to ever more land and resources. Present-day land claim settlements go far beyond legal entitlement. To the extent that they do, the legal entitlements of the rest of society are diminished. This is unfair and unjust" (8).

Focusing largely on BC, Smith asserted that legal decisions and principles had nullified Indigenous claims to the land. If Aboriginal title existed at all, it had been extinguished before the province joined Confederation in 1871. He held to a Lockean notion of land title – the right to possess land as property exists only insofar as that land is worked or tilled. And he took a similar line with Aboriginal assertions of an inherent right to self-government. To those who noted that the Royal Proclamation of 1763 referred to "Indian tribes or nations," he pointed out that the proclamation also referred to Indians as the "King's loyal 'subjects'" (151). So there was no legal foundation for Aboriginal self-government.

Smith expressed dismay at post-1980 attempts to expand the definition of Aboriginal rights and to create new rights. Regarding the Council of Yukon First Nations land claims agreement, he drew attention to the creation of "citizens of First Nations" in Bill C-34: "Are native people in the Yukon now to have two kinds of citizenship extended to them under Canadian law? If so, are not conflicting allegiances likely to arise?" (59).

He was, of course, correct that a new category of citizenship has now been recognized. But this sort of dual citizenship exists in all federal states. Residents of BC do not have the right to vote in provincial elections in Alberta or to access student loans from the New Brunswick provincial government. And BC residents don't have to pay Ontario provincial sales tax when they order something over the Internet from a store in that province. In other words, overlapping citizenship is hardly unique in Canada. In fact, it is a core principle of federalism.

Smith reserved especially strong criticism for section 35 of the 1982 Constitution. In his view, it raised Aboriginal rights above federal and provincial law. Supreme Court decisions such as *Delgamuukw* (1997) had strengthened Aboriginal rights; however, Smith argued that they had also specified when federal and provincial laws could defeat Aboriginal title. He argued that national and regional governments must be vigilant in ensuring that Aboriginal rights were not extended unduly and did not interfere with the proper exercise of federal or provincial authority.

Right up to his death in 2000, Smith argued that Aboriginal rights threatened to create political and administrative chaos across Canada. By convincing governments to launch the BC treaty process, Aboriginal leaders had mocked actual legal rights and placed the province on a course for disaster. Each additional step, be it a politically granted right, a signed treaty, or a Supreme Court decision, would further entrench Aboriginal authority, encourage greater and more unreasonable demands, and make Canada even more ungovernable.

In strong contrast to Mel Smith, **Bruce Clark** argues that Aboriginal claims have a far stronger legal basis than is currently assumed. Clark, at one time the lawyer for the Temagamis of Bear Island, Ontario, is a highly controversial Aboriginal rights advocate. His take on Aboriginal powers is simple: Aboriginal sovereignty is intact in Canada; the country's government is illegal, and therefore its court system is unjust; and Aboriginal people have full and incontestable sovereignty over their traditional territories. Clark based his position on a long-forgotten court case from 1704, *Mohegan Indians v. Connecticut*, which he found in the Aberdeen Law Library. In their arguments over the intent of a seventeenth-century treaty, the Mohegans appealed to the Judicial Committee of the Privy Council, the highest court of appeal in the British legal system. England's attorney general, Lord Northey, recommended that a permanent third-party court be established to adjudicate such claims. The recommendations were passed in 1704 by resolution of the Queen in Council. Clark interprets this event to be of the same weight and authority as the Royal Proclamation of 1763.

In Clark's view, the 1704 order established constitutional protection for Aboriginal rights to their lands:

> The single most important fact in the history of aboriginal rights in North America has been the effective concealment by the domestic legal establishment of the existence of the Order in Council (Great Britain) of 9 March 1704 in the matter of *Mohegan Indians v. Connecticut*. By never mentioning the order, the judges and lawyers of the domestic legal establishment have managed to oversee the greatest land theft in human history, all the while pretending to be serving a rule of law society. Under the proclamation, that theft constitutes treason and fraud. But there has never been a prosecution, precisely because the criminals have also achieved a monopoly over the legal process. It is the perfect crime, precisely because the crime is masterminded by the legal establishment. The consequence of the crime has been the genocide of a race and culture. (92)

Having drawn this conclusion from his research, Clark refined it into a legal argument, but First Nations refused to let him test it in court. An unsuccessful court case had led to his falling out with the political leaders on Bear Island. Eventually, he found several First Nations, including the Lil'wat people in BC and some members of the Bear Island community, to support his approach. With remarkable determination, he challenged the right of the courts to rule on Aboriginal title questions, arguing that they would be directly violating the 1704 proclamation if they did so. He told Aboriginal groups that the British government had recognized their full sovereign rights, that they should assert them without delay, and that First Nations leaders who did not do so were selling out to the Canadian legal and political establishment.

Clark is nothing if not persistent, and he took his information and argument to international Aboriginal rights groups, the UN, and the

International Court in The Hague, as well as to Aboriginal groups across Canada and the United States. His efforts ran into constant resistance from First Nations leaders and legal opponents. His high-profile stand with First Nations at Gustafsen Lake, BC, brought him and his political arguments into disrepute, even though the assertions of First Nations protesters were later found to be substantially true. Truth be told, Clark's confrontational style and contentious arguments in court undermined his public and legal credibility. Eventually, he would be disbarred.

Clark's ideas have not been accorded much attention. That is unfortunate. His basic point is that since the early eighteenth century, British and Canadian authorities have systematically ignored British law in their handling of Aboriginal lands. In other words, the system has ignored its own rules, and that has led to the occupation of Aboriginal territories without proper authority. Whatever the historical merits of all this, it is remarkable that a well-trained historian and lawyer would believe that contemporary courts – Aboriginal *or* non-Aboriginal – would accept his analysis. Political realities matter, and as Supreme Court decisions reveal time and again, the legal rights of Aboriginal peoples are tempered by the competing interests of contemporary non-Aboriginal peoples.

Clark's arguments, which have ruined his legal career and led to his banishment from many First Nations communities in Canada, point to one extreme in non-Indigenous approaches to Aboriginal title. By Clark's interpretation, *Mohegan* means that the Government of Canada and its legal system lack jurisdiction, that non-Aboriginal occupancy and use of traditional Indigenous territories have no legal foundation, and that the sovereignty of Aboriginal peoples over their lands remains absolute. Few Aboriginal leaders would seriously offer a similar argument, and most advance far more limited claims and demands. Clark will continue to find a small number of people and bands willing to support his approach, but he remains a political and legal outsider, unable to persuade the court system, Aboriginal peoples, or the general public to accept his analysis. He deserves more respect than he has received for his tenacity but not for his tactics or for his harsh criticisms of those who oppose him.

## THE MORAL RIGHTS APPROACH

Do Aboriginal legal rights exist? Even if we could somehow all agree that they did, it would not tell us whether they *ought* to exist. To answer that question, we must turn to political philosophers. Several contemporary scholars have addressed the more basic question of whether minority rights, including Aboriginal rights, are compatible with liberal democracy. On such questions, Canadian philosophers and political scientists such as Charles Taylor, James Tully, and Will Kymlicka are recognized world leaders. Two basic schools of thought have emerged. One challenges the premises of liberal democracy as practised in Canada and other Western democracies because of their heavy emphasis on individual rights. The other, strongly associated with Will Kymlicka, argues that Aboriginal and other minority rights are consistent with liberal democracy and for that reason ought to be accommodated.

**Charles Taylor,** a political philosopher at McGill University, and James Tully, a political philosopher at the University of Toronto, offer strong and consistent critiques of the liberal equality-of-individual rights approach, arguing that Aboriginal rights should be recognized. In the 1970s and 1980s, Taylor challenged mainstream thinking about the primacy of individual rights in liberal democracy. He asserted that more attention needed to be paid to ethnopolitical groups. These collectivities existed, operating beyond the realm of the individual, and they had their own meaning and social value. Successful liberal democracies, he argued, require that the dignity and worth of these groups be recognized and that mechanisms be created to accommodate them. He referred to this as the politics of recognition, one consequence of which is that the rights of groups, including the rights of specific minorities, may have to be defended by the state and by the courts.

This approach burst onto the Canadian political landscape during debates over the rights of French Canada – more specifically, over Quebec's highly controversial language laws. Critics of those laws argued that they were an assault on individual rights, including freedom of expression, and as such were unacceptable in a free and democratic society. The Quebec government's position was intensely unpopular among English speakers both inside and outside Quebec. Taylor entered the fray, arguing that it was justifiable to take dramatic legal steps to protect a minority linguistic or cultural group, even if it meant placing that group's interests over the rights of individuals. Stepping in to protect the social, cultural, and in this case linguistic rights of the minority represented an implicit recognition of a power differential. The act of recognition – and this was Taylor's key point – gave the group and its members greater dignity. This might limit individual rights to some degree – on that Taylor was clear – but a greater social good would be achieved.

For Taylor, debates over the rights of minorities illustrated the limits of individual rights and the need for governments to step in to protect the rights of threatened groups. The identity and existence of a group – here, French-speaking Québécois – held enormous significance for Quebec and Canadian society. Confronted with the argument that linguistic protections were necessary to ensure cultural survival, society and its political agents could and should step forward and make clear moral choices. For Taylor, Quebec and Canada were better off with a strong and stable French Canadian minority. It followed that humanity was served by the passage of legislation that defended the group rights of French Canadians, even if such actions infringed on the rights of individuals. Taylor's proposition, nurtured in the heat of Quebec politics, represented a radical Canadian critique of classical liberal democratic thought, which identified strongly with individual rights.

Taylor later extended his analysis to Aboriginal debates. In the political furor surrounding the Nisga'a treaty, he asserted that the arguments he had advanced for Quebec's situation extended to the Aboriginal one. Critics – and there are many – argued that the Nisga'a agreement was race-based, privileging one group over all others, and therefore it undermined individual freedoms. In "On the Nisga'a Treaty" (1998–99), Taylor pointed out that, under the agreement, "certain powers of self-government will be given to a group that is defined by descent; that is a group that others can't join at will. A minute's reflection will show that this is an essential part of any serious proposal for Aboriginal self-rule" (37). The argument, reduced to its essence, was that it was politically acceptable to empower a distinct political minority. Furthermore, membership codes based on ancestry were morally defensible. In making this argument, Taylor was advancing a position quite similar to that of Mohawk scholar Taiaiake Alfred.

Taylor argued that a steadfast defence of individual rights was not consistent with the sociocultural goals or moral choices that a country such as Canada must make. In particular, minority groups had unique claims on the body politic and had the right to expect their specific needs to be attended to legally and politically. A society like Canada was large and powerful enough to protect itself from social and cultural decay. The country could accept immigrants by the tens of thousands and could insist of the newcomers that they integrate into the broader social order through schools, language, and participation in economic and political activities. The Canadian mainstream – its values, social system, economic order, and the like – was not threatened by immigrants precisely *because* the federal and provincial governments had the authority to regulate the activities of citizens and residents. But Aboriginal communities lacked the size and power to protect themselves and their heritage. If specific Aboriginal communities did not have the right to control membership on the basis of ancestry or blood quantum, they would be overrun, undermined culturally, and destroyed socially. Accordingly, to control membership was justifiable and was not racist: "What would the average Canadian say if some outside group demanded the right to enter the country, to be given instant voting rights, without accepting any obligation to learn the language, or accepting the central values of the society, or accepting any other condition that we now impose? And when we refuse, they would call us 'racist'" (38).

For Taylor, Aboriginal communities are unique and special, like Quebec. They are distinct from mainstream Canadian society, with a long heritage and specific cultural and social systems they wish to preserve and enhance. They are not merely Canadians with a few attributes different from the mainstream society. Taylor would not accept, for example, that an immigrant minority should have the same rights of self-determination, self-government, and special legal status that he advocates for Aboriginal peoples. Immigrants choose freely to come to Canada and therefore should be expected to adhere to the mores of the broader society (although there have been many instances of new Canadians resisting social norms in favour of their traditional ones). The difference, for Taylor, is that Aboriginal communities predate the arrival of Europeans by thousands of years and that newcomers imposed their social and political systems on often unwilling and demographically small Indigenous populations. Because of this unique and historical circumstance, Canada has no moral choice but to acknowledge the existence of these political communities, identify and respect their unique needs, and accept the political reality that these small societies must have the legal authority to defend themselves against the culturally different and much larger majority.

Like Taylor, **James Tully** argues that Canadian constitutionalism can and should accommodate the mutual recognition of Aboriginal and non-Aboriginal political communities. In *Strange Multiplicity* (1995), he eloquently employs Bill Reid's famous sculpture *The Spirit of Haida Gwaii* (on display in Vancouver International Airport) to illustrate the importance of mutual recognition of cultural diversity as the basis of constitutional development in Canada and elsewhere:

> The sculpture is a black bronze canoe, over nineteen feet in length, eleven feet wide, and twelve feet high, containing thirteen passengers, *sghaana* (spirits or myth creatures) from Haida mythology . . . *Xuuwaji,* the bear mother, who is part human, and bear father sit facing each other at the bow with their two cubs between them. *Tsaang,* the beaver, is paddling menacingly amidship, *qqaaxhadajaat,* the mysterious, intercultural dogfish woman, paddles just behind him and *Qaganjaat,* the shy but beautiful mouse woman, is tucked in the stern. *Ghuuts,* the ferociously playful wolf, sinks his fangs in the eagle's wing, and *ghuut,* the eagle seems to be attacking the bear's paw in retaliation. *Hlkkyaan qqusttaan,* the frog, who symbolizes the ability to cross boundaries (*xhaaidla*) between worlds, is, appropriately enough, partially in and out of the boat. Further down in the canoe, the ancient conscript, brought on board from Carl Sandburg's poem "Old Timers," paddles stoically (up to a point). *Xuuya,* the legendary raven – the master of tricks, transformations and multiple identities – steers the canoe as her or his whim dictates. Finally, in the centre of this motley crew, holding the speaker's staff in his right hand, stands *Kilstlaai,* the chief or exemplar, whose identity, due to his kinship to the raven (often called *Nangkilstlas,* the One who gives orders), is uncertain. Bill Reid asks of the chief, "Who is he? That's the big question." So the chief has come to be called "Who is he?" or "Who is he going to be?" (17–18)

Tully suggests that the paddlers' journey mirrors our national odyssey in Canada. The voyagers' cultures interact without any losing their identity. There is change. Contestation and negotiation are commonplace. All members are recognized and accommodated.

Aboriginal rights, Tully contends, can be accommodated within three common conventions of constitutionalism: mutual recognition, continuity, and consent. Mutual recognition, in the spirit of Taylor, refers to the recognition of the equal worth and dignity of other peoples – their cultures, social practices, and systems of governance. Continuity recognizes that the values and practices of a people should be allowed to persist within a common constitutional framework, unless that people chooses to change those values and practices. Finally, the principle of consent is closely linked to the convention of mutual recognition. How peoples are recognized is important in determining the nature of their consent to common constitutionalism. In North America, the early British treaties represented a specific form of consent. Aboriginal peoples recognized one another as political communities, and the British recognized the prior and continuing self-determination of Aboriginal peoples as nations. Tully argues that successful reconciliation in Canada requires a return to these principles.

The arguments brought forward by communitarians such as Taylor and Tully are compelling philosophically but are significantly at odds with the political values of many if not most Canadians. Many Canadians, especially in English Canada, cherish the Charter of Rights and Freedoms, particularly its emphasis on individual rights. They are skeptical of arguments that raise group rights over individual rights. One only has to remember the impact of the interventions by Trudeau during the Meech Lake and Charlottetown Accords in turning public opinion against the two agreements precisely on the point of group versus individual rights. The Taylor and Tully approaches provide powerful arguments in favour of special arrangements.

**Will Kymlicka**, a political philosopher at Queen's University, has made a comparable effort to advance Aboriginal rights within a liberal rights framework. His work came into prominence at a time when liberalism was out of fashion in intellectual circles, somewhat swamped by a worldwide infatuation with communitarianism. Because he defends Aboriginal and other minority rights within a framework that is recognizable and acceptable to most Canadians, his work deserves special attention.

Kymlicka argues that all Canadians belong to at least one cultural community. Most French-speaking Quebecers view themselves as Québécois and place great attachment to the norms, values, institutions, and shared history of Quebec. The same is true for most English-speaking Canadians outside of Quebec, who have a strong attachment to the norms, values, shared history, and institutions of Canada and to the unique histories of their various parts of the country.

From his liberal philosophical perspective, Kymlicka argues that membership in a cultural community is basic to human existence and frames our life choices. Members of the dominant culture tend not to realize how Canada's social and political institutions are imbued with the particular cultural values of Europe (particularly England) and with the values that evolved with the settler populations in North America. People in the dominant society do not notice the cultural biases because they reflect their fundamental cultural assumptions. However, they are essential in guiding our *individual* life choices. They help anchor individuals and give meaning to a person's social existence.

The reality in Canada, of course, is that there is not one cultural community but at least three: English Canada, Quebec, and a multitude of First Nations. The English and French groups are divided further by geography, history, culture, and economy. Many Quebecers value their place in the Canadian polity but see their principal cultural community as Quebec. The same is true for First Nations peoples, who see their cultural communities as primary. Because cultural communities are essential to individual well-being and social existence, they ought to be defended. On this point, Kymlicka differs from Taylor, who defends group rights, even at the expense of some individual rights, as vital to collective survival. Kymlicka defends group rights insofar as they advance the well-being of the collective. In this regard, his position is compatible with the prevailing views of liberal democracy held by most Canadians.

A question remains: Why should Aboriginal peoples have special rights that other Canadians do not? Does this not elevate one set of cultural communities over others? Kymlicka argues that special rights are necessary for minority nationalities, such as Quebec and Aboriginal peoples. He does not include individuals who belong to ethnic groups and who have immigrated to Canada since its founding. Like Taylor and Tully, he notes that these individuals, by choosing to come to Canada, have implicitly accepted the values, norms, and institutions of their new home. This choice was *not* available to Aboriginal people and the Québécois, in that the former were dominated by newcomers and the latter were conquered by the British.

Kymlicka argues that Aboriginal people and the Québécois need special rights to ensure that their cultural communities survive and thrive within the dominant cultural community. He offers the example of Aboriginal land claims. The Canadian state holds title to vast Crown lands and natural resources. It also gathers large resources through taxes (including on Aboriginal Canadians). With these vast resources, the Canadian state is in no danger. The English language and the political values of the dominant culture are promoted; we see this every time we turn on a hockey game and see Canada geese flying in a beer commercial or watch *Anne of Green Gables* as a CBC miniseries. Minority cultural communities do not have the same resources. Collectively held Aboriginal land title may provide sufficient financial resources – through natural resource rents, for instance – to enable Aboriginal governments to promote their cultural communities. In this light, Aboriginal land claims are important not because some court discovered that a legal right exists but because this legal right is essential to a vital end, namely, the protection of Aboriginal cultural communities.

With regard to national minorities such as Aboriginal peoples, Kymlicka argues that special representation and self-government are among the most important rights. Special representation refers to some form of guaranteed seats in provincial legislatures or in Parliament. Because they are only 3 percent of Canadians, Aboriginal peoples have few opportunities to elect candidates who can represent primarily Aboriginal interests in the most important decision-making bodies in our political system. Special representation would at least guarantee a minimal number of seats for Aboriginal peoples. Moreover, such representation is not likely to heighten Aboriginal peoples' separateness from the rest of Canadian society; indeed, it is likely to strengthen their commitment to Canada by ensuring their meaningful representation within its political system. (New Zealand has had this arrangement with the Māori for over a century, with generally positive results.) This would be consistent with the existing Canadian political practice. Prince Edward Island has a smaller population than many suburbs around Toronto and Vancouver, yet it is guaranteed four seats in the House of Commons and another four in the Senate – and few Canadians go into high dudgeon about that constitutionally entrenched overrepresentation. Aboriginal people are more than ten times the population of Prince Edward Island, yet they have no guaranteed seats in either the House of Commons or the Senate.

For Kymlicka, Aboriginal self-government is also desirable because it would give a cultural community the capacity to make decisions on matters that most directly affect its members. He acknowledges that it might promote separation, but he does not see this as inevitable. Independence from Canada would be almost impossible for Aboriginal peoples in Canada because of their small population and lack of resources. Kymlicka's key point is that all individuals belong to a cultural community and that such membership is essential to their well-being. Therefore Aboriginal rights, insofar as they enhance Aboriginal cultural communities, are consistent with liberal democracy and ought to be defended.

**Alan Cairns** is a pre-eminent Canadian constitutional expert and has been involved in every major constitutional debate in Canada for the past fifty years. In the mid-1960s, he worked on the *Hawthorn Report,* which was commissioned by Ottawa to identify political, legal, and economic alternatives for Aboriginal people in Canada. The report called for recognition of the unique legal status of Indigenous people, referred to by the authors as "citizens plus." Their recommendations were ignored by Ottawa and trampled by the 1969 White Paper. Cairns believed that the concept deserved a wider hearing and prepared *Citizens Plus* (2000), a thoughtful analysis of the idea's applicability in modern Canada.

Cairns is uncomfortable with the current division between Aboriginal concepts of nation-to-nation relations and the assimilationist model proposed by political scientist Thomas Flanagan. He argues that the current approaches are recipes for confrontation and bitterness. Worse, they do not adequately reflect the real needs of Aboriginal peoples and the political realities of Canada. Returning to the concept of citizens plus, Cairns points out that the idea enjoyed considerable support from Aboriginal leaders at the time the *Hawthorn Report* was published and that it closely reflected Indigenous political demands.

It also recognized a central fact of Aboriginal–non-Aboriginal relations in Canada – that both groups are Canadians, with all of the
rights and responsibilities that citizenship entails.

Cairns's findings are supported by a systematic analysis of the historical constitutional relations between Aboriginal people and the
Government of Canada and reflect a deep concern about prevailing
social and economic trends. He is especially worried about the steady
increase in the urban Native population, although he overstates the
degree of cultural separation that a move from reserves to towns or cities entails. He offers a biting critique of the Liberal government's willingness (continued by the Conservatives after they came to power in
2006) to virtually ignore the *Report of the Royal Commission on
Aboriginal Peoples*. He points to the limited attention paid to urban
Aboriginal people and to empowering reserve-based political organizations. This latter mistake, he argues, has disempowered a large and
growing number of Aboriginal people, including many of the best
educated and most economically active. In emphasizing the nation-to-
nation concept, he argues, the royal commission largely ignored the
need for a rapprochement between Indigenous and other citizens, as if
Aboriginal people were expected to address and resolve their issues in
isolation.

Cairns's citizens plus is a principle and a process, not a list of recommendations. He is calling for a third option between the existing
extremes. Recognition of Aboriginal people as citizens plus, he
argues, would lead to the acknowledgment and funding of Aboriginal
self-government, but only in the context of Canadian political and
legal structures. He sees no nation-to-nation relations in the future,
which – and here he agrees with Flanagan – would result in the with-
ering of national loyalties. By accepting the reality of Canadian citizenship and of partnership with the country as a whole, Aboriginal
people would be able to negotiate arrangements that "enhance the
compatibility between Aboriginal nationhood and Canadian citizenship" (213).

Cairns calls for a meeting of Aboriginal and non-Indigenous
Canadians around the middle ground of citizenship. He argues that
Aboriginal peoples have unique rights, recognized in the Constitution
and well-established in Canadian law, arising from their Indigenous
heritage. Aboriginal people will always have a "plus" – that is, they

will always have specific entitlements and constitutional authority not available to other Canadians. Most importantly, future political relationships must take into account the basic fact that Aboriginal people and other Canadians are already closely interrelated (and here he devotes considerable attention to linkages through marriage and the migration of reserve residents into cities and towns). He argues:

> We are all part of one another, although not always harmoniously so. The future of Aboriginal peoples, whether or not they have a land base that is a requisite for effective self-government, is within Canada. If that "withinness" means that Canada is to be more than a container, or a mini-international system, we need bonds of empathy so that our togetherness is moral as well as geographical. The obvious moral bond is a shared citizenship, although there may for some time be variations in allegiance to it. Constitutional policy, accordingly, should be both sensitive to Aboriginality leading to Nunavut and a third order of Aboriginal government, and supportive of a Canadian dimension of belonging. We should not so structure our institutional arrangements that every Aboriginal interaction with the state – third order, territorial, provincial, federal, municipal – has to be suffused with Aboriginality. (211)

Cairns holds a quintessentially Canadian view of a vexing problem, at once worried and optimistic, pragmatic and philosophical. He offers a vision of a more united Canada while recognizing the hard work, political compromises, and social initiatives required to create a better and stronger future. He does not offer specific solutions; his goal, instead, is to shift the debate from the extremes of assimilation and nation-to-nation relations to a fuller discussion of common citizenship and economic and political realities. He attacks the politics of separation, offering in its place a vision of a shared future in which Aboriginal people would enjoy an effective and prosperous presence within Canada, which would be bound more closely together instead of being driven apart. His appeal is, finally, to common citizenship, one that stresses the benefits of stronger bonds of nationhood between Aboriginal people and other Canadians.

## WELL-BEING

Political theory seeks to explain broad political issues. For most political theorists, Aboriginal and non-Aboriginal alike, abstract questions are of crucial importance, for they underscore the values and assumptions that govern political relationships.

But for some observers, theoretical questions are less relevant than the pressing issues of Aboriginal life today. First Nations, Métis, and Inuit leaders consistently observe that their communities face tremendous problems of high unemployment, violence, alcoholism, and poverty. They and their supporters desire self-government not for broad philosophical or political reasons but because it is the only workable means to address those problems. There are pragmatists among political scientists as well. In that regard, **Tom Pocklington**, a University of Alberta political scientist (now retired), has long wondered why the debate about Aboriginal governance has been dominated by questions of rights instead of well-being. Law and policy, he argues, could easily flow from a desire to address difficult social, economic, and cultural problems and leave for another time the more philosophical questions that have shaped public debate for the past forty years.

Those who favour self-government for Aboriginal peoples tend to emphasize the politics of recognition and the moral value of maintaining distinct cultures. In other words, Aboriginal people have an historical *and* legal and moral right to govern themselves. Opponents, by contrast, have argued that Aboriginal self-government would tilt the balance between individual and collective rights in favour of the latter. Both arguments, though, miss a critical question: Will self-government enhance the well-being of Aboriginal peoples? For Pocklington, it is vital to answer that question. To proceed with self-government without ensuring that Aboriginal communities would be better off would be a major mistake, but to deny Aboriginal people the right of self-government on the basis of philosophical or legal principles when the revived system might improve their lives would equally be in error.

For Pocklington, a substantial gulf exists between rights-based debates and debates about well-being. A right is something an individual or group either possesses or does not. It is either respected or denied.

Degrees of rights do not exist. Importantly, though, this is not true of well-being: an individual can be more or less well off than another, and a community or group can be more or less well off than another. A focus on well-being, he asserts, would remove the debate from the world of absolutes and constitutional rigidities, to say nothing of the "winner take all" judgments of the legal system. In *Democracy, Rights, and Well-Being in Canada* (2000), he suggests that "Native collectivities should have a right of political self-determination to the extent that recognition of that right promises to enhance their well-being without seriously reducing the well-being either of Native people who are not members of such collectivities or of non-Natives" (111).

Much of the current debate about Aboriginal rights as *legal* rights involves taking sharp, unalterable positions. Aboriginal people either do or do not have certain rights. If, for historical, legal, moral, or constitutional reasons, they have them, then they are to be asserted and protected, whatever the costs and the implications. Conversely, if those rights do not exist under the law, then they are not to be applied or granted, even if empowering Indigenous communities would clearly improve Aboriginal lives. "Appeals to rights are conducive to intransigence and uncongenial to dialogue, negotiation, and compromise" (107). For Pocklington, the focus on well-being instead of precise rights and obligations would promote public discussion about the options available to all governments. Extending jurisdiction, creating new institutional arrangements, and finding other means to enhance community life could proceed without the formality and permanence of the rights-based debates and negotiations.

Pocklington advocates a pragmatic, grounded approach to Aboriginal empowerment, not an idealistic and philosophical one. A rights-based approach pursues "one size fits all" legislation; a well-being approach would encourage communities to consider exactly how much autonomy they want or need. Communities would operate and plan in terms of their needs and competencies instead of with an abstract, right-based emphasis. Moreover, well-being approaches would take into account the needs and conditions of other communities or interests that might be affected by self-governing Aboriginal communities. In this way, the well-being model would encourage cooperation and mutual understanding between Indigenous and non-Indigenous peoples.

The well-being approach, as defined by Tom Pocklington, would see the right of Aboriginal self-government extended on the basis of the following eight principles:

> The case for aboriginal self-government is strongest where a Native collectivity (community, band, tribal council) has a territory over which it can exert jurisdiction.
> Aboriginal self-government is strongest in respect of those areas in which Aboriginal people are economically and socially worse off than non-Natives.
> The case for self-government is stronger the more it holds the promise of enhancing the self-esteem of the Aboriginal people involved.
> The case for Native self-government is stronger where members of a collectivity are better able than outsiders to identify the nature and causes of their problems.
> The case for Native self-government is stronger where members are better able than outsiders to deal effectively with the problems that confront them.
> The case is stronger where Aboriginal collectivities have distinctive world views and aspirations which are not easily or widely accepted by outsiders.
> The greater the political and administrative skills among a collectivity's members, the stronger the case for self-government.
> The greater the economic independence the greater the case for self-government. (110-13)

For Pocklington, Aboriginal self-government is not a "right" that should simply be asserted by Aboriginal people and accepted without challenge by all other Canadians. Instead, it is merely one political and administrative tool among many, to be used as appropriate. Rights-based approaches would grant Aboriginal self-government in many situations where it might well fail, and indeed, that has happened often in Canada – community well-being has declined as a result of political change and the assertion of Aboriginal rights. Pocklington is a pragmatist who seeks common sense political solutions that will improve Aboriginal people's lives in Canada. In his mind, the eight conditions he spells out provide a basis for determining where and when the specific right of Aboriginal self-government should be granted, recognized, or applied. He is one of the few political thinkers who emphasize relations between Indigenous and non-Indigenous communities, reflecting his clear understanding that relationships between communities might hold the key to Aboriginal aspirations.

Pocklington might not have supported Canada's Liberal government in 2001–02 regarding its approach to Aboriginal questions, but he might have approved of some its goals. Under **Robert Nault**, minister of Indian affairs and northern development, the government shied away from constitutional approaches and turned to a "results-based," community-by-community approach. For Nault, and especially for Prime Minister Jean Chrétien, who seemed determined to make improved Aboriginal lives a hallmark of his third term, a focus on well-being rather than lofty principles held a great deal of promise.

Nault sought to improve social and economic conditions, address growing tensions between Aboriginal and non-Aboriginal people, and reinvent the role of government and administration. It seems that he intended to use self-government and other "rights" as *tools* in this enterprise rather than as intellectual starting points for reviving Indigenous communities. He made some progress but was unable to implement his pragmatic goals in full. When Paul Martin succeeded Chrétien as prime minister, he migrated away from incremental and practical decisions towards comprehensive and symbolic actions, such as the 2005 Kelowna Accord. The approach taken by the Conservative government since 2006 fits neatly with Pocklington's views: ministers Prentice, Strahl, and Duncan have all emphasized practical, achievable results rather than the quest to enshrine high-level legal rights.

**Menno Boldt** is one of the most straightforward, provocative, and creative thinkers in Aboriginal politics. He has challenged conventional wisdom, criticized both government policy and Aboriginal organizations, and provided a blueprint for how Indigenous peoples might better control their affairs. He writes with an unwavering commitment to the survival of Indigenous cultures and communities. All of this reflects his belief that current approaches, both federal and Aboriginal, are undermining the very societies they purport to be protecting. His major work, *Surviving as Indians* (1993), is one of the single most important books in the field.

Boldt's analysis rests on his distinction between Indians (as defined by the Indian Act and as governed under the Department of Indian Affairs) and *Indians* (a cultural term referring to people who adhere to traditional values and beliefs). The former is, to Boldt, a legal and political construct and is not the proper focus for the long-term management of Aboriginal affairs. *Indian*, by contrast, is a cultural descriptor and represents the desire of ages-old Indigenous societies to survive in postcolonial times. The *Indian*, according to Boldt, should be the focus of government and Aboriginal political action. Simply put, he believes that the goal should be to ensure that the Indians survive as *Indians,* an approach similar to those of Taiaiake Alfred and Patricia Monture-Angus.

His approach is predicated on a critical analysis of how Canadian Aboriginal policy evolved. He argues that Canadian policy has been rife with injustice, designed to serve the state rather than Aboriginal people. The Indian Act and other federal laws served an economic and social elite and were meant to ensure that national priorities, such as the railway, Western settlement, and resource development, were not impeded. Where Boldt differs from most analysts is in his often biting criticisms of present-day Aboriginal governments. Fully aware of what he is doing, he steps into a political minefield and tackles Aboriginal leadership and power structures.

He starts by criticizing today's Aboriginal governments for deviating (in his terms, "radically departing") from traditional Indian forms of governance. He suggests that Aboriginal elites have internalized the value systems and political assumptions of the nation-state. Leaders lead, elites dominate, and – this is key – elites govern in their own best interests. Traditional *Indian* governments were consensus-based; the current systems are hierarchical, deriving their authority and structure from federal law. Communities that had once been egalitarian have found themselves being managed by a self-sustaining ruling elite that is reluctant to surrender authority to or share power with the community.

Boldt's critique, derived from very different foundations than Tom Flanagan's (discussed in the following chapter), includes a sharp indictment of current efforts to establish Aboriginal self-government. This power shift, he argues, would simply replace a national or federal elite with an Aboriginal elite; for the community, very little will have changed, despite impressive rhetoric to the contrary. Aboriginal leaders and communities, he asserts, have to wake up to the significance of this or pay a severe cultural penalty: "Concerned Canadians cannot close their eyes to the possibility that 'Indian self-government' may serve to cloak or to legitimate an Indigenous tyranny that harms the mass of band/tribal members" (118).

These are harsh words, designed to spark debate and attract attention. Boldt's motives are clear. Indians will survive, he asserts, but the persistence of *Indians* is very much in doubt. Without political structures that reflect the values, traditions, and customs of the communities, cultures with roots that stretch back in time for hundreds of years, *Indian* cultures will have lost a golden opportunity to ensure their continuation. The maintenance of language – which is no certainty, given current trends – is utterly essential: "When a language dies, a world view is lost" (187). With that loss, the culture of *Indian* communities will be replaced by the colonizers' culture. Boldt may be overly pessimistic on this account, for there is much debate about the importance of language to cultural persistence. But his main point remains: without political structures that respect traditional values, Aboriginal governments, be they colonized or self-governing, are doomed.

Boldt goes on to consider the economic role of Aboriginal people within Canada. Somewhat surprisingly, given his emphasis on cultural persistence, he argues aggressively for greater interaction between Indigenous and non-Indigenous Canadians. For him, economic self-sufficiency is essential for both personal and community well-being. Aboriginal self-government without economic independence (i.e., from the federal government) would be largely meaningless, for Ottawa retains a significant measure of control over any economically dependent unit. He encourages greater integration of Aboriginal Canadians into the mainstream economy, contending that this need not interfere with cultural survival. And he argues that Indians and *Indians* should be taxed both on and off the reserve so as to ensure the financial sustainability of Aboriginal governments.

The debate over Aboriginal policy in Canada generally falls into two camps: those, such as Flanagan, who oppose special rights and arrangements for Indigenous Canadians, and those, like all of the Aboriginal thinkers discussed earlier, who believe to varying degrees that Indigenous autonomy is essential and inevitable. Boldt does not fit conveniently into either camp. His hard-hitting critique of Aboriginal self-government rests on a firm commitment to the cultural survival of *Indians*. He supports Aboriginal self-government, but only if it is truly freed from the cultural imperatives of the dominant society and does not simply result in the replacement of a non-Indigenous elite with an Indigenous ruling class. He favours economic integration, but as a means to strengthen Indigenous culture, not as a means of assimilation into the mainstream. His ideas flow from a deep appreciation of Aboriginal cultures and years of work with Indigenous communities and organizations. His conclusions have provoked and in some quarters offended Aboriginal leaders, but even his critics can see that he is motivated by a desire to see *Indian* cultures flourish in an often-hostile and unfavourable political landscape.

# 5

# political and institutional
# approaches

**FOR MANY SCHOLARS**, regardless of whether they favour expanding the authority of Aboriginal people, the answer to current issues lies in the exercise of institutionalized political power. They emphasize the need to reform existing political structures and provide Aboriginal governments and organizations with the powers they need and are warranted. But there are widely divergent ideas about where to go from there, and Canada's political parties reflect this lack of consensus.

Terms such as *First Nations* and *Aboriginal self-government* are flung around so freely these days that most Canadians have forgotten how recent this discussion has been. Before the 1970s, the idea that Aboriginal peoples had distinct rights as political units had little following outside Indigenous communities and a small band of political radicals. The political ferment of the 1970s and 1980s, however, brought new ideas forward, including a number of non-Aboriginal statements about the importance of empowering Aboriginal peoples. **Michael Asch** has long been one of the most sympathetic non-Indigenous advocates for Aboriginal rights. He broached the idea of Aboriginal rights as special or "group-differentiated" rights in his book, *Home and Native Land* (1984), long before the concept became mainstream. His book is an eclectic set of arguments about the nature of Aboriginal communities, the legal basis of Aboriginal rights, and the evolution of Aboriginal policy in Canada. He offers a compelling discussion of the different models of liberal democracy and argues, like Kymlicka, that Aboriginal rights as special rights can be accommodated without violating the tenets of liberal democracy.

Asch discusses two competing understandings of liberal democracy. The first sees liberal democracy as based on *universalism*. In other words, liberal democracy is a political system in which universal norms apply to all citizens equally. The equality of rights, including equality before the law, is a hallmark of this conception. He cites the United States as a prime example of this type of liberal democracy, although he could have easily added Britain or France. This form of liberal democracy tends to be strongly assimilationist in that it demands that all citizens adhere to identified core values and political concepts. Uprisings among immigrant populations in France today, and public protests against legal and illegal immigrants in the United States, suggest that assimilation is more an ideal than a reality in these countries.

In the second conception of liberal democracy, a nation is composed of different ethnic, linguistic, and religious communities. The state then provides mechanisms to ensure that these different cultural communities can coexist and thrive. This form of liberal democracy is called consociationalism. Asch draws heavily on the work of Arend Lijphart and G.E. Smith, who studied how ethnically, linguistically, and/or religiously divided societies can nevertheless maintain healthy and stable democracies in which groups are at peace with one another and tolerant of their differences. Political success in these settings requires accommodation among the political elites of the different groups through institutional mechanisms, such as veto rights and guaranteed representation in legislatures.

The third model of liberal democracy is simply a compromise between the first two. This model acknowledges the universal principles of liberal democracy but has institutional mechanisms to accommodate the different segments in society. Switzerland is a good example of this third way. Asch argues that either the strong or the modest version of consociationalism can accommodate the aspirations of Aboriginal peoples without compromising liberal democracy.

He looks at how the accommodation of Aboriginal peoples in Canadian liberal democracy would play out both in the provinces and in the territories. This may necessitate at least three consociational practices.

First, whatever other initiatives or rights may emerge for Aboriginal peoples, the single most important institutional arrangement is territorial-based self-government. Asch posits that because Aboriginal people will always be a minority, their governments require some form of veto power (what is referred to today as paramountcy) over laws. This mechanism of direct consociation is similar to what Belgium practises.

Second, guaranteed Aboriginal seats in national, provincial, and territorial legislatures, based on proportionality, may be desirable.

Third and finally – and Asch admits this is the most controversial – the right to vote and to run for office may be limited to those who belong to a particular Aboriginal political community. In other words, non-Aboriginal residents of Aboriginal communities would not have the right to political representation until they had lived in the region for a specific and extended period of time. A truncated version of this approach has been used in Nunavut.

The approach to consociational accommodation that Asch identified in 1988 came to pass a decade later. The Eastern Arctic (now Nunavut) and the Western Arctic (the remaining Northwest Territories) vary in their approaches because of differences in their demographics and historical development. But in both, indirect mechanisms of consociationalism are at least part of the political equation. In Nunavut, the Inuit are close to 85 percent of the population. Accordingly, the Inuit can control their destiny through indirect consociational means, that is, through public self-government. By contrast, Asch outlines how Aboriginal peoples in Northwest Territories have been seeking a mix of direct and indirect consociational mechanisms. On the regional level, public self-government (indirect consociation) would be supported through a lower house called the National Assembly. In this assembly, Aboriginal peoples would be guaranteed a minimum of 30 percent of the seats, regardless of their percentage of the total population. An upper house, the Senate, would be composed only of Aboriginal members who would have the power to veto the legislation of the lower house (direct consociation). Other provisions of direct consociation might include official status for Aboriginal languages.

What is clear in both Nunavut and Northwest Territories is that because of their larger Aboriginal populations, there is greater flexibility for direct and indirect means of consociation than is advocated for Yukon and the provinces.

For demographic and constitutional reasons, the territorial North allows Canadian and Aboriginal politicians considerable room for experimentation. Although highly dependent on federal transfer payments, the region enjoys a considerable measure of self-government. Also, the large, permanent Aboriginal population provides an effective counterbalance against the large but mostly transient non-Aboriginal society. Although Asch's specific proposals have not been implemented, the territorial North has fostered a variety of accommodations between Indigenous and non-Indigenous peoples. In Yukon, the Council of Yukon First Nations exercises considerable authority, both moral and practical. All political parties pay close attention to Aboriginal constituencies. In Northwest Territories, the consensus-based government structure respects and reflects Aboriginal values and decision making and has (so far) avoided the partisan divisiveness of southern-style political parties. And in Nunavut, the Inuit enjoy preponderant political power and run the territorial government according to an Indigenous agenda although, again, with a consensus-style government that avoids partisan politics. Kativik, the emerging public regional government in northern Quebec (Nunavik), implements these same concepts.

Asch's vision of consociation has found few supporters in the South. It is not well-suited to provinces where Indigenous peoples are only a small percentage of the population. But as the Aboriginal population in Saskatchewan and Manitoba continues to grow, demographic realities may one day make such political accommodations more attractive. The important point is that with the right political will and justification, as exists in the territorial North, it is possible to adjust existing political systems to accommodate Aboriginal political aspirations. These accommodations, in their different forms, can function effectively within a Canadian federal system.

In *On Being Here to Stay* (2014), Asch offers a strongly argued commentary on Aboriginal treaty rights and the need to re-examine the fundamental relationship between Indigenous and non-Indigenous peoples in Canada. As he writes:

> My thesis comes down to this. Treaties offer us the means to rec-
> oncile the fact that we are "here to stay" with the fact that there
> were people already here when we first arrived . . . Had we acted
> in accord with what we promised at that time [of signing treaties],
> we might now be well on the way to establishing a good relation-
> ship with our partners. (152)

Asch outlines the history of treaty making, arguing that the government has moved away from its central promises. His analysis, while
historically appealing, would convince few non-Aboriginal critics of
Aboriginal rights, who see many reasons for not opting to reopen historical treaties and redress political and administrative decisions made
over the past 150 years.

**Thomas Flanagan,** a political scientist at the University of Calgary and
one-time adviser to Stephen Harper, is Canada's leading critic of
Aboriginal political proposals. He challenges the current trend towards
Aboriginal self-government and the entrenchment of Indigenous legal
rights. Often criticized by Aboriginal leaders for his views, he has stayed
his course, providing extensive analyses of such hot topics as Métis
rights in Manitoba and the Lubicon land claim in Alberta. In his award-
winning *First Nations? Second Thoughts* (2000), he criticizes what he calls
the Aboriginal orthodoxy and offers a contrarian view of the place of
Indigenous peoples in Canadian politics. In his book, he refutes the
"orthodox" Canadian view, while providing a detailed commentary on
Aboriginal politics. His critique hits the mark in several key areas but
crashes against legal and political realities in others. Generally, with his
emphasis on specific trouble spots (which admittedly deserve more attention than they have received to date), he overestimates the significance of
unfavourable examples, and he does not balance them with positive accounts of Aboriginal governance. Even so, his criticism of Aboriginal
politics is gaining a broader audience in Canada.

Here, in summary form, is Flanagan's eight-point critique of the position that he contends enjoys widespread support among Aboriginal
politicians, Canadian academics, and government officials. He views

this approach as well-meaning and politically successful but also as wrong-headed and counterproductive and as not accurately reflecting Aboriginal history or contemporary realities. For that reason, he considers it a weak foundation for relations between Indigenous and non-Indigenous peoples.

First Nations    *Orthodoxy:* Aboriginal people were the first inhabitants of the land and for that reason have special legal and political rights, including the right to self-government.
*Flanagan:* Indigenous peoples moved widely over the land, and many Aboriginal settlements today are far from their people's ancestral homelands. "To differentiate the rights of earlier and later immigrants is a form of racism" (4).

Civilization    *Orthodoxy:* Aboriginal peoples were advanced societies, and any attempt to argue that Europeans were more "civilized" reflects racist assumptions.
*Flanagan:* European nations were technologically much more sophisticated, with more complex social organizations as well as formal governments. So it was inevitable and justifiable that the Europeans would occupy North America, bringing with them the benefits of their society, economy, and technology.

Sovereignty    *Orthodoxy:* Indigenous peoples exercised sovereignty over the land and retain key rights related to that sovereignty, including the "inherent" right to self-government.
*Flanagan:* In international law, sovereignty is attached to statehood, which Aboriginal communities have not attained. To offer it to them now would be to grant Aboriginal groups more power than they enjoyed before Europeans arrived. Limited sovereignty would be acceptable, if it were clearly subordinate to the internationally recognized sovereignty of Canada.

| | |
|---|---|
| Nations | *Orthodoxy:* Before the Europeans arrived, Aboriginal societies were nations in the broad cultural and political understanding of that term. |
| | *Flanagan:* Indigenous societies were "tribal communities," not nations. At best, they could be subordinate to the Canadian nation-state; to extend any further recognition to Aboriginal political communities would result in the Balkanization of Canada. |
| Self-government | *Orthodoxy:* Aboriginal communities can manage their affairs effectively, and self-government would provide the resources and authority for effective local administration. |
| | *Flanagan:* Aboriginal self-government – given economies of scale, among other reasons – is unworkable, expensive, and a generator of serious divisions within communities. Self-government would depend on unsustainable levels of federal financial support. |
| Aboriginal property rights | *Orthodoxy:* Aboriginal control over land and resources should be on par with other public ownership rights in Canada, and these property rights should not be extinguished through land claims settlements. |
| | *Flanagan:* For legal reasons, it is impossible for Aboriginal people to make productive economic use of their land and resources, particularly given that Supreme Court decisions have added to uncertainty about Aboriginal property rights. This idea is gaining currency and has been reinforced in a recent book, *Beyond the Indian Act* (2013), co-authored by Flanagan, Christopher Alcantara, and André Le Dressay. |
| Modernization | *Orthodoxy:* Aboriginal people want pre-1950 treaties to be rewritten so as to capture contemporary conditions and to establish "living relationships" between Aboriginal governments and the Government of Canada. |

*Flanagan:* Modernizing the treaties, which were signed in good faith by all participants at the time, would be expensive and disruptive. Also, it would only perpetuate the debate into the next generation and beyond.

Prosperity   *Orthodoxy:* The key to Aboriginal economic and social well-being is the creation of sovereign, self-governing, reserve-based Aboriginal communities.

*Flanagan:* Integration, not separation, is the key to economic and social success. Moreover, the current trend at the reserve level is to separate Indigenous groups into a small, well-paid, political elite and a much larger welfare-dependent population. The "flight" of Aboriginal people from reserves into cities and towns has been a logical response to the failure of reserve economies.

Flanagan's arguments are often criticized for being anti-Aboriginal. This is not a fair assessment. It would be better to say that they reflect Flanagan's political philosophy and deeply held beliefs. A fervent defender of individual rights and responsibilities and a classic free market liberal thinker, he believes profoundly that the current approaches to Aboriginal governance are wrong for Canada and wrong for Aboriginal people. He sees no constructive future for Aboriginal people who blame non-Aboriginal people for their misfortunes. However justified that perspective may be, it provides no avenue for personal or collective improvement. In *First Nations? Second Thoughts,* he states:

The aboriginal orthodoxy is at variance with liberal democracy because it makes race the constitutive factor of the political order. It would establish aboriginal nations as privileged political communities with membership defined by race and passed on through descent. It would redefine Canada as an association of racial communities rather than a polity whose members are individual human beings. The "third order" of aboriginal government would not mesh with existing federal and provincial levels because aboriginal government would be based on a closed racial principle, whereas Canada's other governments are based on open individual and territorial principles. Because the aboriginal element is small relative to Canada's population, the third order of aboriginal self-government might not destroy the country, but it would be a continuous irritant. Its very existence would also be a standing invitation to other racial or ethnic communities to demand similar corporate status. (194)

Flanagan's analysis – and he predicted as much – generated a sharp response. Most Aboriginal leaders reject his conclusions and argue that his selective emphasis on a few negative examples does not undercut the Aboriginal position. Academics and government officials – the other pillars of the "orthodoxy" – have likewise found his arguments to be unacceptable. Yet by stating the opposition case in a logical, coherent, and academically informed way, he has enriched the debate on Aboriginal rights in Canada. His arguments have a 1960s resonance to them and would have fit nicely into the debate over the 1969 White Paper. His emphasis on examples of mismanagement and exaggerated claims is crucial, for the discussion about Aboriginal people within Confederation has for too long proceeded without a public airing of its "dark side." Open dialogue, to which Flanagan has contributed a great deal, is vital if a healthy national discussion is to proceed.

A number of Flanagan's key arguments are dead in the water in Canada. Even so, among the positions discussed in this book, it is his that has been discussed the most. As he anticipated, Aboriginal leaders have rejected of all his proposals. The Canadian Alliance accepted the broad contours of his analysis, but its successor, the Conservative Party of Canada, clearly has not. Prime Minister Harper's government may have rejected the Kelowna Accord as a policy document, but it has committed itself to many of the values and goals expressed in that accord.

It must be said that Flanagan is right in key areas, even if he is wrong in others. The legal rights gained through the courts are not as clear, definitive, or extensive as Aboriginal people believe. Self-government has not been – and will never be – an unvarnished success. The economic needs of many reserve communities are too complicated to be addressed simply by establishing local self-government.

Finally, Flanagan has given voice to widespread non-Indigenous (and some Indigenous) dissent over the current trajectory of Aboriginal rights and politics in Canada. To dismiss his arguments is to miss the critical point that these views are widely held in Canada and that support for a tougher stance on Aboriginal demands and political aspirations seems to be building.

**Frances Widdowson**, a Marxist analyst of Aboriginal affairs and professor of political science at Mount Royal University in Calgary, has been shaking up the polite and cautious academic discussion of Indigenous affairs in Canada. While she is no Flanagan, her sharp commentary on the shortcomings of Aboriginal policy has certainly raised eyebrows. Her approach includes a frontal assault on the so-called Aboriginal industry, a biting critique of Indigenous politics, and a healthy wake-up call about liberal approaches to Aboriginal problems. Few people in the discipline, from political theorists to band managers and bureaucrats, escape her vitriol. She is, in fact, the polar opposite of Bruce Clark and closer to a Marxist version of Thomas Flanagan, if such a thinker can be imagined.

In *Disrobing the Aboriginal Industry* (2008), which Widdowson co-authored with Albert Howard, and in other publications, she contends that recent Canadian policies are profoundly wrong-headed, that major conceptual errors underpin Canadian approaches to Indigenous issues, and that the current policies will only perpetuate heartache and despair among Aboriginal Canadians. Moreover, she argues (and this position is not unique to her) that an "industry" has developed around this consensus about Aboriginal affairs. She agrees with Flanagan that that industry is now a large part of the problem, for it is blocking strong and coherent action that might actually make a difference. Put simply, she approaches contemporary Aboriginal affairs with the convictions and frustrations of Smith and Flanagan, but from a decidedly orthodox left-wing perspective.

Many Canadian writers on the social democratic side of the political spectrum have written angry denunciations of Canadian policy, but they tend to be sympathetic to Aboriginal politicians and Indigenous objectives. Widdowson, in contrast, applies the political logic of Marx, Engels, and Trotsky to Aboriginal policy and throws her darts as much at Aboriginal leaders as at the federal government. She and Howard apply a historical materialist framework to shape their analysis – that is, they start from the position that the economic organization of a society determines how it operates politically, socially, and culturally. As the economic underpinnings of a society change, this line of argument goes, it outgrows the social and political structures; this in turn generates revolutionary change through which new institutions are created.

Drawing on Trotsky, the Russian revolutionary and theorist and an ally of Lenin during the Russian Revolution, Widdowson and Howard address the concept of uneven and combined development, in which "backward" societies adopt the technological advances of more developed ones and thereby make dramatic leaps forward. In these circumstances – including that of North America's Aboriginal peoples – assimilation to the new order is often not wholesale but rather partial and uneven. This is a classic Marxist analysis of the kind that gained widespread academic currency in the 1960s and was a dominant academic paradigm in the 1970s.

Widdowson and Howard differ from their colleagues on the left, however, in that they apply this approach to Aboriginal communities and policies. They save many of their sharpest words for those left-wing scholars who, instead of applying a materialist framework, opt for postmodernist approaches, including an uncritical cultural relativism that argues that no society or culture is superior to another. This, they argue, has deflected attention from the shortcomings of Aboriginal societies. If, as Marx contended, societies move from savagery to barbarism to civilization, Aboriginal societies had not moved beyond barbarism by the time Europeans arrived in North America.

One can readily imagine Aboriginal people and non-Aboriginal analysts gnashing their teeth at this. According to the authors, Aboriginal peoples failed to integrate fully into the capitalist order and thus retained many elements – right through to the present – of Neolithic societies. The battle to preserve Aboriginal cultures, social systems, and traditional practices is simply perpetuating outdated and inappropriate social conditions. Indeed, they suggest, the social pathologies in most of today's Aboriginal communities can be traced to premodern traditions and values. Only by bridging the development gap between the Neolithic stage and late capitalism will Indigenous communities enjoy progress and social success. Widdowson and Howard are not arguing that all Aboriginal peoples are backward, barbaric, or mere vestiges of Neolithic times. They point out that for several centuries they interacted with Christian churches, fur traders, government schools, modern technologies, and contemporary Western societies. But they add, and this is key, most Aboriginal peoples are consumers, not producers, of modern technologies and are only marginally connected to the industrial economy. "Isolation from economic processes has meant that a number of Neolithic cultural features, including undisciplined work habits, tribal forms of political identification, animistic beliefs, and difficulties in developing abstract reasoning, persist despite hundreds of years of contact" (13).

Anticipating that they might be labeled racists for challenging well-rooted assumptions about Aboriginal societies, Widdowson and Howard take pains to distinguish between race or ethnic origins and culture. They point out that individuals have no choice about their race or ethnic origins; it is something they are born with. Culture, however, is a socially defined pattern of behaviour, not a biological given. Culture reflects the economic foundations and historical development of a society. It is something that changes and that can be changed, by individuals or by collectivities. Too often, they argue, analysts conflate race with culture, leading to the situation where people who critique specific practices of a cultural group are wrongly accused of being racist.

Widdowson and Howard's book draws its title from the Hans Christian Andersen story "The Emperor's New Clothes." In that oft-told story, con men convince the Emperor that he is wearing clothes made of threads that are invisible only to those who are incompetent and stupid. The whole town accepts this fabrication, based on taboos that prevent them from stating the obvious. The ruse holds, until a child cries out that the emperor has no clothes (and is actually stark naked). Regarding what they call the Aboriginal industry, Widdowson and Howard see themselves as that child. They decry the influence of the clergy, lawyers, consultants, anthropologists, economists, and others who have feasted off the land claims and legal grievances of Aboriginal people. In their view, these outsiders have helped create an Aboriginal political elite, a powerful group of individuals who derive their influence from the status quo. These con men and women, they argue have made it taboo to criticize current imperatives like self-government and traditional ecological knowledge, even though both have shown severe shortcomings. By advocating Aboriginal self-government and land claims settlements, the industry members profit handsomely while condemning their communities to dependency and poverty. Chapter headings in *Disrobing the Aboriginal Industry* provide a blunt indication of Widdowson and Howard's views: "Land Claims: Dreaming Aboriginal Economic Development"; "Self-Government: An Inherent Right to Tribal Dictatorships"; "Justice: Rewarding Friends and Punishing Enemies"; "Child Welfare: Strengthening the Abusive Circle"; "Health Care: A Superstitious Alternative"; "Education: Honouring the Ignorance of Our Ancestors"; and "Environmental Management: The Spiritual Sell-Out of 'Mother Earth.'"

Widdowson offers critique rather than policy advice. She seems single-mindedly determined to find little more than malevolence, incompetence, and wrong-headedness in the current approaches to Aboriginal issues. Although her overwrought language will win praise from the handful of analysts who share her views, her overly harsh attacks have generated far more hostility than interest, more rejection than acceptance. Important thoughts are embedded in her analysis – the uncritical adoption of Aboriginal cultural assertions merits far more attention than it is receiving from most analysts, and so do some of the structural problems in Indigenous governments. But these are largely lost in the vitriolic stew. Widdowson is quite clear about what Canada should *not* be doing – effectively, anything that looks at all like the current approach – but she is far from helpful when it comes to providing a road map for future policies and practices. In that sense, she fits well within the mainstream of Canadian academic assessments of Aboriginal policies, in that she provides a powerful (if contrarian) view of Indigenous affairs while pulling back from offering practical and useful advice on what to do next.

Given the extensive Aboriginal engagement with the police, the courts, and the prison system, it is not surprising that scholars have devoted considerable effort to understanding how Indigenous communities could improve the clearly dysfunctional relationship between Canadian law and Aboriginal peoples. Patricia Monture-Angus devoted much of her professional life to this theme. **Jane Dickson-Gilmore**, a professor of law at Carleton University, and **Carol La Prairie**, a senior researcher with the federal Departments of Justice and the Solicitor General who died in 2010, view Indigenous approaches to justice as crucial to their efforts to regain control of their communities. In *Will the Circle Be Unbroken?* (2005), they examine the role of restorative justice, which focuses on healing rather than punishment and which brings victim and accused together with the community with the goal of repairing relationships. Many advocates claim that this process reflects traditional Indigenous values and thus represents a reassertion of Aboriginal culture.

As many do, Dickson-Gilmore and La Prairie argue that sentimentalism and cultural caution may have overtaken good analysis and proper understanding. They worry that the present-day enthusiasm for restorative justice is not well-founded. Aboriginal peoples, they tell us, have been ravaged by imposed political and legal systems and are now being presented with an alternative that proponents assert is based on Indigenous principles. In other words, Indigenous peoples are being "saved" administratively by the same system that caused them grief and difficulty in the first place. Dickson-Gilmore and La Prairie make a crucial contribution in that they show how transforming Indigenous governance and justice systems is a complex process and that simplistic appeals to Aboriginal culture can easily miss crucial practical issues.

Drawing on many years' experience with Aboriginal people and the justice system, they offer a valuable corrective to overly quick assertions about the suitability of restorative justice – and, by extension, other political initiatives supposedly inspired by Indigenous traditions. They emphasize the importance of local capacity in tackling major political changes, point out the disconnect between Aboriginal traditions and restorative justice as currently proposed or practised, and highlight the disruptive potential of major failures in the transformation of legal practices.

*Will the Circle Be Unbroken?* provides a practical perspective on some of the ideas now circulating about revitalizing Aboriginal communities through local empowerment. While Dickson-Gilmore strongly supports a reimagining of legal systems and a transformation of the Aboriginal experience with Canadian police and court procedures, she has doubts about the utility of "traditional" values and customs. Given the changes that have occurred over the past centuries, it is by no means clear that the traditional systems now being proposed actually reflect long-standing practices. This is a crucial point worth serious examination. Many Aboriginal communities, and many scholars of Indigenous affairs, argue that a return to traditional practices is essential if communities are to reconstitute their cultures. Dickson-Gilmore and La Prairie suggest that a reality check may be in order. These are, they demonstrate, hurting and even damaged communities. Traditional systems have eroded over time, mainly because of the depredations of the Canadian state. Rushing to re-establish an earlier system – one that may well have been better suited to Indigenous peoples in the past – when the capacity of the communities is in doubt and when understandings of the traditions are weak could well do much more harm than good.

Dickson-Gilmore and La Prairie offer a valuable caution about proceeding too quickly and recklessly to re-establish "Indigenous" customs and traditions. Many political commentators argue that Aboriginal communities need to reassert their cultural practices and norms. Dickson-Gilmore and La Prairie demonstrate that there are significant risks in that approach. Circumstances vary, of course. Traditional practices are perhaps more relevant in the Nass Valley, an isolated corner of northwestern British Columbia, than in heavily transformed regions of the Maritimes, but even in the former case there are reasons for moving slowly. In the end, Dickson-Gilmore and La Prairie's analysis leads to this crucial question: If the current system is a failure, and re-establishing traditional systems may be highly problematic, what is to be done? They make a strong case for moving slowly, working community by community, and restraining the enthusiasm for reintroducing traditional practices. But they also make it clear that the problem at hand – Aboriginal overrepresentation in the justice system – is extremely serious, and that time is running out.

That the conversation on Aboriginal political aspirations has been raging intensely for over four decades often obscures two crucial facts: that real progress has been made, and that the national and political context in which these debates have taken place has shifted considerably. **Gabrielle Slowey**, a political scientist at York University, understands that the global rise of neoliberalism has done more than change national political dynamics. It has also tested the flexibility, acuity, and political acumen of Aboriginal governments. In *Navigating Neoliberalism* (2007), she focuses on the Miskew Cree of northern Alberta and their efforts to secure greater autonomy. Concentrating on what has happened rather than what might happen (which is the perspective adopted by most thinkers in the field), she makes some critical discoveries. The rise of neoliberalism impeded the efforts of the federal government to dictate the terms of local government and Aboriginal autonomy to communities. Slowey shows that the Miskew Cree capitalized on changes in government policy and mindset to advance their own agenda, securing greater autonomy than might have otherwise have been the case.

Slowey makes two important contributions in her work. First, she documents how neoliberal policies create additional space for community-centred political initiatives. With the federal government backing out of the picture, and with resource companies and governments needing some sort of organized presence in the area, Aboriginal governments such as the Miskew could step into the emerging void. "Self-determination is consistent with normative and neoliberal goals of economic, political and cultural self-reliance" (xv). She also asserts the fundamental importance of developing a community economic base, especially in a neoliberal age. She highlights the importance of economic development for self-determination: "Economic development is essential to contemporary First Nations governance. It exposes the dual importance of political autonomy and capitalization. As well, it shows how self-determination functions as a vehicle for First Nations community-governance beyond the simple parameters of institutional arrangements to one of market-inspired governance" (xvi).

The idea that neoliberal or free market governments might advance Aboriginal self-determination has little currency in academe and even less among Indigenous leaders. For several generations of researchers and Aboriginal leaders, schooled in the Liberal Party's pattern of fiscal generosity, the link between development and autonomy is not immediately obvious. Slowey's work emphasizes the creativity of the Miskew Cree (and other communities that followed comparable paths). More importantly, she makes a compelling case that the autonomy brought about by economic development can provide a major boost to both self-determination and material well-being.

A political scientist at Wilfrid Laurier University and coauthor of *Beyond the Indian Act* with Tom Flanagan and André Le Dressay, **Chris Alcantara** is among the most pragmatic of the scholars working on Aboriginal governance. He is often in the same camp as Tom Pocklington

and Bonita Beatty. Although he clearly supports Aboriginal cultural traditions, he would likely call himself a realist, and he focuses on contemporary challenges, including land claims agreements and property rights. He
believes that the existing structures and the intense struggles with the
Government of Canada are distractions from the effort needed to address
quality-of-life issues in Indigenous communities. Most analysts emphasize the need for comprehensive land claims agreements; Alcantara
argues, instead, that Supreme Court decisions, self-government agreements, the First Nations Land Management Act, and various administrative measures could easily provide stronger and more effective solutions
than these negotiations. By focusing on outcomes rather than symbolic
settlements, he shifts attention to practical matters that could have a
quick and substantial impact.

Alcantara summarized his views in an opinion piece in the *Toronto
Star* on December 1, 2011. Responding to the Attawapiskat controversy,
he agreed that remote communities had few economic prospects. Then
he asked a question that few academics had raised publicly: Should federal and provincial governments continue to support remote and uneconomical settlements? True, the federal government had a fiduciary
responsibility to Aboriginal peoples – effectively, a moral commitment
to recognize and fund Indigenous self-determination, including the
right to decide where to live. But he then continued that the discussion
should not stop with these high-level principles. Instead, governments,
scholars, and Aboriginal communities should explore alternatives that
would provide a higher quality of life. A special investment fund could
be established for viable enterprises (perhaps located outside traditional territories) to support local needs, and incentives could be offered to convince community members to move to more economically
viable communities. The concept that Aboriginal peoples and communities have portable rights is already entrenched in Canadian practice, an example being urban reserves on the Prairies. Alcantara
specifically rejects the idea that these measures could be imposed on
Aboriginal communities. Required instead would be open and frank
discussions among Indigenous leaders and federal and provincial
officials.

Alcantara accepts the constitutional and political legitimacy of
Indigenous governments. But he is not constrained by today's
Aboriginal agendas. His focus is on quality-of-life issues, and he is

much more willing than many commentators to contemplate and support radical solutions. He has written about the practicalities of land claims negotiations, the importance of introducing private policy regimes in Aboriginal communities, and the possibility of closing isolated reserves in order to improve economic and social opportunities for Indigenous Canadians. His work on Indigenous development corporations (conducted with Gary Wilson of the University of Northern British Columbia) is an excellent example of his emphasis on practical and business-related solutions to the challenges facing contemporary Canada. His ability to blend support for Indigenous constitutional and political rights with practical solutions to contemporary challenges is part of a growing trend among scholars to focus on more practical outcomes.

## POLITICAL PARTIES

The positions espoused by Aboriginal political organizations have consistently strong philosophical elements. In sharp contrast, non-Aboriginal political parties are much more cautious and pragmatic. Also, their proposals have yet to express themselves as policies. Since the early 1980s, governments have been content to let Aboriginal people and organizations challenge government policy in the courts. When the court system has found government approaches to be wanting – as has happened with increasing frequency – those same governments have moved slowly to translate Supreme Court decisions into practical legislative or regulatory action.

For the 2006 federal election, held shortly after the negotiation of the Kelowna Accord, the three main politic parties went to the hustings with the political platforms we discuss below (and provide in Appendix D). Between 2006 and 2011, those party platforms did not change significantly, but they did become shorter and punchier. In the main parties' documents prepared for the 2011 federal election, Aboriginal issues received very little attention.

The now-defunct Canadian Alliance Party followed Flanagan's general approach. It opposed any further entrenchment of Aboriginal rights and expressed a preference for ending special status for Aboriginal peoples. In some quarters, this was a popular position. It was also consistent with the party's small-government, laissez-faire approach to governance. But it is worth noting that the Canadian

Alliance had its strongest support in the parts of the country where there was the greatest conflict over Aboriginal rights and aspirations: BC, Alberta, and Saskatchewan.

The Conservative Party of Canada, born out of a merger of the Progressive Conservative Party and the Canadian Alliance, dropped the more ideological elements of the Canadian Alliance platform relating to Aboriginal rights. The first minister of Indian and northern affairs appointed by Prime Minister Harper would be Jim Prentice, a Calgary lawyer with years of expertise on the Aboriginal file, who strongly supported the resolution of Indigenous claims in Canada.

The Conservative's 2006 party platform was more conciliatory than that of the Canadian Alliance. It included measures on matrimonial policy and educational choice for Aboriginal children. While few First Nations leaders would have embraced it, it was not wildly out of step with the positions of other national political parties and mixed the ideas, positions, and ideological formulations of the various political philosophers described earlier. It was, in sum, a compromise document, designed to be pragmatic and to emphasize well-being over lofty constitutional principles.

The Liberal Party of Canada (which has an Aboriginal Affairs Commission that provides leadership on Indigenous issues within the party) entered the 2006 federal election with a clear statement on Aboriginal policy. An agreement it signed with the Assembly of First Nations, the Inuit Tapiriit Kanatami, the Métis National Council, the Congress of Aboriginal Peoples, and the Native Women's Association of Canada in 2005 provided an outline of its priorities. The Liberal Party's actual 2006 election platform on Aboriginal policy drew heavily on the Kelowna Accord, rejected broad philosophical issues, and focused on practical questions: health care, education, and self-government.

Realizing that it had no realistic prospect of forming a government, the federal New Democrats were the most open to bold visions and broad pronouncements. Party policy on Aboriginal affairs for the 2006 election included a comprehensive list of high priorities as well as a searing indictment of the previous federal governments.

On balance, the three national parties differ little in terms of Aboriginal policy and priorities, with minor variations in language, emphasis, and philosophical approach. The Conservatives favour greater individual choice and freedom and place considerable value on transparency and accountability. The NDP clearly believes that direct government intervention is the best means of addressing real issues. The Liberals, reflecting on a lengthy period of managing the country's affairs, have opted to draw attention to multiparty (federal, provincial, Aboriginal) accords as the best means of addressing contemporary challenges and opportunities. The various policy platforms reveal how crowded the middle ground is in Canadian politics, how pragmatic considerations win out over philosophical ones, and how the primary objective on the Aboriginal file appears to be avoiding angering either Aboriginal or non-Aboriginal voters.

The policy statements of the national political parties indicate that they have shied away from the philosophical debates raging across Canada on this issue as well as from the visions laid out by Indigenous leaders and organizations. A key consideration here is that as an issue, Aboriginal affairs is not a vote-getter in Canadian politics. Too strong a position in favour of Indigenous rights could push some voters away; overt support for Aboriginal aspirations will draw few people to the party who are not already there. This is not to say that the political ideas, Aboriginal and non-Aboriginal, discussed here do not matter – in fact, they have had a profound effect. Among policy makers, politicians, and Aboriginal leaders, these debates have had considerable influence, with the arguments in favour of encouraging Aboriginal people's integration into the political and economic mainstream drawing more attention and support over time.

## CONCLUDING THOUGHTS

Ideas matter, because they reflect national and regional mindsets and because, in many subtle ways, they influence how Canadians think about Aboriginal issues. People who have never read Taiaiake Alfred or Sákéj Henderson, or who have never heard of Tom Pocklington or Frances Widdowson, may nonetheless have been exposed to their ideas, albeit in a limited and incomplete form. The intellectual swirl around Aboriginal affairs in Canada is filled with strongly held positions. Amidst all of the writing and pondering are gems of insight and vision that will, collectively and individually, affect how Aboriginal and non-Aboriginal Canadians relate to each other in the coming decades. At this point, however, there is consensus on only a handful of items: that Aboriginal peoples are suffering, that the status quo is not working effectively, that government funds are not being applied properly, and that Canadians need to consider bold steps if they want things to get better for Aboriginal people and if Canadians ever hope to become treaty peoples and transform themselves into a treaty nation. We share all of these assumptions – but we also believe that high-level theorizing avoids the most basic elements of this issue: that Aboriginal peoples are hurting, that Canada continues to embarrass itself through its ineffectiveness on this file, and that practical, reasonable steps are needed to a provide a greater measure of justice and opportunity for Indigenous peoples and communities in this country.

In the past few chapters we have reviewed the work of several of the leading thinkers in Aboriginal politics and the law. The diversity of opinion is staggering, particularly within the non-Aboriginal intellectual community (from Clark to Flanagan) and between Indigenous and non-Indigenous political theorists (contrast Cairns with Alfred). What is more, few of the proposals we have discussed so far were drafted with a particular concern for their political and financial practicality. Canada has gone far enough down the road of Indigenous–non-Indigenous debate to know what the two sides need and expect from each other. The political challenge of reconciliation now involves moving beyond philosophical or rhetorical positions into the realm of administrative practicalities and financial realities.

Limits matter. Even if Flanagan's plan for integrating Aboriginal people into the Canadian polity were appropriate, it would founder on the basis of Indigenous resistance alone. Aboriginal people represent a formidable political force in Canada, and their aspirations cannot be brushed aside. The integrationist model, which shares with the Trudeau White Paper the belief that special status is inherently wrongheaded, would never get the support of Aboriginal leaders, and no federal government is likely to find the resolve it would take to force through the required political and constitutional changes. It would be flying in the face of recent legal precedent, constitutional structures, history, and contemporary realities.

But the same applies to the more assertive Aboriginal proposals of Alfred and Monture-Angus, which fall short, just like those of Flanagan and Clark. There is widespread Aboriginal support for Indigenous "nations" and parallelism, for autonomous political structures and power sharing with Ottawa, but this simply isn't going to happen – regardless of whether it is the morally, historically, or politically correct thing to do. Even if these proposals were the right ones for Indigenous communities, and even if they were certain to bring those communities economic opportunity, political peace, and cultural strength, Canadians as a whole would not accept them. These are blunt realities. Non-Aboriginal tolerance for Aboriginal agendas is today near the breaking point, and the federal government's reluctance to respond to the *Report of the Royal Commission on Aboriginal Peoples* rests largely on the realization that there is almost no non-Indigenous support for expanding Aboriginal powers or government spending on Aboriginal affairs. Proposals like those from Alfred and others speak with conviction to Aboriginal dreams and aspirations and resonate with assumptions about the precontact dignity and authority of Aboriginal societies. But that is not going to translate into political acceptance by non-Aboriginal Canadians of the lofty ambitions and extensive demands of Aboriginal people. If anything, the rhetoric of Aboriginal sovereignty and nation-to-nation relations has hardened non-Indigenous resolve and is the principal reason for today's widespread resistance to the expansion of Aboriginal authority in Canada.

The debate is highly political, and venturing forth with new proposals makes one a target for critics from all sides. For many years, Canadian critics of Aboriginal proposals whispered their complaints behind their hands, fearing to offer negative comments in public settings. This intellectual paternalism served no one's best interests, certainly not those of Aboriginal politicians and leaders, who deserved to have their ideas contested openly, frankly, and honestly. Flanagan and Clark have both been criticized sharply for bringing their views forward – in Clark's case, the manner in which he aired his ideas was the main target of the criticism. For their part, Aboriginal political philosophers – like Monture-Angus, with her critique of current Aboriginal governments and male political leaders – have faced intense scrutiny for bringing into the open ideas that many Aboriginal politicians do not want to hear. Widdowson has certainly attracted a large measure of unwarranted venom for offering her strongly held views for debate.

That there is public engagement – and disagreement – with Aboriginal people about models for future relations is a sign of strength and political maturity among all participants. Aboriginal people are not naive enough to believe that, in the complex Canadian political environment, they will achieve all of their objectives and see the implementation of their ideal strategy. To bring ideas forward and have them ignored – as happened with the Royal Commission on Aboriginal Peoples – is insulting and patronizing. Ideas warrant a response, and response generates a debate. In this way, limits will be defined, negotiations will commence, and compromises will eventually be found. That opponents, both Aboriginal and non-Aboriginal, of Aboriginal governments, policies, and proposals now routinely speak their minds is of vital importance to the development of a healthy and meaningful dialogue. Canada will not resolve the conundrum around Aboriginal rights unless and until there is a full, free, and highly engaged airing of different opinions. As is now being discovered, this debate can often be acrimonious, and those courageous enough to venture forward with radical or creative ideas may well find themselves the subject of intense criticism and personal attacks. Aboriginal people have felt the effects of these attempts at silencing for quite some time, and political leaders and thinkers feel them still.

Since the 1990s, critics have used the emergence of local opposition to elected chiefs as a sign that Aboriginal people are not "ready" for self-government. The reverse is closer to the mark. Opposition is essential to effective (and democratic) decision making and to successful local administration. Mature political units learn from criticism and political battles and develop policies that draw diverse elements of the community together. Outspoken criticism is a sign of sharpened local expectations and oversight, which are essential to effective administration. Conversely, non-Aboriginal criticism of Aboriginal policies and politics is a critical sign of engagement. The criticisms voiced by the BC Liberal Party (before Premier Gordon Campbell shifted gears and introduced the most progressive and innovative provincial Aboriginal programs in the country) and the Conservative Party only bring into the public view the assumptions that have long circulated in Canada and that Aboriginal leaders confront routinely in nonpolitical settings. High-level, deeply ideological public debates about Aboriginal rights are a sign that political communities are taking Indigenous aspirations, demands, and achievements seriously. This may *look* like a backlash against Aboriginal people who are straining at the shackles of colonialism (which they are, to be sure), but the country as a whole is better off, for it helps define a national position on critical issues.

There are plenty of good, thoughtful, and creative solutions to the political challenges facing Aboriginal people in Canada. Most of these ideas operate at the level of ideals and political philosophy and are not yet grounded or tested in practice. At present, they represent idealized and diverse notions of what Canada *could* be. All agree that the issue is of great national importance. All agree that the status quo is not viable. All agree that major changes are in order, even as they disagree profoundly about what those changes should be. A merging of political ideals with practical realities could accomplish much.

The disjuncture between political ideas and action is not unusual in Canada. The country has rarely been driven by clear ideological agendas and has instead worked on the basis of compromise and negotiation. This pattern of conciliation has been a national strength at times, but it has also made the country loath to consider bold visions, dramatic solutions, or sharp policy departures. It has made the country cautious to the point of being inactive on many important national files. While debate will undoubtedly rage on about the usefulness of compromise and discussion as a foundation for Canadian political life, it is increasingly clear that further delays present an unfair and unjust burden on Aboriginal people. Bold steps are required. Acts of political leadership and diplomacy are required. Major declarations of positive intent and openness to meaningful partnerships are essential if Aboriginal people are to escape the difficult conditions that history, racism, injustice, and political lethargy have imposed on them. Reconciliation, to put it more simply, is no longer an option. It has become a necessity.

# coming at it from a different direction – aboriginal success stories

# 6

# culture and education

IT IS EASY to get depressed about Aboriginal conditions in Canada. Scarcely a day passes without another sensational headline. If the story is not about impoverished conditions on a reserve then it is documenting urban violence, a child welfare crisis, or an Aboriginal protest. Politicians routinely highlight the statistics of despair, and First Nations leaders, struggling to get the nation's attention, speak openly of endemic drug and alcohol abuse and decry the overrepresentation of Aboriginal people in the prison system. And on it goes, from a glue-sniffing epidemic at Davis Inlet to filthy water at Kashechewan, from corruption in Aboriginal organizations to the difficulties attracting teachers to isolated northern reserves, from unemployment rates above 90 percent on some reserves to bitter battles over child apprehensions and Aboriginal control of social welfare, from multimillion-dollar legal bills for fighting the government to gut-wrenching descriptions of the evil acts of pedophiles in residential schools. There is no need to recite the familiar and depressing statistics, all of which originate in crises and conflicts affecting Canada's Aboriginal communities. Make no mistake on this critical point: Inuit, First Nations, and Métis people in this country are facing serious, systematic, and some would say intractable problems. Canadians hear about them often.

But something vitally important is missing: there are profound reasons for optimism. Hardship, social collapse, and economic despair are very real, but not all Aboriginal communities, families, and individuals are engulfed in sorrow, resignation, and cultural decay. The Aboriginal experience in Canada has a surprisingly large number of positive elements that are rarely noted. Cumulatively, these successes suggest that Aboriginal people are rebounding: through perseverance, cultural conviction, and simple hard work, they are re-establishing themselves as a national force. This is due not to the efforts of Aboriginal politicians – whose greatest victories came during the constitutional battles of the 1970s and 1980s – but rather to the thousands of Aboriginal women, men, and children, working largely at the community level, who are rebuilding confidence and optimism in a population wracked for too long by despair and disappointment. Perhaps this is why Chief Shawn Atleo, when he was chief of the Assembly of First Nations, shifted his focus from high-profile political battles to practical, on-the-ground problem solving. It is here that the greatest changes are occurring. Atleo's approach faced considerable opposition from chiefs from across the country, particularly over the First Nations Education Act introduced in 2014. In fact, opposition to his support for the government was so strong that Atleo felt compelled to resign his office. His successor, Chief Perry Bellegarde of Saskatchewan, elected in December 2014, favours a rights-based approach to government relations. The desire to fight with the government lives on. Many Aboriginal people, however, are getting on with business. The next three chapters describe how they are doing that in the realms of culture and education, business and entrepreneurship, and governance and civil society.

## ABORIGINAL CULTURAL RENEWAL

For more than two hundred years, newcomers predicted the demise of Aboriginal cultures. Analysts today are no different: in Canada, and indeed globally, there is a death watch over Indigenous languages. Although a handful of Indigenous languages remain vibrant in Canada – Cree, Inuktitut, Gwich'in, Innu – the vast majority have few native speakers, and few of those are under sixty. This decline reflects a global pattern – Indigenous languages are being erased by majority ones. There were once more than six thousand languages spoken worldwide; many today are gone, and others are threatened with extinction. Most of the world's languages have fewer than one thousand speakers and are threatened by cultural encroachment and the impositions of national education systems. Some analysts tell us that the death of a language marks the death of a culture – that without the richness, diversity, and cultural references embedded in their language, a people can only be a broken shell of themselves. Others – including us – are less pessimistic and believe that cultures can persist even without language.

In 2011, the National Household Survey of Aboriginal Language Knowledge reported that only 17 percent of Aboriginal people (around 240,000) can hold a conversation in an Aboriginal language. Close to 64 percent of Inuit can do so – in their case, in Inuktitut – and almost all Inuit elders can do so. Overall, though, language competence among Aboriginal children is dropping. In 2013, the community of La Loche, Saskatchewan, reported a catastrophic drop in Aboriginal language use among preschoolers, suggesting an imminent linguistic crisis. There was evidence that an Aboriginal Head Start program was helping preschoolers gain some competency, but home use of the language remained the most critical consideration. According to Statistics Canada, 90 percent of Inuit said that language retention was important to them; however, only 66 percent of First Nations and 50 percent of Métis said the same. The data cited here reflect off-reserve Aboriginal language use. There is other evidence that Aboriginal language is more common on reserves.

The key point is that Aboriginal communities *are* concerned about cultural loss, including language loss. Unfortunately, the diversity of Indigenous Canadians works against large-scale and consistent efforts to rebuild language fluency. One of the strongest language initiatives in the country is in Yukon. There, through the Yukon Native Languages Project, the territorial government and First Nations educational authorities have invested heavily in teacher training and classroom instruction in Indigenous languages. And there are many similar initiatives across the country, including the Ojibway and Cree Cultural Centre, the First Peoples' Cultural Foundation (which maintains the FirstVoices Language Archive), the First Nations Confederacy of Cultural Education Centres, the Yinka Déné Language Institute (Carrier Sekani), Sma'lgyax Living Legacy Talking Dictionary

(Tsimshian), Aboriginal Languages of Manitoba, and the Mi'kmaq Online Talking Dictionary. Perhaps the strongest of all these programs are the ones supported by the Nunavut government. Some communities have Aboriginal immersion day care centres and preschools (although nothing on the scale of the Māori preschools established in New Zealand several decades ago). Many more now offer language instruction in elementary and high schools, typically with elders as instructors, who often incorporate ceremonial and traditional activities into their classes.

Despite these efforts, the battle against linguistic decline is being lost. Language competence among Aboriginal peoples continues to slide, and few Aboriginal languages in Canada will survive the twenty-first century. But Indigenous groups are making strong efforts to address this.

The same pattern does not hold for Indigenous cultural practices. Hunting, fishing, and gathering activities remain strong, although reduced interest among youth is noticeable here as well, just as it is in the non-Aboriginal community. But key cultural ceremonies – potlatches on the West Coast, powwows and the Sun Dance on the Prairies, complex political organization among the Mohawk, and the sharing of food harvests – all of these remain important to Aboriginal people. Efforts have been made to incorporate Indigenous cultures into the justice and health care systems. Aboriginal healing and sentencing circles are becoming common. In a number of Indigenous communities and organizations, elders have regained prominent positions. Few Canadians realize just how strong Indigenous cultural practices still are today. Seasonal ceremonies are still a vital part of Indigenous communities, and long-standing traditions and activities are still important.

Aboriginal Canadians take part in a wide variety of social and recreational activities at the community, regional, and national levels. Many mainstream Canadians have stereotyped Aboriginal peoples as obsessed with bingo. But for them, bingo halls play much the same role as church basements do on the Prairies. They are places where relationships are maintained and where community news is shared. Bingo is a social event for Aboriginal women in particular. A few years back, Saskatchewan banned smoking in public spaces. As an unexpected consequence of this, many bingo halls closed in the province, leaving Aboriginal women without a regular meeting place.

Aboriginal people are heavily involved in sports, both regionally and nationally. The annual all-Native basketball tournament in Prince Rupert, British Columbia, is a winter highlight on the Northwest Coast. Provincial and regional Native hockey tournaments are extremely popular on the Prairies, and so is, increasingly and surprisingly, golf. (The Dakota Dunes course, owned by the Whitecap First Nation, has been named one of the top fifteen courses in Canada by Golf Digest, out of some 3,500 courses.)

The North American Indigenous Games, first held in Edmonton in 1990, attract competitors, artists, and cultural performers from across the country and, in recent years, around the world. The 1997 games in Victoria, BC, drew more than 5,000 competitors, coaches, and managers along with some 2,500 Aboriginal artists. A World Indigenous Games was held for the first time in Australia in 2000. Although the next games, scheduled for Montreal in 2004, were cancelled, they were staged again in Victoria in 2008. Plans for an even larger World Indigenous Games in Winnipeg in 2012 were dropped for lack of funding. The North American Indigenous Games re-emerged, however, in July 2014, with the hosting of a successful competition, involving more than 4,000 competitors, in Regina, Saskatchewan. The games demonstrated the determination of Aboriginal people to build confidence and community through sport.

The scale of Indigenous sports activities is worth noting. The Thirty-Seventh Saskatchewan First Nations Games, held on the Thunderchild First Nation in August 2011, required the construction of soccer pitches, renovations to baseball diamonds, and improvements to a running track. Teams from thirteen tribal councils participated, and more than 4,500 athletes (ages ten to seventeen), 400 volunteers, and thousands of spectators attended the six-day event. Equally impressive was the long list of corporate sponsors: the Saskatchewan Indian Gaming Authority, Gold Eagle Casino, Peace Hills Trust, PotashCorp, BHP Billington, Cameco, Affinity Credit Union, the *Star Phoenix* and *Leader-Post* newspapers, CARC Resources, and others, representing most of the province's leading Aboriginal and non-Aboriginal businesses. These activities have done much to strengthen Aboriginal pride and solidarity.

There is plenty of evidence of Aboriginal cultural persistence, as well as growing evidence that Indigenous people are eager to share their cultures with other Canadians. There is, for example, a growing Aboriginal tourism industry in the country, emphasizing experiences with Indigenous guides and elders on the land and in communities. The Yukon International Storytelling Festival is a good example. It extends beyond Indigenous storytelling to provide a powerful cross-cultural blend of this vital art. Since 1988, the National Aboriginal Achievement Awards have celebrated Indigenous accomplishments and drawn attention to many individual success stories. The annual list of recipients reflects the richness and vitality of Indigenous accomplishments in Canada.

Indigenous Canada is generating a multitude of talented and politically engaged artists and entertainers. Aboriginal dance troupes, drum corps, artists, carvers, storytellers, and musicians have been working hard to build community and public interest in Indigenous cultures. The Le-La-La (Travelling from here to there) Dancers from the Kwakwaka'wakw Nations of Vancouver Island has built a strong international reputation. So have the Dancers of Damelahamid, also known as the Masked Dancers of the Gitxsan Nation. Wanuskewin Heritage Park near Saskatoon, built around an important archeological site, is a renowned cultural centre that celebrates Plains history and culture through dance. The Wanuskewin International Dance Troupe is one of the best known on the Prairies.

On the literary front, there is growing interest in Indigenous prose. Writers such as Thomas King, Joseph Boyden, Jeannette Armstrong, Lee Maracle, Rita Mestokosho, Louise Halfe, Armand Ruffo, Margo Kane, and Drew Hayden have found critical praise and commercial success. The En'owkin Centre in Penticton develops Aboriginal writers, and an affiliated press, Theytus Books, publishes their work. Pemmican Publications supports Métis writers, with an emphasis on their cultural heritage. One of CBC radio's more popular programs, *Dead Dog Café*, written by Thomas King, took a light-hearted approach to First Nations issues. *North of 60*, a TV drama about life in the North, produced with extensive Indigenous involvement, sparked Canadian viewers' interest in Aboriginal themes. Tom Jackson, one of the stars of *North of 60,* has since established himself as a prominent community activist.

There is considerable interest in Aboriginal music, both traditional and cross-over. Talented musicians from Robbie Robertson (formerly of The Band) to Inuit singer Susan Aglukark and Yukoner Jerry Alfred blend Indigenous languages, Aboriginal themes, and traditional music with contemporary instruments. There are many others, including Tanya Tagaq (Nunavut), Wolfpack (Six Nations), North Wind (Ojibwa), Asani (Cree and Métis), Digo (Tlicho/Dogrib), Don Amero (Métis), Eagle and Hawk (First Nations from Winnipeg), and Eekwol (Muskoday First Nation, Cree).

Tomson Highway, the trilingual Cree, French, and English speaking playwright and novelist from northern Manitoba, and Métis writer Maria Campbell have gained critical acclaim in Canada and abroad for their theatre work. September 1999 saw the launch of the Aboriginal Peoples Television Network, the world's first national Aboriginal broadcasting company. One of its most popular programs, *Cooking with the Wolfman,* combines a standard cooking show with a unique perspective on Aboriginal culture and traditions. APTN is not the only Aboriginal broadcaster making an impact. Northern Native Broadcasting Yukon is one of the most consistently impressive Aboriginal cultural operations in the country. The Inuit Broadcasting Corporation, formed in 1981, brought Inuit language and cultural programming to the North. It joined with other Northern broadcasters to form TV Northern Canada. It helped found APTN in 1999. *Atanarjuat (The Fast Runner)*, a feature film produced in Inuktitut by Zacharias Kunuk and Igloolik Isuma Productions, gave Kunuk a high profile on Canada's cultural landscape and on the world's stage. The plaudits from critics did not, however, pay the bills. Kunuk's company closed down in 2011 – a not uncommon fate for Canadian filmmakers.

Every major museum and art gallery in the country routinely hosts exhibitions of traditional and contemporary Aboriginal art. The latter is some of the most arresting and challenging work being done in this country. In 2006, when important collections of Indigenous artifacts were placed on auction around the world, Canadian and provincial museums launched strong campaigns to repatriate that material to Canada. Inuit art – especially prints and soapstone carvings – has become internationally renowned (perhaps a little overpromoted), and West Coast carvings and masks have found critical and commercial success. It is fitting that the nation's most prominent cultural venue, the Canadian Museum of History in Ottawa, showcases early Aboriginal culture and is housed in a complex designed by First

Nations architect Douglas Cardinal. Canada is almost, but not quite, at the point where the work of a successful writer, singer, artist, or performer need not be prefaced with "First Nation" or "Aboriginal." Aboriginal creators are now accepted as part of the country's artistic fabric.

**Aboriginal Spirituality.** Indigenous Canadians have deep and diverse spiritual traditions. Over the past three centuries, they have cultivated unique relationships with Christianity and with other faiths. Especially in the North, Aboriginal interest in the latitudinarian Baha'i Faith has surged. Pentecostal churches have also found many adherents, occasionally dividing communities in the process. In 2006, controversy raged in northern Quebec over constraints on the teaching of evolution in schools. The mainstream churches – Anglican, United, Roman Catholic – continue to attract a considerable following, although their Aboriginal congregations are shrinking and growing older, as with the church membership at large. The United Church holds an All Native Circle Conference that coordinates the activities of First Nations ministries, as well as an annual First Nations Day of Prayer. The famous Lac Ste. Anne Catholic pilgrimage attracts thousands of Aboriginal followers to the shores of a lake northwest of Edmonton every June. Even in the midst of the sustained controversy over residential schools, Aboriginal church members have retained their confidence and active membership. Matthew Coon Come, the former grand chief of the Assembly of First Nations, has spoken openly about his belief that being an evangelical Christian is not incompatible with being Aboriginal – and an assertive Aboriginal at that.

At the same time, there has been a resurgence in traditional spiritual values – including, it should be added, among New Age enthusiasts and other non-Aboriginal people, what some call "spiritual tourism." Indigenous spiritual blessings (often with Christian elements) have become commonplace at Aboriginal gatherings. Spiritual teachings and ceremonial practices, often of a pan-Indian (as opposed to culture-specific) nature, have been integrated into healing programs on reserves, at friendship centres, and in prisons. For example, the Alberta-based Nechi Training, Research and Health Promotions Institute uses Aboriginal spirituality extensively in its recovery and support programs, including those targeting alcohol and drug abuse.

Nechi, which describes itself as part of the "biggest Aboriginal health promotions network committed to wellness in the world," participates in some 640 Native alcohol prevention and treatment programs across Canada. Comparable initiatives in other provinces include the First Nations of Quebec, the Labrador Health and Social Services Commission, Ontario's Aboriginal Healing and Wellness Strategy, and the Indigenous Health Research Knowledge Transfer Network. All of these apply Indigenous knowledge and spirituality to healing.

Many Aboriginal communities are again sending young people out onto the land with elders so that they can learn more about traditional values and the spiritual dimensions of their world. Because Indigenous spirituality is not as formal or codified as Christian faiths, many observers have failed to notice Aboriginal peoples' spiritual strength and continuity. Many Aboriginal peoples went to great lengths to maintain their spiritual and religious ceremonies, even when these practices were prohibited by law. In today's environment, Indigenous spirituality is celebrated rather than oppressed and there is great potential for new growth.

**Community Renewal**. What matters most to Indigenous communities and leaders, of course, is the quality of Aboriginal life. And it is here, with stories of high rates of domestic violence, teen suicide, substance abuse, and rising rates of tuberculosis and sexually transmitted diseases, that even the most hardened Aboriginal leaders find reasons for despair. Although the problems are real – and no communities in Canada discuss their challenges as openly and honestly as Aboriginal people do – the situation is not uniformly grave. Some communities have turned themselves around, moving back from the brink of disaster towards health and vitality. Alkali Lake in central BC remains the icon of such a transformation. The people of that community confronted a deeply entrenched culture of drinking, largely eradicated the scourge of alcohol, and have become proselytizers for sobriety.

There are many similar examples. Inuit villages have found ways to reintroduce youth to life on the land, including by founding cultural schools. West Coast families have resurrected artistic and cultural traditions, enhancing local pride and creating employment at the same time. The strengthening of the powwow circuit on the Prairies speaks loudly to the vitality of traditional culture in that region. Even the Maritimes, where Indigenous peoples suffered severe cultural loss through prolonged contact with Europeans, has seen an explosion in local interest in Mi'kmaq and Maliseet language, culture, and traditions.

Communities that once had decrepit public buildings and homes have been substantially rebuilt, with modern houses and attractive public spaces. The village of Carcross, an hour south of Whitehorse, Yukon, is presently riding a major economic renewal that promises to transform the community. Urban Aboriginal communities are slowly improving, some faster than others, and are renewing themselves in line with the growing confidence and optimism of the Aboriginal population at large. Huge problems remain, even so. Housing is an ongoing crisis in most First Nations and Inuit communities. But amidst all the turmoil and problems, Indigenous renewal is under way across the country. More and more communities are confronting their challenges and seeking more positive futures.

**The Other Side of Urban Aboriginal Life.** Much has been written about the plight of Aboriginal people in cities. While the bad news is true enough – the lives of many Indigenous people in towns and cities are often bleak – there is more to the story. Over the past two decades, a substantial Aboriginal middle class has developed in Canada. The media almost never recognize its existence, let alone comment on its accomplishments and contributions. Violence, substance abuse, and grinding poverty are more newsworthy than examples of achievement. As we discuss below, more and more Aboriginal youth are graduating from university or college, and many of them are securing solid middle-class jobs in the private sector, especially in the fields of law and resources, and in government, with education and health leading the way. There are more and more Aboriginal tradespeople as well.

Many Aboriginal organizations are urban-based, and rural communities often maintain offices and provide services in larger centres. The Indigenous staff in these companies and organizations have decent salaries – and let it be pointed out that contrary to the national myth, they pay taxes, unless they are employed on-reserve. As would be expected, Aboriginal professionals tend to live in nicer homes in suburban areas, and their children attend the local schools. In other words, they defy Canadian stereotypes about urban Aboriginal people. And to a degree that few non-Aboriginal people recognize, these professionals maintain strong connections with their communities, welcoming visitors, returning home for ceremonies, and supporting social and economic renewal.

## EDUCATION

The litmus test for education, of course, is how well students do in school and whether they succeed in society after they leave. In this regard, Aboriginal people face formidable challenges. Reserve schools and core area urban schools have more than their share of students with disabilities, and many families are unable to provide much help with school work. Two major studies – a joint one by the AFN and Ottawa, and a separate one by the Saskatchewan government – reported in 2013 on the shortcomings of the Aboriginal education system, especially in terms of outcomes, and recommended significant improvements, including an emphasis on children under five years old. Both reports sparked a national debate about how to fund Aboriginal education, as well as a series of heated exchanges over education reforms that the Canadian government brought before Parliament in 2013–14.

Although these debates highlight ongoing issues, they draw attention away from major progress on the educational front. Indigenous communities across the country are steering substantial resources towards education. They have worked extremely hard to train and retrain Aboriginal teachers – often from their own villages – to work in local elementary and secondary schools. This effort rests on the assumption, now proved out, that Aboriginal teachers are more likely to *remain* in the communities and face fewer adjustments to life on reserves. The University of Saskatchewan alone has graduated more than one thousand Aboriginal teachers over the past quarter century. Over eight hundred of them are still teaching in the province. There are special Aboriginal teacher education programs across the country, and many of them offer students the opportunity to spend all or a large part of their time working in their home communities. Add to all this the continuing expansion of culturally appropriate curricular materials, many of them rooted in a specific Indigenous culture and/or language, and the seeds of a supportive and encouraging educational system can be seen.

The Canadian government has supported the transfer of authority to local Aboriginal governments. It had long focused more on on-reserve than off-reserve education. An early initiative to bridge this gap was the National Working Group on Education, whose 2002 report, *Our Children – Keepers of the Sacred Knowledge,* called for a holistic approach to Aboriginal education from kindergarten to postsecondary, for greater attention to Indigenous cultures, and for expanded training of Aboriginal teachers. By 2003, only 8 of 502 reserve schools in Canada were *not* managed by Aboriginal governments.

Most Aboriginal communities are entrenching Indigenous traditions in their schools, a process that is well advanced in some parts of the country. In 1996, the Mi'kmaq negotiated the transfer of control of education from the Department of Indian Affairs, thus gaining control over a five-year, $130 million budget. What a marked change this is from only a few decades earlier, when department officials ran the schools, when teacher turnover in those schools was alarmingly high (which remains a problem in many remote and northern settlements), and when educational materials had little if any culturally and regionally appropriate content. Schools that had not produced a high school graduate in several decades have relaunched convocation celebrations. Some communities, such as Benchoko in Northwest Territories, with its impressive Chief Jimmy Bruneau Regional School, have been highly competitive in sending their students on to college and university.

Schools have, in fact, become symbols of the revitalization of Aboriginal communities. Many new schools have been constructed on reserves in recent years, typically after extensive consultations with community leaders and members and usually with a view to establishing a multipurpose facility that both students and adults will use. These new schools, often controlled by bands, incorporate Aboriginal motifs and cultural values into their design and have become sources of community and cultural pride. Good examples are the attractive facilities at Saanichton and Mission, BC. Farther north, at Skidegate on Haida Gwaii, First Nations and non-Aboriginal community members got together to build a facility on reserve land that would serve the entire community. The Nisga'a of northern BC's Nass Valley have been running such schools for more than a quarter century. Band schools have helped overcome Aboriginal distrust of education, a painful legacy of residential schools and of the less well-known Indian day school system. Not surprisingly, facilities run and maintained by Aboriginal people have fewer of the negative connotations typically associated with education. This positive development has contributed significantly to increased attendance and higher graduation rates at the high school and college level.

Although dropout rates remain high by national standards, more Aboriginal students are completing high school and, with strong family and community encouragement, they are continuing their studies at the postsecondary level. Enrolment rates at colleges and universities for Registered Indians aged seventeen to thirty-four stood at 7 percent in the late 1990s, well below the rate for the country as a whole, but a strong increase from a decade earlier. Yet the increasing participation of Indigenous people in the postsecondary system – potentially a cause for national celebration – has often been the focus of criticism.

In the late 1980s, the Mulroney government committed itself very explicitly to providing financial support for Aboriginal people who wanted to attend college or university. Aboriginal people took up the offer in dramatic fashion: the number of federally supported students shot up during the 1980s and 1990s, to the point where the government began to soften its commitment. In 1989–90, Department of Indian Affairs and Northern Development funded 18,500 Registered Indians and Inuit to attend postsecondary institutions – an increase of close to 15,000 students over 1977–78. By 1995–96, that number had increased to over 27,000, at which point Ottawa capped funding. Federal funding is now administered by the bands (a source of often bitter local contention). Financial difficulties notwithstanding, Aboriginal people responded enthusiastically to educational opportunities as they arose. New institutions developed out of the funding program, including the Nicola Institute in Merritt, BC; the Métis-focused Gabriel Dumont Institute in Saskatoon; and, also in Saskatchewan, the First Nations University of Canada, the largest Aboriginal postsecondary institution in the country.

Aboriginal interest in postsecondary education has increased even more dramatically than high school graduation rates. Two forces have combined to bring this about: growing Aboriginal awareness of the importance and value of advanced education, and outreach initiatives by universities and colleges eager to meet the needs of Aboriginal students. Some context is needed here. For much of the twentieth century, young Aboriginal adults lost their Indian status simply by attending university, because earning a high-quality education signified that an individual had joined the Canadian mainstream. Those few students who, before the 1970s, ventured onto university campuses found themselves lost in a non-Aboriginal sea, participants in academic programs with little Aboriginal content. Now, in the early twenty-first century, universities and colleges across the country have established special Aboriginal recruitment and transition programs. Elders are a regular fixture today on a number of Canadian campuses. Most institutions have specialized Aboriginal programs, especially in social work and social services, public administration, law, and education. Aboriginal centres provide meeting places for students, which has helped create and sustain community in institutions where Aboriginal people are still greatly outnumbered.

Universities and colleges are now working closely with Aboriginal communities. Community colleges have been especially active in bringing their courses and programs to First Nations communities, but universities have been offering such services as well. Brandon University's Northern Teachers Education Program brings full degree programs to northern communities, allowing students to spend a portion of their time on the Brandon campus but otherwise study close to home. As a result, there are now Aboriginal teachers at almost every First Nations school in northern Saskatchewan. The University of Northern British Columbia has a variety of community-based teaching programs, and the University of Winnipeg works closely with urban Aboriginal groups to create opportunities for Indigenous residents in the inner city. A small number of schools, including the University of Saskatchewan, Brandon University, the University of Winnipeg, and UNBC, have made service to Aboriginal students central to their mission. In New Brunswick, St. Thomas University has a strong Mi'kmaq and Maliseet program, and several Quebec institutions and Lakehead University in Ontario have made special efforts to accommodate Indigenous knowledge. Northern colleges, led by Nunavut Arctic College, Aurora College in Northwest Territories, and Yukon College, and now including the new University College of the North in Manitoba, are providing excellent adult basic education services as well as a variety of technical, business, and pre-professional programs to a largely Aboriginal clientele. The First Nations University of Canada, the largest Aboriginally controlled institution in the country, made great strides for a decade before becoming caught in an internal political quagmire that slowed progress for several years. The university survived, however, and is making important steps towards sustainability.

Other institutions have worked with Aboriginal and regional governments to develop specially targeted programs, ranging from St. Mary's University's MBA program to the University of Victoria's law program, both designed for and delivered in Nunavut. Brokered social work and education programs for Native students are offered at Yukon College in conjunction with the University of Regina. And, because of the high level of Aboriginal engagement and influence in the region, UNBC and Northwest Community College are working with the Wilp Wilxo'oskwhl Nisga'a (Nisga'a House of Wisdom) to provide university and college programming in the Nass Valley.

Universities and colleges are doing more than just educating Aboriginal people. They are *learning* from them as well. More and more institutions are developing Aboriginal studies programs for both Aboriginal and non-Aboriginal students. Some of these programs, especially on the Prairies, have become the cornerstone of efforts to strengthen Indigenous language use. The best of these programs incorporate traditional knowledge with Indigenous learning styles and allow students to experience contemporary Aboriginal cultures through participation in dances, potlatches, and other community events. Many schools have been working hard to attract Aboriginal faculty, a task made difficult by the enormous pressure on these highly trained individuals to return and help their own communities.

Also, scholarship *about* Indigenous peoples is beginning to take new approaches, such as community-based research. Researchers now share their findings with the people they are studying and are training community members as assistants. The emergence of Aboriginally focused scholarship, based on information provided by elders and community members and incorporated into mainstream academic work, has brought Canada to the forefront of Indigenous knowledge (IK) studies, led by scholars such as Marie Battiste. This has ensured that the lessons and learnings from Indigenous peoples will be widely shared.

But again, the core message is in the numbers. In 2011, according to Statistics Canada, 48 percent of Aboriginal people had some form of postsecondary qualifications, including a university degree (9.8 percent), college diplomas (21 percent), trades certificates (14 percent), and some university study (3.5 percent). By way of comparison, 65 percent of non-Aboriginal people between the ages of twenty-five and sixty four had some form of postsecondary education, including a university degree (26 percent), a college diploma (21 percent), and a trade certificate (12 percent). In the past three decades, hundreds of well-trained Aboriginal lawyers have entered the legal profession, to the point where the percentage of Indigenous lawyers is higher than the percentage of Aboriginal people in the Canadian population. Meanwhile, hundreds of Aboriginal teachers are graduating each year, and most of them are returning to their communities to teach. Special programs in nursing, community health, and medicine are attracting growing numbers of applicants. The University of Manitoba's program for Aboriginal doctors is enjoying considerable success in this regard. The deservedly popular tripartite nursing program offered by the University of Saskatchewan, the Saskatchewan Polytechnic, and the First Nations University of Canada has to turn away dozens of well-qualified Aboriginal applicants each year. The University of Saskatchewan's Native Law Centre remains the preeminent entry point for Aboriginal students seeking to study law. Business programs were somewhat slow to respond to Aboriginal people's needs, although they have been working hard to catch up. Canada now has several Aboriginal-focused undergraduate and MBA programs.

In the second decade of the twenty-first century, Aboriginal students continue to be underrepresented at colleges and universities; even so, the improvements in this area have been dramatic. With close to thirty thousand Aboriginal people (First Nations, Métis, and Inuit) currently in postsecondary education, advances in employment and careers will likely be considerable in the coming decades. The effects of having tens of thousands of well-trained and highly educated Aboriginal people in the workforce are only now being felt, but they will be noticeable in the years to come.

# ——— 7 ———

# business and
# entrepreneurship

Aboriginal people are among the most entrepreneurial in Canada. In recent years, a great deal of commentary has been offered about the poor economic performance of Indigenous people and communities. There is considerable truth to it. But Aboriginal business is growing steadily, and a number of Aboriginal communities have established vibrant and profitable enterprises. Indigenous communities have been experimenting with a wide array of economic models, from band ownership to cooperatives, from individual enterprises to community shareholding. Some have worked, spectacularly. There are reserves in Canada where the unemployment rate is lower than the provincial rate. The holding company for the Inuvialuit in Northwest Territories has annual revenues exceeding $100 million and assets of close to $500 million. commercial entities formed by the James Bay Cree after their land claim settlement have become cornerstones of the regional economy, investing in commercial entities such as Air Creebec, tourism operations, and other ventures. Other enterprises have failed, though, just as dramatically. Over the past two decades, the federal government has invested heavily, and not always wisely, in Aboriginal economic development. Critics of Canada's Aboriginal policy often point to the lack of consistent success. There are major issues at play here, from the difficulties involved in raising investment capital for reserve projects to difficulties associated with federal regulation of band companies. There are problems and opportunities attached to the special legal status of reserves, especially when it comes to getting a mortgage and to the advantage that Registered Indians working on reserves enjoy because they are not required to pay income tax. Adding to the difficulties, many First Nations reserves and Inuit communities are isolated and thus unattractive locations for business. And Indigenous businesses must balance the competing demands of family, community, and profit making. Despite all of these challenges, an impressive number of Aboriginal businesses have emerged in recent years. Some are independently operated, others are run by band and tribal council officials. All have tackled the formidable challenge of carving out a space for Indigenous people in the Canadian economy. There are reasons for optimism.

Aboriginal people must live with oppressive stereotypes. Among the most prevalent is the notion that they seek government "handouts," lack entrepreneurial drive, and are not interested in gainful employment despite tax benefits that most Canadians view (wrongly) as stunningly generous. The evidence suggests that different forces are at play. The free enterprise economy provides few opportunities on remote reserves; even for the most aggressive and business-minded, there are few jobs to be had. Decades of workplace discrimination severely restricted private sector opportunities, and young Aboriginal people have grown up with considerable distrust of non-Aboriginal businesses and employers. When Aboriginal people land skilled jobs, their counterparts often assume that they did so through affirmative action. Without question, Aboriginal unemployment is extremely high – scandalously so on small and remote reserves. Welfare dependency remains very strong among many First Nations communities, despite three decades of effort to provide alternatives.

But there is another side, and it provides a more promising image of Aboriginal realities and futures. Aboriginal entrepreneurship is taking root across the country and is generating jobs, wealth, and opportunity on reserves and in the towns and cities. The Carcross-Tagish First Nation in Yukon, the Lac La Ronge Indian Band in Saskatchewan, and Membertou First Nation in Nova Scotia are just three of many communities that are embracing entrepreneurship and local business development. The Canadian Association of Native Development

Officers and the Canadian Council for Aboriginal Business are truly impressive business promotion organizations. Business leaders who had long ignored Aboriginal workers, business people, and commercial opportunities are becoming increasingly aware of the opportunity to work with Indigenous communities.

This is best seen in the North, where joint ventures, corporate training programs, Aboriginal hiring initiatives, and arrangements with Indigenous communities have become commonplace for almost all resource developers. Syncrude, one of the first big companies to work the Alberta oil sands, and Suncor have exemplary systems for working with Aboriginal communities and employees. First Nations communities (especially Fort McKay First Nation) around Fort McMurray, the heart of the oil sands development, have become commercially active. The rise of entrepreneurs such as Chief Jim Boucher and Doug Golosky in the oil sands economy is a sign of things to come. (Golosky, who made a sizeable fortune in the Alberta oil sands, sold his firms, took a short hiatus, and then re-emerged to develop an impressive network of partnerships with Aboriginal communities.)

There is dramatic evidence of a business transformation, and not just in the rapidly expanding energy sector. The northern Saskatchewan communities of Lac La Ronge Indian Band have demonstrated impressive entrepreneurial acumen and are busy creating opportunities for local residents, particularly through Kitsaki Management Partnerships. The start-up rate for Aboriginal business is more than two-and-a-half times the national average: between 1981 and 1996 the number of self-employed Aboriginal people grew by 170 percent, compared to the national rate of 65 percent. This is truly impressive for a cultural group viewed by many Canadians as non-entrepreneurial. This effort has its critics. Some Aboriginal observers oppose integration with the mainstream economy and worry that Indigenous values and community stability may be at stake.

The transformation is only beginning. In 2006, there were around thirty-seven thousand Aboriginal business owners in Canada, a stunning 85 percent increase over 1996. Almost 20 percent of self-employed Aboriginal people are under thirty, a rate that is twice the average for the country as a whole. Many Aboriginal companies, such as stores, are reserve-based and serve local markets. In the past, the profits from these local enterprises left the community; now they are being reinvested locally. At the other end of the scale, major

Aboriginal corporations in Alberta and BC are attempting to convert Aboriginal-controlled resources or royalty payments into jobs and profits. How many Canadians know that one of the largest farming operations in Canada, One Earth, works in partnerships with First Nations people, farming largely on First Nations land? In the Arctic, the Inuit cooperative movement has set a standard for community engagement, solid management, and innovation that is attracting global attention. Many of the leaders in the successful Inuit land claims and self-government movement gained valuable managerial experience through their work with Arctic cooperatives. For a glimpse of the unique combination of accomplishment and commitment to community that underlies Aboriginal business, check out the individual winners of the annual CANDO awards.

The growing number of partnerships between Indigenous communities and Canadian businesses is a sign of successful reconciliation. Some of these partnerships are well known. Syncrude's employment arrangement with the people of Fort Chipewyan has been a model of successful collaboration. So, too, has been the close partnership between BHP's Ekati diamond mine and the Aboriginal people of the Northwest Territories. Almost 20 percent of that mine's workforce is Aboriginal, and efforts are being made to ensure that Indigenous workers progress beyond unskilled, entry-level positions. Cameco and Areva have impressive collaboration agreements with First Nations and Métis communities in northern Saskatchewan that include training, employment, and business development arrangements. Similar efforts involving the Tahltan of northern BC ran afoul of internal politics, especially a bitter division between reserve-based elders and off-reserve adults. The Tahltan National Development Corporation, under the guidance of Jerry Asp, nonetheless established a series of productive and mutually beneficial joint ventures with resource developers in the region. The Tahltan went from widespread unemployment to near zero unemployment within twenty years.

Although difficulties remain in parts of Canada – especially with regard to the controversial Ring of Fire development in northern Ontario – the reality is that resource developers now realize they have to work with local Indigenous groups if they hope to see their projects proceed. Similarly, Aboriginal groups recognize that development brings employment and commercial opportunities and promises long-term revenues through royalties, taxes, and other financial arrangements. For their part, Canadian corporations understand that they have no choice but to collaborate with Aboriginal communities when operating in northern and remote regions, and they have developed the techniques and the credibility required for successful partnerships.

The best example of all this – showing how much has changed in recent years – relates to pipeline development in the North. In the 1970s, the proposed Mackenzie Valley Pipeline became a flashpoint for conflict between Aboriginal aspirations and southerners' development plans. Indigenous protests helped shut down the project. When high energy prices rekindled interest in pipeline projects in the 1990s, it became clear that the situation had shifted. Northern Aboriginal groups, supported by the Yukon and NWT governments, lobbied hard for pipeline construction. In fact, the battle between the Alaska Highway Pipeline and Mackenzie Valley Pipeline unfolded in large measure as a struggle between two groups of Aboriginal proponents. In the case of the Mackenzie proposal, there has been a difficult internal struggle between Dene groups, one of which has repeatedly blocked efforts to launch the project. The Dehcho of the southern Mackenzie have been especially vocal in their criticism of the project, pointing to the lack of government attention to their demands. Aboriginal people in the North are now confident that they can ensure that the pipeline projects will benefit their communities and that they will be able to control any negative consequences of the sort that flowed from earlier resource projects in the region. Indigenous groups are part owners of the proposed Mackenzie Valley pipeline (though now highly unlikely to proceed) and have been given strong commitments with regard to training, construction work, long-term employment, and significant downstream royalties. They share the frustrations of the corporate sector and government with delays in approval processes. Clearly, much has changed.

There are still impressive barriers to Aboriginal business development. One big problem is access to capital to start or expand businesses. The problem here is exacerbated by the legal realities of Aboriginal reserves. Communally held property cannot be used to secure mortgages, and this makes it difficult for individual entrepreneurs to borrow money. The Nisga'a of northwestern BC became, in 2013, the first Indigenous group to allow private ownership of

Aboriginally owned land, thus enabling individuals to use their homes as collateral. Over the past forty years, a great deal of the start-up capital for new companies has come from the Department of Indian Affairs. There have been many federal economic development initiatives, most with mediocre or poor track records owing to the many difficulties facing Indigenous businesses. But government assistance is still forthcoming, and the amount of federal capital available has increased in recent years.

However, a growing share of the investment money is coming from Aboriginal sources, including resource royalties, land claim settlements, and other revenue streams. Besides this, there are now nearly four dozen Aboriginal-controlled financial institutions, which include Aboriginal capital corporations and Aboriginal-controlled community futures development centres. In 1993, seven Aboriginal capital corporations formed a network to address common challenges. By 1997, that network had eighteen members, who founded the National Aboriginal Capital Corporation Association. By 1998, all thirty-one corporations had joined the NACCA. Having expanded its membership to include futures development centres, the NACCA now has more than fifty financial institutions members. NACCA members today include Peace Hills Trust (Alberta), the Saskatchewan Indian Equity Foundation, Tecumseh Development Corporation (Ontario), Anishinabe Mazaska Capital Corporation (Manitoba), Tewatohnhi'saktha Business Loan Fund (Quebec), and All Nations Trust Company (BC).

The major banks and non-Aboriginal credit unions have recognized the commercial spirit and drive in Indigenous communities and are making more money available. Most of the major financial institutions maintain offices devoted to Aboriginal business, and several corporations have established high-level contacts with Indigenous organizations and communities in order to better anticipate their needs. Crown corporations have often taken the lead in this area, especially in Saskatchewan, capitalizing on provincial and federal investments to support and encourage Aboriginal business and personnel development. Little of this support was available twenty years ago.

Aboriginal people are heavily and publicly involved in Canada's casino industry through special arrangements with provincial governments. The largest First Nations casino in Canada, Casino Rama, was established by the Mnjikaning First Nation in Ontario and became the focus of a long legal struggle over the distribution of profits from the facility. In 2003–04, this casino generated almost $500 million in revenues. Manitoba's only Aboriginal casino, the Aseneskak Casino Resort, opened in 2002 near The Pas, is operated by a consortium of six First Nations communities. Saskatchewan has the most extensive Aboriginal casino network, operating under the Saskatchewan Indian Gaming Authority. It employs twelve hundred people (almost two-thirds of them Aboriginal) and has operations in North Battleford, Prince Albert, and Yorkton and at Whitecap First Nation. The authority's net revenues, which exceeded $86 million in 2012–13, are distributed to the First Nations Trust, the Government of Saskatchewan, and the Community Development Corporation. After a proposal for an urban casino was defeated in Saskatoon, Dakota Dunes Casino and Dakota Dunes Golf Links, which hosts PGA tournaments, were built outside the city limits. More than four hundred employees now work there. The government of Alberta approved the development of the first casino in 2004. The River Cree Resort, located just west of Edmonton and run by Enoch Cree Nation, offers a four-and-a-half-star Marriott Hotel, 1,100 slot machines, and thirty-two gaming tables.

Casinos, drawing much of their inspiration from the success of Indian casinos in the United States, have been touted as the gateway to employment and commercial opportunities for many Aboriginal communities (although not, so far, for Inuit settlements). Aboriginal casinos employ hundreds of Indigenous people, return significant amounts of money to the sponsoring communities, create openings for Aboriginal companies, and develop professional managers. They may well have an impact on capacity building comparable to what Arctic cooperatives had on the Inuit. There are well-identified controversies over Aboriginal gambling: proponents argue that gambling has long been part of Aboriginal culture, while critics point out that problem gambling among Indigenous people runs three to four times the national average, thus offsetting some of the gains. If the American experience is replicated north of the border, First Nations casinos will have uneven success. Those located close to major cities – the River Cree Resort is perfectly situated on the outskirts of Edmonton – and those with other attractions (entertainment, golf courses, and so on) are most likely to prosper; those built in smaller communities and that offer only casino operations may encounter difficulties. In general, however, casinos at present are valuable money spinners that also create hundreds of jobs for Aboriginal people and opportunities for Indigenous companies.

Urban reserves have generated further opportunities. A few groups – the Squamish First Nation on Vancouver's North Shore, for example – have been lucky in terms of locations of the reserves they were assigned long ago. The Squamish land holdings now generate large annual revenues from shopping malls, industrial parks, housing, and an unused but highly lucrative federal government lease. Much the same is true in Kamloops and Westbank, BC. By contrast, reserves in New Brunswick are almost all located far from valuable urban or industrial sites. In Saskatchewan, new reserves have been established in urban settings, on lands either purchased with First Nations funds or selected through the Treaty Land Entitlement process, which was launched to address the fact that the government deliberately underreported Aboriginal populations during treaty negotiations in order to limit the size of allocations. From controversial beginnings in Prince Albert, urban reserves have quickly expanded to Fort Qu'Appelle, Yorkton, Meadow Lake, Regina, and North Battleford. One of the most impressive initiatives of this type is the Muskeg Lake urban reserve, established on industrial land in Saskatoon. This reserve, devoted entirely to business, has attracted significant investments, including medical and professional offices, financial institutions, and a trucking company. More than three hundred Aboriginal jobs are based on this reserve, which, despite doubts expressed at the time, has been an important and much appreciated economic engine for Saskatoon. Given that half of Saskatchewan's Aboriginal people live off-reserve, the creation of commercial centres and employment opportunities in the cities has been a boon for them. Whatever the old accusations, these urban reserves *do* pay taxes, in the sense that they pay directly for services provided by the city. Those payments closely approximate the taxes they would pay if the city owned the land.

Many middle-class urban Aboriginals maintain strong connections to their home communities. It is not at all uncommon for visitors and family members from the villages to stay with their urban relatives, often for long periods of time. Those relatives provide a support network for newly arrived reserve members, help them adjust to city living, and mediate relationships with the community at large. They help newcomers find work and assist with child care and other arrangements. They often take in children and young adults who have encountered difficulties back on the reserve and help them adjust to educational and employment situations in the cities. More generally, members of the urban middle-class provide role models for young people trying to find a place in Canadian society. Many take this responsibility seriously. Urban Aboriginal people are often highly active in their communities, and financial flows back to on-reserve family members and friends can be considerable. But because there are few off-reserve concentrations of Indigenous people in Canadian suburbs, they tend to attract little attention and are not appreciated for the contributions they are making to their home communities and to Canadian society at large.

Every specialist in the field knows that education and training are connected with employability and income. It is vital, therefore to note that both Aboriginal educational attainment and employment rates have been rising significantly. In 2006, 63 percent of Aboriginal people fifteen years and older who sought jobs found them; among the Métis, the rate was almost 60 percent, only slightly less than the national average of 61.5 percent. Aboriginal unemployment was much higher than for other Canadians, at close to 15 percent, but this was an improvement over the past. Consider, too, that in 2006, 34,000 off-reserve Aboriginal people held a bachelor's degree, more than 6,100 a master's degree, and more than 1,200 a doctorate. The largest concentrations of Aboriginal students were in commerce and business, education, the social sciences, the health professions and applied sciences, and technology and trades. (The on-reserve numbers were lower: 726 held a bachelor's degree, 140 a master's, and 20 a doctorate.) Aboriginal incomes remained low by national standards – an average of $26,000 in 2001 against a national average of close to $37,000. The 2012 Aboriginal People Survey produced similar results for off-reserve Aboriginals: only 70 percent of those aged eighteen to forty-four had a high school diploma, compared to 89 percent for the country at large. Only 40 percent of this same cohort had a postsecondary qualification, compared to 64 percent for non-Aboriginals. Those who had completed high school, college, or university were doing significantly better in the working world than those who had not. The Métis and Inuit showed similar patterns. The point here is simple: statistics have and can be used to paint a portrait of despair and hardship for Aboriginal people in Canada. Yet the same data also tell us that in some regards – life expectancy, health care, education, employment, business – conditions seem to be improving significantly. Aboriginal peoples and communities have been facing near-critical circumstances for quite some time; their efforts to improve their lot, with help from other Canadians and their governments, are having an impact.

There are a growing number of wealthy Aboriginal people in Canada – individuals who have invested their money wisely, started successful businesses, or otherwise secured their financial future. Doug Golosky, who made a sizable fortune in the Alberta oil sands, sold his companies and is now working on a impressive network of partnerships with First Nations communities. Wealthy Indigenous people often attract a great deal of critical attention. They are singled out for criticism by others within their community, for Aboriginal society has a strong "tall poppy" syndrome, where those who rise well above the mean are brought down a peg or two or called apples (red on the outside, white on the inside). So wealthy Aboriginals are routinely criticized – usually *sotto voce* and behind their backs – for having made so much money. The implication, often, is that they either made their money by manipulating government programs and transfers or, even worse, by taking advantage of their community members. Although these things happen in all segments of Canadian society, most wealthy Indigenous people have money because they earned it. And to put a sharper tone on it, many of them would have made much more money if they had not devoted a large part of their adult lives to working with and for their communities. People such as Darcy Bear (Saskatchewan), Bernd Christmas (Nova Scotia), and Justin Ferbey (Yukon), to name just a few, would have succeeded in just about any organization or business in the country.

# 8

# governance and civic engagement

THE FUTURE of Aboriginal political communities will be shaped largely by the determination of their members to build what political scientist Robert Putnam refers to as social capital. By social capital, he means those "features of social organization such as networks, norms, and social trust that facilitate coordination and cooperation for mutual benefit." Developing networks of civic engagement typically involves creating institutions of civil society – that is, institutions that mediate between state and society. These organizations include everything from Rotary Clubs to labour unions to churches. Without civil society, we cannot expect institutions of governance to flourish. As Putnam notes in *Bowling Alone* (2000), "citizens in civic communities expect better government and (in part through their own efforts), they get it" (346).

Over the past forty years, Aboriginal communities have expanded their civil institutions, developing social, recreational, and political associations. Since participation in these groups is typically restricted to Aboriginal people, many Canadians are unaware of how many there are and what they do. It is also important to note that Aboriginal women dominate many of these organizations, contributing strongly to the social and cultural well-being of their communities.

## ABORIGINAL MEDIA

The coverage of Aboriginal issues in mainstream media has improved in recent years. Although only a handful of Aboriginal journalists work for major newspapers or national broadcasters, Indigenous issues are reported heavily across the country. Journalists such as Jeffrey Simpson of the *Globe and Mail*, Andrew Coyne of the *National Post*, and Stephen Hume of the *Vancouver Sun* routinely address Aboriginal issues. Christie Blatchford, now with the *National Post*, reported heavily on the Caledonia standoff in 2006 for the *Globe and Mail*, offering a biting critique of how it was handled by all sides. Several Aboriginal journalists, most notably Doug Cuthand, report regularly on Indigenous issues and events. Much of the media coverage is sympathetic to the Aboriginal side. Aboriginal political events generate a reasonable amount of coverage, although the emphasis tends to be on crises rather than accomplishments (bad news sells everywhere). Elections for the grand chief of the Assembly of First Nations are generally given considerable attention, as are pronouncements by national and regional Indigenous organizations.

As we noted in Chapter 6, Indigenous Canadians have their own media outlets, which have grown significantly in reach and professionalism. Twenty years ago, Aboriginal TV programming was in its infancy, supported by uncertain federal grants and often mixed in with various training and development initiatives. Among the handful of Aboriginal broadcasters, Northern Native Broadcasting Yukon stood out for the quality of its documentaries and for its coverage of Indigenous issues in the far Northwest. Today, most Canadians have access to the Aboriginal-focused programming on the Aboriginal Peoples Television Network (APTN). Companies such as Pine Needle Productions, an Anishnabe firm; Director General Films; Igloolik Isuma Productions (now closed; the producer of the widely celebrated *Atanarjuat: The Fast Runner*); Nutaaq Media; Big Soul Productions; and First Nations Films produce programs with Indigenous subjects and perspectives. There is also a network of Aboriginal radio stations, including Aboriginal Voices Radio (available online) and Canada's First Nations Radio. And there are a significant number of Aboriginal newspapers and magazines across the country, led by *Windspeaker, Aboriginal Times, Say Magazine,* and *Spirit Magazine.*

The development of Aboriginal media has had little impact on the country as a whole but a significant one on Indigenous communities. Aboriginal documentaries and news and cultural programs find highly receptive audiences, and the circulation of the leading Indigenous publications is strong and apparently growing. As a result, Indigenous peoples are learning more about one another – APTN is key in this regard – and are developing a stronger sense of common cause. Especially in the territorial North, the regular appearance of elders and cultural leaders on television and the production of radio and TV programs in Indigenous languages are raising the status and profile of traditional cultures.

## FRIENDSHIP CENTRES

Friendship centres are among the most important institutions of Aboriginal civil society. There are dozens of First Nations and Métis friendship centres across the country. The Kikinahk Friendship Centre in La Ronge, Saskatchewan, to select one example from dozens, serves hundreds of Aboriginal and other community members. Friendship centres are not as well developed among the Inuit, although there is a significant Inuit gathering place in Ottawa *(Tungasuvvingat Inuit)*. Most Inuit have stayed in the Arctic and have not migrated to southern cities like the First Nations and Métis.

Aboriginal friendship centres provide recreational programs, support groups, counselling, employment services, and – perhaps most important – a focus for local activities. Most of them offer youth programs and drop-in spaces as an alternative to hanging out on the streets. They sponsor and sustain Indigenous cultures, and most of them tap into traditional values and customs when helping their clients. The services on offer differ greatly from centre to centre, but all share a commitment to helping Indigenous people adjust to urban life. Although assistance with government programs, housing, job searches, adult basic education, cultural initiatives, and the like are vital, perhaps these centres' most important function is that they provide an unequivocally Aboriginal "resting spot" in a challenging and often unfriendly non-Indigenous world. Most friendship centres occupy humble buildings in the poorest part of town and depend on uncertain government grants and, increasingly, First Nations support. Their activities are generally low-profile, for they seek to help the often invisible Aboriginal residents of the country's towns and cities. Through their presence and their programs, friendship centres reinforce the Aboriginal presence in Canada and strengthen individual lives and the Aboriginal community at large.

## ABORIGINAL ORGANIZATIONS

Indigenous political institutions, beyond those established by the Department of Indian Affairs, have expanded in the last fifty years. The Assembly of First Nations as a national organization has its roots in the early twentieth century. Critics argue that these institutions exist solely because of government subsidies and grants, when in fact, Aboriginal people have been yearning for generations to address their own issues on a national scale. The founding of other organizations – the Métis National Council, the Congress of Aboriginal Peoples, the Inuit Tapiriit Kanatami, and dozens of regional and provincial or territorial organizations – has been a logical response to changing political times. All of these groups have provided Indigenous peoples with outlets for their ideas and concerns and with venues for debating both. These organizations are not governing bodies. Rather, they exist to represent the wishes of their members and supporters to one another and to the broader Canadian community. Through these groups, Aboriginal people have been able to assert their presence on the national stage and to ensure that Canadians at large are more aware of their concerns and objectives.

The organizational impulse, once focused on national political and lobbying efforts, has become much more diffuse. Many national and regional Aboriginal organizations now operate in Canada, covering various professional and occupational groups. Consider this partial list of organizations: Aboriginal Financial Officers, Aboriginal Nurses Association, Canadian Aboriginal Science and Engineering Association, First Nations Chiefs of Police Association, Indigenous Bar Association, National Aboriginal Forestry Association, National Aboriginal Lands Managers Association, National Indian and Inuit Community Health Representatives, Métis National Council of Women, Native Women's Association, Pauktuutit Inuit Women's Association, Aboriginal Healing Foundation, Aboriginal Sport Circle, First Nations Child and Family Caring Society, National Aboriginal Circle Against Family Violence, National Aboriginal Diabetes

Association, National Aboriginal Health Organization, National Aboriginal Housing Association, National Native Addictions Partnership Foundation, Nechi Training Research and Health Promotions Institute, National Association of Indigenous Institutes of Higher Learning, Aboriginal Human Resource Development Council, Aboriginal Tourism, Arctic Cooperatives, Canadian Council for Aboriginal Business, Canadian Executive Services Organization–Aboriginal Services, National Aboriginal Capital Corporation Association, Centre for Indigenous Environmental Resources, First Nations Environmental Network, Indigenous Environmental Network, First Nations Confederacy of Cultural Education Centres, Inuit Art Foundation, National Aboriginal Recording Industry Association, National Association of Friendship Centres. These organizations are all part of what Paul Hawken, a leading environmentalist and social activist, calls blessed unrest, by which he means the emergence of community and special interest groups to tackle their own present-day challenges.

This partial list of national Indigenous organizations illustrates the changing nature of Aboriginal activism and coordinated action in recent years. While the public remains fixated on national political organizations, the work of professional and other associations provides just as much reason for optimism. That there are enough Aboriginal lawyers, doctors, nurses, engineers, and other professionals to establish national organizations speaks volumes about the impact of post-secondary education on Indigenous communities. That Aboriginal communities are working collaboratively to identify opportunities and solutions is among the most promising developments in the country. Commentators have often spoken about the need for Indigenous communities and organizations to develop greater capacity – that is, the human capital necessary to address the serious challenges they face. The surprisingly good news is that this is happening – and far faster than most Canadians would credit.

## SELF-GOVERNMENT, SELF-ADMINISTRATION, AND CO-MANAGEMENT

For forty years, Aboriginal leaders spoke wistfully about self-government and urged Ottawa to recognize their peoples' right to manage their own affairs. Although the country stopped short of everything Indigenous groups sought – it did not offer constitutional protection for the right to Aboriginal self-government – much has been achieved. Through a number of comprehensive land claims settlements in the North and through dozens of community-specific negotiations, Aboriginal peoples have gained control of their local governments. More than 80 percent of the money spent by Aboriginal Affairs and Northern Development Canada is now disbursed through band and regional offices. Many Aboriginal communities run their own schools and health centres, manage their own water and sewage systems, maintain their own roads and housing, staff their own economic development offices, supervise their own child welfare services, and operate their own income support programs. The vast majority do so quite well, albeit with the inevitable challenges associated with the transition to new and expanded responsibilities. A few communities – the ones described at length in the press – are struggling with these responsibilities. But as Herb George (Satsan), Wet'suwet'en hereditary chief of the Frog Clan and founder of the National Centre for First Nations Governance, has said about the struggle for self-government: "That battle has been won and now it's time to put all that rhetoric into practice. We have a new story – a story of hope – to tell the next generation. We always say that our youth are our future. Now is the time to make that happen. Now is the time for action."

The transition to self-administration, if not full self-government, has been quite remarkable. In the early 1970s, most First Nations communities still had little control over their affairs and operated under the tight supervision of the local Indian Agent. Few Aboriginal people had the training or expertise to manage complex budgets or to handle diverse administrative responsibilities. Professional activities, including health and education, were well beyond the capacity of the communities. This is no longer so, and indeed, some communities have signed comprehensive self-government agreements with the federal and provincial governments. The Sechelt Agreement of 1986, which assigned municipal-style authority and self-government to the band, generated enormous controversy across the country. Many Aboriginal leaders felt that the Sechelt had surrendered too much authority; local leaders believed that it was more important to get on with the business of governing the community. This accord has run into difficulties owing to problems with the negotiation of the Sechelt treaty.

Modern land claims agreements, especially the Council of Yukon First Nations accord and the Nisga'a treaty, have included extensive self-government powers. But Nunavut is the most dramatic expression of this transition, for it gave the Inuit effective control of their entire territory. A comparable arrangement in Nunavik (northern Quebec) has established three regional administrative bodies: the Kativik School Board, the Nunavik Regional Board of Health and Social Services, and the Kativik Regional Government. Critics of these agreements claim that they are sellouts or have given up Indigenous rights and aspirations in return for limited, municipal-like powers. Non-Aboriginal opponents, for their part, contend that these accords have created virtual "principalities" that are threatening the very fabric of Canada as a consequence.

The negotiations between the Westbank First Nation, in BC's Okanagan Valley, and the Government of Canada demonstrate the potential of self-government. Under this 2004 accord, which the community ratified, Westbank's members, who share their reserves with close to eight thousand non-Aboriginal residents, now have the right to establish landlord-and-tenant arrangements, manage local resources and the education system, and impose traffic regulations. The agreement has established a ward system, with an advisory council to secure input from non-Aboriginal residents, several of whom had resorted to the courts in an attempt to stop the negotiations. Westbank, which is one of the wealthiest Aboriginal communities in the country, has gained the full range of municipal powers as well as the right to raise taxes and to control justice, albeit with the official recognition that the Canadian Criminal Code will apply on reserve lands.

In the early twenty-first century, most First Nations governments are exercising some measure of local control. The mismanagement of some communities has attracted the headlines, whereas the quiet and growing competence of the vast majority is generally not mentioned. Aboriginal governments vary widely in ability and impact. Some of the best-run bands – such as Lennox Island in PEI, Six Nations in Ontario, Muskeg in Saskatchewan, Nisga'a in British Columbia, Champagne-Aishihik in Yukon, and the Nunavut government – have done a great deal to ameliorate local social and economic conditions and to inject Indigenous perspectives into governance. Other communities have attracted attention for the serious difficulties they have encountered: accusations of misappropriation of funds are being investigated in the Ermineskin band (Alberta), in several Manitoba communities, in Lake Babine (BC), and at the Virginia Fontaine Addictions Foundation in Manitoba. In Alberta, the Stoney Indian Reserve controversy has been ongoing. There, a judge in a spousal abuse case shocked the participants by ordering an investigation into political corruption in the community. He later wrote a harsh criticism of the government and the First Nations leadership for the chaos on the reserve.

But the reality is that Aboriginal self-government is part of the country's administrative and political fabric and that most communities have risen to the challenge. And in coming decades, many more community managers will have college or university training, perhaps through specialized offerings like the Indigenous Public Administration Program at Carleton University, the master's program in Northern Governance and Development at the University of Saskatchewan, or the programs now being planned by the National Centre for First Nations Governance (where, unfortunately, programming has been reduced significantly due to cuts in federal funding). Aboriginal governance has improved dramatically in recent decades. The potential for continued evolution and greater professionalism is exceptionally strong.

Given the complex challenges facing Indigenous communities, difficulties securing training and experienced managers, and the history of government control and manipulation, it is hardly surprising that the experience has been uneven. It is, quite frankly, still early days. Years if not decades will pass before all Indigenous communities have gained the expertise and perspective they need to manage their affairs well. Most communities recognize the difficulties they face. Unfairly, critics have fixated on the controversies – which are serious and deserve attention and remediation – and have largely ignored the successes. In one of the most promising developments in years, the Kativik Regional Government promises to transform the national debate. That a number of communities there have agreed on a shared regional administrative structure, thus creating administrative economies of scale, is exceptionally promising. Other jurisdictions will be monitoring these developments carefully and, one hopes, following this important lead.

Criticism and community protest are crucial to the proper functioning of governance systems. As communities come to realize what they have a right to expect of governance, their tolerance of unsatisfactory or unethical performance declines. In this regard, opponents of band chiefs and councils are more likely than before to take their complaints to politicians, the government, or the press. And governments are increasingly willing to address abuses within Aboriginal organizations, as the RCMP did when a scandal erupted on the Eskasoni Reserve in Nova Scotia in 2001, as the Saskatchewan government did quite dramatically with a slowly unfolding scandal involving the CEO of the Saskatchewan Indian Gaming Authority in 2000–02, as the Conservative government did in 2006 when it cut off educational funding to the Métis Nation of Saskatchewan, and as the federal and provincial governments did when they suspended payments to the First Nations University of Canada in 2010. These developments indicate that Indigenous governments and agencies are increasingly being held to the same standards as other public institutions. The First Nations Governance Act, developed under Indian affairs minister Robert Nault, was dropped by the Liberal government of Paul Martin, but the Conservative Party has kept the issue very much on the table. Aboriginal and non-Aboriginal people alike are beginning to insist that Indigenous organizations operate in a transparent and efficient manner. The Assembly of First Nations took an important step in this direction when, in 2011, it passed the non-binding recommendation that Aboriginal organizations publish the salaries and expenses paid to their officials.

That First Nations communities are speaking openly about internal difficulties, and that scandals involving financial mismanagement hit the press with some regularity, is often taken as a sign of weakness. It should be interpreted very differently. First, Aboriginal controversies play out in public much more than is the norm. Phil Fontaine, the former grand chief of the Assembly of First Nations, spoke out about the abuse he suffered at residential school, fuelling a national debate about those schools. Matthew Coon Come, for his part, stated on the record that he thought too many chiefs had difficulty with alcohol and personal habits and offered poor role models for their young people. Some Aboriginal people sharply criticized him for perpetuating stereotypes; others applauded him for speaking openly about a chronic problem. Second, the emergence of open dissent is a sign of political confidence and belief in the future. Not so long ago, Aboriginal people felt compelled to maintain a solid, impenetrable front, if only to indicate to the country at large that they were a political force. But as the basic elements of Aboriginal rights become more firmly entrenched in Canadian public life, Aboriginal critics are speaking more frankly and publicly about the shortcomings of their leaders and governments. Those critics have pointed out serious abuses of power and office and have often convinced communities, governments, or the courts to take action. This is a sign of a functioning political system, not of internal weakness or incompetence. Given how recently Aboriginal communities have achieved self-governance, how few leaders are fully trained for their assignments, and how many problems have to be tackled concurrently, evidence of difficulties should hardly be surprising. Evidence of a willingness to do better, far from being a sign of political failure, is best understood as a further sign of the communities' determination to improve the quality of government and political leadership.

On the opposite side of the coin, Aboriginal communities and groups have actively engaged with other governments and non-Aboriginal groups on a variety of resource and wildlife management ventures. While full acceptance of Indigenous knowledge among project planners remains some distance off – Western scientific models remain the basis for these – there has been considerable direct engagement of Indigenous peoples in other venues, especially in the territorial North, where the right of Aboriginal people to be consulted on land use and environmental protection is now codified in land claims settlements. The federal government, for example, established the Climate Change Adaptation Program to draw Northern stakeholders into a region-wide planning and research enterprise. This has been accompanied by a major study called Aboriginal Communities and Non-Renewable Resource Development, which focuses on building sustainable Aboriginal settlements. The Inuit Tapiriit Kanatami is actively involved in climate change planning and monitoring. A growing number of these co-management activities have been established in the provinces as well. In Quebec, the Enhanced Aboriginal Involvement initiative created opportunities for Indigenous (Montreal Lake and Akwesasne) engagement with the Canadian Model Forest

Network. In BC, the Aboriginal Fisheries Commission ensures Indigenous input into the management of the hotly contested West Coast fishery. On a more local level, the Secwepemc Fisheries Commission assists with river monitoring, research, and support in the BC Interior. These are but a few examples of how Aboriginal people and communities are inserting themselves into the management of natural resources and wildlife.

## LAND CLAIMS

Over the past two decades, the Canadian government has negotiated major land claims agreements with Aboriginal groups across the country. A few – like the controversial Nisga'a agreement in BC, ratified by 54 percent of the membership – attracted a great deal of attention and debate. Most of these negotiations, however, took place in the North and received only passing mention in the national press. Yet in a relatively short period of time, Aboriginal and non-Aboriginal leaders have rewritten the legal, political, and organizational map of Canada. Beginning with the James Bay agreement in 1975, followed soon after by the Northeastern Quebec Agreement of 1978, the federal government has settled with the Inuvialuit (Western Arctic), Gwich'in (Northwest NWT), Nunavut (Eastern Arctic), Council of Yukon First Nations, Sahtu Dene and Métis (central NWT), Nisga'a (northwestern BC), Tlicho (central NWT), and Labrador Inuit. In the late spring of 2006, Ottawa tendered a substantial offer to the Dehcho of the southern Mackenzie Valley.

Most of BC remains under claims and, therefore, in dispute, but governments and First Nations have already spent over half a billion dollars on negotiations. A series of interim agreements have allowed development to occur in the absence of final settlements. And while there have been few high-profile successes (the Nisga'a discussions started much earlier and were not covered by the BC treaty process), most of the groups negotiating claims with the federal and provincial governments have continued to work towards agreements. The first group, Tsawwassen First Nation, has a signed treaty, and it moved quickly to convert that agreement into a major community development initiative that includes a large shopping mall. Maa-Nulth, Tla'amin, and Yale First Nations also have signed agreements, and the In-SHUCK-ch, Yekooche, and K'ómoks First Nations have signed agreements-in-principle.

At present, sixty First Nations are proceeding with claims in BC, so much work remains to be done. The Canadian government sparked some controversy in 2011 by announcing that it intended to move to final offers and to finalize outstanding treaty discussions. Although some First Nations decried the move, and were joined in this by Liberal and NDP critics, it is possible that the straightforward Conservative approach may well move stalled discussions forward.

By international standards, these comprehensive agreements are startling documents: they provide First Nations and Inuit governments with sizable cash payments, a share of future royalty revenues, control over substantial portions of traditional territories, and funds for training and transition. They also offer a broad range of self-government powers. The Tlicho (Dogrib) Agreement, signed in the Northwest Territories in 2003, saw that First Nation gain control of 39,000 square kilometres of land, in addition to $152 million and a share of future resource royalties. The same agreement recognized the Tlicho government and granted it broad authority over language, culture, lands, and resources.

But the best-known settlement in the country remains the one with the Nisga'a. That agreement included a payment of almost $200 million (1996 dollars), more than 2,000 square kilometres of land, a substantial yearly allocation of salmon for both local consumption and commercial sale (the latter being extremely controversial with area fishermen), guaranteed hunting harvests, money for conservation and management of the local area, and almost $40 million in transition funding. For the Nisga'a, the most important provisions included the recognition of the Lisims government, the ability to make laws subject to the superiority of the Constitution and the Criminal Code, and funding of over $32 million per year, initially to provide health, education, and social services to the Nisga'a people of the Nass Valley. Besides dropping their claims to traditional territories, the Nisga'a gave up their income tax and sales tax exemptions; also, they are now responsible for funding a portion of their governmental costs.

Contrary to critics' warnings, the land claims resolutions have not resulted in administrative or political chaos. In fact, they have generally been welcomed by regional and national businesses. They are neither an instant panacea nor a threat to the status quo, but they *have* provided Aboriginal groups with the land, power, and financial resources they argue are essential to engage with the dominant society. Often ignored in the discussion of the land claims is how they have fundamentally altered the relationship between the signatories and the Canadian government. Once the agreements come into effect, the beneficiaries are no longer covered under the Indian Act. In effect, they have voluntarily shed an important vestige of the colonial system. That thousands of First Nations people are no longer managed under the Indian Act has attracted little attention, precisely because it has proven to be noncontroversial and has not disrupted social, economic, or political relations in the treaty areas.

## CONCLUDING THOUGHTS

Canadians have paid far too little attention to one of the most remarkable stories in their recent history. The bitterly sad problems of young people at Davis Inlet, Labrador, attract much more attention than a successful band-run school (and efforts at the new Labrador community, Natuashish, to ban alcohol drew the media back to the settlement). The lingering effects of fetal alcohol syndrome spark far more critical debate than does the effective management of federally funded social assistance programs. The accomplishments of a musician or artist are individualized and understood as a personal achievement; the difficulties of a criminal or alcoholic are generalized as part of the social pathology of a community. Success stories are a vital part of Aboriginal life, yet they are missing from the picture in Canada. The revitalization of potlatches and powwows, the achievements of band-managed health care centres, the investment activities of community economic development offices, and the educational achievements of thousands of college and university students speak to a different future. There is a pattern worth noting: crises are noisy; accomplishments are quiet. But when the national pattern is identified, and individual Aboriginal achievements are viewed, properly, as elements in the successful response of communities and peoples to changing times, the importance of underscoring these successes becomes even more evident. Something important, and positive, is going on among Indigenous Canadians. There is far more to Aboriginal communities, families, and individuals than the social pathology that dominates public commentary. These impressive and expanding accomplishments must be factored into the picture if non-Aboriginal Canadians hope to understand the healthy optimism and anticipation that runs deep in Canada's Aboriginal communities.

It is commonplace to emphasize the troubles facing Aboriginal people in Canada. We should instead consider first what Indigenous communities have done *despite* the burdens of history and *despite* contemporary attitudes, often with the support of governments and non-Aboriginal groups. A battle to sustain language and cultural traditions is being waged, and communities are taking greater responsibility for education, health care, and local government. Aboriginal educational institutions exist across the country, ranging from First Nations day care centres to independent postsecondary institutions. Economic opportunities are expanding, largely through Indigenous entrepreneurship and joint ventures. Little of this was in place forty years ago. The prospects for continued improvement of Aboriginal circumstances remain very strong.

Statistics have long been used to document the serious crises facing Aboriginal communities – and they certainly tell a tale of social and economic despair and provide a wake-up call for the nation. But far too much time has been spent dwelling on the clear and obvious negative elements, for that sort of commentary leaves the impression across the country that nothing positive or significant is happening. Aboriginal communities have accomplished a great deal in recent years, with the financial support of the Canadian government, growing interest at the provincial level, largely unrecognized contributions from the Canadian business community, and the remarkable dedication of Indigenous community leaders and politicians.

Things are happening, and the success stories coming out of Aboriginal communities across the country deserve to be told. More than half of Canada's Aboriginal people live off-reserve. They are mingling and cooperating with other Canadians in countless new and often positive ways. In no way is it fair to characterize the move into the cities as one of unrelenting despair and hardship, although the Aboriginal areas of Winnipeg, Saskatoon, Regina, Edmonton, and a few other centres belie this observation. But even here there are signs of change. The impressive steps taken by President Lloyd Axworthy of the University of Winnipeg to connect that institution to the social and economic challenges of urban Aboriginal people are creating change. That Don Iveson, elected as mayor of Edmonton in 2013, committed his city to addressing the challenges faced by its Aboriginal people points to new energy and determination on the part of non-Aboriginal politicians. Serious health problems, especially the near-epidemic of diabetes, have been identified in Aboriginal populations, and major research and treatment programs have been launched to address some of the causes and consequences. Indigenous life expectancy has been rising rapidly – from less than sixty-one years for Aboriginal males in 1980 to a forecast of over seventy-four years in 2021. The gap in life expectancy between Aboriginal and other Canadians was almost 11 years in 1980 but is expected to fall to 5.2 for Indigenous men and 3.8 for Indigenous women by 2021. Infant mortality rates that stood at a scandalous 23.7 per 1,000 in 1980 – over twice the national average – had fallen to 6.4 by 2000. That was only 0.9 higher than the Canadian average of 5.5. While on-reserve housing remains a serious problem, the number of "adequate units" increased from 45.7 percent in 1993–94 to 53.2 percent in 2002–03, although this latter number was a drop from a high of 56.9 percent in 1999–2000. Aboriginal people are still significantly overrepresented in the justice system – they were 21 percent of all custodial and community admissions in 2003, an increase of 3 percent over four years. In recognition of the ongoing challenges, the federal justice system has been seeking new ways (not always with success) to accommodate Aboriginal culture, spirituality, and healing practices.

More and more developments aimed at Aboriginal peoples are being initiated and managed by Indigenous organizations. Indigenous communities know of the severity and depth of their problems. They know that, whoever is at fault for causing their difficulties, they are responsible for finding viable and sustainable solutions. To those who wonder if anything can or will change, there is a simple answer: change is already happening.

steps towards social, political, and economic equality

# 9

# global lessons

AS WE ARGUE throughout this book, the relationship between Aboriginal and non-Aboriginal peoples requires substantial rethinking. Historical arrangements clearly failed, and although contemporary arrangements include substantial improvements over those of the past, continued and thoughtful change is still required. We argue that there are several pillars that must underlie the path forward. The goal, it seems to us, is quite simple: Aboriginal people in Canada deserve nothing less than full equality of opportunity with other Canadians in the social, political, and economic realms as well as recognition of their cultures, traditions, and Aboriginal and treaty rights.

Much Canadian Aboriginal policy is structured around the goal of making Indigenous peoples look, live, and act like other Canadians. The inherent paternalism of such approaches belongs in the historical dustbin of government policy making. The goal, instead, should be to create situations where Aboriginal people can achieve equality of status, equality of political liberality, and equality of economic opportunity, situations where they can create and determine their futures within the laws, structures, and political processes of the country as a whole. To achieve this, we must set the stage for real and sustainable equality of opportunity. The prospect of achieving these goals is much more realistic than it was thirty years ago but will still require unprecedented commitment to rejecting the colonial and racial assumptions of the past, stepping aside from long-standing government policies and structures, and accepting Indigenous peoples and their governments as full participants within the Canadian political, economic, and social system.

There are many reasons to be optimistic, but we also acknowledge that Canada faces tough choices about the future of Aboriginal–non-Aboriginal relations, and the past century does not provide a clear model for positive coexistence. Current proposals for rebuilding First Nations and improving relations are unlikely to provide acceptable solutions, although the situation is not as gloomy as most Canadian think. It is true that ideas with historical, practical, or moral merit tend to be rejected by one side or the other, deepening the divide and enhancing the intensity of debate. At the same time, almost all Canadians agree that the status quo is not workable and that the social and economic problems facing Aboriginal people must be addressed.

Given that the past provides few workable models and that many of the current approaches are unacceptable to one side or the other, the country is in a difficult spot. Positions harden, conflicts intensify, anger flares, political will dissipates, and social, cultural, and economic gaps remain. This does not serve the country. Many analysts put great faith in continued negotiations and the refinement of legal and constitutional positions and, indeed, growing political and legal power has brought some gains to Canada's Aboriginal communities, with more to come as new generations grow up in more optimistic conditions. But this progress has also heightened non-Indigenous people's anger and frustration. One lesson from the past, in Canada and elsewhere, is that laws and the courts offer declarations of intent, not assurances of conduct. Canada's long history of neglecting its political commitments and legal responsibilities suggests that constitutional and legislative agreements may well be a weak foundation for reconciling Aboriginal and non-Aboriginal Canadians. Transforming ourselves into a treaty nation will require more than treaties.

More than anything else, the path towards common ground will require openness and creativity. Few Canadians recognize just how remarkably open Aboriginal people are to a renewed partnership.

They remain at the negotiating table. They work within the Canadian legal and political system. When confronted with strong rhetoric and the vestiges of colonialism, they remain calm. The most important lesson to be drawn from Idle No More, a nationwide celebration of the cultural survival of Aboriginal people in Canada, is that the thousands of Indigenous people who came forward to share their views did so with drums, not guns, with songs, not violence. Non-Aboriginal Canadians, to give the rest of the population their due, have also been generally non-violent (if sometimes verbally aggressive) in their approach to Indigenous people. If non-Aboriginal Canadians share a collective fault, it is their idea that providing federal money is a substitute for engagement.

Things can and will improve. Accommodations can be found and have been found. Solid partnerships have emerged, especially in Yukon, Northwest Territories, and Saskatchewan, though tensions remain in all three places. There are bright spots on Cape Breton Island, in northern Quebec, on Haida Gwaii, and in the Okanagan Valley. The increasingly skilled Aboriginal population continues to win court battles, negotiate agreements, work with resource companies, improve urban conditions, and cooperate with governments. If the country has not yet found common ground, there is a growing awareness that it is *somewhere* out there. But solutions will not come without effort and a broad commitment to creating a better and lasting partnership.

Part of this country's problem has also been the assumption that the problems facing Aboriginal people are exclusively *Canadian* and that their solutions can only be found *within* Canada. In fact, Indigenous people's problems are global, and Canadians could learn a great deal from the experience of other peoples and nations. Many countries have struggled with the political and social problems associated with colonialism and its aftermath. Countries around the world, incidentally, follow Canadian legal and political practices closely and have learned from our example to take a more liberal and generous approach to the affairs of their own Aboriginal peoples. Several years ago, a delegation of northern Canadian Aboriginal people visited Russia and met with Indigenous leaders and communities. On their return, they made two commitments: to continue to help Indigenous people in Russia, and to reconsider their approach to the Canadian government in light of the lack of respect and support shown by Russian authorities for Indigenous rights. A first step in developing a new and sustainable vision for Canada is to realize that positive examples and answers may well lie outside this nation's borders.

## NEW ZEALAND

Arguably the best example in the world of peaceful and cooperative coexistence between Indigenous and non-Indigenous peoples comes from New Zealand. That country has some significant advantages: small size, a unitary government (i.e., no provinces), one major Indigenous group with a common language, and a long history of cooperation and coexistence. The Māori resisted European settlement, negotiated a strong treaty (the Treaty of Waitangi of 1840), and later took up arms against settlers who ignored that treaty. The Māori lived largely outside the Pākehā (non-Māori) mainstream, although never to the degree that is commonplace in North America. Many joined in with the miners, loggers, whalers, and farmers who uncovered New Zealand's economic potential. They participated in national politics, largely because in 1867 they were guaranteed representation in Parliament (albeit this provision was intended more to reward Māori political loyalists than to uphold moral or ethical principles).

The situation facing the Māori today is far from ideal. Māori communities have a lower standard of living than the Pākehā. They are far more likely to be arrested and sentenced to prison than Pākehā, and social conditions are often difficult. The graphic and disturbing movie *Once Were Warriors* (1995) offers a brilliant introduction to the realities of Māori urban life. Discrimination remains a fact of life in the country, although far less so than in Canada. Many Māori responded to rural economic malaise by migrating to the cities, where they often married Pākehā, Māori from other *iwi* (tribes), and Pacific Islanders. Today, urban Māori are a distinct and politically influential group in New Zealand, often at odds with iwi-based political organizations regarding the distribution of the country's power and resources. There have been dramatic debates between Māori sovereigntists and more pragmatic politicians, with the former claiming that the Treaty of Waitangi guaranteed the Māori full partnership in the nation.

In the 1970s, the New Zealand government acknowledged that it had wilfully ignored the Treaty of Waitangi, a sweeping document that had committed the British to the shared development of the land. The Treaty of Waitangi Commission, an arm's-length agency with the authority to investigate Māori claims regarding land and other treaty rights and to make recommendations about them, provided a useful forum for debating and resolving grievances. (As in Canada, it also led to accusations that the process established a profitable grievance "industry.") Beginning in 1995, modern treaties were negotiated that transferred resources and responsibilities to the Māori people. In recent times, debates *among* the Māori have been drowning out arguments between the Māori and the national government as the main focus of Māori political action.

Perhaps more important than political and financial arrangements (involving far less money than in Canada) has been the degree of social respect and accommodation. Māori people do not have reserves, and they generally live among the broader New Zealand population. Schools and workplaces are highly integrated, and Māori graduates have been filling key professional posts for decades. Māori sports stars are widely hailed, as are leading Māori artists and cultural figures. There is genuine national acceptance of Māori culture within national institutions, highlighted by the brilliant Te Papa (The People) museum in Wellington. Not all Pākehā support biculturalism, and it takes little effort to find outspoken critics of that concept. In the main, though, New Zealanders accept biculturalism as a fact of national life, a basic political reality, and an enrichment of the country's social and cultural fabric. The Treaty of Waitangi itself has become generally accepted as fundamental to New Zealand's national existence.

## AUSTRALIA

Across the Tasman Sea, Australians face a different reality. Relations between Aboriginal and other Australians remain strained. High-profile debates over Aboriginal rights, demands for the government to apologize for removing Aboriginal and half-caste children to foster homes and boarding schools, and the national government's refusal for years to provide a statement of reconciliation are only the most recent manifestations of a long-simmering dispute over Indigenous rights. It was considered a major advance when Prime Minister Kevin Rudd offered a formal apology in 2008, soon after taking office. Aboriginal Australians secured citizenship and voting rights only in 1967, and there was no legal recognition of Aboriginal land rights until the *Mabo* decision in 1992.

Unlike New Zealand, Australia has experienced little cultural mixing and integration. Most Aborigines still live in the outback, and many live modified traditional lives on the land. There are not many urban Aborigines, although the numbers have been growing over the past twenty years. With non-Aboriginal Australians based largely in the cities and Aborigines living mainly in the back country, contact between the groups has been limited. Governments make no particular effort to cultivate the Aboriginal vote, and Indigenous issues are not high on the national agenda. (Australians are highly sensitive to international criticism of their Aboriginal policies. When the UN Committee on Human Rights criticized Australian practice in 2000, the government flatly rejected the criticism and withdrew from several key UN organizations.)

Australia settled some land claims and granted Aboriginal groups considerable autonomy – but only in the vast desert reaches of South Australia and the Northern Territory (which has subordinate constitutional status, much like Yukon, Northwest Territories, and Nunavut). The state governments in Queensland and Western Australia have historically opposed Aboriginal rights for fear that expanded authority would harm the mining and cattle sectors. A central government agency, the Aboriginal and Torres Strait Islanders Commission, was tasked with developing new policies for the Aborigines, but it lacked a high public profile and strong government support. The Liberal-National government of John Howard eliminated the commission in 2005, arguing that its activities were emphasizing Indigenous separation and entrenching welfare dependency. Strong public demonstrations erupted when the commission was cancelled, but the general sentiment seemed to be that the proper course was to eliminate special status and targeted programs. The Australian government's blunt willingness to end elements of Aboriginal people's special status has attracted considerable interest among Canadians who are critical of current federal policies. Howard's government ran its course late in 2007 and was replaced by a Labor administration that was openly critical of the Liberal-National government's Aboriginal policy. The election result signaled a return to a more collaborative approach, which lasted, albeit without major changes in Aboriginal policy, until the defeat of Labor in 2013.

## SCANDINAVIA

Participants at international Indigenous rights meetings are typically impressed with the Sami representatives. Although clearly committed to their culture – representatives often speak Sami and wear traditional dress – they are fluent in other European languages, are comfortable in complicated international settings, and offer articulate and heartfelt appeals for the preservation of their lands and rights. The Sami of northern Norway, Sweden, and Finland (and Russia) faced considerable development pressure in the post–Second World War era. Like Indigenous peoples in other regions, they fought back, organizing themselves politically and taking their rights campaign to southern audiences. Generally, the Sami are better educated than most Indigenous peoples and typically are strongly affiliated with their national society. However, their traditional practices, such as reindeer herding, have been strongly influenced by the development of roads, railways, and hydroelectric dams as well as by environmental changes. In particular, the Chernobyl nuclear disaster of 1986 affected large expanses of the reindeer habitat.

The small "s" social democratic governments of Norway, Sweden, and Finland have tried to accommodate Sami aspirations, especially at the cultural level. There is strong support for Sami cultural initiatives, including Sami-language schools (as in New Zealand, this effort is aided by the existence of a more or less common Sami language, although there are distinct regional dialects). Some protection has been offered to traditional Sami harvesting practices, although not to the point of interfering with national economic priorities. Wide-ranging government programs aimed at *all* citizens have helped ameliorate some of the difficulties associated with cultural transition and the struggle to maintain traditional values and activities in the face of severe development pressures.

Scandinavian governments have tried to provide the Sami with some measure of political influence. Norway has a Sami parliament, funded by the Norwegian government, which advises the Norwegian parliament and government on matters relating to and affecting the

Sami. Although the Sami parliament is advisory and does not have self-governing authority, it has had a surprising level of success (and some notable failures) making sure that Sami concerns are considered in the development of national legislation. One of the most important accomplishments has been the Sami parliament's role in the creation of the Finnmark Act. The act transfers ownership of 95 percent of the land of Finnmark County, the largest and most northerly county in Norway, to all residents. The land is managed by the Finnmark Estate, and the estate operates on the basis of co-management and has a six-member board of directors, three appointed by the Sami parliament, three by the Finnmark County Council. Although co-management is fairly extensive, the arrangement excludes saltwater fishing, mining, and oil and gas rights. Along with participation in governance, the Sami parliament is active in program delivery. The parliament provides funding to Sami University College (located in the Sami town of Kautokeino), which provides a variety of university programs tailored to meet the Sami population's needs. Political structures in Sweden and Finland are less formal and strictly advisory, designed to provide the Sami with an opportunity to influence, although not direct, national policy and to ensure that government leaders understand Sami positions.

Perhaps the greatest external strength underpinning the Sami struggle to maintain cultural integrity is widespread national support for their cause. Among Scandinavians, there is an openness to cultural accommodation and flexibility that is rare in most of the world. This is due, in some measure, to the long history of positive relations between the Sami and their southern neighbours, highlighted by extensive intermarriage, and to the fact that the Sami occupy the mysterious, iconic northern fringe of Scandinavia, an area that figures prominently in Scandinavian folklore and national culture but little in the day-to-day lives of citizens.

The Sami differ in important ways from Aboriginal peoples in Canada and Australia. The Scandinavian countries have accommodated their cultural rights (e.g., language education) and economic rights (e.g., reindeer herding). However, the Sami do not possess legal rights to land or territorial-based self-government, nor are they likely to attain either. In this regard, Aboriginal peoples in Canada and Australia have greater political autonomy.

## THE UNITED STATES

The United States does not have a good historical record with Indigenous people, yet it has been fairly progressive in terms of self-government and political autonomy. The entire world has been raised on a steady diet of movies about the American conquest of Indian territories that accompanied the westward expansion and settlement of the nation. American history is full of tales of broken promises, treaties signed and ignored, Indians forcibly removed from their lands, attacks by an army dedicated to protecting settlers and travelers, and the social and economic isolation that followed. The United States attempted in the 1880s to eliminate Indian reservations and separate status for Indian people. That policy failed due to Aboriginal resistance. Like Canada, it tried interventionist programs to assimilate Indians into the American mainstream; more recently, it has devoted considerable resources to affirmative action programs in education, state and federal employment, and the awarding of government contracts. As with Aboriginal people in many other parts of the world, Indians in the United States remain substantially apart from other Americans, although the rate of intermarriage is high.

Most significantly, the United States is politically comfortable with the notion of limited Native American sovereignty. Canadian officials fret about the term and its application to First Nations reserves; the Americans accepted long ago that Indians should be able to govern themselves. On most of the small and scattered reservations in the United States, this governance amounts to little more than self-administration. A few reservations, blessed by strategic location, have used their right to self-governance to establish highly profitable casinos, several of which generate tens of millions in profits for small communities. Larger and more isolated Indian reservations, such as the Navajo in the West, enjoy sufficient economies of scale to fund their own schools, colleges, police forces, and court systems. Metlakatla, Alaska, a unique experiment in Indigenous self-government dating from the nineteenth century, has demonstrated that local administration and responsible government can be effective. Within the constraints imposed by federal and state laws, Indian reservations enjoy considerable freedom to chart their own course. In Alaska, for example, several communities have declared themselves to be officially alcohol-free and impose tough penalties on offenders, including banishment. The system works better in some places than others, typically as a function of the length of time that political autonomy has been exercised and the availability of skilled and experienced administrators. An analysis by the Harvard Project, now co-directed by Manley Begay Jr. and Stephen Cornell, found that where tribes enjoy sovereignty and build effective governance institutions, including effective barriers between business and government, economic development flourishes. Canada has important lessons to learn from south of the border.

Forty years ago, organizations such as the American Indian Movement grabbed international attention with a series of protests and confrontations, most notably a standoff with federal officials at Wounded Knee, South Dakota, and the occupation of Alcatraz Island in San Francisco Bay. At present, Aboriginal rights glow only dimly on the nation's political radar. Highly localized conflicts – over water rights in California, fishing rights in Washington, casinos in various states, and the status of old treaties in the eastern United States – flare up from time to time. Some observers are concerned about the claims that Indians are making to sacred sites and about the capacity of Indigenous groups to interfere with development projects. Overall, though, liberal guilt about past depredations – nicely brought to the fore in the Hollywood movie *Dances with Wolves* (1990) – remains fairly strong. For the most part, tensions are local and involve the emergence or exercise of Aboriginal rights near reservations.

## OTHER NATIONS

There are hundreds of Indigenous groups around the world, and many of them are facing rapid incursions into their traditional territories and consequent social and cultural dislocations. There has historically been so much emphasis on the activities of European powers that much less attention has been paid to the intrusions of countries such as India, Thailand, Botswana, Taiwan, China, and Japan onto Indigenous lands. In most of these countries, the imperatives of resource development have taken precedence over the needs of small, isolated, and politically powerless Indigenous peoples. While some groups attract attention from time to time – the Yanomami in the Amazon Basin and the Penan of Sarawak (Malaysia) are the best examples – there is generally little public appreciation of a simple truth:

the development frontier that displaced Indigenous peoples earlier in Canada, Australia, and other countries continues to wreak havoc on comparable societies in remote corners of the Earth.

The global advance of settlement and development on traditional Indigenous lands has led to a variety of initiatives and approaches, few which have enjoyed much success. Strong international criticism of national policies forced Brazil to create special reserves for Indigenous communities, but poorly regulated logging and gold mining continue to ravage local populations. Countries in Central and South America have drafted strong constitutional protections for Indigenous peoples, but to little practical effect. Other countries, notably Bangladesh and India, face so many pressing demographic, political, and economic pressures that the unique needs and aspirations of Indigenous cultures generally get very short shrift.

In Russia, the collapse of the national economy in the 1990s and the weakening of the government resulted in severe reductions in financial support for the small and widely scattered "small-numbered peoples" of the North. But even Russia – a state with a complicated federal structure – has lessons to teach Canada. In Russia, clans can make claims on traditional territories even if these territories are widely separated. Although land rights are weak compared to Canada, they nevertheless address a basic problem. Because not all First Nations have the same system of land occupancy and ownership, flexible arrangements for accommodating these differences need to be implemented if reconciliation is to be achieved.

Other innovative policy developments include the creation of expert commissions in the Sakha Republic (Yakutia) in eastern Siberia. These expert commissions evaluate the potential social and cultural impacts of developments on Indigenous communities as a separate process from environmental impacts, and their recommendations are based on appropriate mitigation and compensation mechanisms. In Canada, by contrast, assessments of potential social and cultural impacts are typically collapsed into the environmental impact assessment process, where they often receive a lower level of attention. Officials in the Sakha Republic (Yakutia) looked to Canada and learned what *not* to do. Canada may now want to look to Russia's example in the development of new assessment processes for resource development projects. More recently, the Russian government's efforts to suppress and control the Russian Association of Indigenous Peoples of the North (RAIPON), the national organization of Russia's Indigenous peoples, have limited that group's ability to work with other Indigenous organizations and Western NGOs.

Because government programs and legal protections have generally been ineffective, Indigenous groups have entered the international political arena in their search for support. This has embarrassed some governments into action – especially Brazil – but has resulted in few changes on the ground. Only in the more prosperous First World countries have the pleas and demands of Aboriginal people had much impact on public policy. In the rest of the world, these groups face perennial economic hardship, suffer the ill effects of contact with the outside world (diseases continue to ravage many groups), and experience repeated incursions by settlers and developers onto traditional territories. Conflict has erupted in places, but most of the time the power and military might of the nation-state has succeeded in suppressing Indigenous protests.

Other nations provide models of attempted reconciliation and evidence of the ongoing difficulties involved in reaching a compromise between Indigenous peoples' needs and the prerogatives of the nation-state. Taiwan has made significant strides in supporting Indigenous aspirations. Japan, by contrast, has recognized the existence of the Ainu as a separate people for less than a decade and is only now beginning to develop suitable policies. So long as nations are driven by the pursuit of material gain, it is impossible to imagine their original inhabitants withstanding development pressures.

By most objective political, economic, and social standards, Indigenous peoples in Canada, Australia, New Zealand, the United States, and Scandinavia are better off than most. Even so, Aboriginal politicians from the First World are among the loudest protesters at international meetings and the strongest supporters of the UN Declaration on the Rights of Indigenous Peoples. Māori representatives from New Zealand routinely offer strongly sovereigntist appeals at these sessions, and Canadian representatives have been quick to accuse the government in Ottawa of racism and genocide. But First World Indigenous leaders overestimate the impact of their strongly worded rhetoric on other Indigenous organizations. Groups in Central America facing government suppression and Indigenous

peoples in the Philippines or Indonesia coping with the direct occupation of traditional lands often dismiss efforts by the comparatively
"rich" Indigenous groups of the First World to make common cause.
At a UN meeting held in northern Canada in the mid-1990s, when a
northern Canadian First Nations leader excoriated the federal government for its racism, genocidal practices, and refusal to sign a land
claims deal, representatives from Central America asked whether he
wanted his people to change places with them.

Indigenous groups around the world spent more than two decades
working on the UN Declaration on the Rights of Indigenous Peoples.
Strong disagreements about key concepts – such as a definition of
*Indigenous,* which is ambiguous enough that the Boers of South Africa
tried to claim that label – and the enormous gulf between Indigenous
demands and the willingness of nation-states to meet those demands
added to political delays. The declaration (reprinted here in Appendix E)
was finally approved by the UN Humans Rights Commission in 2006
and by the UN as a whole in 2007, over the objections of the governments of Australia, Canada, New Zealand, and the United States.
Media commentary aside, this Canadian position was not a reflection
of the Conservative government, for the previous Liberal administration had also expressed significant concerns about the declaration.
Even so, all four First World governments had signed it by 2010.
Although the declaration is nonbinding on UN members and therefore lacks even the limited force of UN resolutions, Aboriginal groups
have shown that they intend to resort to its strong language. The declaration is repeatedly cited by Indigenous peoples as if it has the force
of law, mainly because it is the strongest and clearest global statement
available to them.

The declaration includes a number of clauses that Indigenous
peoples considered crucial at the time it was being drafted (see especially its preamble). Overall, it is a powerful and evocative statement
of Indigenous hopes and expectations. The process of drafting it
brought together Indigenous peoples from around the world and gave
voice to cultures and societies long ignored. Anyone wishing to understand the passion and commitment of Indigenous political leaders
would do well to study the declaration and to appreciate the deep historical and cultural understanding it reflects. All of that said, it is
stronger about the past than it is about the future.

Canada, the United States, New Zealand, and Australia opposed the document when it was first tabled. Why? Because unlike some of the countries that supported it early – nations that routinely ignore UN declarations – the leading industrial nations generally attempt to abide by UN resolutions. The declaration demanded too much of them and would not have secured majority support back home. Overall, though, the declaration is a meaningful and influential indication of Indigenous dreams. It also illustrates the global mobilization of Aboriginal people over the past twenty years.

## RECONCILIATION IN CANADA

Other countries have provided examples of what Canada could do – or, equally important, should not do. But no nation has yet got everything right when it comes to fully reconciling Indigenous and non-Indigenous world views, values, and expectations. Aboriginal demands are based on an attachment to traditional territories and on the desire for autonomy over internal affairs. By contrast, non-Aboriginal expectations rest on making productive (i.e., economic) use of available resources and managing land in the best interests of all citizens. There is an inherent contradiction in these priorities, one that is deeply embedded in the long-standing Canadian practice of combining administrative responsibility for Indigenous peoples with western and northern development. No Western nation can make substantial concessions to Aboriginal people without potentially infringing on the rights of other citizens. And while some steps can and have been taken – especially during good economic times – broader initiatives have been slowed by the perceived need to balance Aboriginal and non-Aboriginal interests, with the former typically seen as less important.

Aboriginal Canadians, for their part, have been emboldened by court decisions (which do not, however, guarantee subsequent government action). They have also been propelled by the growing frustration and cultural despair in their communities. Non-Aboriginal Canadians, for their part, have been angered by the same court decisions and wonder where the upward trajectory of Aboriginal rights will end. Importantly, the move towards greater Aboriginal empowerment seems to have slowed if not stalled. Governments, especially Ottawa, feel caught between their legal responsibilities to the First Nations, the political imperatives of non-Aboriginal resistance, and

the desire to ensure that Aboriginal rights do not interfere with economic development. The result is a complicated and often frustrating
whirlwind that shows no evidence of dissipating. The Canadian response has been to patch things together, work on one problem at a
time, avoid the broad picture, and hope that time will solve all difficulties. The evidence is overwhelming that the opposite is happening.
Canada has reached a point where the very persistence of the problems is leading to less government action, fostering more public uncertainty, and heightening Aboriginal frustration.

The solutions currently on the table are contradictory and wide-
ranging and provide no coherent or definitive answers. Canadians have
become used to constitutional wrangles and negotiations but few non-
Aboriginal people believe that further constitutional change will address
current problems and needs. Aboriginal notions of "parallelism" – of
Indigenous communities living alongside the rest of the nation – do
not accord with social and economic realities and trends. While our
suggestions for moving forward will, like all others before them, be
limited in nature and potential impact, we offer them as contributions
to a vital national debate. Canada must steer itself off the current legal
and constitutional track and consider a much broader package of initiatives and approaches, founded on the full recognition of Aboriginal
legal and constitutional rights but not limited to this realm.
Furthermore, it is essential that there be greater recognition of contemporary Aboriginal concerns and of the need to develop realistic
responses. It is also essential that the next steps towards resolving this
issue demonstrate a commitment to compromise, mutual understanding, and innovation. The next decade will be critical in determining
the future shape of Canada. But it is certain to be only a start down a
long and complicated path, with many bumps, twists, and turns to be
navigated before reconciliation becomes a fact of life in the country –
before Canadians become truly treaty peoples.

The following assumptions or considerations are fundamental to
any meaningful effort at reconciliation:

> Indigenous peoples in Canada are distinct political communities with
  unique expectations, circumstances, and rights. They are mature political groups with identifiable goals and options and, as such, they deserve respect and accommodation.

> The changes necessary to address Aboriginal aspirations are, in the main, relatively straightforward and can be accommodated within existing Canadian constitutional, legal, and political frameworks.
> Aboriginal peoples are equals in Confederation – not in a structural, constitutional sense, but in the context of citizenship and partnership in Canada. When charting a mutually beneficial future, it will be critical that Canada understand and build on this political reality, but without obsessing about it.
> There is no future in a relationship built on grievance and guilt. That path has led only to acrimony as well as to a broadening of the gap between Indigenous people and other Canadians, especially new Canadians, who are separated by history from responsibility for the distant past. The guilt card was essential in the 1960s and 1970s, and it carried a great deal of weight with the largely Euro-Canadian population. It is counterproductive in the multicultural Canada of the twenty-first century.
> The Canadian debate has been conducted too much in the context of colonialism and the need to develop coherent responses to colonial realities. Colonialism may be a very good way of understanding Canada's past, but it does not provide a useful analytical tool for building Canada's future.
> The nation's search for appropriate models and options should not be constrained by relations between Indigenous and majority populations; rather, it should include reference to broader structural and social relationships within multicultural states.
> Finally, the options considered for Indigenous peoples must not establish a higher standard than is held out for the rest of the population. The tendency to expect perfection from programs aimed at Aboriginal communities is unfair and unwise and reinforces a double standard.

# —— 10 ——

# equality of status

THERE IS NO perfect or exhaustive list of what can and should be done to develop a more mutually beneficial relationship between Aboriginal peoples and other Canadians. In the following chapters, we turn to important questions such as political arrangements and economic relations. We believe, however, that there are some symbolic steps that could provide the foundation for reconciliation. Prime Minister Stephen Harper's formal apology to Aboriginal people, delivered in an emotion-filled House of Commons in 2008, demonstrated the power of symbolic gestures and the receptiveness of Aboriginal Canadians to sincere remorse. We, as a country and as people, could do more. Canada needs to commit itself to the principle of equality of status, recognizing and celebrating Aboriginal peoples as equal partners in the past, present, and future of Canada.

## PARLIAMENTARY REVIEW OF THE *REPORT OF THE ROYAL COMMISSION ON ABORIGINAL PEOPLES*
Between 1991 and 1996, a group of talented and committed commissioners travelled the country to review the state of Aboriginal affairs in Canada. Their work resulted in the *Report of the Royal Commission on Aboriginal Peoples,* released in 1996, a comprehensive and often

controversial evaluation of public policy and government programming directed at and for Aboriginal people in Canada. The Canadian
government has never converted its dozens of recommendations into a
program of action. Even so, its values, assumptions, and ideas have
worked their way into the nation's consciousness.

The Royal Commission took its members to dozens and dozens of
Aboriginal communities, where they sought input about the problems
facing Indigenous peoples as well as potential solutions. Some of its
recommendations were speculative or even inappropriate; others
merited immediate consideration. By failing to acknowledge and respond to the report, the federal government showed profound disrespect for the commissioners and for the Aboriginal people who shared
their stories and offered constructive suggestions. That disrespect has
become a major political irritant – indeed, a huge barrier to any subsequent consultation with Aboriginal peoples. It is noteworthy that the
first time Jean Chrétien was involved in a major Aboriginal consultation, in 1968–69, he ignored input from Aboriginal people. As prime
minister, he did so again following the commission's report. So did
Prime Minister Martin, and so has Prime Minister Harper.

In the wake of the Idle No More movement that swept across
Canada in 2012–13, Aboriginal leader Mary Ellen Turpel-Lafond
argued that the federal government should revisit the RCAP recommendations as they related to nonconstitutional approaches to
renegotiating relations between Indigenous peoples and the government. Others such as James Mulvale and Peter Russell have pointed
out that Canada has ignored the commission's advice that Ottawa
focus on consultative public policy development with Aboriginal
people.

Ottawa should turn the Royal Commission over to the appropriate
parliamentary committees of the House and Senate and encourage
those bodies to hold nationwide hearings to ascertain public interest
in the recommendations. Otherwise, the federal government's credibility in future consultations will be seriously eroded, perhaps ir-
reparably. Asking the committees to examine the report does not
commit either governments or Aboriginal peoples to its recommendations. But doing so would open a dialogue based on practical, specific
suggestions and move both sides away from exhausting and open-
ended discussions of policy and the constitution.

The Royal Commission *did* have an impact. It raised the profile of Aboriginal issues, even if its lengthy and complicated policy suggestions put to rest any idea that there were easy or obvious solutions to the challenges facing First Nations, Métis, and Inuit people. And the forestry and natural resource management sectors seem to have adopted the spirit of the Royal Commission's recommendations. Others have pointed out that the spirit of reconciliation reflected in the Royal Commission's work was later reflected in the 2005 Kelowna Accord and in the Truth and Reconciliation Commission tasked with investigating residential schools.

Over time, valuable critiques of the commission's report have emerged, regarding, for example, its emphasis on reserve-based First Nations as the foundation for Aboriginal–government relations, an approach that disenfranchises urban Aboriginal people. In her article, "Negotiated Inferiority" (2001), Kiera Ladner, a critic of the Royal Commission, argued that the

> RCAP should be shelved in its entirety. We need to chart a new course and begin the process of decolonization. We need to create a renewed relationship based upon a true partnership in Confederation, which is based upon a realization of a postcolonial vision and not a perpetuation of colonialism through the creation of negotiated inferiority and an unequal partnership. To do so, we need to escape the assimilationist, primitivist, and colonialist ideologies that have confined most attempts to envision a new relationship between Aboriginal peoples and the settler society. In so doing, we must begin the process of "thinking against colonialism" and creating a postcolonial vision of the future. While I offer no such vision of the future, it should be noted that James (sakej) Youngblood Henderson, Patricia Monture-Angus, and Taiaiake Alfred have begun the process of "journeying forward." (262)

Because the passage of time has seen major changes in political, legal, and other relationships between Aboriginal people, public governments, and the Canadians at large, it is impossible to resurrect the Royal Commission's report in full. Aboriginal peoples are especially sensitive to some aspects of it, especially its perceived imbalance in understandings of reserve and urban realities. That said, the report offers many recommendations worthy of detailed review and public discussion. To address that report's missed opportunities, the Canadian government and its Aboriginal partners should together re-examine its recommendations. This review, with a time window of perhaps one year, would examine each of the recommendations, comparing the public policy and programming situation in 1996 with present circumstances. The data collected by the National Household Survey and the Aboriginal Peoples Survey could provide the necessary statistical background. Importantly, this review would inform Canadians about how much change has transpired since the Royal Commission conducted its work. It would also honour the contributions made by the Aboriginal people who were consulted during the hearings and show respect for the work of the commissioners.

## NATIONAL STATEMENT OF RECONCILIATION

The federal government, provincial governments, and Aboriginal representatives should craft a statement of national reconciliation. Australia did this after a major report was released on Aboriginal deaths in custody. Its government established an organization called Reconciliation Australia and crafted hundreds of organizational and institutional Reconciliation Action Plans. In doing so, it gave national reach and real substance to efforts to rebuild relationships with Aborigines and Torres Strait Islanders. Canada should take similar steps, including a sincere public apology for historical injustices, a common declaration of intent to live cooperatively, and clear goals for public policy and future negotiations. At the present time, Canadians have been hamstrung by the absence of a statement of goals. Billions are spent annually on Aboriginal affairs, but there is no clear understanding of the purpose of this spending. Similarly, land claims negotiations and other settlements are concluded without identified common objectives. It is time to spell out exactly how Aboriginal people and other Canadians intend to relate to each other in the years and generations to come. Such a statement, properly written, disseminated, and celebrated, could provide a critical foundation for future relations.

Aboriginal politics has been rooted deeply in the assumption that non-Aboriginal Canadians continue to feel guilty about their past misdeeds. But we cannot expect younger Canadians and recent immigrants to share a sense of historical responsibility for actions carried out dozens if not hundreds of years ago. Guilt is a weak foundation for future relationships. At best, it generates paternalism and shallow zeal for resolving the social pathology that has arisen from historical injustices. At worst, it stimulates a national debate about responsibility for the past, one that is increasingly unlikely to be resolved entirely in the Aboriginal peoples' favour. Besides, over the past fifty years the country has addressed its most serious historical wrongs. That said, past government and public actions have left a legacy, and Canadians should have their responsibilities clarified and enumerated in ways that acknowledge that legacy.

As time passes, the issues will become smaller, more complicated, and less one-sided. As the focus shifts to these more controversial topics, public sympathies will become divided and support for the Aboriginal cause will fade. For example, the most hideous examples of sexual and physical abuse in residential schools attracted widespread public horror and anger. The federal government established the Truth and Reconciliation Commission to learn more about the residential school experience. At the same time, it earmarked more than $2 billion in compensation to former students, which took much of the political sting out of the issue (although the payment of hundreds of millions of dollars to lawyers representing the students angered many Canadians). Few Canadians are now paying much attention to the commission. In the minds of many Canadians, past injustices have already been addressed.

The far more attractive option, and one that is likely to enjoy support and success, is to use the historical legacy as a constant reminder of why these issues are on the table and to turn attention towards the future. Quebec's "Je me souviens" provincial motto is a good illustration of the political potency of keeping the past alive. Former prime minister Pierre Trudeau, in an ill-founded witticism, once said of Indian rights that he was not interested in "historical might have beens." This harsh and arrogant position exacerbated a situation that in hindsight could have been resolved much more quickly and cheaply but for his obstinacy. But it is just as wrong to think that the Canadian government should accept its guilt for all past social, cultural, and economic ills. So the federal, provincial, and Indigenous governments should consider including in the statement of reconciliation a commentary about the historical relationship, crafted to recognize national responsibility for the challenges facing Indigenous peoples and to acknowledge that the entire country is prepared to move beyond debate about the past and towards a search for common solutions.

## SPECIAL ISSUES FACING ABORIGINAL WOMEN

The challenges facing Aboriginal women require special attention. For the past few years, Aboriginal leaders have been calling for a national inquiry into the fate of missing and murdered Aboriginal women, pointing out that hundreds of such cases have not attracted enough attention from investigators. So far, these calls have been rebuffed. At times in the past, particularly relating to demands that the Charter of Rights and Freedoms apply on reserves, Aboriginal women have mobilized on a national level. The Royal Commission addressed this issue and proposed solutions brought forward by Indigenous women, but, as noted earlier, that document has never been accorded the attention it deserves. A fair and frank assessment of Aboriginal women's issues has yet to be conducted in Canada. The commitment of these women to their communities has been remarkable. Consider the exceptionally large number of Aboriginal men incarcerated in the Canadian prison system, and then consider how much of the responsibility for family and community has fallen on the shoulders of wives, partners, daughters, aunts, and grandmothers.

There is no need for another detailed inquiry on this matter. Aboriginal women know the issues and have been discussing solutions for decades. The Canadian government and the Assembly of First Nations should convene a high-level meeting, inviting Aboriginal women from across the country, including representatives from Indigenous women's organizations, Aboriginal scholars, and activists in the fields of health care, education, business development, and culture. The gathering would be an opportunity to identify national priorities and to assign various committees to develop community and regional initiatives to address the most pressing questions facing Aboriginal women. That meeting would in all likelihood produce some pointed critiques of the male-dominated political systems both across Canada and within Aboriginal communities.

That meeting would serve as both a starting point and a national consciousness-raising event. By giving Aboriginal women a clear, prominent, and separate platform to speak to Ottawa and the Assembly of First Nations' leaders, it could launch a crucial national dialogue on Indigenous women's issues. Such a focus is seriously overdue. Almost anyone familiar with the challenges facing Aboriginal communities will tell you that women are the bedrock of those communities, even as they bear the brunt of the crises and social pathologies that affect Aboriginal populations. Women provide much strength to Indigenous peoples in Canada; they must play a pivotal role in laying out a strategy for the future.

## CITIZENS MINUS, CITIZENS PLUS

Canadians need to accept that Aboriginal people have certain legal rights that other citizens do not. People can argue – and they do – about a "level playing field" and "one law for all Canadians," but the likelihood of changing the status quo in this regard is negligible. The Supreme Court of Canada has consistently recognized the importance of Aboriginal and treaty rights. Whatever the critics might say, the learned justices are not making this stuff up! These rights are integral to Canadian law, as well they should be. Opposing special status will solve nothing and will only exacerbate an already tense situation. As political scientist Alan Cairns has argued persuasively, Aboriginal people in Canada are and should be citizens plus (see Chapter 4). They are Canadian citizens with the attendant rights and responsibilities, but they are also Indigenous people with a separate list of rights established by law (and, it must be noted, with separate responsibilities that other Canadians do not share). These cards are in the Canadian deck. It is time to get used to playing with the full set.

The concept of differentiated citizenship – of one group of Canadians having more rights than another – is not unique in Canadian history and law. For many years, Canadians readily accepted the idea that Status Indians were citizens minus. They were Canadians – and many served with distinction in the Canadian armed forces – but they lacked certain basic human and civil rights, including the right to vote, to own property, to get a business licence, and to attend university. Few Canadians raised their voices in protest over the many decades that citizen minus rules were in existence. Small wonder that demands that citizen plus legal rights be revoked fall on deaf ears.

Even more importantly, First Nations people are not as unique in this regard as most Canadians seem to believe. For many years, First Nations shared their citizen minus condition with other Canadians. Chinese and Japanese Canadians did not have full citizenship rights until after the Second World War. Women fought for many years to overcome legal and political barriers to full citizenship. During times of war, the rights of many Canadians, ranging from Jehovah Witnesses to German immigrants, were abrogated and ignored. Aboriginal peoples are not unique in being excluded, historically, from full participation in the Canadian system.

Similarly, the citizen plus concept is not restricted to Aboriginal people. French-speaking Canadians have certain specific rights across the country – for example, to expect court services and education in their own language. Catholics on the Prairies, in Ontario, and in Yukon have special educational privileges that are not uniformly available, including full government funding for their schools. There is no more chance of changing Aboriginal legal rights than there is of removing the rights of women, the special legal status of Quebec, Prince Edward Island's unequal representation in Parliament, or the provinces' right to collect revenues from natural resources. As with Aboriginal rights, these are legal *group* rights that have been extended to an identifiable subset of the provincial or national population.

These examples are introduced not to lessen the Indigenous claim but to make it clear that Aboriginal people's expectations are not especially precedent setting. Furthermore, the Aboriginal transition from citizen minus to citizen plus reveals a fundamental weakness in the attack on Aboriginal legal status: reducing that status would reinforce a historical legacy that disempowered First Nations for generations. Given that Indigenous rights have been achieved through open negotiations or legal challenges, it would also strip away those rights based on the demonstrably false proposition that First Nations had gained special status within Canada. The attack on the special status of First Nations lacks legal merit and is politically untenable. It would be far more useful to define and flesh out the citizen plus concept.

## RIGHTS AND GRIEVANCE TRIBUNAL

The federal government needs to establish a mechanism for addressing Indigenous grievances. Some of those grievances are frivolous and deserve to be set aside quickly. Others reveal enormous abuses of power by past governments and need to be resolved expeditiously. Most cases, good and bad, valid or spurious, languish in government offices, surfacing from time to time at negotiating tables or in the courts, and seem to defy resolution. The Indian Claims Commission has set a precedent here; it needs a broader mandate and more authority.

The Indian Claims Commission and the Royal Commission report both recommend a permanent, arm's-length tribunal to handle the claims backlog. Such a tribunal could act without the full apparatus of the law and could either provide binding arbitration or collect and hear evidence and render its own judgments. Properly funded and empowered, this tribunal could quickly resolve existing and future cases. When cases linger for years and years, Aboriginal people's sense of injustice builds, non-Indigenous costs and uncertainties carry on, and anger and frustration result. A properly constituted tribunal could solve a serious and long-standing problem in Canada. The Specific Claims Tribunal established in 2008 by the Canadian government with the participation of the Assembly of First Nations has had mixed results in achieving this goal. Challenges include friction over costs, which are carried by the provinces, even though the tribunal is composed of federal judges. A less legal approach, designed to provide more prompt resolution, would be better, especially when one considers the costs to communities of hiring lawyers.

## A THOUSAND ACTS OF GOOD WILL

Canada cannot escape the legacy of the last few hundred years. The nation needs to recognize the pain that exists within Aboriginal communities. By stepping aside from the culture of guilt and reparations and responding to the needs of Indigenous people as fellow citizens, Canadians could do a great deal to help Aboriginal communities address their challenges. Government programs can go part of the way and provide important assistance; missing, though, has been evidence that the country as a whole cares about the aspirations of Indigenous people and their communities.

A thousand acts of goodwill – spontaneous, individual, creative, heartfelt – could be among the most important initiatives ever undertaken in Canada. This goodwill need not spring from guilt; rather, it could emanate from interest and compassion. It should reflect a shared interest in a better future rather than be a specific response to a historical grievance. Other Canadians must not be paternalistic – the country has been down that path many times before. Initiatives should rely, wherever possible, on input from Indigenous groups and organizations. Within the United Church of Canada, for example, the creation of the All Native Circle Conference was probably of greater long-term benefit than attempts at apology and formal reconciliation, for it established the principle of true and ongoing partnership with Aboriginal church members.

The challenge – and it is just that – is not to create a government agency, funding program, or coordinating committee. Instead, the aim is for spontaneity, for Canadian groups and organizations to identify needs and develop common responses to them. The initiatives might be fairly substantial – the creation of shared schools in Skidegate, BC, and North Battleford, Saskatchewan, point to the enormous promise of meaningful collaboration. Or they might be small, involving little more than a union executive visiting a band council meeting. The good works might include a service club building and maintaining a sports facility for a nearby Aboriginal community or a business offering to sponsor an Aboriginal soccer team or travelling Inuit cultural group.

Although people often think otherwise, a nation is built by its citizens, not its politicians. Leaders provide frameworks; whether they flourish or wither is determined by the people. Official bilingualism carried the country only partway down the path towards linguistic tolerance. The Canadian Parents for French and local French and French Immersion school boards have sustained that vision far more than any federal office or political leader. So it is with Indigenous peoples in Canada. Legal, constitutional, and political agreements are only skeletons. They lack flesh and substance. What determines the success of reconciliation efforts is the degree to which non-Aboriginal Canadians are prepared to step outside their comfort zones and find ways to cooperate with and support First Nations.

In this conception of Canada's future, church groups, trade unions, business organizations, service clubs, sporting associations, and community groups are just as important as politicians and Supreme Court justices. If Canadians turn their backs on the needs and opportunities of Aboriginal peoples, reconciliation will remain a hollow shell. If, conversely, non-Aboriginal Canadians offer examples of goodwill and outreach (from which, incidentally, they will benefit as much as the Indigenous communities), then the political framework will begin to take shape, cultures will identify common ground, understanding will replace misunderstanding, and reconciliation will become both possible and sustainable. Leadership ultimately comes from the bottom, not the top, of the political system. Canada is long overdue for a groundswell of interest in and enthusiasm about Indigenous affairs.

Aboriginal groups, incidentally, have been taking this approach for many years. The openness of their communities to outsiders remains remarkable. Their willingness to share their culture with other peoples is a defining feature of their strategy for survival and rebirth. Hands have been extended many, many times, but reciprocity has been rare. It is vital for Canadians to stop relying on their governments to take all of the measures that are required. Hundreds of small actions by hundreds of groups seeking to rebuild relationships and establish new and strong foundations for the future of Canada would be of incalculable benefit.

## STUDENT AND GROUP EXCHANGES
Contact is an excellent solution to cultural misunderstanding. A remarkable number of Canadians have never visited a First Nations reserve and have had little direct experience with Indigenous cultures. The opportunity exists for Canada to stimulate a broad series of exchanges between Indigenous and other Canadians. These can be done easily at the local level, through school and community exchanges, and could readily be expanded to the national level. Such meetings, which should flow in both directions in order to ensure reciprocity and to create opportunities for mutual understanding, could prove critical to ongoing efforts to improve dialogue between Aboriginal and non-Aboriginal Canadians. It is important for more non-Indigenous Canadians to experience First Nations culture first-hand. Aboriginal Canadians have a great deal of contact with the non-Indigenous world, but rarely in such exchange settings. Exposure to potlatches, powwows, Aboriginal feasts, hunting and fishing expeditions, round dances, band meetings, Native hockey tournaments, and the other activities and rituals of First Nations life would be a strong

reminder of the diversity, complexity, and vibrancy of contemporary Indigenous societies. The impressive Dechinta Bush University Centre for Research and Learning, based in Northwest Territories, is one of the best examples of this approach in the country. It offers Aboriginal and non-Aboriginal students alike the opportunity to learn from Indigenous people in a culturally appropriate setting. The Pen Pal Project, which involves children from Six Nations and Caledonia, is another example.

It is difficult to conceive of mutual respect and long-term understanding developing through arm's-length relationships and cultural distance. Parallelism, if maintained in everyday life, can only deepen and broaden the chasm between Aboriginal and non-Aboriginal peoples. Canadians need a stronger awareness of contemporary Indigenous realities, not further negotiations and politicking moderated through the media. The goal of such exchanges is not to create a common social reality but rather to generate a deeper awareness of Canadian's cultural diversity and of the real distinctiveness of Aboriginal societies. There is a reason why Aboriginal communities typically immerse visiting politicians in the rituals and ceremonies of Indigenous culture. By involving outsiders in their ceremonies, they provide compelling evidence of the survival of Indigenous customs and of the determination of their people to persist and flourish in contemporary times.

Ottawa has long sponsored such exchanges across the country. For years, programs such as Young Voyageurs brought schoolchildren from different parts of the country together. A cooperative initiative with Indigenous communities could go a long way towards knocking down the barriers and removing the cultural blinders that continue to divide Aboriginal and non-Aboriginal people in Canada. Student exchanges could provide the next generation with a more positive and realistic foundation for future relations.

## CELEBRATIONS OF RECONCILIATION

Aboriginal affairs in this country have long been marked by acrimony, not celebration. There have been precious few examples of true rejoicing around First Nations issues. Treaties and settlements come at the end of exhausting negotiations that are generally closed with relief rather than joy. Any celebrations have generally been restricted to Indigenous communities. Treaties and successful negotiations are typically viewed as Aboriginal accomplishments, not regional or national ones. So the celebration of the Nisg̱a'a treaty was held – understandably – in the Nass Valley and not in Victoria or Vancouver, or even Terrace (where it was signed) or Prince Rupert, two of the closest non-Aboriginal communities affected by the agreement.

Societies need benchmarks, points that demarcate significant events and accomplishments. These celebrations provide residual goodwill and a public declaration of new beginnings. Canadians are capable of grand celebrations that generate national memories, such as Expo 67, the Calgary and Vancouver Winter Olympics, and the 1972 Canada–Russia Summit Series. The country now needs to extend such celebrations into the Aboriginal arena. National Aboriginal Day is a slow start in this direction. Major events involving schoolchildren, community leaders, and mass public participation are one way that communities and countries celebrate their achievements. The opening of the University of Northern British Columbia in Prince George in August 1994 received national and international attention, in large measure because of the presence of Her Majesty Queen Elizabeth II. Memories of that day in the regional consciousness are strong. Activities like these create community buy-in and approval and have a way of resolving whatever debates, hard feelings, and anger may remain.

Canada should recognize that major accomplishments are diminished if they are not widely celebrated. Two examples from New Zealand illustrate the point. When the Tainui signed a land claim deal with the national government in 1995 – the first modern accord in the country – its passage in Parliament was highlighted by passionate speeches and much emotion on all sides. The nation's collective memory of the historic event is strong. Nothing as significant was done in the Waikato, the home territory of the Tainui, however, and very few local non-Māori participated in the celebrations. A short time later, on a much smaller scale, the University of Waikato reached an agreement with the Tainui regarding the long-term leasing of the campus grounds from the Māori group. The celebration marking the event was reported to the university community after the fact, and in this way a vital opportunity was lost to bring the students, faculty, and staff together with the Tainui to mark the truly historical occasion. The same thing has happened in Canada. Major agreements in Canada, like the Nisg̱a'a deal, have typically been marked by political back patting and local celebrations, but not by activities that reach out to non-Aboriginal Canadians.

In the future, to ensure that memories of major events and acts of reconciliation become embedded in the collective historical record of the citizenry at large, Canadian and Aboriginal governments should ensure that appropriate celebrations are held. These should be joyous, inclusive, and culturally rich events, designed to recognize a sharp break with the past and new foundations for the future.

## ACCOMMODATING ABORIGINAL CULTURE IN THE WORKPLACE

A common non-Aboriginal criticism of Indigenous peoples relates to matters of work. Commentators routinely decry the stunningly high unemployment rates, especially in remote and northern communities, and complain that the culture of entitlement or welfare dependency has resulted in self-imposed isolation from the workforce. Rarely, it seems, is thought given to the possibility that the typical Canadian workplace is a culturally specific and often culturally hostile environment, unfamiliar with Indigenous values, traditions, and obligations and unresponsive to Aboriginal needs. In the mid-1990s, non-Aboriginal people in the Maritimes routinely complained that Indigenous people lacked a strong work ethic. Then, in 1997 and 1999, the *Paul* and *Marshall* court cases gave Aboriginal people the right to harvest timber (temporarily) and to fish (permanently) for commercial purposes. Overnight, Indigenous people headed into the forest or onto the ocean, capitalizing on their re-established rights. Almost as quickly, non-Aboriginal people complained that the Aboriginal folks were working too hard and too fast, putting resources at risk. The difference, of course, was that Aboriginal people in the Maritimes finally had the right and opportunity to work close to their communities, for themselves, and without recourse to the mainstream work environment.

Adjustments, relatively minor in most instances, to the standard approach to work could make the Canadian workforce more attractive to Aboriginal workers and thereby address one of the fundamental challenges facing Indigenous Canadians.

It is easy to forget how far Canada has come in the past forty years in responding to and respecting Indigenous cultures and values. Some

medical systems, especially in Manitoba, Saskatchewan, and the territorial North, have made accommodations for Indigenous healing and
spirituality. Aboriginal cultural activities figure prominently in pris-
oner rehabilitation programs. Elementary and high schools, colleges,
and universities have expanded the study of Indigenous issues. They
are also providing more balanced and favourable portraits of
Indigenous peoples than in the past and are finding ways to acknowledge Aboriginal values in classrooms. The Christian churches now
understand and respect Indigenous spiritual traditions and encourage
Aboriginal spiritual expressions within traditional Christian services.
Overall, the country has done more than it realizes to recognize the
unique values and contributions of Aboriginal peoples.

Perhaps the widest remaining gap is in the workforce. Indigenous
people, especially in remote and northern areas, have different obligations than most non-Aboriginal Canadians. Some of these reflect
family and community challenges; many others are embedded in culture, including obligations to attend lengthy potlatches and ceremonial and rite-of-passage events, as well as harvesting obligations.
Canadian workplaces have trouble accommodating cultural ways that
do not involve a regular work week, advanced scheduling, and specific
holidays. Some of the larger employers, Suncor in northern Alberta
being a well-known example, have made significant adjustments to
accommodate Indigenous workers. Many bosses and supervisors have
found ways to recognize the needs of individual employees.

The Canadian workplace has adapted successfully to other groups,
such as new Canadians and the disabled, and maternity or paternity
leave is now standard almost everywhere. There have been quite
remarkable efforts to recruit Aboriginal employees, especially by governments and resource companies, but less has been done to
accommodate Indigenous cultural needs. On a corporate or organizational and national level, it is crucial that efforts be made to identify
appropriate strategies for Aboriginal employees. For unskilled and
semi-skilled workers, fluid employment systems work quite effectively.
For more highly skilled and professional employees, companies need
to work out appropriate arrangements on an individual level. These
arrangements would take into account yearly harvesting cycles, in the
case of remote and northern communities, but would generally focus
on clearly articulated family and community responsibilities. Given

the cyclical nature of resource employment, it is possible (as has been done in Fort Chipewyan) for northern communities to negotiate crew arrangements with companies that would allow Aboriginal people to work a less structured schedule by rotating workers through the company. Individualized plans for Aboriginal employees would provide most employers with a unique opportunity to understand the dynamics of Indigenous family and community life. The mutual learning that would develop from such dialogues would go a long way towards eliminating the resistance and misunderstandings that often accompany efforts to honour Aboriginal employees' requests. More positively, such arrangements would help educate companies and their employees about the vitality and diversity of Indigenous cultures and community obligations.

## REDEFINING CANADIANS AS TREATY PEOPLES

Our proposals for a new foundation for relations with Indigenous peoples are optimistic and forward-looking. In many ways, they also stand at odds with current Aboriginal and non-Aboriginal proposals for changing the relationship between Indigenous and other Canadians. Perhaps the greatest point of departure is this: the future of Aboriginal people in Canada will be sunnier if we drop the language of guilt, paternalism, colonialism, and Aboriginal uniqueness. This language should be replaced with the concepts of equality, cultural reconciliation, recognition of Aboriginal peoples' specific needs, and the renewal of Indigenous communities. Aboriginal people will always be part of Canada's political landscape. They have rights, as Canadians and as Aboriginal peoples, that must be respected. Historical circumstances created the present day's difficulties and challenges. It follows that the structures, values, approaches, and rhetoric of colonialism and anticolonialism are ill-suited for defining future relationships. The language, concepts, and assumptions connected with treaties offer a much stronger conceptual framework for improving the position of Indigenous people in Canada.

Aboriginal people and other Canadians *can* coexist and *can* cooperate to a much greater extent than they have in the past. Connections, not separation, would strengthen all groups and create a situation in which cultural understanding and mutual support are built over time. Indigenous communities from coast to coast to coast have demonstrated that they can live close to non-Aboriginal peoples, adopting many of the features of Western material culture while remaining true to their own. The future will not be one of self-imposed isolation or enforced segregation, as in the past. Instead, Indigenous peoples in Canada will expand on their current strategy of selective integration, whereby they pick the points and degree of contact. They will retain reserve communities, even if many of their residents move freely between reserves and urban environments. By building institutions and relationships that respect the uniqueness of Indigenous cultures and certain common standards and expectations, Canada and its Aboriginal people could develop a structure that benefits all. By moving beyond history and beyond grievances to build relationships and a shared future, Aboriginal and non-Aboriginal Canadians can begin separating the country from its historical legacies. It is time to build the country we want, not simply to accept the country we inherited.

# 11

# citizenship and a commonwealth of aboriginal peoples

THE RECOGNITION of Aboriginal peoples as partners in Canada is important; so is the acceptance of Aboriginal cultures as fundamental to the country. But these things are not by themselves sufficient. Canada needs to build new political relationships with Aboriginal peoples and must create opportunities for them to govern their own political communities. Before the arrival of Europeans, Aboriginal peoples existed as distinct political communities on their own territories. Even after generations of dislocation and social change brought about by relations with newcomer societies, Aboriginal peoples survived as political communities. They found common cause in their opposition to assimilationist government policies, their determination to sustain their cultures and languages, and their desire to protect their homelands. Aboriginal political organizations had a significant impact on the national political agenda only in the 1960s, but Aboriginal peoples had been organizing locally, regionally, and nationally for years before then – even as early as the 1920s, at a time when they were legally banned from doing so.

But since then cracks have developed in the Aboriginal social fabric, widened by the bitter legacy of residential schools, government interference in cultural and economic activities, the gradual erosion of traditional practices, and rapid postwar migration into towns and cities. Many communities that once prided themselves on their cohesiveness and social solidarity must now cope with poverty, cultural decay, and social disintegration. Local, regional, and national Aboriginal organizations continue their activities, helping to push the Canadian government away from the paternalist and interventionist approaches embodied in the national welfare state. These same organizations mobilized aggressively after the release of the 1969 White Paper, which called for an end to special status for Aboriginal Canadians. At several points in the last forty years, especially during times of constitutional consultations and political controversy, Aboriginal leaders such as Ovide Mercredi, Matthew Coon Come, Phil Fontaine, Shawn Atleo, and Perry Bellegarde have been better known than most provincial leaders and all but a handful of federal cabinet ministers. Most Canadians, however, are tired of what is perceived as incessant bickering and conflict between Aboriginal people and the federal and provincial governments. Support for Indigenous causes seems to be declining sharply.

Canada can do better. Equality of opportunity requires political liberty. In Canada, political liberty means the liberty of individuals *and* political communities. We cherish individual freedoms – freedom of speech, freedom of conscience, and the freedom to run for political office. But we also value freedom as groups and regions. One of the biggest stumbling blocks to Aboriginal peoples achieving equality of opportunity is the lack of political power equivalent to that enjoyed by other Canadians. As we discuss in the next two chapters, there are several possible ways to greatly strengthen the ability of Aboriginal people to build political communities with vibrant futures, operating within and contributing to a renewed Canada. These include redefining Aboriginal citizenship, replacing Aboriginal and Northern Development Canada with a national Aboriginal Commonwealth, creating more space for Aboriginal self-government (including a third order of government), addressing questions of accountability and, importantly, accommodating the political needs of Canada's urban Aboriginal population.

## CITIZENSHIP AND MEMBERSHIP

Perhaps the most challenging task facing Aboriginal political communities relates to membership. There have been nasty fights, some of them ongoing, about the right of individuals to belong to specific

Aboriginal communities. At issue are competing authorities and legal entitlements. The Indian Act defines official status for Indians and Inuit, and its clauses and subclauses have been intensely debated over the years. Conflicts and debates will only grow as more and more Aboriginal people marry outside their communities. Bill C-31, passed in 1985, which allowed many women and their children who had been stripped of their Aboriginal status by the Indian Act to regain their standing, has created a situation in which many Aboriginal women and their children have full status but are not accepted as members of a specific Aboriginal community. The same bill has returned official status to several hundred thousand Aboriginal people – a much higher number than the federal government anticipated. As a consequence, the children of a man who received status under Bill C-31 but who is married to a non-Aboriginal woman are not eligible for Indian status under existing Canadian law. Several commentators have suggested that the Indian Act provisions will lead to a precipitous decline in the number of Status Indians in coming years. In fact, some see this as a deliberate goal of government policy and as a way to bring about assimilation within a few generations. Actually, it reflects the dynamics of Aboriginal marriage patterns, in that large numbers of women are marrying outside their communities.

Official and legal approaches to status run counter to how Aboriginal people want to define membership. Through land claims settlements, assertions of traditional rights, and control of electoral processes, their communities are demanding the right to determine membership, separate from any federal government mechanism. Ottawa, for its part, is prepared to respect Aboriginal decisions concerning citizenship (such as the right to vote and to run for office), but it refuses to place ineligible individuals on band rolls, for this would make them eligible for government support, including entitlements to education, social services, and housing. In New Zealand, mass migration to the cities after the Second World War created a large body of urban Māori who lacked clear lines of ancestry back to a particular *iwi* (tribe). Much the same is happening in Canada today: the "urbanizing" of Aboriginal peoples is rapidly blurring traditional cultural and community connections. An Aboriginal child with official Indian status might have grandparents from four different reserves or even from four different cultural groups. The government's obligations to individuals under the Indian Act may be quite clear, but it is not at all obvious which community, if any, should assume administrative responsibility for any given person.

Issues such as this became clear in 1999 during the Supreme Court's decision in the *Corbiere* case, a successful challenge to the management of band elections and political processes brought by First Nations living off-reserve. The claimants argued successfully that off-reserve First Nations people should hold political rights in their official home community, something that reserve-based First Nations contested for fear that it would change political relationships and alter the allocation of community funds and programs. With over 50 percent of Status Indians now living off reserve, the *Corbiere* judgment re-empowered those members living away from the reserve (although some communities dealt with the legal requirement by insisting that individuals come back to the reserve to vote, a substantial barrier for people living a long distance from their home community). The *Corbiere* case demonstrates an emerging reality of Aboriginal political life, namely, that intragroup tensions are likely to become more prominent in the future, particularly as Indigenous governments gain additional resources and authority.

Membership and the rights associated with such status are volatile issues that have the potential to divide communities and deepen the rifts between Indigenous and non-Indigenous people. There is a strong and often illogical belief that Status Indians enjoy an inordinate number of financial benefits from being on a membership roll. Much is made of their income-tax-free status, for which most Indigenous people would qualify anyway because of their low incomes. Mention is also often made of Aboriginal people's exemption from cigarette and sales taxes, their "free" houses (which are rarely free and cannot be mortgaged), and Ottawa's support for postsecondary education (which is far less generous than Quebec's massively subsidized postsecondary system). What frustrates non-Aboriginal Canadians is that these benefits, if they can be called that, are not available to all. Anyone who envies Alberta's no-sales-tax regime or Quebec's postsecondary tuition fees can simply move to those provinces. Because of membership requirements and Status Indian regulations, there is no opt-in opportunity for other Canadians when it comes to reserves.

Another significant legal and political challenge has emerged, one related to the re-emergence of Métis membership and status as a major issue. Métis legal challenges, now before the Supreme Court of Canada, argue that the Métis, as a constitutionally recognized Indigenous people, should have comparable rights and status to Indians, as defined under federal government legislation. If accepted, this approach, which does not sit well with First Nations, would transform Indigenous political affairs in the country, in large measure because Métis membership and identity is only loosely defined at present. For the most prominent Métis populations, membership requires having ties to the historical Métis communities of the southern plains and fur trade posts from the nineteenth century. For others, being of both Aboriginal and non-Aboriginal ancestry, without the same cultural and linguistic characteristics, is sufficient. The courts, to date, have added requirements that Métis should be living in a Métis community, living in a traditional Métis way, and be generally recognized as Métis in order to qualify for certain harvesting rights.

There is no easy solution to the membership conundrum. Should Aboriginal communities have full control over membership? Must every Aboriginal person be linked to a community? Could Aboriginal communities place on the Indian Act rolls a person who does not qualify under existing rules, thus increasing Ottawa's financial responsibility? Should Aboriginal groups that want to add individuals to their membership lists bear the full cost of providing services for them? Recent land claims settlements and modern treaties bear out that Aboriginal people insist on the right to control membership. There is growing concern that the Status–non-Status divide will widen because of the strictures of the Indian Act and that the "official" Aboriginal population will continue to shrink as a consequence. With these and related questions hanging over the discussion, several recommendations stand out as reasonable and responsible.

**Change the Indian Act Provisions**. For obvious financial reasons, Ottawa does not want to tinker with the Indian Act – for example, by opening official status to community-controlled mechanisms. On this issue, many Aboriginal communities are on the same page as the government – they want to maintain Indian Act definitions of membership based on blood quantum. Status Aboriginal people, whose rights and privileges are defined by the Indian Act, have been reluctant to expand their membership rolls, realizing that the resources available to communities are unlikely to expand accordingly.

But to base citizenship and membership solely on blood is intolerable in a liberal democracy. There is no reason not to expand the Indian Act's definition to allow for "naturalized" Aboriginal citizens. Provision could be made for individuals who have resided on an Aboriginal community's territory for a continuous period of time – say ten years – and who can demonstrate a thorough knowledge of that community's customs, traditions, and (where appropriate) language. This would silence claims that Aboriginal governments are race-based, which they are under the current Indian Act. It would also prevent the creation of "instant Indians" and thus end the federal government's worries about the financial implications of a strong influx of new Status Indians. And finally, it would prevent small Aboriginal communities from being overwhelmed by outsiders, for the threshold to become an Aboriginal citizen would be quite high. Canada does not grant citizenship on the basis of race but rather on the basis of a commitment to defined values and culture. Aboriginal communities within Canada's liberal democracy should follow the same principles.

**Community-Controlled Membership.** It is equally important that communities have culturally appropriate means of identifying and selecting their members. The individuals thus identified may not have access to government-funded programs, but there is nothing to stop communities from providing locally supported services for them. As community funding of services expands through taxation and other revenue streams, more and more Aboriginal members could be accommodated by Aboriginal governments. In the interests of fairness and accountability, these mechanisms would need to be fully and publicly defined, have clearly articulated requirements, and be ratified by the community. Membership mechanisms that are not transparent, culturally appropriate, and fairly administered will invariably generate a strong and harsh reaction.

**Aboriginal-Controlled Appeal Procedures**. Small communities guard their membership rolls very carefully – at times, too carefully. Given the importance attached to band council elections, some communities have conducted intense debates about whom to allow on the rolls – especially when it comes to women who regained their status through Bill C-31. There must be culturally and politically appropriate means of appealing local government decisions about membership, except where the appeal procedures are already spelled out in treaties or land claims agreements. This would be an obvious role for the Commonwealth of Aboriginal Peoples (see below), which could establish regional tribunals to review appeals relating to membership in an Aboriginal community.

**Urban Aboriginal Membership**. To put this issue in perspective, here are some numbers. There are more than 50,000 Aboriginal people in Edmonton, many more than in all of Nunavut. Vancouver has well over 40,000 First Nations residents, substantially more than the First Nations, Métis, and Inuit populations of the Northwest Territories. Toronto and Calgary both have more than 25,000 Aboriginal residents, close to three times the Aboriginal population in Yukon. At present, these people are significantly underrepresented.

Modern membership provisions must recognize modern realities. Thousands of Aboriginal people lack obvious community affiliations or would choose a broader, less band-focused membership, typically because they are urban dwellers. These people urgently require a political voice. One of those voices is the Congress of Aboriginal Peoples. The opportunity exists to create, on a city, town, or regional basis, a new form of membership in an Aboriginal community. That membership would be open to individuals who have official status under the Indian Act. These new political communities would be pan-Aboriginal, with members whose cultural roots go back to Aboriginal groups across the country. These new groups would form a powerful and influential urban political community and would quickly develop the capacity and resources to manage their own programs and services. Most reserve-based governments would prefer to strengthen community affiliations and would criticize this idea. But the reality is that urban Aboriginals, some of them now two or three generations removed from reserve life and married to non-Aboriginal people or to people from other Aboriginal groups, *already* exist in a separate social and political space. It is urgent that Canadians recognize this and that services and political opportunities be extended to them.

**The Métis**. No group faces greater membership challenges than the Métis. Although there are distinctive Métis communities across the country, many Métis are interspersed among other Aboriginal and non-Aboriginal populations. The very definition of *Métis* – a person of mixed ancestry – suggests there is no precise definition of a Métis person. The Métis Nation of Canada has its own membership or citizenship provisions: "Métis means a person who self-identifies as Métis, is of historic Métis Nation Ancestry, is distinct from other Aboriginal Peoples and is accepted by the Métis Nation." The Métis Nation has begun determining membership, albeit in an environment where the Métis have few clearly demarcated Aboriginal rights and limited access to government programs. The Métis National Council's membership identification procedures are appropriate, but its appeal mechanisms and the cultural standards it applies require external discussion and acknowledgment if they are going to be definitive. It is safe to assume that as the Métis secure further Aboriginal rights (as they have already done in the harvesting sector), and as their community grows in profile and confidence, the number of applicants for Métis status will rise dramatically. This issue took a dramatic turn in 2013, when the Federal Court accepted the Métis argument that they and non-Status Indians are "Indians" under the Constitution Act, 1982. This crucial case has been appealed to the Supreme Court of Canada.

## A COMMONWEALTH OF ABORIGINAL PEOPLES

Genuine political innovation is rare. History weighs heavily on the future, and the attractions of precedent are extremely strong. Radical new ideas are quite unusual and seldom move beyond high-level theorizing. So the debate about Aboriginal rights in Canada has long been framed in terms of long-established concepts such as colonialism, the nation-state, municipal-like self-government, and provincial status, all of which are bandied about freely. For a decade, Aboriginal intellectuals and political leaders have been enthralled by the language of nationhood and have identified a strong continuity between pre-European practices and today's aspirations. That the federal government – and governments around the world – are not going to move down this path has not stopped many from demanding national status for Aboriginal peoples (sometimes, but not always, in the context of the Canadian federal system).

A model can be proposed that takes into account fiscal and political realities, Aboriginal aspirations, non-Aboriginal expectations, and legislative and constitutional commitments. The model will be less than perfect, for there is no way to accommodate all dreams, visions, frustrations, and uncertainties. But a different approach to Aboriginal rights in Canada might well open debate on a broader range of options and priorities. Aboriginal peoples require a new political structure that fits within Canada's existing constitutional and political framework. Such a structure would have to recognize Aboriginal rights to self-government and would have to be able to function effectively. It would have to be fiscally realistic and accountable, and it would have to be democratic. Some have proposed that an Aboriginal province be established, representing all of Canada's Indigenous peoples, but this option will never gain sufficient political and public support.

We recommend creating a Commonwealth of Aboriginal Peoples. This organization would represent all Indigenous groups in Canada and would be managed through an elected body of Aboriginal representatives (the Inuit, who already control Nunavut and are moving towards regional government for Nunavik in northern Quebec, might or might not choose to participate). These representatives would be selected on a regional basis, with the structure (size, regional distribution, composition) of the body determined by a combination of demographic and cultural factors. This political unit would not be province-like in its scope and constitutional authority, but it would have enough administrative capacity and political authority to address the needs of Aboriginal people across Canada. The Commonwealth would establish a national administration, largely along tribal and cultural lines, with attention to the needs of urban Aboriginals. It would operate within the constitutional and legal boundaries of the Canadian constitution, which is to say it would accommodate existing Aboriginal and treaty rights as well as human rights laws and the Charter of Rights and Freedoms.

This Commonwealth would entirely replace Aboriginal Affairs and would have a stronger mandate, but it would not be a province, nor would it be a nation. It would not exercise sovereignty, nor would it replace federal or provincial authority, except where it exercised delegated power on behalf of these governments. Instead, it would be a unique, Aboriginal-controlled, Canada-specific organization tasked with overseeing all Aboriginal programs and services in Canada. It would also supervise all Aboriginal lands, membership lists, and trust funds. The organization would not own First Nations lands; these would come under the control of the appropriate local or regional Aboriginal authorities. Thus the Commonwealth would not have a nationwide land base of its own. Aboriginal groups could, individually or collectively, transfer administrative responsibility for their lands to the Commonwealth, thus creating such a land base, but that arrangement would be neither compulsory nor implicit. But within its frame of reference, the Commonwealth would have complete autonomy, subject only to parliamentary approval of its annual budget. It would have more power than the Assembly of First Nations or Aboriginal Affairs and would carry heavy and specific responsibilities for managing the affairs of Aboriginal people in Canada, answerable to an Aboriginal electorate from across the country.

The Commonwealth would have a broader political mandate than the ministry now does. To address a major shortcoming of the current structure, it would be responsible for Status *and* non-Status Indians as well as Métis and, perhaps, Inuit. This would entail a redefinition of Indian status and the legal rights and responsibilities attached thereto. It would also entail providing services both on and off reserve and both to culturally specific groups (as in communities) and mixed Aboriginal populations (as in major cities). As the Congress of Aboriginal Peoples has long argued, the Status/non-Status distinction is a historical artifact that needs to be reviewed. Establishing a broad mandate for a new organization would help address perennial complaints about identity, status, and membership.

The new Commonwealth would shoulder the same wide-ranging responsibilities as Aboriginal Affairs, but in line with the principles of self-government, it would have the flexibility to allocate resources as it sees fit. Its objectives would be set by the people elected to set them, who would almost certainly give priority to cultural and linguistic vitality, as Aboriginal peoples have done for years. The Commonwealth would be tasked with maintaining appropriate standards in areas such as education, health care, policing, and infrastructure. It would also have the freedom to shift priorities on a national, regional, or community basis. It would be responsible for building and sustaining relationships with regional Aboriginal governments, with federal and territorial governments, and with municipal and other local authorities. In this way, it would become the primary point of contact between public governments and Aboriginal peoples.

In accepting a Commonwealth, the federal government would be moving away from its previous (nonconstitutional) guarantees to provide housing (a service it has managed unsatisfactorily) and post-secondary education (where it has been more successful). This is an important point. Except in specific treaty situations – and even then, far less than Indigenous peoples believe – Ottawa has no legal requirement to provide the full range of Aboriginal services. There is no reason why, under a Commonwealth, Aboriginal Canadians would have fewer or poorer services than other Canadians, a situation that currently exists in many Indigenous communities. Like other elected bodies, the Commonwealth would have the power to establish scholarships, bursaries, and social-housing programs if it wished. Or it could use resources previously committed to these areas to develop other initiatives for creating healthy, self-sustaining communities.

Within its areas of responsibility, the Commonwealth of Aboriginal Peoples would have a broad mandate and considerable freedom of administrative action. The national, elected body would draft and implement policies and regulations. It would have a direct financial and political relationship with Aboriginal communities and band governments. The actual administration of many Commonwealth initiatives would probably be carried out through local Aboriginal governments and regional bodies. In the former case, and following on the recommendations of the Royal Commission on Aboriginal Peoples, Aboriginal governments would have to move away from the idea that each community should operate all of its own programming – an approach that is financially unsustainable and that tends to result in villages becoming even more administratively top-heavy.

Under the structure outlined above, the Commonwealth would be able to organize program delivery efficiently and collaboratively. After all, dollars spent unwisely on administration are dollars that cannot be spent on programs. Administrative services currently provided by Aboriginal Affairs would be apportioned to the regions. New communications technologies would enable the Commonwealth to operate online; in this way, key leaders would be able to stay in their communities and regions, with no need for a central "capital."

Such a Commonwealth would be the key representative body for Aboriginal people in Canada. Other purely political organizations such as the Assembly of First Nations and the Native Council of Canada could well continue to be funded by Parliament or Aboriginal people, but the Commonwealth's stature as an elected body and its administrative authority would give it considerable heft in national politics. It would represent Canada's Aboriginal people in their negotiations with federal and provincial authorities (with appropriate local and regional representation as required) and in future constitutional discussions. It would, as well, serve as the primary liaison with other federal and provincial departments. Because of its autonomy, expanded authority, and Aboriginal control, it would likely be more successful than Aboriginal Affairs in attracting and holding talented Aboriginal employees. Over time, this would help develop top-quality managers and administrators.

The Commonwealth of Aboriginal Peoples would exercise considerable political and administrative autonomy. It would be able to adapt its political structure and administrative services to fit with Indigenous cultures. It would also have clearly identified sources of funding, sufficient to develop and implement Aboriginal programs in Canada. The founding of a Commonwealth would acknowledge and respect the fact that Indigenous peoples are distinct political communities within Canada and that they have the rights and responsibilities of self-government. It would report to the House of Commons on an annual basis, and its financial affairs would be subject to a public audit just like all political agencies and governments in Canada. One hopes it would do better than some current federally administered programs. It could hardly do worse than the long gun registry and the sponsorship program! But responsibility for ensuring that the Commonwealth provides the services expected by Aboriginal peoples would rest with Indigenous voters, not with Ottawa. With the right to self-government goes direct responsibility to the people being served.

This outline for a new political and administrative unit is without precedent in Canada, but the individual elements fall well within both Aboriginal and nationwide structures, experiences, and practices. It would not require constitutional change, would not result in the creation of a new province, and would not involve recognizing individual First Nations as "nations" in the theoretical *or* practical sense of that term. The arrangement would address many prominent Aboriginal and non-Aboriginal concerns about Indigenous affairs in Canada and would provide an autonomous, properly funded, arm's-length organization free to address the needs of Aboriginal people as its elected representatives saw fit. With a high level of political and financial accountability, the Commonwealth would hold Aboriginal politicians to the same level of public responsibility expected of all Canadian politicians – no more and no less. It would, moreover, disentangle the historical relationship between Aboriginal Affairs and Indigenous peoples, a relationship rife with ill will, distrust, and uncertainty. Certainly, the Commonwealth might face some birthing difficulties, but it is difficult to imagine an Aboriginally run organization doing much worse that the federal government has done with its mandate over the past century and a half. Indigenous communities, politicians, and governments have repeatedly stated that they could do a much better job than Ottawa in managing the affairs of Aboriginal peoples. They are right. Those who oppose further empowering Indigenous Canadians should recognize that this arrangement would make Aboriginal people responsible for their own future. No more complaining – at least no more than one hears routinely from provincial premiers – about the inequities of Confederation.

*Funding the Commonwealth:* Almost every year, a minor public outrage arises over federal funding of Aboriginal programs. Critics love to throw around the $11 billion figure, as if they have unearthed a national scandal. The analysis is rarely sophisticated and skips over the crucial fact that federal responsibility for Aboriginal people requires large provincial-like expenditures on health, infrastructure, education, and economic development (funnelled through Aboriginal Affairs) and that governments routinely spend large amounts of money on people in poverty or at risk. The public commentary is generally highly critical, implying that the money is wasted on Indigenous people and communities and that major program changes are needed. Setting aside arguments about the size of the payments (for the harsh assessment of many non-Aboriginal observers is the polar opposite of the position advanced by Aboriginal leaders), the major problem with the current funding arrangements is that the money is seemingly discretionary and is provided as an annual federal allocation. This makes funding subject to political uncertainties. It has also led to a weak financial and conceptual basis for supporting Aboriginal governments and programs in Canada.

The arguments surrounding funding are frustrating. It is intriguing that there is so much opposition to federal support for Aboriginal college and university students and virtually no comment on the remarkably low university tuition maintained, for political purposes, in Quebec. Both are subsidies: Quebec's program is funded largely by equalization payments, yet it is the Indigenous program that is singled out for criticism. This is mainly because the setting of tuition fees is seen as a provincial matter and entails raising tax revenues or reducing other government programs. For Aboriginal people, no such relationship is seen to exist. Furthermore, the implication that all Aboriginal students get a "free" education misrepresents the amount of funding, underestimates the significance of many mature learners returning to university, and ignores the fact that many ambitious Aboriginal students are not funded each year because of caps on the program.

Aboriginal initiatives could be supported financially from an annual, block-funded budget from the federal government. The funding could come – and this is symbolically significant – based on the wealth generated from land and resources and on a percentage of Ottawa's gross revenue or Canada's GDP. Aboriginal leaders routinely assert that they deserve a share of resource wealth derived from their traditional lands and should share in the benefits derived from the use of their territories. Of course, most resource rents go directly to provincial coffers, making it impossible for the federal government to track and transfer the necessary funds. But provincial resource rents are only a small percentage of the wealth derived from resources and economic activities on traditional Aboriginal lands. The federal income tax on businesses and individuals involved in those industries, the salaries and wages themselves, and individual and company profits all figure into the wealth produced. Establishing a formal and fixed connection between Canada's overall wealth and Aboriginal funding would address a critical Aboriginal demand and establish a firm and clear financial relationship based on sharing the country's wealth. This approach would, in effect, institutionalize the resource-revenue sharing so strongly desired by Aboriginal peoples.

One measure of resource wealth is GDP. Agriculture, fishing, mining, oil and gas, and forestry account for about 10 percent of Canada's

GDP. Aboriginal people are about 4.3 percent of the Canadian population. A fair share based on population would be approximately $8 billion – roughly what Aboriginal Affairs and Northern Development Canada currently spends each year on Aboriginal programs. Alternatively, the formula could be based on total federal revenues. The 2014 federal budget estimated revenues of $264 billion. Based on a "fair share" percentage of the total, Aboriginal people would have received between $11 billion (revenues) or roughly the currently total amount of spending by Ottawa on Aboriginal programs (AANDC and other departments). (These numbers do not recognize that Aboriginal peoples share in the benefits of many other federal expenditures.) Not all of this money would be available for direct Aboriginal expenditures, and a sustainable formula would need to be worked out. The percentage would then be established as the base for Aboriginal expenditures in the future, with downstream sums tied to the growth in national wealth and changes in the Aboriginal population. In other words, this approach need not automatically cost the Canadian government more, save for expenses legitimately tied to growth in the Indigenous population and improvements in Canada's economic position.

The symbolism of this approach should not be underestimated. Current arrangements have rendered Aboriginal Canadians supplicants to the federal government. They are seen as constantly requesting funds and demanding greater support. Under the present structure, there is almost no chance of Aboriginal people escaping Ottawa's budgetary control. Indigenous Canadians argue that some portion of Canada's wealth properly belongs to them. Acknowledging this basic principle – that financial allocations to Indigenous peoples are a matter of right, not national or political generosity – would extend permanence and solidity to Aboriginal governments. The funding would not be capped at this level but would rise or fall in line with future federal revenue streams. Note here that the redistribution of tax revenues based on wealth and need is an established principle in Canadian politics.

Additional funding for the Commonwealth of Aboriginal Peoples would require a profound change in federal taxation policy. Aboriginal people's exemption from income tax is an enormous irritant for many Canadians, even though most First Nations people do not earn enough to pay taxes, those who work off reserve do pay taxes, and the signatories of modern treaties have surrendered their tax exemptions. Full partnership in Confederation will require Aboriginal people to pay taxes when they are financially able to do so, just like other Canadians. With the Commonwealth, the remaining Aboriginal exemptions from federal taxation would be lifted. Again, federal transfers based on resource wealth and income taxes might not be enough to cover the full costs of the Commonwealth (at present, only three provinces and none of the territories are able to finance their administrative and program costs from normal revenue sources). In such situations, federal compensatory payments would be required, on the basis of the kind of fixed formula funding currently used for the provinces. If Aboriginal income and federal revenue transfers were to exceed actual expenses at some point, a portion of the excess would flow back into federal coffers.

The Commonwealth of Aboriginal Peoples, working with regional authorities and local Aboriginal governments, could establish other revenue streams: sales taxes, business taxes on reserves and settlement lands, and the like. These funds would go to support Aboriginal programs and to ensure their continuity. Even with all of these revenue sources, the Commonwealth would not be self-sustaining, at least in the short term. Note here that most Canadians are unaware that most municipal governments are not sustainable based on their own source revenues. Across Canada, about 40 percent of municipal revenues come from transfers from the provincial and federal governments. Financially, the Commonwealth would be closer to the model of Yukon, Northwest Territories, and Nunavut, three jurisdictions that must cope with vast distances, scattered populations, and severe social and economic difficulties. The kind of arrangement proposed, then, is well within Canadian precedent. Furthermore, it would allow the provision of national-standard programs for Aboriginal people across the country, with these programs designed, implemented, and administered by Aboriginal people themselves.

A properly funded Commonwealth of Aboriginal Peoples would have the resources to support a variety of national and regional programs. It would be able to fund Indigenous governments tasked with administering specific Aboriginal programs. It would, therefore, be able to support both Canada-wide initiatives as well as respond to local needs and opportunities. It would achieve enormous economies of scale relative to current arrangements and thereby remove the intense localism (the "politics of smallness") that often impedes effective governance in Indigenous communities. Most importantly, its finances would be substantially independent from federal or provincial control. The Commonwealth, like all other constitutionally guaranteed governments, would possess a secure source of financing tied to Canada's general prosperity and not to Ottawa's whims.

# 12

# aboriginal self-government

FEW CLOSE OBSERVERS of Aboriginal affairs in Canada doubt the importance of self-government. Most also understand that the attainment of self-government is a process, not a single event, and also understand there will be bumps along the road. Self-government, fundamentally, is about building political community. It involves managing duties and responsibilities as well as acquiring, through government transfers, local taxes, and other revenue streams, the resources to pay for those services. Most importantly, self-government is a strong reality across the country. There have been difficulties and even spectacular failures: the Kashechewan water fiasco of 2006 was largely a consequence of the band's poor management of its own water supply, and the hugely expensive relocation of Davis Inlet revealed fundamental weaknesses in band administration and accountability. That said, most Aboriginal communities in Canada manage their affairs with integrity, public accountability, and a sincere commitment to the best interests of their members.

It is important that the Canadian government and the provinces and territories maintain their commitment to measured, timely, and carefully managed Aboriginal self-government. Although there are some communities whose reach exceeds their capacity to grasp their duties, most Aboriginal governments are strongly aware of their limitations in terms of trained personnel, the capacity to handle additional tasks with existing resources, and management challenges. The transition to self-government will be uneven – the Mohawk and the Nisga'a will move much more quickly than most Aboriginal groups – and quite slow over-all. Skills learned in the first areas selected for devolution – especially education, health, and economic development – will help communities cope with more challenging duties later on, especially policing, social services, and child welfare. The process will not be in one direction. Some communities will accept certain governmental responsibilities and, finding them beyond their capacity at the present time, will pass them back to the federal, provincial, or territorial authorities.

Aboriginal self-government is a reality in Canada and will only expand in the coming years. The degree to which other levels of government assist with the process will be crucial to any successful transition. There are many examples across the country of positive and constructive working relationships. Municipalities, the often forgotten level of government in the Aboriginal governance puzzle, have been especially important in forging strong partnerships that serve all residents well. Some critics of self-government still worry about the constitutional and political ramifications of empowering Aboriginal groups, but each passing year renders their concerns less compelling. Some Aboriginal activists demand full sovereign powers and complete autonomy, which is simply not going to happen. Far from the glare of publicity, however, Aboriginal communities and other governments are working quietly, carefully, and constructively on the development of Indigenous governance capacity and on the transfer of specific government responsibilities and resources to Aboriginal authorities. The City of Powell River and the Tla'amin First Nation have developed strong inter-government relations. The process to date has been a significant success, although marred by some serious failures in some communities. The prospects for continued expansion and improvement remain high.

## A THIRD ORDER OF GOVERNMENT

Accommodating Aboriginal rights within shared political institutions is not simply possible, it is desirable. One of the boldest and most creative ideas being floated is to establish Aboriginal self-government as a third order of government. It is no surprise that not all Canadians accept this notion.

It would help to start with a shared understanding of the concept.

It is useful to think of self-government in the context of modern federal and unitary states. Before the French Revolution, states were weaker than they are now. They were not highly centralized, nor were they staffed by a professional bureaucracy recruited according to merit. Moreover, the populations of these early states were divided by status – peasants were subjects, not citizens. Traditional authority was vested in the monarch, who in France was the embodiment of the state. Born in the aftermath of the French Revolution, the unitary state became the most powerful, centralized form of political organization in the history of human societies. The modern state does not just claim sovereignty; it *exercises* it. Ninety percent of the world's contemporary states are unitary.

The federal state evolved as a more decentralized structure. The distinction hinges on sovereignty. Canada is one of a minority of countries that divide sovereignty between a central government and regional (sometimes even local) governments. *Sovereignty* can be defined as the authority that overrides all other authorities. *Authority* can be defined as the right to command. A *right* is an entitlement to do or refrain from doing something, which others have an obligation to respect. From this perspective, sovereignty is a bundle of rights rather than a lofty, abstract concept. A useful metaphor is to view each right of command as a tree branch. A number of branches can be tied into a distinct bundle. Another bunch of branches can be tied into another bundle. The two bundles can then be tied together. From a distance, the bundle looks like a single whole, but when the outer string is untied, it become apparent there are actually two bundles. That is the nature of sovereignty in a federal state. Citizens of federal states have a tangible sense of how sovereignty, as the right of command, is divided between the central government and regional governments. Albertans know that control over natural resources falls within provincial jurisdiction. Canadians are aware, through the constant bickering over health care funding, of the distinction between federal taxation powers and the provinces' financial obligations to provide health services. Most Canadians are unaware of the theoretical labels attached to such things, but they intuitively understand the concept and practice of divided sovereignty.

In federal states, because sovereignty is divided between two or more orders of government, decision-making authority has to be clearly articulated. Federal states, by necessity, have written constitutions that divide sovereignty and clarify the respective areas of jurisdiction of each order of government. In Canada, the manner in which sovereignty would be divided between Ottawa and the provinces was first outlined in Sections 91 and 92 of the British North American Act, 1867. The United States failed to spell out governmental responsibilities quite as clearly in the first instance. That country moved fairly quickly to bring in a series of amendments to clarify key governmental powers. The American Civil War was fought, not over slavery as is commonly believed but rather over a long-standing disagreement about the rights of the states and the rights of the national government.

Federal states are premised on concepts that require definition. The first is *concurrent law-making*, which relates to whether one level of government can make laws affecting the other's area of jurisdiction. If there is a conflict between the central and regional government in this regard, the constitution typically specifies whose law prevails. This is called *paramountcy*. A final, albeit crucial, feature of federal states relates to *constitutional protection* of each order of government. Basically, neither order of government can unilaterally dissolve the other. Thus, Canada's federal government cannot unilaterally dissolve a province or provinces, nor can a province or provinces unilaterally dissolve the federal government. There is, of course, a perennial debate as to whether a province can unilaterally secede from Canada, an issue addressed by the Chrétien government in the Clarity Act of 2000.

In Canada, as in most federal states, the federal and provincial governments are not the only governments. Local governments play an important role in the nation. They are the creations of the provincial governments. Local governments exist only when provincial governments pass laws to create them. The powers that local governments possess, however broadly or narrowly defined, are determined by each province. Constitutionally, the Saskatchewan government could make a postal clerk from La Ronge the sole administrator of the City of Regina. In practice, of course, this is unlikely to happen, though many in the North would take some delight in such an event. Local governments have no constitutional standing, nor do they have constitutionally defined areas of jurisdiction. They have authority, but it is delegated from the province. This is the *delegated* (municipal) model of self-government.

This does not mean that local government is unimportant or ineffective. Local governments provide vital services to citizens. They are catalysts of economic growth, and most importantly, they build community. But the fact that local governments have no share of sovereignty and constitutional protection makes them fundamentally different from provinces in Canada. (This model is not universal. Germany and Russia recognize local government in their respective constitutions.)

A third order of government exists if it satisfies at least two conditions. First, it must be constitutionally protected. This means that no other order of government, federal or provincial, can unilaterally dissolve it. Second, it must have specific areas of jurisdiction over which it exercises ultimate, though not necessarily exclusive, decision-making authority. In other words, it must have *paramountcy* in some jurisdictional areas. Canada already has third-order governments, arising from lengthy land claim and treaty negotiations. The Nisga'a Final Agreement is one of them.

In the late 1990s, the Nisga'a agreement was the subject of passionate debate. This is understandable, for it marked a fundamental change in Aboriginal–state relations in Canada. The treaty granted a strong measure of Aboriginal self-government. It also established the constitutional authority of the Nisga'a government (which was used in 2013 to establish the right to create private landholdings). The Nisga'a agreement was not the first self-government agreement. More than a decade earlier, the Sechelt Indian Band came out from underneath the Indian Act through the Sechelt Indian Band Self-Government Act. The Alberta–Métis Settlement Accord (1989), negotiated in the only province that has a specific Métis land base, was followed by self-government in 1990, based in provincial legislation. In both cases, however, self-government was delegated by legislation and was not constitutionally protected. Neither can be characterized as a third order of government.

Given that the Nisga'a agreement ushered in a new era of Canadian politics by directly recognizing a First Nation as a third order of government, it is hardly surprising that it generated strong reaction. Some observers likened the agreement to a constitutional amendment and demanded a referendum. Other critics said it would lead to a nation of mini-states, with Ottawa and the provinces powerless to control Aboriginal "nations." On the other extreme, advocates of greater empowerment for First Nations declared the treaty meaningless, for it fell far short of recognizing the full and inherent sovereignty of Aboriginal peoples. The same debate made it clear that despite the strong opinions and vociferous arguments, few people had actually read the treaty or understood its highly technical language. A review of some of the key articles in the agreement illustrates the degree to which the Nisga'a Final Agreement represented a radical departure from Canadian practice.

One requirement of a third order of government is that it be constitutionally protected. Paragraph 2.1 of the agreement states: "This Agreement is a treaty and a land claims agreement within the meaning of sections 25 and 35 of the *Constitution Act, 1982.*" The following paragraph then states: "This Agreement is binding on the parties." In other words, the agreement's provisions are explicitly recognized as constitutionally protected Aboriginal and treaty rights. None of the parties can unilaterally amend the agreement. One of the rights stated in the treaty is the right to self-government. Paragraph 11.1 states: "The Nisga'a Nation has the right to self-government, and the authority to make laws, as set out in this Agreement." In other words, the right of the Nisga'a to self-government is now constitutionally protected.

The second requirement of a third order of government is that there be areas of law-making authority over which that government has the ultimate (though not necessarily exclusive) right of command. The Nisga'a agreement establishes a concurrent law-making model. The Nisga'a Lisims government has no areas of exclusive jurisdiction. All areas in which the Nisga'a can make laws are areas in which the federal and provincial governments will continue to make laws of general application. In this regard, the Constitution has not changed. Even so, the scope of law-making authority held by the Nisga'a Lisims government is quite broad. For example, according to Paragraph 11.75, the "Nisga'a Lisims Government may make laws in respect of solemnization of marriages within British Columbia, including prescribing conditions under which individuals appointed by Nisga'a Lisims Government may solemnize marriages." This is an area of provincial jurisdiction identified in Section 92 of the Constitution. However, Paragraph 11.76 states that "In the event of a conflict between Nisga'a law under paragraph 75 and a federal or provincial law of general application, the federal or provincial law prevails to the extent of the conflict." Here, the Nisga'a do not have paramountcy. There are many provisions like this in the agreement, covering such topics as environmental assessment and protection, social services, health services, public order, traffic and transportation, fish and wildlife sales, and the regulation of intoxicants. It is also important to note that in some areas, the Nisga'a have no lawmaking authority. These include national defence and security, international treaty making, immigration, and international trade.

But the Nisga'a do have paramountcy in a number of other areas. One of the most important involves Nisga'a citizenship or political rights, including the right to vote in Nisga'a elections and the right to run for office. Paragraph 11.39 of the agreement states: "Nisga'a Lisims Government may make laws in respect of Nisga'a citizenship"; moreover, "[i]n the event of an inconsistency or conflict between a Nisga'a law under paragraph 39 and a federal or provincial law, the Nisga'a law prevails to the extent of the inconsistency or conflict." In other words, the Nisga'a have primary jurisdiction in determining who may or may not be members of the Nisga'a political community. The number of areas in which the Nisga'a have paramountcy is limited: they include areas that are principally internal to the Nisga'a, such as language and culture, lands and assets, and administration. Nevertheless, the Nisga'a agreement has established the only third-order government in Canada that can overrule federal or provincial law in certain areas.

Establishing Nisga'a *paramountcy* in selected areas does not mean that the Nisga'a have no obligations to other levels of government. Education, another area of provincial jurisdiction, is a prominent example. The agreement states:

> Nisga'a Lisims Government may make laws in respect of preschool to grade 12 education on Nisga'a Lands of Nisga'a citizens, including the teaching of Nisga'a language and culture, provided that those laws include provisions for:

a. curriculum, examination, and other standards that permit transfers of students between school systems at a similar level of achievement and permit admission of students to the provincial postsecondary education systems;

b. certification of teachers, other than for the teaching of Nisga'a language and culture, by:

i. a Nisga'a Institution, in accordance with standards comparable to standards applicable to individuals who teach in public or independent schools in British Columbia, or

ii. a provincial body having the responsibility to certify individuals who teach in public or independent schools in British Columbia: . . . (Para. 11.100) In the event of an inconsistency or conflict between Nisga'a law under paragraph 100 and a federal or provincial law, the Nisga'a law prevails to the extent of the inconsistency or conflict. (Para. 11.101)

So although the Nisga'a have paramountcy in this area, they must still meet or exceed provincial standards.

Clearly, the Nisga'a agreement represents a sharp departure from past self-government agreements. It *does* constitute a third order of government. But this is nothing more than an extension of Canadian political practice.

### STRENGTHENING CANADIAN DEMOCRACY

Little attention has been given to how Aboriginal self-government might strengthen, not diminish, Canadian democracy. In the 1830s, the French political philosopher Alexis de Tocqueville observed in his travels across America how essential local government was to democracy, liberty, and citizenship. In fact, he argued, "municipal institutions constitute the strength of free nations." First Nations are political communities in their own right, and this distinguishes them sharply from municipalities. However, First Nations typically are local communities and are similar in that sense to the New England townships Tocqueville observed long ago.

Central to Tocqueville's argument is that citizens will engage in political life if local political communities have both autonomy and authority. He observed that in America, municipal bodies were kept alive and supported by town spirit. For him, a township in New England possessed two advantages that strongly excite the interest of citizens: independence and authority. Its sphere was limited, but within that sphere actions were unrestrained. This independence gave it a real importance.

Tocqueville argued that the small scale of local government is what makes it accessible and encourages civic participation. Without strong and meaningful participation in the democratic process, he asked, how can we seriously expect a healthy democracy? Town meetings are to liberty what primary schools are to science. They bring it within the people's reach; they teach people how to use and enjoy it. A nation can establish a free government, but without municipal institutions, it cannot have what Tocqueville referred to as the "spirit of liberty."

Tocqueville made another important observation: being born into a community does not guarantee a commitment to ensuring a healthy polity. Local autonomy and authority are necessary for a healthy community, but in themselves they are not enough.

He wrote that a New Englander was attached to his township not so much because he was born in it, but because it was a free and strong community of which he was a member and that deserved the care spent managing it. In Europe, those who were in power often regretted the absence of local public spirit. Everyone agreed there was no surer guarantee of order and tranquility, yet nothing was more difficult to create. It was feared that if municipal bodies were made powerful and independent, they would become too strong and anarchy might break out.

Healthy democracies require engaged citizens, not passive subjects. In this vein, many reasons have been advanced for explaining Canadians' growing indifference to politics. Few have suggested weak municipal governments as an important explanation. The past two decades have seen substantial cuts in transfers to municipalities, which are struggling to provide the basic services that citizens expect. In its 2002 policy statement on the future role of municipal government, the Federation of Canadian Municipalities described the problem this way: "Municipal government is the bedrock on which Canadian democracy rests . . . Despite citizens' expectations that municipal institutions should act as though they constitute an order of government, the Canadian constitution does not recognize them as such. As a consequence, municipal governments do not have the autonomy required to exercise adequate powers or command adequate resources to meet local needs or expectations." With this in mind, some contend that local governments require constitutional protection.

We should not be surprised that where municipalities – "schools of democracy" – are weak, citizen trust and engagement are low. Building political community is unceasing toil. It requires long-term planning and huge investments of human resources. It is difficult to imagine long-term commitment to building political community without a reasonable degree of predictability that the institutions that will be built have a reasonable chance to endure. When a provincial or federal government has the authority to dismantle the powers of an Aboriginal government, that predictability is damaged, if not lost.

For many, the dismantling of an Aboriginal government may seem highly unlikely, so constitutional protection is unnecessary. Most political scientists have long shared that view. In a textbook written in the early 1990s, the authors observed that "the government of Ontario has the power, that is the legal authority, to abolish the government of the City of Hamilton, but obviously it does not have the positional power to do so. If it tried, it would fail." Experience shows how much circumstances can change. The provincial government forced amalgamation on the communities surrounding Toronto, creating the mega-city of Toronto, exercising its constitutional power even in the face of loud and well-organized community opposition. In Quebec, the provincial government did the same to Montreal. Given these examples, one can understand why some Aboriginal people are not interested in delegated self-government. If Canadians care about local self-government, then it is in everyone's interest to accommodate Aboriginal people's demands for it.

## CULTURE AND GOVERNANCE

A fundamental problem with Aboriginal administration has long been the imposition of standard, Western governance systems on communities with long histories of managing their own affairs. Band governments – initially dominated by Indian Agents, later elected "first past the post" – deviated dramatically from traditional leadership structures based on clans, elders, and hereditary chiefs, as well as on women, who often had powerful and clearly defined roles. The Department of Indian Affairs' structure lent itself to abuses, such as the manipulation of local elections; and in many smaller communities, one strong extended family could assert control over the entire population. But the greatest problem with the system was that it did not respect local traditions and Indigenous values. This generated tension between traditional leaders and cultural norms and the new, democratic means of governance.

There is no single transferable model for Aboriginal governance in Canada. What works for the Mohawk will not work for the Inuit. The house-based Gitxsan system is not the same as the preferred structures of the Plains Cree. In quite a few communities, British-style elections have become the norm, and there is little pressure to change this. Most of these communities, though, have developed prominent roles for elders and traditional chiefs. Some have used land claims settlements to entrench culturally specific Aboriginal governments; examples are the Nisga'a Lisims government and the clan-based system implemented by the Teslin First Nation in Yukon.

When it comes to local self-governance, there is bound to be strong variation between Aboriginal groups. Some very small communities will establish their own structures and essentially go it alone in terms of managing their affairs. More and more, though, will coordinate significant parts of their administrative and political work with regional bodies, such as tribal councils or regional settlement boards. The governance system adopted by an Aboriginal group will either sustain or weaken its cultural strength and vitality. Where governance structures reflect long-held community values and lines of authority, cultural traditions are enhanced. Communities that shift from systems that incorporate elders and internal cultural structures towards simple, Western-style democratic systems can find it harder to sustain and enhance their culture.

For many Aboriginal citizens, it is essential to incorporate the teachings of elders and to revitalize moribund governance structures, even when these are a poor fit with Western systems and controversial among community members – especially those living off reserve, who will worry about losing political power. Non-Aboriginal Canadians will find the diversity of Aboriginal governance systems bewildering, and few will take the time to understand the cultural roots and contemporary importance of these systems. It is likely, though, that stronger, more cohesive, and culturally richer communities will result when Aboriginal traditions of leadership and decision making are incorporated into governance.

## INTERNAL ACCOUNTABILITY

Critics of contemporary Aboriginal policy have focused on the need for greater accountability – by which they mean accountability to Ottawa and the Canadian citizenry at large. This level of accountability is undoubtedly important, but it must take a back seat to local accountability. The procedures in place today emphasize the relationship between Aboriginal Affairs – a distant, complex, and historically unpopular bureaucracy – and Aboriginal governments. Governments have consistently demanded greater accountability, both on specific files such as the First Nations University of Canada and more generally. Lines of responsibility, oversight, and financial review are fuzzy at best. Efforts by the Harper government to establish accountability measures hold considerable promise. The AFN's 2011 decision to pass a nonbinding resolution recommending that band governments disclose salaries and expense payments is an important though incomplete step in the right direction.

Communities themselves are beginning to demand greater accountability. In the country as a whole, political scandals typically arise from interventions by whistle-blowers, federal oversight agencies (particularly the Auditor General of Canada), or investigative journalists. On Aboriginal reserves and within Indigenous organizations, the vast majority of the revelations come from community members. Most Aboriginal governments do not at present have mechanisms for public review and oversight of spending. As a consequence, accusations of favouritism, nepotism, misspending, or corruption emerge in a relative information vacuum. Hotly contested items – a prized job in the band administration, a new house, an education grant – become matters for intense public debate and, often, anger. When questions are not answered, as often happens, members have little recourse but to go public with their complaints. In recent years, these battles have become increasingly acrimonious, in part because there are few resources to spread around and in part because the needs are often so pressing. Band offices are occupied, public protests are held, and, increasingly, band elections are bitterly contested amid accusations of bribery and threats of violence, with the struggles often continuing in the courts after the elections. All of this is compelling evidence of dysfunctional government.

. But Canadians should take these protests as signs of *strengthening* Aboriginal political communities. People are more aware than ever of Aboriginal governance issues, and expectations are rising. Elected officials are being held accountable in ways they were not twenty years ago, and voters are demanding clear and public explanations for major decisions. The results can be messy as communities adjust to changing political realities in the emotional pressure cooker of Aboriginal public affairs. Many communities and Aboriginal organizations have established stricter accountability measures and operate their affairs in a manner consistent with accepted accounting and political practices. The public rarely hears about these governments.

Aboriginal organizations will have to provide consistent, open, and transparent accounting to their communities. Non-Aboriginal observers, for their part, must learn to acknowledge the intensity of local governments. Aboriginal administrators face staggering demands on their time and resources, and the band governments are being held increasingly accountable for weak federal funding and questionable national policies. These increased requirements do not come with more resources. Few non-Aboriginal political jurisdictions in Canada are as tough on politicians as Aboriginal communities. So it is important that Canadians be reassured that public funds are being spent properly. But it is more important that Aboriginal people have a grasp of the plans and spending activities of their own governments.

## ACCOMMODATING OFF-RESERVE FIRST NATIONS

The 1999 *Corbiere* decision by the Supreme Court of Canada presented Aboriginal communities with a major challenge. For decades, Aboriginal governments had been reserve-based, providing the vast majority of their programs and services for members living on the reserve. Community after community argued that reserves were central to the survival of Aboriginal cultures, even though most were holdovers from post–Second World War government programs. Members who had left for towns and cities, sometimes hundreds of miles away, lacked (so it was said) connections to land, people, and community that were necessary to sustain a strong identity. So bands restricted access to services and the right to vote to people living on reserve. The *Corbiere* decision changed all of this dramatically by ordering First Nations to find ways to allow off-reserve members to vote.

Because there were so many bands that had a majority of members living off-reserve, most communities assumed that *Corbiere* would require them to extend services, programs, and expenditures to all members, wherever they lived. This, many band leaders assumed, would accelerate out-migration from reserve communities and cripple Aboriginal cultures across the country. Furthermore, critics of the decision fretted that the empowerment of off-reserve members would inject different priorities into band affairs – more short-term, less community-based, and more economically driven ones. Community elders argue that this is what happened in the case of the Tahltan in northwestern BC, whose leaders have taken a pro-development stance over the continued objections of some reserve residents. In the northern Ontario community of Attawapiskat, the 2013 band elections allowed people living off reserve to vote – but controversially, they had to do it in person, a major deterrent to members living in the south.

It is ironic that so many Aboriginal leaders are standing behind a much-hated piece of legislation – the Indian Act – that defines membership and that was used to establish the reserves that have so strongly shaped Indigenous life in most of Canada. *Corbiere* suggests that major changes are coming. Voting arrangements have generally been made, and programs are expanding slowly. A significant number of Aboriginal communities have already adjusted to the new realities of rural–urban migration. Many First Nations people from outlying communities in Yukon live in Whitehorse; indeed, it has become quite common for band chiefs to live in Whitehorse and visit their home reserves on a regular basis. The Nisga'a Lisims government has established political and administrative places for off-reserve Nisga'a in Terrace, Prince Rupert, and Vancouver, who together outnumber those actually living in the Nass Valley. In the Maritimes, many key Mi'kmaq leaders are based in Halifax or other major centres but continue to work on behalf of their traditional communities.

Aboriginal communities will face major adjustments as they adapt their programs and political systems to meet the needs of off-reserve members. As population dictates, communities will have to commit themselves to staffing and financing housing projects, support services, and other activities in distant towns and cities. Money spent off reserve will inevitably cut into resources available on reserve, potentially making the reserve less attractive again and encouraging more migration. Off-reserve Aboriginal people often marry outside their community, and even tend to marry non-Indigenous people, and this too will change the demographic composition of the population and weaken connections to the home community.

But the situation is not all negative. Off-reserve programming will help migrants adjust to town and city life while ensuring that individuals remain engaged with their government. Similarly, the political life of individual communities could be strengthened by the inclusion of off-reserve members, whose urban experiences may well broaden the scope of policy options. Although the possibility exists of sharp reserve–off-reserve splits, family and clan ties will moderate this danger. Moreover, once reserve-based governments come to terms with their obligations to off-reserve members, conditions for individuals living in towns and cities should improve significantly as they gain better access to training, education, and support programs.

Aboriginal governments would be well advised to respond constructively to the requirement that they expand services to off-reserve members. A tardy response will only heighten tensions and ensure that the reserve–off-reserve division plays out aggressively in band politics. Individual communities lack the human and financial resources to address all of their commitments in towns and cities, since their members are scattered among many urban centres. Given that reality, collaborative programs and services are the only way to serve the population properly. Tribal councils, other regional governments, or even the Commonwealth of Aboriginal Peoples (or a comparable group) could shoulder the responsibility for service delivery, working on a chargeback basis to the various Aboriginal communities they serve. The thought of coordinated, well-planned services and support programs for off-reserve First Nations is attractive, for it would acknowledge a present-day reality while encouraging collaboration among Indigenous groups.

## BRIDGING ABORIGINAL AND NON-ABORIGINAL COMMUNITIES

Ultimately, though, the most important political communities in Canada will be the ones that bridge cultural and ethnic boundaries. In Canada's big cities, business, political, and social organizations have reached across ethnic barriers to draw new Canadians into the social fabric. These somewhat preliminary efforts to engage new Canadians in national and provincial political life are a promising sign that this steadily increasing population is finding common cause with other Canadians. Comparable efforts have been made on the Aboriginal side. For decades, the federal Liberal Party has benefited from substantial Aboriginal support, albeit without devoting much effort to securing their backing. The Conservative, Liberal, and New Democratic Parties have all offered themselves as vehicles for inclusion and engagement with non-Aboriginal people. Although relations between communities and nearby reserves have become more positive, in most cases broad cultural divides continue to separate Indigenous people from other Canadians. From church groups to unions, from chambers of commerce to anti-poverty campaigns, the integration of Aboriginal people into broader, non-Aboriginal political communities is progressing more slowly than it should.

A challenge for all Canadians, Aboriginal *and* non-Aboriginal, is to recognize the importance of reaching out to one another. Separation does not protect cultures; in fact, it fosters misunderstanding, social distance, and political neglect. Respectful collaboration can go a long way towards ensuring that the concerns of Aboriginal peoples are heard, understood, and converted into community priorities. There are many positive examples of this process, ranging from Westbank to Whitehorse to Saskatoon and including the consensus-style government in Northwest Territories. In those places, and in more and more others, non-Aboriginal people and governments have recognized that their future rests on positive, constructive, and mutually beneficial arrangements with Aboriginal residents. These crosscultural communities typically start by focusing on high-profile issues such as economic development, skills training, local services and infrastructure, and crime and poverty.

But it is cultural and social ties that are ultimately crucial. In Westbank, housing developments on First Nations land have brought Aboriginal and other Canadians into close proximity. Physical distance creates misunderstanding; being neighbours helps undermine negative stereotypes. In Saskatoon, Aboriginal cultural venues – the Wanuskewin Heritage Park, a First Nations theatre company, festivities geared to the general public – are helping build permanent bridges. In Whitehorse, events such as the annual storytelling festival and the renaming of the Whitehorse campus of Yukon College as Ayamdigut ("she got up and went" in Tlingit) have elevated the profile and social status of Indigenous cultures throughout the territory.

Aboriginal people need to strengthen their own political communities but also work with non-Aboriginal people to do the same. The responsibility is a shared one. Aboriginal groups have generally been open when it comes to sharing their culture and social events with others. This needs to continue. Besides this, they need to invite social, political, cultural, athletic, and economic groups to engage with them. And non-Aboriginal people and community leaders need to step forward and make positive and constructive overtures to local and regional Aboriginal populations. This can be in formal ways, such as a request for Aboriginal representation on civic committees, organizations, task forces, or planning groups. It can also be less formal, through information sessions for union members, church groups, or service clubs. Sporting events that draw Aboriginal and non-Aboriginal teams and competitors together and cultural activities that showcase and celebrate all parts of the Canadian social fabric can also be enormously constructive.

A shortcoming of constitutional debates, legal challenges, and high-level politicking is that they divert us from a fundamental truth: reconciliation must be based on positive and constructive relations between individuals across Canada's cultural divides. The opposite is also true. The bitter standoff between Six Nations protesters and non-Aboriginal residents in Caledonia, Ontario, that started in the spring and summer of 2006 and was ongoing in 2012 created scars that will last for decades. The matter can be put more bluntly: water, sewage, and fire-fighting arrangements matter to more people than the technical details of a Supreme Court decision. Being involved in community-planning activities, celebrating Aboriginal culture alongside other cultural events, competing in athletic events, and collaborating on economic development matter more than the nuances of federal government policy or high-level political pronouncements. The bridges that can – and must – be built between Aboriginal and non-Aboriginal Canadians hold the key to this country's future, just as the bridges between Quebec and the rest of the country, and between new Canadians and others, are crucial to national prosperity, stability and identity. Canadians have, on the Aboriginal file, a long-standing tradition of leaving reconciliation to government officials; they can absolve themselves of responsibility no longer. Canadians can become treaty peoples, as many communities and regions in the country have demonstrated, when hands of friendship, collaboration, and mutual interest stretch across the cultural divide.

# 13

# community-based economic well-being

**FOR RECONCILIATION** to succeed, it must be based on equality of opportunity. The previous chapters addressed the steps required to achieve equality of opportunity in terms of status and respect and also in terms of political liberty, enabling Indigenous people to make decisions affecting their own lives and communities. These steps would be consistent with – indeed, they would enhance – Canadian values and principles and enrich Canadian federalism and democracy. But bridging the gap between Indigenous and non-Indigenous Canadians will also require close attention to economic relations. Stereotypes and national mythology notwithstanding, Aboriginal people and communities are anxious – sometimes desperate – for economic opportunity.

Everyone wants to end the culture of welfare dependency, wherever it is found. This problem has been as intractable for Aboriginal people as for other Canadians in economically depressed parts of the country, if not more so. Canadians have historically viewed it as shameful to depend on government largesse, to be at the mercy of administrative rules and the requirement to "report in" to bureaucrats on a regular basis. This reflects the values of many Canadians. The basic concept – a largely ineffective one – is that welfare is supposed to tide people over between periods of paid employment, with the rates and conditions set so as to discourage individuals from remaining on government handouts.

Welfare systems do not suit Aboriginal people. Their historical relationship with Indian Agents turned welfare into a multigenerational reality (as it is in parts of eastern Canada, as well as in Britain and other countries). The policies and assumptions of a capitalist, colonial power have also carried little weight with Indigenous people, even as their own politicians argue that income supports are an Aboriginal entitlement. Finally and perhaps most importantly, many Aboriginal people live in economically remote communities where there are few jobs, except in the band office.

In these circumstances, there are limits to what can be accomplished. Aboriginal leaders generally agree, though, that community members need to take more responsibility. There have been plenty of efforts to create jobs through government subsidies and joint ventures, but those jobs tend to be low-skilled, temporary, and seasonal. The most motivated and most highly skilled individuals have many incentives to relocate to urban centres, where there are many more opportunities. Remote reserves cannot be written off, although more and more Aboriginal workers live off reserve and visit on a regular basis. Many send money and other resources back to their communities, much like recent immigrants to Canada. There is no perfect solution for communities that are essentially "uneconomical" in a capitalist sense. These villages, incidentally, tend to depend heavily on harvesting activities, which rarely count as financial ventures but which contribute both culturally and economically to the people.

Governments today are spending large sums on welfare and other support payments in remote communities, with all the Western ideological baggage that entails. There are alternatives. One is to eliminate welfare, with its "shame" foundations, and replace it with community-based responsibility. At present, funding is fragmented into a variety of programs and dispersed to individuals. That funding could instead be allocated, as block grants, to regional or local Aboriginal governments. It could then be earmarked for community building (part of what Stephen Cornell of the University of Arizona calls a nation-building strategy). People without paid employment independent of the local government would be eligible for modestly paid jobs aimed at building the community's economic and social infrastructure, with their wages set so as to ensure that other regional jobs remain attractive. These jobs could include repairing roads, clearing brush, and helping with community development projects. They could also include cutting wood for elders, gathering country food, collecting elders' stories, working as cultural resource people in schools, taking lessons from elders in traditional cultural or harvesting practices, and providing cultural or social services to the community. In non-Aboriginal towns and cities across Canada, millions of dollars are invested in exactly the same kinds of jobs – building and repairing roads, providing elder care, maintaining parks and other city properties, and so on. These services, paid for by tax dollars, provide vital services and promote civic pride. Why should it be any different in Aboriginal communities?

In this way, Aboriginal governments could foster healthy, sustainable communities. The communities themselves would gain a valuable workforce. And if the usual assumptions about productive work hold true, individuals would develop greater confidence, a stronger sense of responsibility, and marketable skills. In this regard, the definition of "marketable" would need to be broadened to include work of particular value to Aboriginal people. In many remote communities, a program like this might continue for many years as the primary source of employment, given that many settlements are unlikely to attract regular, salaried employment. But when mining, logging, exploration, construction, and tourism enterprises come to these areas, they would find well-served and well-kept communities whose members have a strong work ethic, a sense of social responsibility, and increased connectedness to their culture and society. Also, if meaningful employment were available in Aboriginal communities, Aboriginal elected officials would face less pressure to allocate jobs on the basis of personal relationships rather than merit.

Australia long ago implemented a scheme like this, the Community Development Employment Projects (CDEP). Since 1977, this voluntary program has provided individuals and communities with alternatives to "the dole." By 2006, more than 32,000 Aborigines had participated in the program – almost one quarter of all Indigenous workers in the country. The program works through community organizations, emphasizes local control and decision making, and focuses on community economic enhancement. It covers a wide range of work, from artistic and traditional activities to housing repair and road construction. CDEP supports traditional cultural activities while placing emphasis on preparing Aborigines for work away from their communities and in the mainstream economy. Critics have labelled it "work for welfare." The program was revamped in 2009, so that CDEP continues in remote regions, with Aborigines in areas with "established" economies directed towards national employment services.

Critics of Aboriginal policies in Canada tend to focus their vitriol on the continued existence of remote and isolated reserves. The debacle over the water supply at Kashechewan, Ontario, in 2005, which ended up costing many millions of dollars, generated a nationwide debate about the logic of preserving these communities. Analysts suggested that reserves such as Kashechewan were economic wastelands requiring endless government support. In the past, some non-Aboriginal communities have been sacrificed on the altar of economic transition: Joey Smallwood closed many Newfoundland outports, and the Romanow government in Saskatchewan made the tough decision to withdraw government services from dozens of small Saskatchewan towns. Aboriginal leaders react with anger to such suggestions, which have surfaced regularly for many decades. There is a widespread belief that economic efficiency should govern the placement of Indigenous communities. This argument is reinforced by the continued migration of Aboriginal people, especially women and children, from remote communities to towns and cities. More than half of all Status Indians now live off reserve, and Aboriginal urban populations continue to grow. Most Nisga'a – one of the strongest and best-organized Aboriginal groups in the country – live outside their isolated Nass River homeland in northern BC. The numbers of Aboriginal people in Toronto, Edmonton, Winnipeg, Saskatoon, Regina, and Vancouver continue to climb.

Isolated reserves will not disappear quickly, and certainly not because critics want them to. Attachment to place is extremely strong in Aboriginal society. Even people who have moved away retain a strong attachment to their traditional homelands. Nor, it must be added, are the remote villages necessarily economic basket cases. There are plenty of ways these reserve settlements could provide jobs and strengthen their economies. Few reserves will become industrial powerhouses unless a mine, pipeline, or other resource development starts nearby.

The same could be said of many non-Aboriginal parts of Canada, including much of rural Atlantic Canada, rural Quebec and Ontario, some of the agricultural districts on the Prairies, small towns in the BC Interior, and non-Aboriginal settlements in northern Canada, all of which struggle economically. Put differently, the economic challenges facing Aboriginal communities are almost the same as those in these places. But they are also different, in the ways we discuss below.

Culture is one of the fastest-growing sectors of the Aboriginal economy. Inuit art (printmaking and carving) is only the best-known element in a broad network of Aboriginal artistic commercial ventures that are producing healthy revenues for artists and their communities. Indigenous tourism has expanded; Aboriginal people are providing guided tours, cultural experiences, and access to Aboriginal spiritual and world views for a growing market in North America and farther afield. West Coast carvings and related artworks are a multimillion-dollar industry. Indigenous writers, many based in smaller communities, are finding audiences for their work, as are Indigenous singers and filmmakers. The federal and provincial governments could do much to promote Aboriginal cultural endeavours and would likely find considerable international interest in them. For their part, Aboriginal governments will have to realize – as many already do – that participation in the commercial economy requires close attention to quality, service, timeliness, and so on. The private sector is quite unforgiving of those who forget this.

As we noted earlier, reforms to transfer payments and the welfare system could quickly create a different cast to Aboriginal employment. Beyond this, the repatriation of administrative responsibilities to bands and tribal councils is generating stable and well-paying jobs, and so is the recruitment of Aboriginal (often local) teachers, police officers, doctors and nurses, and other employees who until recently were always drawn from the non-Aboriginal workforce. Carefully managed reserve-based job creation can stimulate commercial activities by providing training and experience and by raising the overall level of professionalism in the community. Commentators have often criticized government-based employment on Aboriginal reserves, failing to recognize that most Aboriginal governments are taking on responsibilities that in other jurisdictions would be handled by village, municipal, provincial, or federal governments, as well as health authorities, school boards, and related agencies. It is just that Aboriginal governments aggregate the work into one organization, whereas in other communities there are typically several different employers. Care will have to be taken to guard against nepotism and patronage – a difficult challenge in what are often tiny communities – and to ensure that incoming employees have the training and experience to succeed in their posts. A promising development in recent years has been the establishment of the National Centre for First Nations Governance, an organization committed to training and professionalizing the employees of Aboriginal organizations. However, this centre has lost most of its federal funding in recent years and has had to scale back.

Aboriginal communities are different from others. Communal imperatives run strong. In many First Nations and Inuit communities, individual prosperity is routinely subordinated to the best interests of the group. The Inuit are enthusiastic about cooperatives, which were introduced after the Second World War and are still prominent in the northern economy. Programs that emphasize community economic well-being instead of individual prosperity are highly valued in these villages and towns. Many of the initiatives arising from land claims, joint ventures, and resource development emphasize the economic well-being of the whole community rather than opportunities for the few. Much of this well-being will develop organically, out of land claims settlements, and meanwhile government programs should shift their emphasis from individual entrepreneurship to increased support for broadly based commercial ventures.

The standard Western metrics of community success include employment rates and income levels. Things like these make little sense in Aboriginal settlements, where there is growing support for using wellness and happiness indexes instead. This approach, which reflects a much broader assessment of achievement, has been referred to as social prosperity. Its assessment tools allow communities to define the appropriate measures for themselves instead of having a rigid financial model imposed on them. A possible social prosperity evaluation system for Aboriginal peoples would likely incorporate cultural characteristics (such as language retention), country food production, community health, reductions in violence and substance abuse, redistribution of resources within the community, and other measures that are more appropriate than simple income and employment statistics. Some communities that currently show up as being in serious difficulty might already be meeting local and cultural objectives quite well. Old Crow, in Yukon, is one example; another is La Ronge, in Saskatchewan. The ultimate goal of political, economic, and social systems, after all, is to deliver what the people want and need, not to meet some artificial and quantitative standard set by and monitored from Ottawa.

One axiom of economic development is that investment in education produces the most lasting and significant returns. So it is with Aboriginal Canadians, as the evidence of the past three decades demonstrates. For northern and remote communities, the challenges are different. To capitalize on educational opportunities, most students have had to relocate to southern cities, and this has drained many talented people from isolated settlements. New developments promise to change this pattern. Brandon University's Northern Teacher Education Program provided face-to-face instruction in northern communities for decades. Many variants of that program are now available, ranging from the NORTEP initiative in northern Saskatchewan to the international University of the Arctic Bachelor of Circumpolar Studies program. Colleges in the territorial North and across the northern provinces are expanding face-to-face, Internet, and television-based opportunities for reserve residents. The legacy of residential schools and unhappy experiences in provincial and territorial classrooms have left deep scars among Aboriginal people across the country. Educational improvements have come slowly, but opportunities for continued development in this field remain very promising.

The federal and provincial governments should emphasize distance-delivered education and training programs, focusing initially on adult basic education so that adults can catch up, then going on to provide certificate, diploma, and degree programs. There should be much more effort on practical, work-related training, in keeping with the needs of industry and tied to local economic realities, but with the expectation of a shift towards degree opportunities as capacity and training levels improve. Few of the jobs currently on offer in the North require a university degree. The vast majority require technical or entrepreneurial skills, and the emphasis should be on these. A promising development has been the emergence of master's programs, often available to bright and talented adults whose life experiences make up for less formal education. These career-related and practical programs have been highly effective in responding to the needs of the emerging North.

Country food production contributes significantly to Aboriginal economies in Canada's northern and remote regions. Aboriginal hunters, fishers, and gatherers remain highly valued in their communities, even though the number of people who draw their living from the land has dropped precipitously in the past few decades. It would be useful to support hunters to remain on the land, in terms of providing healthy food supplies and helping communities maintain their connections to the land and its wildlife. Given the often extremely high cost of replacement foods in these communities, there is considerable economic merit in working with the hunters, fishers, and gatherers to ensure they remain in the field and that young people are recruited into these time-honoured pursuits. A comparable model evolved in Curitiba, Brazil, where civic leaders, fearing a mass migration from the countryside into the city (as had happened in São Paulo and Rio de Janeiro), paid small rural farmers slightly above market rates for their produce, thus encouraging them to stay on the land. The food was used to feed the homeless in Curitiba, and this helped the city achieve a balance with the countryside. In a world where high agricultural subsidies by advanced nations have distorted national and international markets for farm produce and where exceptionally generous employment insurance arrangements keep Maritime fisheries workers in their communities, the concept of subsidizing country food production is hardly a radical step. In fact, it would be a double-standard to treat Aboriginal communities differently. Furthermore, the financial crisis in Aboriginal harvesting has come about largely as a result of international campaigns against the sealing and fur industries, which have harmed many personal hunting and trapping operations. Support for country food production could come in the form of subsidies for actual harvests or guaranteed annual incomes for hunters, fishers, and trappers. If this support is delivered through an Aboriginal government, there should be clear expectations about sharing the harvests with community members.

Canada has critical national problems related to Arctic sovereignty and surveillance. Canadians know surprisingly little about their northern and remote regions – except for Aboriginal residents, who know a great deal. By extending the model of the Canadian Rangers – volunteers who help the Canadian Armed Forces defend the country and who are well-known for their work in the Arctic – Ottawa could develop a cadre of skilled observers, who would collect data for a variety of government and academic research purposes. This work would be occasional and part-time, but it could be combined with other seasonal and harvesting activities to produce a viable and sustainable level of activity for northern residents. This work would have the added benefit of capitalizing on Aboriginal skills and knowledge and thereby recognizing Indigenous people's understanding of their environment. Canada would gain priceless information about conditions in the Arctic and Subarctic. Many scientists and researchers currently employ Aboriginal technicians and research assistants, but these programs are haphazard, besides being unreliable as sources of income. In this era of growing debates about global warming and Arctic sovereignty, the development of a core of trained observers would provide the country with a unique means of monitoring a variety of natural phenomena in the vast Arctic and Subarctic regions.

◇◇◇◇◇◇◇◇◇◇◇◇◇◇

Critics of Aboriginal policies emphasize the reality of poor economic prospects in remote and northern communities and the equally serious challenges facing most urban Aboriginals. Cities offer more employment opportunities, but urban Aboriginals often lack the education, skills, and means to take advantage of them. Some – particularly those with postsecondary education – do well in urban settings. However, both urban and rural Aboriginal people face daunting personal and community-wide problems, including systemic racism. The nation needs to develop economic strategies that produce decent results in both remote and northern communities and in cities and towns.

There are reasons for optimism. Now that they have substantial assets from comprehensive and specific claims settlements, agreements with resource companies, and returns from Aboriginal economic development corporations, Aboriginal communities are increasingly taking the initiative to create income, jobs, and economic opportunities. Aboriginal communities located close to major cities (Squamish First Nation, for instance) or resource projects (like Fort McKay First Nation) have impressive opportunities to exploit close at hand. Remote communities, by contrast, must make investments outside of their traditional territories to produce a profitable return and create the cash needed for community initiatives.

Inuvialuit's investments in southern cities are an example of this new wave of economic development. Similarly, the Muskeg First Nation in Saskatoon has selected some of the land owed to them through the Treaty Land Entitlement Process in the form of an urban reserve, on which more than a dozen Aboriginal businesses have generated more than three hundred jobs for Aboriginal people. Urban reserves have become increasingly popular, especially on the Prairies, and should be encouraged. Whether the land is purchased or received through a land claims settlement or some other process, these reserves provide vital opportunities for Aboriginal communities. Rental and commercial activities can provide a steady flow of cash to Aboriginal governments. Whatever the fear mongering that accompanied their development, urban reserves have benefited Aboriginal people and their surrounding communities.

But the cornerstone of Aboriginal economic development has to be the upgrading of education and job skills, and there is no excuse to delay this. National and regional initiatives will be required to address the education gap, especially in adult literacy and skills training, to ensure that Aboriginal people will have access to the full range of trades, careers, and professional and academic programs. There is a false understanding in Canada regarding the level of financial and institutional support currently available for Aboriginal students. It is overestimated, when in fact, that funding leaves many eager students without the assistance they require. This is especially true for single mothers – one of the largest groups of Aboriginal students – who often struggle to support themselves on the limited funding available through their bands. Many such initiatives are under way, although often with little coordination and insufficient attention to best practices. Prioritizing literacy and skills training would involve a significant overhaul of current educational initiatives.

The model proposed for remote communities – hiring local residents for community enhancement and culturally relevant tasks instead of simply providing income assistance – could be applied in urban centres as well. Many community-based tasks, from improving the physical environment to offering cultural training and sharing knowledge, could be converted into positive work experiences.

The greatest problem in urban settings relates to the social and cultural challenges facing the Aboriginal population. Non-Aboriginal people typically see urban Indigenous residents as a largely undifferentiated population when in fact they are drawn from dozens if not hundreds of communities representing many different language and cultural groups. Tensions within urban Aboriginal societies – between Métis and First Nations on the Prairies, for example – often interfere with collaborative community building. Community enhancement initiatives would have to be sensitive to cultural differences and realities and would have to be undertaken with a view to supporting individual cultural groups and facilitating cooperation between them.

In several Canadian cities – Winnipeg, Regina, Saskatoon, and Edmonton being the best examples – Indigenous people are a large and highly visible part of the population. To date, urban Aboriginals have been viewed as a serious social problem rather than as an integral part of the community. When steps have been taken to develop a positive and proactive approach to Indigenous residents – Saskatoon is the leading example, though Edmonton is making strides as well – Aboriginal people are viewed instead as a vital and growing part of the workforce and as critical to future prosperity.

Especially in Saskatchewan, the business community understands that the long-term viability of their enterprises rests on their ability to mobilize Aboriginal people as both workers and consumers. A positive attitude towards Aboriginal people and their cultures can go a long way to encourage their greater engagement and economic integration. Much has been done in the cultural and political spheres to recognize the Aboriginal presence in Canadian cities; there has been less engagement by business. Chambers of commerce or their counterparts could play a significant role in encouraging companies to hire and train Aboriginal workers, respond to Aboriginal markets, and celebrate successful collaborations with Indigenous employees, groups, and communities. So far, municipal governments have devoted most of their well-meaning efforts to the social pathology of urban Indigenous populations. It is time to shift the emphasis towards creating equality of opportunity in the broader economy, through employment, business development, and the serving of Aboriginal markets, and, more generally, through embracing Aboriginal consumers and workers.

Canada's towns and cities are home to surprisingly large numbers of successful Aboriginal businesses and employees. For a variety of reasons, including the sad but real possibility of a backlash against Aboriginal businesses, Indigenous business people and employees generally keep a low profile. It is time to reverse that and to provide a much higher profile for Aboriginal success stories. Indigenous leaders typically encounter strong pressure to handle a wide range of community responsibilities. At the risk of adding to an already sizable burden, it is time for business leaders and successful employees to allow themselves to be held up as role models for the youth in their communities. Aggressive and prominent role modelling could do much to provide Aboriginal people in towns and cities with greater optimism about the prospects of securing a place in the local economy. Lynco, a Saskatchewan-based firm founded on partnerships with Aboriginal governments and businesses, is developing such a model.

# 14

# finding common economic ground

INDIGENOUS LEADERS often speak out against the welfare culture that saturates their communities. Canada's first comprehensive land claim, tabled by the Yukon Native Brotherhood in 1973, included a prelude about the importance of breaking the pattern of welfare dependency. Phil Fontaine and Bill Wilson, candidates for the Assembly of First Nation's leadership in 2006, spoke of the need for much greater economic opportunity. Shawn Atleo, before he stepped down as the AFN's national chief, spoke eloquently about the need for jobs, Aboriginal businesses, and economic opportunity. Aboriginal entrepreneurship is growing rapidly. Land claims and resource settlements are providing new foundations for commercial engagement. Although new approaches and understandings will be required, especially for remote and Northern communities, let there be no question: Aboriginal Canadians attach a high priority to the creation of sustainable economic opportunity. Equally importantly, Indigenous communities tend not to see economic growth as an end in itself but rather as a tool for creating stronger families, healthier populations, and greater political autonomy. Aboriginal people, to put it succinctly, see economic development from a social-economy perspective; they see wealth and opportunity as cornerstones of cultural revival, stronger governance, and safer and healthier people.

Poverty as a cause or a consequence, or both, is at the core of many issues facing Aboriginal people in Canada. Many Canadians are appalled by the Third World conditions in too many Aboriginal communities and by the impact of long-term welfare dependency. Directly aware of the reality of Indigenous poverty, Aboriginal leaders are demanding greater national and provincial attention to the low wages, high unemployment, and much lower living standards experienced by most Aboriginal people. Although there are signs of improvement in some regions, the simple truth is that for certain parts of the year some Aboriginal people are not sufficiently connected to the Canadian economy. Finding a path from welfare dependency to self-sufficiency remains a formidable challenge for too many of them.

Canada's current system of economic support and encouragement for Indigenous peoples has many flaws, the most basic of which is that it does not work. In the broadest terms, Ottawa's economic support is quite generous. The federal government spends billions of dollars each year on a large number of support programs, ranging from welfare and the Old Age Security pension to job training and income assistance. But this support comes with a price – and a large bureaucracy. Aboriginal people who cannot support themselves financially and who rely on government payments spend a great deal of time navigating the bureaucracy, increasingly that of their own band or tribal council. They have to fill in forms, demonstrate that they are seeking employment, account for paid work, and otherwise justify ongoing income assistance. Any Aboriginal person who tries to start a new business is quickly drawn into the vortex of the economic development agencies, again having to complete applications, liaise with government development officers, and report on progress or difficulties on an ongoing basis.

Canadians generally view income assistance or business development grants as a last resort. In some parts of the country, especially the Maritimes and rural Quebec, long-term unemployment has fostered a dependency on the state quite similar to that of Aboriginal Canadians. Critics deride the Maritime culture of entitlement and complain that individuals and entire communities don't try hard enough to get off the welfare rolls. But no Canadian group faces as much sustained criticism for their reliance on government assistance as do Aboriginal Canadians. For many people, Aboriginal communities' dependence on welfare flies against the self-reliance and personal responsibility that are supposedly the bedrock of the Canadian economy. People are supposed to prepare themselves for the workforce, seek work, moving if they must, and hold on to their jobs, resorting to unemployment assistance or welfare only as a last resort.

All of this rests on ideological assumptions about individual responsibility and on the belief in a strong link between work and self-worth. Regular paid employment or ownership of a business is accorded the highest possible value; long-term unemployment or the refusal to look for work is equated with failure. Not surprisingly, governments' practices reflect these basic Canadian values and assumptions. Those practices, though, do not always fit comfortably with traditional Aboriginal values, which emphasize strong links to traditional territories and communal responsibilities, and which are based on less materialistic needs and more flexible approaches to work.

Canada should not change or abandon its assumptions about work, employment, and business development. Indeed, our success as a nation likely requires an even more aggressive and competitive approach to business and economic development than the country has taken to date. Aboriginal people and communities acknowledge that decades of welfare dependency have not served the population well. Many thousands of Aboriginal people have sought a permanent place in the wage economy or have established their own businesses. Many Aboriginal communities have started cooperatives, joint ventures, or community-owned businesses. Aboriginal engagement with the economy continues to strengthen at a sometimes impressive pace.

Creating economic common ground does not require rigid conformity in either direction. Non-Aboriginal Canadians should understand and respect Indigenous approaches to work, employment, and business development and ownership. They should seek ways (some outlined below) to strip the ideological intensity and inherent criticism from current approaches to income support and welfare. Aboriginal people, for their part, should recognize the increasing diversity in their own communities on this issue. Many people *want* steady employment or *want* to operate their own businesses. Much of the success of recent northern resource development, and much of the recent migration from remote reserves to cities, rests on this simple reality. Canada requires a new approach to including Aboriginal people and communities in the national and international economy, but no single model will work. Indigenous people's participation in the economy will require approaches that respect their traditional economic values, support their entry into the market economy, and encourage them and their companies to join the mainstream business environment.

At this point, it is important to be clear about one central element: the role of government investment in Aboriginal and Canadian development. In recent years, assumptions have developed about "limited government" and the primacy of the private sector. The rhetoric of economic liberalism is attractive in some quarters, but the reality is that government still matters a great deal in Canada's economy. The economic crisis of 2008–09 reminded people around the world that governments play a vital role in protecting and growing national economies. It is not just Aboriginal communities that depend heavily on government spending. In Yukon, for example, spending by Ottawa, Whitehorse, and municipal governments' accounts for more than two-thirds of the gross territorial product. As is well known, the Maritime provinces depend on equalization payments and other government transfers (including direct transfers to individuals, often in the form of EI payments). A closer look at federal and provincial spending in the Maritimes – including subsidies for private business through organizations such as the Atlantic Canada Opportunities Fund – makes it clear that many Maritimers draw their paycheques directly or indirectly from governments.

Heavy reliance on government spending is not unique to Aboriginal communities or the Maritime provinces. Which province has the highest per capita spending on government programs? It is not Newfoundland and Labrador or even Prince Edward Island. Alberta leads the pack. That province's supposedly right-of-centre Conservative government continues to eat through oil revenues at a ravenous pace. Alberta and BC have formidable private sector economies, but many private sector activities in both provinces are substantially, sometimes massively, subsidized by governments. Completely unsubsidized private sector operations are quite rare – including, let it be said, in the oil and gas industry, where a lot of exploration and development activity is underpinned by generous tax breaks. (BC's impressive – by volume and income generated – marijuana industry is one of the few sectors that operates without much government input.) So, recognize the impressive amount of public spending that fuels the economies of BC and Alberta, two of the fastest-growing provinces in the country. Add up the expenditures on health care, education (including universities), highway maintenance, public transit, social services and social welfare, pensions, and other government activities. Do not forget major investments in infrastructure. Consider only BC's situation, which was shaped by major spending on the 2010 Winter Olympics, including $600 million for the Sea to Sky Highway, hundreds of millions on rapid transit in Vancouver, and another billion, give or take, on the Asia-Pacific Gateway and Corridor Initiative and hundreds of other large government projects. It is difficult to identify the percentage of economic activity in BC and Alberta attributable directly or indirectly to government spending, but it would likely exceed one third of the total economic activity in Canada's most free-enterprise provinces.

The point here is not to criticize Alberta, BC, or any province or territory or to suggest that they have become dependent on government spending. Rather, it is to highlight a simple truth: the Canadian economy is strongly influenced by government spending. To a degree we rarely acknowledge, it depends heavily on direct and indirect government expenditures. Aboriginal economies are often criticized for relying on transfers from Ottawa, band and tribal council jobs, and investments fuelled by land claims settlements and resource royalties. In some areas, such as Westbank (BC), Whitecap (Saskatchewan), Tsuu T'ina (Alberta), Membertou (Nova Scotia), and Squamish (BC), transfer payments play a lesser role in local economic activity; other income sources help support social, employment, and commercial operations. Other communities, especially those in northern and remote locations, rely much more heavily on government payments to individuals and the local Aboriginal authorities. Northwest Territories and northern Saskatchewan depend much more on government support than downtown Toronto or Calgary. So in this regard, the Aboriginal experience mirrors that of the country as a whole – the river that runs through the Canadian economy is filled in part with government spending on projects and services and with direct payments to individuals. Some of the poorer Aboriginal communities are at the extreme end of the spectrum in terms of dependence on government, but they are not completely off the Canadian scale.

Aboriginal people in Canada are poor – significantly so by national standards. Federal programs have not really solved this problem. Over the past forty years, Canadians have learned that government-led economic development initiatives aimed at job creation rarely work. The reasons for this often have as much to do with administration and local economic conditions as with any lack of drive among Aboriginal people. There is plenty of evidence that government spending is at best only a partial answer to the economic problems facing Aboriginals. There is also evidence that property ownership and individual responsibility are key elements in the generating of personal and collective wealth. Writers such as Hernando de Soto have argued that the absence of property rights is responsible for a significant portion of global poverty; in this regard, the land tenure regime on Indian reserves in Canada is without question part of the problem. Without embracing all the free market ideology that dominates today's world, it is clear that all people, whatever their culture or country of origin, respond best when they are rewarded for their personal efforts. The landholding system on Aboriginal reserves arises as a factor here – many Aboriginal people want to remain on their traditional territories, which complicates Aboriginal economies. But the basic principles still hold.

There is evidence from the United States that Aboriginal communities that adopt "job and income" strategies fail to ameliorate their desperate social and economic conditions. The job and income approach – which has been tried repeatedly in economically depressed regions in Canada – identifies the problem as not enough jobs and not enough income and the solution as starting businesses. This approach fails for a number of reasons: investors get caught up in local politics and decide to pull out; the tribal government shifts profits from the enterprise to cover shortfalls in other areas; or a tribal leader uses the business as a patronage tool so that people are hired on the basis of political loyalty rather than business acumen.

Tribes that adopt a "nation-building" strategy are far more successful. This approach, too, recognizes that jobs and income are a big part of the problem, but it tackles the problem in a fundamentally different way – by building a nation where businesses *and* people can prosper. This approach tries to create an environment in which people want to invest. The US experience indicates that sovereignty – in Canadian language, self-government – is a necessary condition though not in itself a sufficient one. Effective governance is also required. That includes stable institutions and policies, fair and effective dispute resolution systems, the separation of politics from business management, a competent bureaucracy, and a cultural "match" between governing institutions and the community's political culture. Perhaps the best Canadian example of this approach is casinos, which generate substantial revenues, provide jobs and training opportunities, and support related Aboriginal businesses (although this activity also has its drawbacks).

These elements of Indigenous nation building parallel the situation of Third World developmental states, which include the "Asian Tigers" – Taiwan, South Korea, Hong Kong, and Singapore – as well as Botswana and Mauritius, which in the last quarter of the twentieth century experienced even higher annual growth rates than those four. Developmental states focus on nation building. Their elites create effective bureaucracies and then insulate them from societal pressures, including business interests, so that planning decisions can be in the long-term interests of the nation. These countries do not blame the international system for economic injustice, nor do they resign themselves to dependency. Instead, they make political choices that are conducive to long-term economic growth and that engage with the international economic system. These countries have done much better at guarding against the rampant patronage, kleptocracy, and theft of state resources that have plagued Zimbabwe, Sudan, and the Philippines. Quality of life measured by jobs, incomes, and equality tends to be much better in developmental states, which need not be authoritarian, as demonstrated by Botswana and Mauritius. Canada's Aboriginal communities and governments need to consider closely the economic models of the successful developmental states.

Future initiatives also need to consider how the politics of economic development create economic opportunities for individuals. Future initiatives should draw on that knowledge. Two basic elements should be given high priority in future nation building: education and training, and strong governance institutions.

The first priority has to be education and training. Examples from around the world have demonstrated that effective education is the single best way to foster hope in communities, as well as marketable skills. Aboriginal people have worked hard in this area – indeed, their efforts amount to a revolution in First Nations education. Meanwhile, colleges and universities have made great strides in serving the needs of Indigenous students. Aboriginal school boards and colleges and the First Nations University of Canada are playing a more prominent role, though admittedly, they are encountering some growing pains as they adjust to new realities. In any event, they are providing places for Aboriginal students to study in an Indigenous environment if they so choose. These institutions have forced non-Aboriginal institutions to pay greater attention to Aboriginal students' needs and expectations. First Nations students are not required to attend Aboriginal institutions, and the choices now open to them have enriched both individual students and the nation's colleges and universities.

Greater attention must also be paid to the legal, financial, and institutional foundations of economic activity. There is evidence that property rights are vital to economic development. Hernando de Soto's *The Mystery of Capital: Why Capitalism Triumphs in the West and Fails Everywhere Else* (2003) is instructive here. He argues that without institutionalized property rights, we cannot expect capitalist economies to flourish. In this regard, Canada should change its property ownership rules on First Nations reserves to permit the individual ownership of houses and land. This initiative would create personal responsibility for privately held property. The present system effectively prohibits Status Indians from capitalizing on their primary economic asset – their land, which they cannot mortgage. Clearly, this limits their economic options. Aboriginal governments have been developing new models for landownership, including new strategies for promoting homeownership and local real estate markets. The Okanagan Lake Band in BC has allocated land to families; many have, in turn, leased waterfront properties out commercially to non-Aboriginal people, which provides them with handsome annual rents.

There are already promising signs of new approaches. Recent efforts to establish Aboriginal banks and credit unions are very important. Countries around the world have enjoyed considerable success with micro-lending organizations, which emphasize the ready availability of money as well as strict rules for repayment of loans. A Canadian version of this approach might involve providing a loan to purchase a truck, boat, or other piece of equipment for economic development purposes. By introducing financial resources and clear personal financial responsibility into local economies, these initiatives would support the current expansion in Aboriginal entrepreneurship. Some caution would have to be exercised in this area. Canada is an entrepreneurially weak nation, and the free market spirit does not run deep through the nation's soul. For the past forty years, federal economic strategies for First Nations and Canadians in depressed economic zones have focused on providing support for entrepreneurs, without first recognizing that this mindset and its associated skills are in short supply across the country. Cooperatives, led by the Arctic cooperatives of Inuit art fame, have great potential. National cooperative organizations have been working to expand their presence in Aboriginal communities.

Non-Aboriginal business leaders have been playing an increasingly active role in assisting Aboriginal companies. The number of successful joint ventures between Aboriginal and non-Aboriginal companies continues to grow, especially in the northern resource sector, and this is providing an excellent foundation for economic activity. This is a little-known yet vital area for national reconciliation, since it can help budding entrepreneurs overcome their inexperience and trepidation about heading into the untested waters of capitalism.

Self-interest is clearly part of the reason – it is difficult to proceed with resource projects without Aboriginal backing and participation, especially under the new "duty to consult and accommodate" requirements established by the Supreme Court. That said, it is also important to acknowledge that the Canadian business community has changed its attitude. From Voisey's Bay to Dease Lake and BHP's Etaki diamond mine in Northwest Territories, Aboriginal companies and employees are working cooperatively on major development projects. In some instances, Aboriginal communities and organizations hold an equity stake in the project. In other cases, they have negotiated training and employment arrangements with resource and supply firms, thus creating opportunities for local Aboriginal workers.

Joint ventures bring tremendous benefits to all parties. Companies gain access to local workers, who are more strongly committed to the region than their largely transient non-Aboriginal counterparts. Aboriginal employees gain access to decent, well-paid jobs, often with significant training opportunities and the prospect of long-term work, in areas where such prospects are often bleak. Indigenous communities gain access to commercial and technical expertise. Governments benefit from the reduction in unemployment, lower welfare payments, and help in training Aboriginal workers. The most successful of these ventures – Syncrude/Suncor's relationship with the community of Fort Chipewyan is a good example – are many years old and have provided a flexible, culturally sensitive, and mutually beneficial opportunity for Indigenous engagement with the workforce. According to Suncor's corporate website, it employs more Aboriginal people than any other industrial employer in Canada: almost 8 percent of its workers are Aboriginal. Furthermore, over the past twenty years, Suncor has done more than $1.5 billion in work with Aboriginal-owned businesses.

When stimulating joint venture initiatives, there is no need for major policy initiatives. The critical elements in joint ventures have been the empowerment of Indigenous communities and greater awareness among resource companies. Strengthened by land claims agreements, especially provisions requiring consultation with and the support of local Aboriginal peoples for any significant resource development, Indigenous governments have been able to negotiate mutually supportive joint venture agreements. During the construction of the Voisey's Bay nickel mine, for example, 40 percent of the workforce came from the Innu and Inuit communities of Labrador. The Northwest Territories' diamond mines have developed comparable mutually beneficial relationships with Aboriginal companies and individuals. Communities do not always take equity positions in the development, nor do they always start service and support companies. Many collaborative arrangements are limited to employment and training. For their part, companies have learned that stable developments on and near Aboriginal territories require harmonious relationships with Indigenous peoples and governments. It is clearly in their corporate interest to proceed in a constructive and forward-looking manner – a lesson that many firms across the country have learned.

Joint ventures and collaborative arrangements will feature prominently in the economic future of Aboriginal communities. The skills, training, and experience gained in these situations will carry over productively into future commercial activities. Aboriginal workers are becoming better prepared to compete for jobs, Aboriginal companies have a stronger foundation for competitive operations, and a culture of wage work is being established in communities long separated from the market economy. Although there is no question that some companies have opted into these initiatives to forestall protests and legal impediments to resource projects, most appear to have concluded that it is possible to establish mutually beneficial relationships with Aboriginal communities. Observers interested in the future of Aboriginal commerce, especially in northern and remote regions, would do well to pay close attention to collaborations between Indigenous peoples and corporations.

Our recommendations and optimism are tempered by the recognition that there will be no overnight transformation of Canada's Aboriginal economies. Job discrimination, inadequate training, and the absence of regular jobs in most remote communities will ensure that Aboriginal people continue to lag behind national averages in employment and earnings. Not all Aboriginal people are looking for a partial or total immersion in the wage economy. They are content, instead, to continue their current pattern of harvesting with occasional work for cash and are unwilling to relocate, seek training, or otherwise adapt to the mainstream economy. That said, there are abundant signs of significant changes in Aboriginal communities as individual and collective entrepreneurship takes root, as communities discover the commercial possibilities of Indigenous culture, and as young people, fully immersed in the contemporary popular culture, come to share widespread North American expectations. The thousands of Aboriginal businesses and the emerging pattern of joint ventures across the country are signs of improved realities for Aboriginal people.

Going to the next level – that is, providing greater opportunities for individuals and communities – will require a shift from the current preoccupation with training programs and government loans to small businesses, towards restructuring the approach to funding Aboriginal governments and communities and providing financial support for individuals and families. The previous two chapters have outlined a variety of options, from developing a new approach to welfare payments to creating a royalty-based funding formula for Aboriginal governments, that could well be part of a reconceptualization of

Aboriginal economies in Canada. Aboriginal leaders, government officials, and other observers undoubtedly have other ideas that should
be considered. It is important to get off a track that has produced
more poverty and isolation than positive and respectful economic
engagement. Over time, Aboriginal participation in the mainstream
economy, combined with a more culturally supportive approach to
government support programs, could serve as a cornerstone of reconciliation in Canada.

The goal of becoming a treaty nation will not be achieved if
Indigenous people remain poor by national standards and if they continue to depend on government-administered, shame-based handouts.
Changes need to be made in key areas, especially taxation and property-
holding arrangements. The development of private property regimes
cannot be forced on Indigenous peoples, but the option, as some
First Nations and the federal government are currently promoting,
for individual First Nations to move in this direction is essential.
Attention should be paid to opportunities for greater cooperation
among Aboriginal communities and between those communities and
non-Aboriginal businesses. The groundwork has been laid for many of
these initiatives. Steps taken in recent years in the North suggest that
the business community is actually ahead of governments in finding
productive and mutually beneficial ways to work with Aboriginal communities. Educational attainment continues to rise, offering substantial hope for the next and subsequent generations.

The alleviation of poverty and dependency is perhaps the most formidable challenge facing Aboriginal policy makers. A tragedy of the
past forty years is that this area has attracted far less attention than
constitutional reform, legal processes, and political relationships. The
most promising development is that, with comparatively limited government engagement or direction, Aboriginal people and the business
community in Canada have recognized the benefits of collaborative
arrangements. There are, finally, reasons for hope. The proposals outlined here – based on strong, autonomous Indigenous communities
using strength in governance to enhance economic development and
well-being – are not ideas for the 2030s or the 2050s. We have ample
evidence across Canada, today, that this approach works. The treaty-
based transformations underway among the James Bay Cree in northern Quebec or the Inuvialuit in the Mackenzie Delta/Beaufort Sea

area show that political and economic empowerment go hand in hand. So do the achievements of the Lac La Ronge Indian Band and the Meadow Lake Tribal Council, both in Saskatchewan. The significant accomplishments of the Vuntut Gwitchin First Nation (Old Crow in Yukon, and owners of Air North) point to the capacity of isolated but political sound communities to seize control of their future, just as the highly praised achievements of Osoyoos First Nation in south-central British Columbia illustrate how talented and committed leadership can remake community both economically and politically. The rapid emergence of Aboriginal development corporations as major players in the Canadian economy (watch for future expansion by these power-ful, beneficiary-controlled organizations) and increasingly extensive collaborations and joint ventures between Indigenous communities and the private sector illustrate the ability of well-managed Aboriginal governments to bring about substantial improvements in community well-being.

# conclusion

SUSTAINABLE RECONCILIATION in Canada will require extending equality of opportunity to Aboriginal peoples, rather than equality of result or circumstance, which has failed as an objective. This in turn will require attention to three crucial elements: respect for Indigenous cultures, political reform, and economic opportunity. For Aboriginal peoples to want to belong to this country, progress must be made on all three fronts. Any steps taken will need to reflect basic Canadian political and social values. If arrangements with Aboriginal peoples and governments are seen as departing strongly from those values, the backlash from non-Aboriginal Canadians will grow stronger, and reconciliation will be delayed. Canada can and must do better than in the past at accommodating Indigenous cultures, and it has the tools to do so.

Conflict and willful ignorance clouded much of the past century. Partnership will be achievable in the next one. Reconciliation will take commitment, patience, and courage on all sides, but it is increasingly possible. Many of the solutions will have to be found and implemented within Aboriginal communities themselves. Others will require the goodwill and support of Canadian society. The goal is to create political and social space within Canada for Aboriginal people and communities to succeed. That success will be measured not just in terms of lower unemployment rates and higher educational attainment, as important as these are. *Social* prosperity – a concept based on wellness, happiness, and less rigid measurements of material success – will provide a much better measure. Success must also be measured in terms of how well Aboriginal peoples and their cultures emerge as valued and integral parts of the country we call Canada. Below we summarize the ten general conditions that would put Canada on the path to becoming a treaty nation.

## FOCUS ON THE FUTURE AND SUCCESS, NOT ON THE PAST AND FAILURE

Much of the debate about Aboriginal issues in Canada focuses on past failures. As we have discussed, a powerful non-Aboriginal constituency has emerged that is highly critical of Aboriginal relations in Canada. These people argue that Canada has gone too far in recognizing Aboriginal rights to land and self-government. Their solution is to turn the clock back, legally and constitutionally. In their view, federal policy is being managed by a bloated bureaucracy that perpetuates ill-conceived programs based on an outdated paradigm of welfare paternalism. They want to end subsidies to Aboriginal governments and encourage Aboriginal people to migrate from reserves into the broader Canadian society. They assert that too many Aboriginal leaders are corrupt, incompetent, and dictatorial and that Indigenous self-government will lead to fiefdoms that further fracture the Canadian political system. For these critics, the alternative is integration into the Canadian political system through municipal-type band governments, coupled with voluntary participation in the national economy.

Meanwhile, powerful Aboriginal politicians and groups remain wedded to the arguments of the past. Some of them focus on historical injustices as the sole source of contemporary problems and encourage a dialogue built on newcomer guilt. This approach was effective in the 1970s and 1980s, when many non-Aboriginal Canadians were shocked to learn about the impact of residential schools, the Indian Act, and other federal initiatives on Indigenous people in Canada. But guilt fatigue set in for many Canadians. Moreover, many new Canadians do not share the general sense of collective responsibility for past injustices – a crucial point, given how formidable new Canadians are as a political force. Other leaders want to turn the clock back to the days when newcomers viewed Aboriginal peoples as allies. For them, the solution is coexisting solitudes, with other Canadians recognizing the full sovereign rights of Aboriginal societies. But approaches rooted in the past are neither realistic nor achievable.

For reconciliation to succeed, it will have to be *forward* looking. A relationship based on guilt fosters a sense of victimization and resentment. For Canadians to live together as treaty peoples, we must foster mutual respect and an earnest desire for a better future. As Canada struggles to find an appropriate course for the twenty-first century, it will have to develop strategies that include Aboriginal people in that future.

We also need to place greater emphasis on success. Talk of failure is a self-fulfilling prophecy, for it lowers expectations and rationalizes lack of progress. Serious problems are confronting Aboriginal communities, but their many successes are just as real. More and more Aboriginal communities are establishing profitable businesses and efficient, competent governments. Aboriginal people increasingly excel in education, the arts, and sports, yet policy makers' attention still focuses almost exclusively on problems and crises. Schools, the media, and other institutions need to emphasize the success stories of Aboriginal communities with the same energy and attention they devote to the stories of crisis. Success models success.

## ACCEPT ABORIGINAL PEOPLE AND CULTURES AS INTEGRAL TO CANADIAN SOCIETY

Canada celebrates itself as a community of communities. That is the cornerstone of our identity and of our political institutions. In this context, Canadians have always viewed Aboriginal people as a marker of their country's diversity and cultural wealth and have used them as such in the international arena. If only this superficial celebration of Indigenous art, culture, and knowledge could be internalized by the nation as a whole! Reconciliation requires strong and sustainable Aboriginal cultures that are accepted as integral to Canadian society. As political philosopher Will Kymlicka has noted, our life choices are framed by our culture. Members of the dominant society rarely notice that their choices are made within cultural reference points set by British or French traditions. Community is valued not simply for itself but because it provides a reference point for individual choices and thereby improves one's life chances. A country of treaty peoples will find ways to include Aboriginal cultures as Canadian communities. From a more local perspective, Aboriginal cultural vitality is essential to strong Indigenous communities. People need to feel proud of their cultures, and to believe they are respected and honoured. Strong Aboriginal cultures and communities are absolute prerequisites for Indigenous success, both personal and collective.

All of this has two repercussions. First, Indigenous cultural survival is up to Aboriginal peoples themselves, not governments, granting agencies, and urban art galleries. Second, Indigenous peoples must *want* their values, traditions, and cultures to survive into the twenty-first century. Aboriginal activism offers overwhelming evidence that they do want this. But this does not mean that Aboriginal cultures are locked in the past. All cultures are dynamic – they adapt to new social and economic realities, and they absorb elements from the cultures that surround them. The Scots have a strong sense of identity and national purpose, as do the Japanese, Koreans, Basques, and many other cultural groups, large and small. But none of them are culturally frozen; all have developed strong connections to the contemporary world. In other words, Aboriginal cultures are fundamentally modern phenomena with roots to the past. They are not trapped in their own history, either by themselves or by outsiders. The Aboriginal culture that manifests itself in contemporary Indigenous art, sports, politics, and social organization is no less authentic than the Aboriginal cultures of the fifteenth century.

The Idle No More movement, a loosely connected, largely spontaneous series of rallies that spread across the country with remarkable speed in 2012–13, was widely viewed as a protest movement. Actually, those events were profoundly peaceful and more resembled celebrations of Aboriginal identity. The drumming, dancing, and pride that infused these events, which were dominated by women and their children, surprised most Canadians, who were long used to focusing on Aboriginal people's anger at Ottawa. Clearly, Indigenous culture is alive in Canada.

The broader Canadian society must acknowledge the richness, vitality, and contemporaneity of Aboriginal society. Although it is wonderful that collectors value traditional Haida totem poles and

Inuit carvings and prints, contemporary works by Aboriginal paint-
ers, sculptors, writers, and singers are equally valid representations of
Indigenous reality. But these images must compete for public interest
and approval on their own merits, not as historical curiosities. If modern art by an Aboriginal person is not good art, it will not sell, nor
should it. For many decades, Canadians have looked on Aboriginal
cultures as if they were utterly foreign. They have not reached out to
Aboriginal people as a central element of Canadian society; they have
not looked for what Aboriginal culture has to offer Canada. This country will be less than whole as long as Indigenous people are kept at
arm's length, as long as they are viewed as historical relics rather than
as part of the country's social fabric. The country will be stronger and
richer when Aboriginal peoples are celebrated as a key element of
Canadian society.

## REBUILD HEALTHY AND ACTIVE
## ABORIGINAL COMMUNITIES

Cultural vitality is difficult to sustain if the people are hurting, if water
systems do not work, if sewage backs up, if there are few meaningful
jobs, and if the education system lags far behind national norms.
Many Aboriginal communities are not healthy; in fact, many of them
are in near disastrous condition. Their housing is overcrowded to a degree that would shock and appall most Canadians if they knew. While
many new schools have been built, staffing problems continue and
teacher turnover is shockingly high. Substance abuse is a serious problem in many communities. Few Canadians have spent so much as a
single day on an Aboriginal reserve or community in Canada. Those
who do are often aghast at the Third World conditions they see and
find it easier to comprehend the anger and frustration of Aboriginal
people at what they view as government procrastination. Few
Canadians would tolerate for a week, let alone a lifetime, the kinds of
conditions that are commonplace in Aboriginal communities across
the country.

Canadians should be embarrassed about current conditions and
angry at themselves for leaving the problems unaddressed for so long.
All the participants in this enterprise (band, provincial, and federal
governments) need to accept responsibility for improving Aboriginal
living conditions as a top priority. The task will be neither easy nor

cheap. The problems are severe, the unmet demand enormous, and the need urgent. The Harper government's post-Kelowna policy has retained some of that accord's core elements, especially around housing, but lacks its symbolism and urgency.

The rebuilding of Aboriginal communities must avoid top-down approaches, with Ottawa imposing national solutions on intensely local problems. Instead, the solutions must reflect the communities and regions where they are applied. Canadians have the right to know that the money (and it will cost billions) is going to be well spent. It would be horribly wasteful to spend vast sums without ensuring that local administrations are up to the task, that the communities want to rebuild where they are, that the needs of off-reserve members are met, and that the developments will support local economies. But the central point remains: there is no reason why Indigenous peoples and communities should be expected to settle for a far worse quality of life than other Canadians. At a minimum, they deserve equality of opportunity.

## ENGAGE ABORIGINAL PEOPLE WITH EDUCATION AND IN THE ECONOMY

Improvements have been made in elementary and high school education for Aboriginal people, but the work remains largely unfinished. The gap is wider than even governments and Aboriginal groups will acknowledge. The conditions facing many young children in the formative first five years of their lives – a result of poverty, domestic struggles, overcrowded and poorly maintained homes, and cultural loss – penalize Aboriginal youth before they ever enter the school system. Little has been done to ensure that Aboriginal students have the skills and aptitudes they need to succeed in the Canadian economy. People familiar with the field realize well that high school graduation from a reserve-based school does not equal, in quality and learning outcomes, graduation from an urban high school. Aboriginal women are increasingly engaged in postsecondary education; there is an urgent need to draw more Aboriginal men into that system. Many institutions, including Canada's three territorial colleges, the University of Northern BC, Lakehead University, and a number of others in Saskatchewan, are providing innovative educational programming to Aboriginal students, both on urban campuses and in their communities. The links between educational attainment and participation in the broader economy are strong. For Aboriginal people to succeed in the broader economy, further investment must be made in Indigenous education and training, often in the form of support for the students and their families.

Major strides have been made in Aboriginal economic development. Indigenous entrepreneurship continues to expand, especially in sectors such as tourism, resource development (primarily through joint ventures), and services to Aboriginal communities. One important success story relates to efforts by Canadian businesses – including Crown corporations, the major banks, and resource firms – to reach out to Aboriginal communities. The sharing of knowledge and expertise has been truly remarkable, and trusting relationships have developed. The prospects for continued improvement are high as Indigenous groups capitalize on the funds they receive through land claims settlements, develop reserve-based opportunities like casinos, exploit market opportunities presented by proximity to major urban areas or vacation resorts, insist on a fair share of jobs and commercial opportunities associated with resource developments, and otherwise work their way into the corporate world. Great strides have already been made. In charting a common future with Aboriginal peoples and communities, Canadian businesses are leaders.

But education and commercial development are only part of the solution. In remote communities, where Aboriginal people retain powerful ties to traditional lands and resources, commercial opportunities are few and a different model is needed. Canada needs to address the welfare dependency that characterizes many of these Aboriginal communities. As noted earlier, even in Alberta, the most free-market province in Canada, a large part of the population is employed by the public sector, including the educational and health care systems. Still others work for private companies that contract services to government. Why, then, is there so much resistance to expanding publicly funded jobs in Aboriginal towns and villages, many of which have about as many free market opportunities as prairie farm villages and Newfoundland outports? Why do Canadians tolerate multigenerational welfare dependency but resist a radical restructuring of the income support and wealth transfer system? An Aboriginal person can receive $20,000 a year in welfare and other support payments, or receive the same amount doing productive and culturally appropriate community-based work. Which approach – continued welfare dependency or community-managed employment focusing on urgent local needs – is most likely to produce proud and healthy societies, strengthen the community's work ethic, and provide a stronger foundation for the economy? The answer seems obvious.

## ACCOMMODATE ABORIGINAL SELF-GOVERNMENT

Aboriginal self-determination is a foundation for reconciliation, not an impediment to it. The capacity to make decisions is fundamental to healthy political communities. It is also a precondition for economic development, though not in itself sufficient. Four key points need to be made about Aboriginal self-determination in Canada.

First, Canadians should embrace the concept of a third order of government as an extension of Canadian political practice. A third order of government would mean that Aboriginal peoples are opting *into* the Canadian political system, not out of it.

Second, far too much attention is being directed towards reserve-based First Nations. Models of self-governance that accommodate Canada's growing urban Aboriginal population need to be developed. This will require flexibility and innovation on the part of existing governments, emphasizing a needs- rather than power-based approach to administrative systems.

Third, Aboriginal self-determination will require the dismantling of the Department of Aboriginal Affairs and the development of something like a Commonwealth of Aboriginal Peoples to oversee program development and delivery *by* Aboriginal people *for* all Aboriginal people – First Nations, Métis, and Inuit, whether they live on reserves or in urban communities. If Canadians want Aboriginal people to trust Ottawa, they will have to let them manage their own affairs.

Fourth, Aboriginal self-governance will require significant self-financing. Local Aboriginal governments will need to have some taxation powers, because financial participation in governance is crucial to the democratic process. But the system will also require funding derived from a fair and equitable distribution of wealth in Canada. This could be achieved by providing Aboriginal peoples and governments with a fixed portion of Canada's resource wealth. With its often contentious equalization formula, Canada has developed a mechanism for redistributing income to provide adequate funding for the provinces. At present, Aboriginal programming is funded by unstable annual allocations from Ottawa. This funding should be regularized, and allocated in a way that recognizes the very different costs associated with delivering services to Aboriginal communities. The shift from variable to formula funding would not necessarily increase costs, except for those associated with increased population. It would, though, provide a level of security that has so far been missing. And no less importantly, it would demonstrate a commitment to share the wealth drawn from Canada's lands and resources.

## INSIST ON ACCOUNTABILITY

Reconciliation is not a one-way street. Just as non-Aboriginal Canadians need to respond to the demands from Indigenous peoples, so do Aboriginal communities need to heed the expectations of other Canadians.

Aboriginal and non-Aboriginal critics alike are correct to assert that accountability measures must be in place before there can be greater public trust in Aboriginal governments. That is not an exclusive concern for Aboriginal governments, as evidenced by the Gomery Report on the Sponsorship Scandal. Non-Aboriginal Canadians must also realize that Aboriginal people are leading the demand for improved government. Most of the scandals we learn about in the media were exposed not by some civic watchdog like the Canadian Taxpayers Federation but rather by outspoken Aboriginal citizens. The blogosphere is alive with detailed and highly critical commentaries on Aboriginal politicians and governments, with many of the comments written by Aboriginal people. There is no reason why the standard for Aboriginal accountability – to their own communities and to the Canadian public at large – should be any different from that applied to other governments. Over the past forty years, Canadians have shown themselves willing to devote large sums of money to Aboriginal affairs, albeit with mounting skepticism about the value of that investment. Expanded and even continued funding will come only with greater accountability and a greater focus on positive outcomes.

It is important, as well, that the Canadian public not overreact to stories of inefficiency, corruption, and government breakdown, Aboriginal *or* non-Aboriginal. Aboriginal governments have emerged from paternalism and colonial management only over the past forty years. Their achievements, in general, have been quite remarkable. There have been serious difficulties, occasionally involving non-Aboriginal advisers and consultants. These issues have to be addressed. National confidence in Indigenous governance rests not on a general witch hunt against Aboriginal leaders but rather on the rapid and fair response to reports of mismanagement or corruption. Canadians, Aboriginal or not, would settle for nothing less. Furthermore, and perhaps surprisingly, revelations about mismanagement in Aboriginal government are crucial signs of political health. Clearly, Aboriginal citizens increasingly feel they have the authority, right, and opportunity to call their governments to account. Public confidence will follow the appropriate prosecution of anyone, Aboriginal or non-Aboriginal, involved in corruption in public government. The resulting improvement in transparency and accountability will strengthen their commitment to their governments and improve public confidence in Aboriginal government.

## CLARIFY ABORIGINAL RIGHTS

In the British North America Act, 1867, the federal government was given responsibility for Indian peoples. Section 35 of the Constitution Act, 1982, holds the key to Aboriginal aspirations in Canada. It says, simply, that Canada recognizes "existing Aboriginal and treaty rights." The Constitution also recognizes three distinct Aboriginal groups: Indians, Métis, and Inuit. At no point does any constitutional document spell out precisely what programs, duties, and responsibilities are attached to these provisions. The Constitution says the federal government has responsibility for Aboriginal programs. But it does not require the Canadian government to provide any particular programs, or even *any* programs, and Ottawa has the right to cancel every single program aimed at Aboriginal Canadians. The same holds for the federal and provincial services for all Canadians. Provinces are responsible for such services as education and health care, but there is no precise definition of the level or quality of service that must be provided.

The reality is, of course, different from the stark constitutional formalities. Most Indigenous groups are covered by historical or modern treaties, which spell out, with greater and lesser degrees of specificity, government obligations tied to Aboriginal land surrenders. The old treaties contain vague references to legal requirements, many of which have been tested over time (does "medicine chest" in a nineteenth-century treaty mean lifetime government-funded health care, for example?), but many such requirements do not have full legal standing. Through the courts, Aboriginal people have won recognition or clarification of many different Aboriginal and treaty rights. Today, hundreds of cases are working their way through the courts as Aboriginal people and governments seek to define Indigenous rights and entitlements. Much as many Canadians would like to see this legal jousting come to an end, the truth is that Aboriginal Canadians, like all other Canadians, have the right to seek a resolution of their disputes through the courts. Something must be done, however, to clarify Aboriginal and treaty rights – something other than endless and costly court battles. Several options are available that would provide a higher level of certainty and a sense of resolution to the many outstanding Aboriginal and treaty rights cases. Those Canadians who recoil at the prospect of empowering Aboriginal peoples through such processes need only look at the United States, Australia, and New Zealand for useful (albeit far from perfect) examples of accommodations based on the recognition of Indigenous rights or sovereignty. Whatever the difficulties, efforts to resolve problems have not borne out the cataclysmic predictions that the Canadian federation will fragment as a result of recognizing Aboriginal and treaty rights.

## EXPAND PERSONAL CONTACTS WITH ABORIGINAL CANADIANS

Despite living together in northern North America for several centuries, and despite considerable intermarriage between Indigenous people and newcomers over the years, there is far too little personal contact across the cultural divide. Most Canadians have not been anywhere near a reserve, and certainly not to one of the isolated communities that show up on the news from time to time. For all the rhetoric to the contrary, they are not inherently terrifying or difficult places. Although many are facing difficulties, these Aboriginal communities are friendly, engaging settlements that wrestle publicly with their community challenges. Conversely, non-Aboriginal communities are more open and accepting of Aboriginal people than many expect, welcoming newcomers into their neighbourhoods and homes in ways that the public discussion of racial divides would not suggest. But there is a caveat that needs to be entered: separation generates misunderstanding and fear. In the United States, it is clear that many people fear African Americans at a fundamental level. This shows up in Canada, too, both at the level of personal safety (although Aboriginal–non-Aboriginal violence is remarkably rare) and in conversations with Indigenous peoples. Canadians, unlike their counterparts in Australia and New Zealand, are often reluctant to speak bluntly to Aboriginal Canadians. Agreeing in public and disagreeing in private is profoundly disrespectful. Frankness is a precondition for reconciliation.

Canada needs far more contact between Indigenous and non-Indigenous people. The country needs Canadians taking holidays in northern and remote regions, service clubs building facilities on reserves, churches playing an even more hands-on role in addressing urban Aboriginal challenges, and businesses continuing their outreach and collaboration. Canada needs exchange programs that bring young Aboriginal students from remote reserves to largely non-Aboriginal southern towns, and vice versa. More and more non-Aboriginal people are experiencing the excitement and cultural richness of traditional Indigenous celebrations. The prairie powwow circuit could become a major attraction based on living, contemporary Aboriginal life. Aboriginal sporting events are drawing greater attention, for they offer a unique blend of high-level competition and cultural engagement. Distance separates people, creating huge vacuums into which misunderstanding and stereotypes quickly breed. When bonds of friendship, collaboration, and familiarity bridge the cultural chasm, the potential for lasting reconciliation rises dramatically – treaty peoples come to like and admire each other, recognizing foibles and differences but celebrating the unity in diversity.

## RESPOND TO SPECIAL CHALLENGES

No single model, or set of solutions, will address all of the needs of Aboriginal people in Canada. Two groups – remote communities and urban Aboriginals – present especially serious challenges. Both have attracted relatively little attention in recent years, for political debates have focused on high-level concepts and practical efforts have emphasized reserves near urban centres or major resource developments.

Tens of thousands of Aboriginal people prefer to remain on their traditional lands, even though economic and social opportunities are circumscribed. Far removed from the public eye, these villages gain notoriety only when a crisis strikes. Then, immediately, all remote communities are tarred with the same brush and described as decrepit, impoverished, and unsustainable. But these communities are far more varied than the general portrait suggests. People move off reserve for work or education, typically visiting often and occasionally returning to live. For all the social problems, they are the places in Canada where Indigenous language use, traditional knowledge, and Aboriginal customs remain most alive. They are, at once, the greatest challenge facing Aboriginal Canadians and the greatest hope for cultural persistence. That is why so much of the Aboriginal political effort focuses on these communities.

Sweeping changes are necessary in some locations – some communities could be closed and their populations relocated to other Indigenous settlements, at their choice of location and timing – but it is wrong to assume that all remote villages are doomed to fail. If some of the prescriptions offered in this book are adopted, especially regarding employment and cultural programming, these remote communities could become or stay vital. Much is at stake here, including the survival of centuries-old languages, the maintenance of rich understandings of the land and its resources, important cultural practices, and many other valuable elements of Indigenous life in Canada. In time, and recognizing that some Indigenous people will always opt to relocate away from reserves (one hopes, in the future, for more positive reasons), these remote communities will serve as beacons of Indigenous cultural survival and adaptation.

With regard to urban Aboriginals, the first thing Canadians need is an awareness of the diversity of this group. Many, perhaps most, Indigenous people living in large towns and cities do not live on the streets, hang out in shelters, or struggle with alcohol and drug abuse. Many, although not yet most, have regular jobs or attend school or training programs and live in typical urban residential areas. Although seemingly assimilated into the Canadian mainstream, the overwhelming majority of middle-class Aboriginal peoples maintain strong ties with their communities and cultures. They often host family and community members visiting the city, return to their reserves on a regular basis, and remain connected to political and cultural events back home. This group – part of the broad Aboriginal success story – attracts almost no attention, in large part because they do not seek any.

It is new arrivals from remote communities, many of them in dire circumstances, who fuel the stereotype of urban Aboriginals. They struggle with substance abuse and poverty, face discrimination, and often find themselves in trouble with the law. They are often disconnected from their communities and families and struggle to eke out a living in a hostile social environment. Special programs for urban Aboriginals often founder on cultural diversity. Aboriginal people from dozens of communities and many language groups flock to the major cities – Toronto, Vancouver, Winnipeg, Edmonton, Calgary, Saskatoon, Regina, Halifax – where they face many problems of adjustment and dislocation.

Until Canadian policy making and Aboriginal political life reflect the needs and aspirations of remote communities and the two very different urban constituencies, and until there is greater awareness of the contributions and life histories of middle-class Aboriginals in towns and cities, Canada's ability to respond to the challenge and the promise of Indigenous people in the country will remain sadly weak.

## MOVE TOWARDS A COMMON FUTURE

Much of the criticism of Aboriginal aspirations focuses on fear of separation – on the belief that self-government, treaties, and other initiatives will drive a wedge even deeper between Aboriginal and other Canadians. This need not be so. Canada's bedrock institutions will hold the country together even as Indigenous aspirations are realized. The concept of the Crown has deep roots that have defined Aboriginal peoples' relations with newcomer societies in North America since well before Confederation. The respect for the Crown embodied in the treaties, the Constitution, and the Charter of Rights and Freedoms underpins the strong commitment of Aboriginal people to Canada. Aboriginal Canadians have as strong a relationship as most Canadians to the Crown and to the Canadian state.

The debate over Aboriginal futures, if handled in a respectful and constructive manner, could build national awareness of the building blocks of Confederation and greater understanding of how a divisible

Crown can operate. A new approach to governance could demonstrate how, if Aboriginal peoples and governments were properly empowered, the new arrangements could bring Canadians together instead of pulling them apart. When we listen closely to the debate, it becomes apparent that Indigenous leaders believe strongly in the Canadian Constitution, which explicitly recognizes Aboriginal and treaty rights. Many Aboriginal women have high confidence in the Charter of Rights and Freedoms, were delighted to have human rights legislation extended to Aboriginal reserves in 2011, and see the Charter as protecting them from patriarchal biases in Aboriginal political cultures. Even those Aboriginal leaders who believe that Indigenous laws and traditions should trump the Constitution and the Charter are very familiar with the content and meaning of these foundational documents.

A better Canada awaits us. Aboriginal people remain at the table despite decades of disappointments. We need recommitment at the federal level to bring about real change. Almost all Canadians agree that the status quo is unacceptable. Many Canadians, either enthusiastically or because other avenues seem closed off, appear to support Aboriginal self-government and the recognition of Aboriginal and treaty rights. The most significant changes in the offing will likely involve health care, education, fire protection, and water treatment – the stuff of local government – rather than lofty philosophizing and politicking of the kind that has consumed the country for most of five decades. A new Canada, one founded on treaty principles and offering a partnership between Indigenous and other Canadians, will be built slowly, growing with each reinvigorated community, each new Aboriginal business, each joint cultural celebration, each reduction in suicide and incarceration rates, and each improvement in Indigenous cultural health. There will be few transformative leaps, if any. Change will come about frustratingly slowly and with more than a few reversals along the way. Improvements will come if political courage remains strong and if Canadians' desire for a better country does not dissipate.

Reconciliation is achievable. Canadians can become treaty peoples. Collectively, we can find the common ground to build new and productive relationships. We can already see these changes across the country, on the fishing docks in the Maritimes, in the classrooms at Trent University and UNBC, on the Saskatoon urban reserve, in the mixed schools of North Battleford, in Suncor's creative employment schemes in northern Alberta, in Cameco and Areva's collaborations with northern Saskatchewan communities, in successful joint ventures at the Etaki mine in the NWT, in important collaborations between the Quebec government and Indigenous communities, in the consensus-style government of Northwest Territories, in negotiations involving land claims implementation teams in Yukon, in collaborative resource development on Tahltan territory in BC, in the high-profile and truly impressive Aboriginal engagement with the 2010 Olympics, in Aboriginal film and writers' festivals, in planning activities for the Mackenzie Valley natural gas pipeline, in residential development along the Sea to Sky Corridor between Vancouver and Whistler, in creative prison reforms for Aboriginal detainees, in the inclusion of Aboriginal spiritual practices in mainline Christian churches, in the crosscultural mixing embedded in the Arctic Winter Games (co-hosted by the Lheidli T'enneh First Nation and the City of Prince George), and in literally hundreds of other examples of Indigenous and other Canadians finding constructive common ground. Reconciliation is happening across the country. It is a clear and powerful element in contemporary Canadian life, not a pipe dream for the Canada of the future.

This book reflects our firm belief that the goal of reconciliation is equality of opportunity for Aboriginal Canadians. It is rooted, equally, in respect for Indigenous cultures, world views, and political aspirations and in the conviction that Aboriginal people's aspirations and cultural commitments can be reconciled with the values, priorities, and laws of the country as a whole. Comprehensive attention to the life chances of Aboriginal people could bring about a sea change in Indigenous relations with other Canadians. But to achieve this, the country will have to address three linked elements of Aboriginal life: economic opportunity, status and honour, and political power. Indigenous communities need the authority to govern their own affairs in such a way that they are accountable to their own people as well as to the country at large. They also need to know they are respected within Canada and that Canadians see Aboriginal cultures as a vital and viable part of Canada's social fabric. Finally, Aboriginal Canadians must have realistic and appropriate economic opportunities that are consistent with their world views, their commitment to their homelands, and the emerging balance between individual aspirations and communal values.

None of these priorities or prescriptions is radical or revolutionary, although their transformative impact on Canada may well be. After all, equality of opportunity within Canada is fundamental to the national political culture. What is proposed here rejects as unworkable and inappropriate the "equality of rights" approach advocated by some commentators on Canada's Aboriginal policies. It is equally divergent from the "equality of results" priorities of Canada's political left, with its overtones of paternalism and central control, which will not work for Aboriginal Canadians. As well, the arguments advanced here reject the "equality of nations" approach of Aboriginal sovereigntists and other intellectuals, for the political relationship they propose cannot be sold to other Canadians and would not likely serve Aboriginal Canadians well. Our vision for future Aboriginal relations with other Canadians may lack rhetorical flourish and intellectual melodrama. We are convinced, however, that a pragmatic, realistic, and moderate approach – one that is founded on real change to the status quo, and built on clear and public respect for Aboriginal cultures and communities, yet saleable to the country at large – could transform the place of Aboriginal people within Canada and create optimism and hope where there has been too much pessimism and despair.

To move the process along more quickly and comprehensively will require courage on all sides – the courage to consider genuine alternatives, to stand firm in the face of resistance to change, and to turn back forces of complaint and criticism that fear the further empowerment of Aboriginal people in Canada. There are many ideas on how to improve relations between Indigenous people and other Canadians. This book covers only a select few of the many suggestions that have circulated among those seeking a better future for this country. As new and better ideas come to the fore, many of the suggestions included here could well disappear into that great void that has absorbed generations of ideas on how to solve the "Indian problem." But there are many positive signs at present, strong indications that the movement towards reconciliation has found a momentum all its own, separate from the actions of governments and independent of Aboriginal plans for autonomy and self-control. The foundation for a new and different Canada can be seen across the country. There *is* common ground. Let's just hope that the country – Aboriginal and non-Aboriginal alike – has the courage and the foresight to seek it out.

# postscript

A KEY TEST of any public policy proposal relates to practicality. Hundreds of idealistic and unrealistic ideas are floating around, likely to founder on financial, political, ideological, or cultural grounds. In this book, we have not been immune to idealism or to fanciful notions of a perfect future. The statistics and politics of poverty engulf all discussion of Indigenous peoples in Canada. One cannot help but be touched by stories of epidemic suicide, entrenched unemployment, cultural loss, and social distress. When, Aboriginal leaders ask – often with anger – will Canada wake up to the developing-world conditions in its own backyard? When will the country finally take steps towards real and sustainable improvements? Just as loudly, non-Indigenous Canadians ask different questions. When, they wonder, will the gravy train from Ottawa be halted? When will Aboriginal Canadians be subject to the same rules, laws, and expectations as other Canadians? When will the remote reserves finally be shut down?

So goes one of the most frustrating, painful, and difficult conversations in national public affairs. The country has been debating these matters aggressively for more than forty years; Indigenous Canadians have been living with the nation's failures for several centuries. Social despair, economic hardship, criminal and violent behaviour, and the like increase almost as often as they drop.

But let your imagination run freely for a moment. Imagine a time when common ground has been identified, when Aboriginal and non-Aboriginal Canadians have developed the capacity to work together, when working as treaty peoples becomes the norm. Imagine a time when the ideas in this book and other studies have been tested and improved, when Aboriginal Canadians have come to believe that the country *does* care, that social justice *is* possible, and that improvements *can* be made and sustained. Imagine, just imagine, a country where these things have come to pass:

> Major landmarks have been renamed to reflect Indigenous nomenclature and cultural values.
> Schools and sporting facilities are designed to meet the needs of Aboriginal *and* non-Aboriginal Canadians.
> Senior representatives of Canada's immigrant communities reach out to Aboriginal people in the interests of building economic prosperity and personal opportunity.
> Large cities develop economic zones where Aboriginal businesses are flourishing and where Indigenous people work, create, and serve.
> The country finds places in its colleges and universities for tens of thousands of Aboriginal students, providing hope for future generations.
> Governments capitalize on new technologies to deliver high-quality medical and government services to remote Aboriginal settlements.
> Authorities find the means to encourage private ownership of property on Aboriginal reserves, breaking the business-stifling rules of the current system.
> Aboriginal and non-Aboriginal governments solve major legal and technical issues without recourse to the courts or public confrontations.
> Schools have stopped teaching about Aboriginal cultures as if they were fossilized remnants of a distant past.
> Communities have found ways to stop the revolving Aboriginal door in the Canadian justice system.
> Education systems work with elders to preserve Indigenous languages and to foster the use of those languages among youth.

> Prominent Canadians have mobilized financial institutions, companies, and business leaders to build networks of successful Aboriginal entrepreneurs across the country.
> Governments and companies have redefined their resource development strategies to ensure that Aboriginal people and communities benefit, primarily in terms of jobs and revenue sharing, and Aboriginal people are able to influence that development on their traditional lands.
> Companies and governments have found ways to incorporate Aboriginal knowledge and experience into resource management systems.
> Participants have moved beyond community-level discussions about Aboriginal self-government and developed more sustainable and practical regional solutions.
> The country has learned to celebrate Aboriginal artistic and cultural achievements and to recognize that these are an important and lasting part of the nation's cultural landscape.
> Legal authorities have adjusted court proceedings so that the understanding and wisdom of oral cultures can be shared in legal processes and given appropriate weight in court decisions.
> Constituencies are electing people of Aboriginal ancestry to public office without viewing them as representing solely Aboriginal interests.

How truly exciting it would be if and when Canada and Aboriginal Canadians broke out of age-old patterns, embraced real change, and began to achieve some of these things.

Now cast your eyes over that list again, but this time from a different perspective. These items are not a distant dream – in fact, they are part of today's Canadian reality. Take careful note of the following:

> The Government of Canada renamed the Queen Charlotte Islands as Haida Gwaii, recognizing the importance of cultural names to First Nations.
> The residents of North Battleford, Saskatchewan, have built a combined public, Catholic, and First Nations school to better serve the community.
> Aditya Jha, former president and former CEO of Karma Candy and one of the most prominent Indo-Canadian leaders in the country, is using his foundation to engage Canadian business leaders in helping Aboriginal young people consider entrepreneurial careers.

> The urban reserve in Saskatoon is providing an excellent model for commercial collaboration and Aboriginal business development and has sparked First Nations entrepreneurship in the province.
> Universities and colleges from Labrador to Yukon have developed special programs for Aboriginal students, attracting tens of thousands of young adults into their classrooms. Large-scale Aboriginal participation in postsecondary education is a reality, not a pipe dream.
> The development of high-speed digital transmission systems in the NWT is allowing the delivery of impressive diagnosis and treatment facilities to remote communities, connected to first-rate physicians and high-quality services in Edmonton.
> The Nisga'a First Nation of northwestern BC has developed a system that permits private ownership – by Aboriginal and non-Aboriginal people alike – of settlement lands in the Nass Valley. It is not alone in changing the rules of reserve life.
> The Indian Claims Commission has settled dozens of potentially controversial disputes through mediation and alternative dispute resolution mechanisms. Most Aboriginal legal challenges are now being solved outside of the courts.
> Teaching about Aboriginal peoples and culture in schools, colleges, and universities has been transformed. Culturally sensitive and Aboriginally inspired instruction, often by Aboriginal writers, teachers, and schools, has become commonplace.
> Treatment systems based on Indigenous traditions and cultures, including sentencing circles, have succeeded in reducing recidivism among Aboriginal offenders.
> Elders across northern Canada are working with school officials to develop locally appropriate curriculum materials and educational programs designed to provide youth with access to traditional languages. Many schools, colleges, and universities have elder-in-residence programs.
> Prominent Canadians, including former prime minister Paul Martin, have committed formidable time and resources to promote Aboriginal entrepreneurship across Canada and have developed formal systems for supporting Indigenous business development. Canada's banks are at the forefront of this effort. A shared non-Aboriginal and Aboriginal effort to address issues relating to murdered and missing Indigenous women is another excellent example of this coming together of talent, commitment, and energy.

> Modern treaties and court decisions mandating the duty to consult Indigenous peoples have resulted in resource developments that incorporate Aboriginal priorities and that return substantial benefits to the local population.
> Recognizing the limitations of small town self-government, Inuit in Nunavik (northern Quebec) have developed a regional government, Kativik, that has the potential to be highly effective in dealing with collective needs and interests.
> Canada is celebrating Aboriginal creative accomplishments. Meanwhile, through events such as the Indspire Awards, many Indigenous artists are being recognized for their impressive talents as painters, musicians, writers, and the like.
> New models of regional development, most evident in the North but also impressively displayed during the lead-up to the 2010 Vancouver Olympics and as part of the proposed Mackenzie Valley pipeline project, are incorporating job creation for local Aboriginal people and are engaging heavily with Indigenous businesses.
> In many parts of the country, but especially in the North, Indigenous knowledge and the wisdom of elders are being directly integrated into regional resource management regimes.
> Canadian courts, including the Supreme Court of Canada, have acknowledged the important insights to be gained from oral tradition and oral testimony and have mandated that judges take Indigenous knowledge and cultures into account when making decisions.
> More and more Aboriginal politicians are being elected at all levels of government. Several Aboriginal people, such as Rod Bruinooge (Conservative, Winnipeg South), have been elected in constituencies that are not dominated by Indigenous electors.
> The BC government, which had instructed provincial counsel to challenge the idea that Aboriginal peoples live in organized societies, has since backed off this controversial and highly offensive legal position. The government's position today is that Indigenous societies were organized and sustainable in the years before the Europeans entered the region.

Canadians can and do live as treaty peoples. The examples above are only a handful. The future is already here. More can be done, of course. So far, we have only visited the common ground. We have yet to occupy it.

# APPENDICES

# APPENDIX A

## VISION STATEMENT OF THE ASSEMBLY OF FIRST NATIONS

*A Declaration of First Nations*

We the Original Peoples of this land know the Creator put us here.

The Creator gave us laws that govern all our relationships to live in harmony with nature and mankind.

The Laws of the Creator defined our rights and responsibilities.

The Creator gave us our spiritual beliefs, our languages, our culture, and a place on Mother Earth which provided us with all our needs.

We have maintained our Freedom, our Languages, and our Traditions from time immemorial.

We continue to exercise the rights and fulfill the responsibilities and obligations given to us by the Creator for the land upon which we were placed.

The Creator has given us the right to govern ourselves and the right to self-determination.

The rights and responsibilities given to us by the Creator cannot be altered or taken away by any other Nation.

# APPENDIX B

In representing Inuit in the coming years, ITK will direct its energies to the following goals and objectives:

1. To function as the collective voice of Canadian Inuit in promoting a better understanding among other Canadians of Inuit rights and culture and of Inuit contributions to Canada.
2. To monitor and prepare responses to constitutional reform issues in Canada that may affect the rights or well-being of Inuit and to maintain Inuit primacy through co-operative and productive relations with national institutions.
3. To pursue, in concert with the Inuit Circumpolar Council (Canada) and in accordance with the *Circumpolar Inuit Declaration on Sovereignty in the Arctic* and the *Circumpolar Inuit Declaration on Resource Development Principles in Inuit Nunaat,* those rights and interest of Canadian Inuit that share both national and international dimensions.

4. To contribute to a significant and sustained improvement in the socio-economic well-being of Inuit in Canada, with a view to closing and eliminating gaps between Inuit and non-Aboriginal Canada; and,
5. To support the promotion of Inuit identity thought the increased vitality and use of the Inuit language.

# APPENDIX C

## VISION STATEMENT OF THE UNION OF BRITISH COLUMBIA INDIAN CHIEFS

### Our Vision

One of the main principles of the Union of British Columbia Indian Chiefs is that, despite our differences, we will be stronger if we work together. The goal of the UBCIC is to support the work of our people, whether at the community, nation or international level, in our common fight for the recognition of our aboriginal rights and respect for our cultures and societies. Our goal, the goal of the people, has been to give the aboriginal people of BC a voice strong enough to be heard in every corner of the world. We have, and we continue, to carry out this mission in a number of different ways.

Another major principle behind our organization is the belief that knowledge is power. We are dedicated to information-sharing as well as to the fostering of fundamental and necessary research skills for Indian people in the province.

### Our Mission

> to improve intertribal relationships through common strategies to protect our Aboriginal Title

> to hold the federal government to its fiduciary obligations and have them change their extinguishment policy
> to support our peoples at regional, national and international forums
> to continue to defend our Aboriginal Title through the revival of our way of life (political, social, economic and spiritual)
> to build trust, honour and respect so we may achieve security and liberty in our lifetime and continue the healing and reconciliation (decolonization) of our Nations.

# APPENDIX D

## PARTY STATEMENTS ON ABORIGINAL AFFAIRS DURING THE 2006 FEDERAL ELECTION (EXCERPTS)

### Conservative Party of Canada

The fundamental obligation of the federal government is to improve the living conditions of Aboriginal Canadians, including the Inuit, in terms of economic opportunity, health, education, and community safety . . .

The Parliament of Canada must develop legislation which governs the delivery of federal governmental programs to Aboriginal Canadians. Both Aboriginal and non-Aboriginal Canadians deserve to know the legislative basis upon which the Government of Canada is expending funds on Aboriginal health, education, social welfare and infrastructure. Legislation should be developed which governs such programs and which prescribes the standards of service which the federal government has undertaken to provide to aboriginal Canadians . . .

The Indian Act (and related legislation) should be replaced by a modern legislative framework which provides for the devolution of full legal and democratic responsibility to First Nations, including the Inuit, for their own affairs within the overall constitutional framework of our federal state.

Such legislative reform should be pursued following full consultation with First Nations, with the objective of achieving a full and complete devolution of democratic authority that is consistent with the devolution of other decision making responsibility within our federal system. First Nations like other Canadians, are entitled to enjoy democratic control over their own affairs within a legislative context that ensures certainty, stability, respect for the rule of law and which balances collective and individual responsibility.

First Nation communities must have the flexibility to determine for themselves, whether and how free market principles, such as individual property ownership should apply to reserve lands. Self government should be accomplished in a manner which takes into account the cultural and linguistic diversity of Canada's First Nations. Within the context of the Canadian Constitution, we should be prepared to make flexible accommodations for the protection of language and culture within self-government agreements . . .

Both Aboriginal and non-Aboriginal Canadians are entitled to complete transparency and accountability in the expenditure of all public funds on Aboriginal programs, services and inter-governmental transfers. Aboriginals, like other Canadians, must have ready access to police and judicial intervention to constrain and check any exercise of governmental authority (whether Aboriginal or non-Aboriginal) which is illegal, corrupt or an abuse of power . . .

We are a nation governed by the Constitution Act, under which the rights of all citizens are protected and advanced by the Charter of Rights and Freedoms. Our future together as a country must be built upon the universal application of that framework.

All Aboriginal rights recognized under Section 35 of the Constitution must be conferred within the four square corners of the Constitution Act and the Charter, with full protection for equality rights, such as women's rights, for both Aboriginal and non-Aboriginal Canadians. Future Aboriginal legislation, policies and programs must balance the collective rights of Aboriginal Canadians under Section 35 of the Constitution with the individual equality rights enshrined in the Charter – which protect all Canadians – whether Aboriginal or non-Aboriginal. Aboriginal Canadians are entitled to the full benefits of Canadian citizenship and the full protection of the

Charter – in areas such as economic opportunity, the delivery of health services, community safety, women's rights, respect for the rule of law, and the education and protection of children. Canada must develop in a manner that ensures constitutional equality and workability . . .

Settlement of all outstanding "comprehensive claims" must be pursued on the basis of a clear framework which balances the rights of Aboriginal claimants with those of Canada – in particular, negotiated settlements must balance the economic and social needs of Aboriginal Canadians with Canada's need for certainty and finality of terms. Self government agreements must reflect Canada's need for both efficacy and practicality in institutional structure, and "constitutional harmony" so as not to impede the overall governance of Canada . . .

The federal government should, as a priority, adopt measures to resolve the existing backlog of "specific" claims so as to provide justice for Aboriginal claimants, together with certainty for Government, industry and non-Aboriginal Canadians. Institutional reform in the specific claim area should be pursued in a manner which resolves claims in a timely manner. The jurisdiction of the Federal Court should be expanded and the arbitrary ambit of the Indian and Northern Affairs Canada (INAC) Minister and the Specific Claims Policy contracted to eliminate the inherent conflict of interest of the Federal Crown in the resolution of "specific claims."

On the matter of Aboriginal land title, the Conservative Party supports the development of a property regime that would encourage lending for private housing and businesses. This will promote economic opportunity and individual freedom.

A Conservative Government, in conjunction with First Nations, would create a First Nations Land Ownership Act, which would transfer Reserve land title from the Federal Crown to willing First Nations.

### Liberal Party of Canada

Relationships/Negotiations – The Government has committed to strengthening the ability of Aboriginal organizations to contribute more effectively to public policy making.

Accountability for Results – The Government will prepare regular "Progress Reports," done in conjunction with Aboriginal groups, and fully disclose federal spending on Aboriginal programs.

Health – We will continue our work to improve the health of Aboriginal peoples with policies that reflect the unique needs and perspectives of diverse populations, regions and communities. The Government also acknowledges the need for a long-term federal commitment to Aboriginal health needs.

Education/Life-Long Learning – We will work with Aboriginal, provincial and territorial partners to encourage school innovation both on and off reserve, support First Nations education systems and create new reporting tools to ensure greater accountability in Aboriginal education. Agreement was also reached on the integration of Aboriginal Early Learning and Child Care programs that will provide more access to programming for children and families and reduce administrative burden.

Housing – We committed to creating Aboriginal institutions and capacity to meet housing needs, while developing skills in land, housing and financial management.

Economic Opportunities – We committed to developing an Aboriginal Economic Development Framework to meet the needs of First Nations, Inuit and Métis Nation communities by removing legislative and regulatory barriers to economic development and ensuring that federal programs and Aboriginal institutions work more effectively together.

### New Democratic Party of Canada

We cannot afford a Canada that does not provide space for these Original Nations to exercise their rights and share their talents and energies. It is time for a genuine commitment to be made and fulfilled.

Despite the hope for the future envisioned in the recommendations of the report of the Royal Commission on Aboriginal Peoples, Liberal policy about Original Peoples has been bogged down in endless processes that go nowhere. It's more of the status quo, more broken promises, more litigation – more denial of rights.

Costly negotiations with no results, self-government discussions that go nowhere, round tables that just go round and round, First Ministers' Meetings to make commitments without mechanisms to guarantee delivery and accountability, and lofty promises in Speeches from the Throne that await budgets and lead to meetings and more promises. Everything but concrete results.

[List of priorities:]

> Recognizing Canada's responsibilities for residential schools abuse by quickly implementing lump-sum compensation, a Truth and Reconciliation process and an apology by the Prime Minister in the House of Commons. Jack Layton and the NDP will stop the federal government from wasting millions of dollars challenging legitimate claims and painting victims as liars.
> Accepting responsibility for efficient resolution of claims by respecting the 1998 Joint Task Force report that recommends an independent, effective system to resolve land claim disputes. Jack Layton and the NDP will establish an Independent Claims Commission to decide on specific claims and a comprehensive claims policy that respects Treaty-based settlements, so that Canada can meet its legal obligations.
> Developing community economies with people as the priority by providing infrastructure for First Nations, Métis, and Inuit peoples to fully participate in Canada's prosperity. This will include legislating financial reforms to provide enhanced access to capital for community economic development and increasing management of natural resources and sustainable development.
> Supporting First Nations, Métis, and Inuit initiatives to improve health.
> Provide adequate housing, water, and infrastructure.
> Respect traditional healing, working together with western medicine to provide quality care.
> Respond to the unique health needs of northern and remote communities.
> Encourage traditional nutrition, fitness, and breastfeeding practices.
> Work with First Nations, Métis and Inuit peoples to develop comprehensive and holistic mental health and wellness strategies with special focus on healing, addictions and suicide prevention.

> Creating approaches to justice that heal and provide opportunity by giving Indigenous youth better opportunities than those provided by gangs and by encouraging healing facilities and systems of restorative justice that also assist victims of crime.
> Ensuring First Nations, Métis, and Inuit communities have infrastructure, sustainable housing, water and other services equal to those that are enjoyed by Canadians by respecting community decisions and knowledge, by training local people to maintain and operate systems and by making clean drinking water and sustainable waste treatment a top priority.
> Respecting implementation of the inherent right to self-governance by creating legal space and recognition for the legitimacy and jurisdiction of Indigenous governments with a properly compensated and trained public service and by promoting supporting systems of government that have the support of communities and nations, including their instruments for accountability, recourse to appeal, human rights, audits, matrimonial property and encouraging the restoration of civil society and community-based non-governmental activity.
> Restoring the health of languages by strengthening First Nations, Métis, and Inuit communities and culture by supporting their efforts to restore – in this generation – the health of Indigenous languages. Jack Layton and the NDP will develop a corps of trained second-language teachers and provide positions for them.
> Making Canada safe for First Nations, Métis and Inuit women, wherever they are, by taking immediate action on the recommendations of the Amnesty International's Stolen Sisters Report and by supporting efforts of native women to develop healing centres and educational and training opportunities.
> Emphasizing education and training of children, youth and adults by encouraging the participation of public and private sectors with the federal government in the development of programs that will move tens of thousands of persons into employment in health, education, social services, sciences, commerce, engineering, trades and entrepreneurial opportunities.
> Ensuring equitable participation of First Nations, Métis, and Inuit peoples and governments in Canada's stewardship of air, water and lands.
> Encourage environmental career choices.

> Provide specific space on boards, commissions and international delegations.
> Ensure equitable  participation in environmental projects and activities, especially those related to climate change.
> Keep governments accountable for their promises and obligations by appointing a Parliamentary Commissioner to use international and mutually-acceptable standards as the basis for regular public report cards on government conduct. The Commissioner will receive and investigate complaints about government actions or omissions, negotiate their resolution, and report to Parliament when recommendations are not accepted and implemented.

# APPENDIX E

## DECLARATION ON THE RIGHTS OF INDIGENOUS PEOPLES, 2007

*The General Assembly,*

*Guided* by the purposes and principles of the Charter of the United Nations, and good faith in the fulfilment of the obligations assumed by States in accordance with the Charter,

*Affirming* that Indigenous peoples are equal to all other peoples, while recognizing the right of all peoples to be different, to consider themselves different, and to be respected as such,

*Affirming also* that all peoples contribute to the diversity and richness of civilizations and cultures, which constitute the common heritage of humankind,

*Affirming further* that all doctrines, policies and practices based on or advocating superiority of peoples or individuals on the basis of national origin or racial, religious, ethnic or cultural differences are racist, scientifically false, legally invalid, morally condemnable and socially unjust,

*Reaffirming* that Indigenous peoples, in the exercise of their rights, should be free from discrimination of any kind,

*Concerned* that Indigenous peoples have suffered from historic injustices as a result of, inter alia, their colonization and dispossession of their lands, territories and resources, thus preventing them from exercising, in particular, their right to development in accordance with their own needs and interests,

*Recognizing* the urgent need to respect and promote the inherent rights of Indigenous peoples which derive from their political, economic and social structures and from their cultures, spiritual traditions, histories and philosophies, especially their rights to their lands, territories and resources,

*Recognizing* also the urgent need to respect and promote the rights of Indigenous peoples affirmed in treaties, agreements and other constructive arrangements with States,

*Welcoming* the fact that Indigenous peoples are organizing themselves for political, economic, social and cultural enhancement and in order to bring to an end all forms of discrimination and oppression wherever they occur,

*Convinced* that control by Indigenous peoples over developments affecting them and their lands, territories and resources will enable them to maintain and strengthen their institutions, cultures and traditions, and to promote their development in accordance with their aspirations and needs,

*Recognizing* that respect for Indigenous knowledge, cultures and traditional practices contributes to sustainable and equitable development and proper management of the environment,

*Emphasizing* the contribution of the demilitarization of the lands and territories of Indigenous peoples to peace, economic and social progress and development, understanding and friendly relations among nations and peoples of the world,

*Recognizing* in particular the right of Indigenous families and communities to retain shared responsibility for the upbringing, training, education and well-being of their children, consistent with the rights of the child,

*Considering* that the rights affirmed in treaties, agreements and other constructive arrangements between States and Indigenous peoples are, in some situations, matters of international concern, interest, responsibility and character,

*Considering also* that treaties, agreements and other constructive arrangements, and the relationship they represent, are the basis for a strengthened partnership between Indigenous peoples and States,

*Acknowledging* that the Charter of the United Nations, the International Covenant on Economic, Social and Cultural Rights and the International Covenant on Civil and Political Rights, as well as the Vienna Declaration and Programme of Action, affirm the fundamental importance of the right to self-determination of all peoples, by virtue of which they freely determine their political status and freely pursue their economic, social and cultural development,

*Bearing in mind* that nothing in this Declaration may be used to deny any peoples their right to self-determination, exercised in conformity with international law,

*Convinced* that the recognition of the rights of Indigenous peoples in this Declaration will enhance harmonious and cooperative relations between the State and Indigenous peoples, based on principles of justice, democracy, respect for human rights, non-discrimination and good faith,

*Encouraging* States to comply with and effectively implement all their obligations as they apply to Indigenous peoples under international instruments, in particular those related to human rights, in consultation and cooperation with the peoples concerned,

*Emphasizing* that the United Nations has an important and continuing role to play in promoting and protecting the rights of Indigenous peoples,

*Believing* that this Declaration is a further important step forward for the recognition, promotion and protection of the rights and freedoms of Indigenous peoples and in the development of relevant activities of the United Nations system in this field,

*Recognizing* and reaffirming that Indigenous individuals are entitled without discrimination to all human rights recognized in international law, and that Indigenous peoples possess collective rights which are indispensable for their existence, well-being and integral development as peoples,

*Recognizing* that the situation of Indigenous peoples varies from region to region and from country to country and that the significance of national and regional particularities and various historical and cultural backgrounds should be taken into consideration,

*Solemnly proclaims* the following United Nations Declaration on the Rights of Indigenous Peoples as a standard of achievement to be pursued in a spirit of partnership and mutual respect.

# REFERENCES AND FURTHER READING

## INTRODUCTION

For excellent general histories of Native-newcomer relations in Canada, see J.R. Miller's *Skyscrapers Hide the Heavens: A History of Indian-White Relations in Canada* (Toronto: University of Toronto Press, 2000) and Olive Dickason and David McNab's *Canada's First Nations: A History of Founding Peoples from Earliest Times* (Toronto: University of Oxford Press, 2008).

On the evolution of Canada's Aboriginal policy, see J.R. Miller, *Compact, Contract, Covenant: Aboriginal Treaty-Making in Canada* (Toronto: University of Toronto Press, 2009) and John L. Tobias, "Protection, Civilization, Assimilation: An Outline of Canada's Indian Policy," *Western Canadian Journal of Anthropology* 6, 2 (1976): 13-30. The Mi'kmaq partnership with the Crown is discussed in William Wicken, *Mi'kmaq Treaties on Trial* (Toronto: University of Toronto Press, 2002) and in Ken Coates, *The Marshall Decision and Aboriginal Rights in the Maritimes* (Montreal/Kingston: McGill-Queen's University Press, 2000).

To read more about the loss of land, health, culture, and people that accompanied colonialism, start with the following: Ingeborg Marshall, *A History and Ethnography of the Beothuk* (Montreal/Kingston: McGill-Queen's University Press, 1996); Bruce Trigger, *Natives and Newcomers: Canada's "Heroic Age" Reconsidered* (Montreal/Kingston: McGill-Queen's University Press, 1986); John Webster Grant, *The Moon of Wintertime: Missionaries and the Indians of Canada* (Toronto: University of Toronto Press, 1984); Cole Harris, *Making Native Space: Colonialism, Resistance, and Reserves in British Columbia* (Vancouver: UBC Press, 2002); J.R. Miller, *Shingwauk's Vision: A History of Native Residential Schools* (Toronto: University of Toronto Press, 1996); John Milloy, *A National Crime: The Canadian Government and the Indian Residential School System* (Winnipeg: University of Manitoba Press, 1999); and Douglas

Cole, *An Iron Hand upon the People: The Law against the Potlatch on the Northwest Coast* (Vancouver: Douglas and McIntyre, 1990). On the Innu rejection of the Catholic Church's apology for abuse in residential schools, see Colin Samson, "Sexual Abuse and Assimilation: Oblates, Teachers and the Innu of Labrador," *Sexualities* February 6, 1 (2003): 46-53.

For the global context on Indigenous rights, see Ken Coates, *A Global History of Indigenous Peoples* (London: Palgrave Macmillan, 2004). The best study on Aboriginal political activism in Canada is Paul Tennant's *Aboriginal Peoples and Politics: The Indian Land Question in BC* (Vancouver: UBC Press, 1990). See also Grace Woo, "Canada's Forgotten Founders: The Modern Significance of the Haudenosaunee (Iroquois) Application for Membership in the League of Nations," *Law, Social Justice, and Global Development Journal* 1 (2003), http://www2.warwick.ac.uk/fac/soc/law/elj/lgd/2003_1/woo/woo.rtf, and Laurie Meijer Drees, *The Indian Association of Alberta: A History of Political Action* (Vancouver: UBC Press, 2002). For a summary of Indigenous attitudes to education, see the Royal Commission on Aboriginal Peoples, *Report of the Royal Commission on Aboriginal Peoples*, Vol. 3, *Gathering Strength*, sec. 5, "Education" (Ottawa: Indian and Northern Affairs, 1996).

To read more about the White Paper and Aboriginal peoples' responses to it, see *Statement of the Government of Canada on Indian Policy* (Ottawa: Indian Affairs, 1969), also available online. For a political memoir by the minister responsible, see Jean Chrétien's *Straight from the Heart* (Toronto: Key Porter, 2007). One of the most influential Aboriginal responses to the White Paper was Harold Cardinal's *The Unjust Society: The Tragedy of Canada's Indians* (Edmonton: Hurtig, 1969), and the best study of the government's motivations is Sally Weaver's *Making Canadian Indian Policy: The Hidden Agenda, 1968-1970* (Toronto: University of Toronto Press, 1981).

Studies that trace the shift towards Aboriginal control of the national agenda include Paul W. DePasquale, *Natives and Settlers Now and Then: Historical Issues and Current Perspectives on Treaties and Land Claims in Canada* (Edmonton: University of Alberta Press, 2007); Tom Molloy, *The World Is Our Witness: The Historic Journey of the Nisga'a into Canada* (Calgary: Fifth House, 2000); and R. Jhappan, "Inherency, Three Nations and Collective Rights: The Evolution of Aboriginal Constitutional Discourse from 1982 to the Charlottetown Accord," *International Journal of Canadian Studies* 7-8 (1993): 224-59. On self-government and its challenges and implementation, see Government of Canada, *Aboriginal Self-Government: The Government of Canada's Approach to Implementation of the Inherent Right and the Negotiation of Aboriginal Self-Government* (Ottawa: Indian and Northern Affairs, 1995); Dan Russell, *A People's Dream: Aboriginal Self-Government in Canada* (Vancouver: UBC Press, 2000); Katherine Beaty Chiste, "Aboriginal Women and Self-Government: Challenging Leviathan," *American Indian Culture and Research Journal* 18, 3 (1994): 19-43; and Frances Abele and Michael J. Prince, "Four Pathways to Aboriginal Self-Government in Canada," *American Review of Canadian Studies* 36, 4 (2006): 568-95.

Non-Aboriginal responses to Charlottetown include Thomas Flanagan's *First Nations? Second Thoughts* (Montreal/Kingston: McGill-Queen's University Press,

2000) and Mel Smith, *Our Home or Native Land: What Governments' Aboriginal Policy Is Doing to Canada* (Victoria: Fraser Institute, 1995).

To read more about the issue of defining Aboriginal peoples in Canada, see Augie Fleras, *Unequal Relations: An Introduction to Race, Ethnic, and Aboriginal Dynamics in Canada,* 7th ed. (Toronto: Pearson, 2011); Maximilian C. Forte, ed., *Who Is an Indian? Race, Place, and the Politics of Indigeneity in the Americas* (Toronto: University of Toronto Press, 2013); Frank Trovato and Anatole Romaniuk, eds., *Aboriginal Populations: Social, Demographic, and Epidemiological Perspectives* (Edmonton: University of Alberta Press, 2014); Christopher Adams, Ian Peach, and Gregg Dahl, eds., *Métis in Canada: History, Identity, Law, and Politics* (Edmonton: University of Alberta Press, 2013); and Robert Muckle, *Indigenous Peoples of North America: A Concise Anthropological Overview* (Toronto: University of Toronto Press, 2012).

## CHAPTER 1: THE TRADITIONALISTS

Over the past twenty years, a growing number of Aboriginal writers and thinkers have brought new perspectives to understanding Aboriginal people's position and opportunities in Canada. In addition to our summary of their thought, see Menno Boldt, *Surviving as Indians: The Challenge of Self-Government* (Toronto: University of Toronto Press, 1993) and Calvin Helin, *Dances with Dependency: Out of Poverty through Self-Reliance* (Woodland Hills: Ravencrest, 2008). Both books provide different but useful perspectives on how Indigenous peoples might respond to contemporary challenges. See also Annis May Timpson, ed., *First Nations, First Thoughts: The Impact of Indigenous Thought in Canada* (Vancouver: UBC Press, 2009).

For further readings by Aboriginal leaders and scholars who can be defined as traditionalists, see Taiaiake Gerald Alfred, *Peace, Power, Righteousness: An Indigenous Manifesto,* 2nd ed. (Toronto: Oxford University Press, 2009); *Heeding the Voices of Our Ancestors: Kahnawake Mohawk Politics and the Rise of Native Nationalism* (Toronto: Oxford University Press, 1995); and *Wasase: Indigenous Pathways of Action and Freedom* (Peterborough: Broadview Press, 2005). See also his "The Politics of Recognition: A Colonial Groundhog Day," discussion paper co-authored with Erin Tomkins for Chiefs of Ontario, August 2010; "What Is Radical Imagination? Indigenous Struggles in Canada," *Affinities: A Journal of Radical Theory, Culture, and Action* 4, 2 (2010): 5-8; "First Nation Perspectives on Political Identity," First Nations Citizenship Research and Policy Series: Building towards Change, Assembly of First Nations, June 2009; "Colonialism and State Dependency," *Journal of Aboriginal Health* 5, 2 (2009): 42-60; "Restitution Is the Real Pathway to Justice for Indigenous Peoples," in *Response, Responsibility, and Renewal: Canada's Truth and Reconciliation Journey,* Aboriginal Healing Foundation Research Series (Ottawa: Aboriginal Healing Foundation, 2009), 179-87; "Warrior Societies in Contemporary Indigenous Communities," co-authored with Lana Lowe, background paper, Ipperwash Inquiry, May 2005; and "Being Indigenous: Resurgences against Contemporary Colonialism," co-authored with Jeff Corntassel, *Government and Opposition: An International Journal of Comparative Politics* 40, 4 (2005): 597-614.

Glen Coulthard's views are encapsulated in *Red Skin, White Masks: Rejecting the Colonial Politics of Recognition* (Minneapolis: University of Minnesota Press, 2014); "Subjects of Empire: Indigenous Peoples and the 'Politics of Recognition' in Canada," *Contemporary Political Theory* 6, 4 (2007): 437-60; and "Placing #IdleNoMore in Historical Context: Three Decades of Indigenous Resistance in Canada Inform Today's Movement," *The Tyee*, 4 January 2013. See also "Resisting Culture: Seyla Benhabib's Deliberative Approach to the Politics of Recognition in Colonial Contexts," in *Deliberative Democracy in Practice,* ed. David Kahane, Daniel Weinstock, Dominique Leydet, and Melissa Williams (Vancouver: UBC Press, 2010), 138-54; and "Beyond Recognition: Indigenous Self-Determination as Prefigurative Practice," in *Lighting the Eighth Fire: The Liberation, Resurgence, and Protection of Indigenous Nations,* ed. Leanne Simpson (Winnipeg: Arbeiter Ring Press, 2008), 187-204. Finally, see Avigail Eisenberg, Jeremy Webber, Glen Coulthard, and Andrée Boisselle, eds., *Recognition versus Self-Determination: Dilemmas of Emancipatory Politics* (Vancouver: UBC Press).

For an introduction to Joyce Green's work, see *Making Space for Indigenous Feminism* (Halifax: Fernwood, 2007). For other works by Green, see (with Ian Peach) "Prescribing Post-Colonial Politics and Policy in Saskatchewan," *in Belonging? Diversity, Recognition, and Shared Citizenship in Canada,* ed. Keith G. Banting, Thomas J. Courchene, and F. Leslie Seidle (Montreal: Institute for Research on Public Policy, 2007), 263-84; "From Stonechild to Social Cohesion: Anti-Racist Challenges for Saskatchewan," *Canadian Journal of Political Science* 39, 1 (2006): 507-27; "Self-Determination, Citizenship, and Federalism: Indigenous and Canadian Palimpsest," in *Reconfiguring Aboriginal-State Relations,* ed. Michael Murphy (Kingston: Institute of Intergovernmental Relations, School of Policy Studies, Queen's University, 2005), 329-52; and "Parsing Identity and Identity Politics," *International Journal of Critical Indigenous Studies* 2, 2 (2009): 36-46.

Patricia Monture-Angus's views are presented powerfully in *Journeying Forward: Dream First Nations' Independence* (Halifax: Fernwood, 1999). See also Patricia Monture-Angus and Patricia McGuire, eds., *First Voices: An Aboriginal Women's Reader* (Toronto: Inanna Publications, 2009) and Patricia Monture-Angus, *Thunder in My Soul: A Mohawk Woman Speaks* (Halifax: Fernwood, 2003).

For works by Kiera L. Ladner, see in particular "Negotiated Inferiority: RCAP's Vision of a Renewed Relationship," *American Review of Canadian Studies* 31, 1-2 (2001): 241-64, and Kiera Ladner and Caroline Dick, "Out of the Fires of Hell: Globalization as a Solution to Globalization – An Indigenist Perspective," *Canadian Journal of Law and Society* 23, 1-2 (2008): 63-91. See also Kiera L. Ladner, "Understanding the Impact of Self-Determination on Communities in Crisis," *Journal of Aboriginal Health* 5, 2 (2009): 88-101; (co-authored with Michael McCrossan) "Whose Shared History?" *Labour/Le Travail* 73 (Spring 2014): 200-2; "Visions of Neo-Colonialism? Renewing the Relationship with Aboriginal Peoples," *Canadian Journal of Native Studies* 21 (2001): 105-35; and "Governing within an Ecological Context: Creating an Alternative Understanding of Blackfoot Governance," *Studies in Political Economy* 70 (Spring 2003): 125-52.

## CHAPTER 2: TREATY FEDERALISM

To read more of these scholars' works and others who share their vision, see Ovide Mercredi and Mary Ellen Turpel, *In the Rapids: Navigating the Future of First Nations* (Toronto: Penguin, 1993). Phil Fontaine's remarks were delivered, on behalf of the National Assembly of First Nations, to the Royal Commission on Aboriginal Peoples on January 7, 1998. Alan Cairns's discussion of the *Report of the Royal Commission* comes from *Citizen Plus: Aboriginal Peoples and the Canadian State* (Vancouver: UBC Press, 2000). See also "Coming to Terms with the Past," in *Politics and the Past: On Repairing Historical Injustices,* ed. John Torpey (Lanham, MD: Rowman and Littlefield Publishers, 2003), 63-90. James (Sákéj) Youngblood Henderson articulates his position succinctly in "Empowering Treaty Federalism," *Saskatchewan Law Review* 58 (1994): 241-329. For other works by Henderson, see *Indigenous Diplomacy and the Rights of Peoples: Achieving UN Recognition* (Saskatoon: Purich Press, 2008); *Treaty Rights in the Constitution of Canada* (Toronto: Carswell, 2007); *First Nations Jurisprudence and Aboriginal Rights: Defining the Just Society* (Saskatoon: Native Law Centre, University of Saskatchewan, 2006); "Constitutional Vision and Judicial Commitment: Aboriginal and Treaty Rights in Canada," *Australian Indigenous Law Review* 14, 2 (2011): 24-48; "Dialogical Governance: A Mechanism of Constitutional Governance," *Saskatchewan Law Review* 71, 1 (2009): 29-73; "Constitutional Supremacy and the Deadbeat Crowns," *Directions* 5, 1 (2009): 40-44; and "Aboriginal and Treaty Rights and Tribunals," *Canadian Journal of Administrative Law and Practice* 19 (2006): 1-37.

Dan Russell outlines his vision in *A People's Dream: Aboriginal Self-Government in Canada* (Vancouver: UBC Press, 2000).

## CHAPTER 3: BRIDGING THE SOLITUDES

To explore the arguments of scholars who advocate bridging the solitudes between Aboriginal and non-Aboriginal peoples in Canada, see John Borrows's *Recovering Canada: The Insurgence of Indigenous Law* (Toronto: University of Toronto Press, 2002); *Canada's Indigenous Constitution* (Toronto: University of Toronto Press, 2010); (co-edited with Alexandra Harmon) *The Power of Promises: Rethinking Indian Treaties in the Pacific Northwest* (Seattle: Center for the Study of the Pacific Northwest/University of Washington Press, 2009); and *Drawing Out Law: A Spirit's Guide* (Toronto: University of Toronto Press, 2010). See also Emma LaRocque's *Defeathering the Indian* (Agincourt, ON: Book Society of Canada, 1975); (co-edited with Paul W. Depasquale and Renate Eigenbrod) *Across Cultures, Across Borders: Canadian Aboriginal and Native American Literatures* (Peterborough, ON: Broadview, 2010); and *When the Other Is Me: Native Resistance Discourse, 1850-1990* (Winnipeg: University of Manitoba Press, 2010).

Calvin Helin outlines his vision in *Dances with Dependency: Out of Poverty through Self-Reliance* (Vancouver: Orca Spirit, 2006). See also his *Dances with Spirits: Ancient Wisdom for a Modern World* (Winnipeg: Premier Publishing, 2014). For Bonita Beatty's approach, see "Integrating 'First' Principles into Aboriginal Administrations," *Policy Options* 18, 2 (1997): 31-34. She also presents her views in the following: "Facilitating Community Engagement in First Nation Governance in Northern Saskatchewan," paper at "Comparing Modes of Governance in Canada and the EU: Social Policy Engagement across Complex Multilevel Systems," University of Victoria, October 15, 2011; (with Loleen Berdahl) "Health Care and Aboriginal Seniors in Urban Canada: Helping a Neglected Class," *International Indigenous Policy Journal* 2, 1 (2011): http://ir.lib.uwo.ca/cgi/viewcontent.cgi?article= 1024&context=iipj; (with Greg Poelzer and Loleen Berdahl); "More Than Voting," *Policy Options* 35, 5 (2014): http://policyoptions.irpp.org/issues/beautiful-data/ poelzer-et-al/; and (with Loleen Berdahl and Greg Poelzer) "Blended Aboriginal Political Culture in Northern Saskatchewan," *Canadian Journal of Native Studies* 32, 2 (2012): 121-39.

Finally, see Dale Turner's *This Is Not a Peace Pipe: Towards a Critical Indigenous Philosophy* (Toronto: University of Toronto Press, 2006); "What Is Native American Philosophy? Towards a Critical Indigenous Philosophy," in *Nature of Philosophy: Whose Knowledge? Which Tradition?,* ed. George Yancy (Lanham, MD: Rowman and Littlefield, 2007); "Oral Histories and the Politics of (Mis)recognition," in *American Indian Thought: Philosophical Essays,* ed. Anne Waters (Malden, MA: Blackwell, 2003), 229-38; and "Vision: Towards an Understanding of Aboriginal Sovereignty," in *Canadian Political Philosophy: Contemporary Reflections,* ed. Ronald Beiner and W.J. Norman (Don Mills, ON: Oxford, 2001), 318-31. Also of interest in this field are Caroline Dick's review of Peter Russell's *Recognizing Aboriginal Title: The Mabo Case and Indigenous Resistance to English-Settler Colonialism, Canadian Journal of Political Science* 40, 3 (2007): 771-72, and her "The Politics of Intragroup Difference: First Nations' Women and the *Sawridge* Dispute," *Canadian Journal of Political Science* 39, 1 (2006): 97-116.

## CHAPTER 4: LEGAL RIGHTS, MORAL RIGHTS, AND WELL-BEING

Non-Aboriginal analysts and academics have reflected, at length, on the non-Aboriginal side of Native-newcomer relations. We discuss a selected list of the major authors and books. For a provocative but uneven view, see John Ralston Saul's extended and controversial essay *A Fair Country: Telling Truths about Canada* (Toronto: Viking, 2008). See also his "A Different Model of the Nation-State: Canada in the World and the Aboriginal Influence," *Saskatchewan Law Review* 75, 1 (2012): 3-12, and his latest work, *The Comeback* (Toronto: Penguin Random House, 2014).

To read more on the legal rights approach, see Melvin H. Smith, *Our Home or Native Land? What Governments' Aboriginal Policy Is Doing to Canada* (Toronto: Stoddart Publishing, 1995) and *Aboriginal Land Claims in British Columbia: Serious Concerns about the Nisga'a Deal* (Vancouver: Fraser Institute, 1999); and Bruce Clark, *Justice in Paradise* (Montreal/Kingston: McGill-Queen's University Press, 1999). For Clark's less polemical and historical work, see *Native Liberty, Crown Sovereignty: The Existing Aboriginal Right of Self-Government in Canada* (Montreal/Kingston: McGill-Queen's University Press, 1990).

On moral rights, see Charles Taylor's *Multiculturalism and "The Politics of Recognition,"* expanded paperback ed. (Princeton: Princeton University Press, 1994) and

"On the Nisga'a Treaty," *BC Studies* 120 (Winter 1998-99): 37-40. See also James Tully, *Strange Multiplicity: Constitution in an Age of Diversity* (Cambridge: Cambridge University Press, 1995); "Modern Constitutional Democracy and Imperialism," *Osgoode Hall Law Journal* 46, 3 (2008): 461-93; and "Property, Self-Government and Consent," *Canadian Journal of Political Science* 28, 1 (1995): 105-32. For a good introduction to Will Kymlicka's thought, see *Liberalism, Community, and Culture* (Oxford: Oxford University Press, 1989) and *Multicultural Citizenship: A Liberal Theory of Minority Rights* (Oxford: Oxford University Press, 1995). See also his *Multicultural Odysseys: Navigating the New International Politics of Diversity* (Oxford: Oxford University Press, 2007); (with Keith Banting) "Canadian Multiculturalism: Global Anxieties and Local Debates," *British Journal of Canadian Studies* 23, 1 (2010): 43-72; "Categorizing Groups, Categorizing States: Theorizing Minority Rights in a World of Deep Diversity," *Ethics and International Affairs* 23, 4 (2009): 371-88; and "Theorizing Indigenous Rights," *University of Toronto Law Journal* 49, 2 (1999): 281-93. Finally, see Alan Cairns's *Citizens Plus: Aboriginal Peoples and the Canadian State* (Vancouver: UBC Press, 2000) and *First Nations and the Canadian State: In Search of Coexistence* (Kingston, ON: Institute of Intergovernmental Relations, Queen's University, 2005).

For scholars and thinkers whose calls for change stem primarily from a concern for Aboriginal people's well-being, see Don Carmichael, Tom Pocklington and Greg Pyrcz, *Democracy, Rights, and Well-Being in Canada,* 2nd ed. (Toronto: Harcourt Brace, 2000) and Menno Boldt, *Surviving as Indians: The Challenge of Self-Government* (Toronto: University of Toronto Press, 1993). Boldt's earlier works may also be of interest. See J. Anthony Long and Menno Boldt, *Governments in Conflict: Provinces and Indian Nations in Canada* (Toronto: University of Toronto Press, 1988) and Menno Boldt and J. Anthony Long *The Quest for Justice: Aboriginal Peoples and Aboriginal Rights* (Toronto: University of Toronto Press, 1985).

## CHAPTER 5: POLITICAL AND INSTITUTIONAL APPROACHES

For the work of Michael Asch, see, in particular, *Home and Native Land: Aboriginal Rights and the Canadian Constitution* (Toronto: Methuen Publication, 1984) and *On Being Here to Stay: Treaties and Aboriginal Rights in Canada* (Toronto: University of Toronto Press, 2014). See also "Reflections on Relations between Indigenous Peoples and the Canadian State," *American Anthropologist* 106, 1 (2004): 165-68; "Governmentality, State Culture and Indigenous Rights," *Anthropologica* 49, 2 (2007): 281-84; (with Shirleen Smith) "Consociation Revisited: Nunavut, Denendeh and Canadian Constitutional Consciousness," *Etudes/Inuit/Studies* 16, 1-2 (1992): 97-114; and "Indigenous Self-Determination and Applied Anthropology in Canada: Finding a Place to Stand," *Anthropologica* 43, 2 (2001): 201-7.

Tom Flanagan articulates his vision fully in *First Nations? Second Thoughts* (Montreal/Kingston: McGill-Queen's University Press, 2000; 2nd ed., 2008). See also *Metis Lands in Manitoba* (Calgary: University of Calgary Press, 1991); "Adhesion to Canadian Indian Treaties and the Lubicon Lake Dispute," *Canadian Journal of Law and Society* 7, 2 (1992): 185-205; (with Christopher Alcantara and André Le

Dressay) *Beyond the Indian Act: Restoring Aboriginal Property Rights* (Montreal/ Kingston: McGill-Queen's University Press, 2010); (with Terry L. Anderson and Bruce L. Benson) *Self-Determination: The Other Path for Native Americans* (Palo Alto, CA: Stanford University Press, 2006); and "The History of Métis Aboriginal Rights: Politics, Principles and Policy," *Canadian Journal of Law and Society* 5 (1990) : 71-94.

Frances Widdowson's views are presented in Frances Widdowson and Albert Howard, *Disrobing the Aboriginal Industry: The Deception behind Indigenous Cultural Preservation* (Montreal/Kingston: McGill-Queen's University Press, 2008) and in "Separate but Unequal: The Political Economy of Aboriginal Dependency," which she presented at the annual conference of the Canadian Political Science Association, Dalhousie University, Halifax, Nova Scotia, June 1, 2003. See also (with Albert Howard) *Approaches to Aboriginal Education in Canada: Searching for Solutions* (Edmonton: Brush Education, 2013); "Corruption North of 60," *Policy Options/Options Politiques* 20 (1999): 37-40; "The Aboriginal Industry's New Clothes," *Policy Options/Options Politiques* (March 2002): 30-34; and "The Disaster of Nunavut," *Policy Options/Options Politiques* (January-February 1999): 58-61.

For Jane Dickson-Gilmore and Carole La Prairie's views on restorative justice, see *Will the Circle Be Unbroken? Aboriginal Communities, Restorative Justice, and the Challenges of Conflict and Change* (Toronto: University of Toronto Press, 2005); Jane Dickson-Gilmore, "Aboriginal Communities and Crime Prevention: Confronting the Challenges of Organized Crime," *IPC Review* 1 (March 2007): 89-110, and "Whither Restorativeness? Restorative Justice and the Challenge of Intimate Violence in Aboriginal Communities," *Canadian Journal of Criminology and Criminal Justice* 56, 4 (2014): 417-46; and Carol La Prairie, "Seen but Not Heard: Native People in the Inner City," Department of Justice, Communications and Consultation Branch, 1995.

Gabrielle Slowey explores the impact of the rise of neoliberalism on debates and developments in *Navigating Neoliberalism: Self-Determination and the Miskiswe Cree First Nation* (Vancouver: UBC Press, 2007). See also "Federalism and First Nations: In Search of Space," in *Constructing Tomorrow's Federalism: New Routes to Effective Governance*, ed. Ian Peach (Winnipeg: University of Manitoba Press, 2007), 157-70; "Boom Not Bust: Self-Determination and the Mikisew Cree First Nation," *Boom and Bust in Regional Development,* ed. Heather Myers (Prince George: UNBC Press, 2003); "Globalization and the Dispossessed: Impacts and Implications for First Nations," *American Review of Canadian Studies* 31, 1-2 (2001): 265-81; "America, Canada and ANWR: Bilateral Relations and Indigenous Struggles," *Native Americas* 18, 2 (2001): 26-32; and "Aboriginal People, Self-Government and the Extinguishment of Title: The Effective Elimination of 'Other'?" *Native Studies Review* 13, 1 (2000): 1-17.

Christopher Alcantara's pragmatic look at Aboriginal governance is outlined in *Negotiating the Deal: Comprehensive Land Claims Agreements in Canada* (Toronto: University of Toronto Press, 2013). See also (with Thomas Flanagan and André Le Dressay) *Beyond the Indian Act*; *Negotiating the Deal: Comprehensive Land Claims*

*Negotiations in Canada* (Toronto: University of Toronto Press, 2013) and (with Gary N. Wilson) "Mixing Politics and Business in the Canadian Arctic: Inuit Corporate Governance in Nunavik and the Inuvialuit Settlement Region," *Canadian Journal of Political Science* 45, 4 (2012): 781-804.

## CHAPTER 6: CULTURE AND EDUCATION

The emphasis, perfectly justified, on Aboriginal people and communities in crisis has not been balanced by comparable studies on major achievements and progress. On Aboriginal education, see Marie Battiste's important body of work, including *Decolonizing Education: Nurturing the Learning Spirit* (Saskatoon: Purich, 2013). There are many initiatives across Canada to revitalize Aboriginal languages. For just a sample of their achievements, see the books in UBC Press's First Nations Languages series and the University of Regina Press's *Cree: Language of the Plains* (2004) by Jean L. Okimasis. Statistics Canada tackles the challenging issue of Aboriginal language retention in "Aboriginal Languages in Canada," 2011 Census in Brief, and "Aboriginal Peoples and Language," both available online. The Atlas of Canada and CBC News also maintain online, interactive maps of Aboriginal languages. To read more about the continued practice and revitalization of hunting, fishing, and gathering traditions, see Thomas McIlwraith, *"We Are Still Didene": Stories of Hunting and History from Northern British Columbia* (Toronto: University of Toronto Press, 2012).

On justice and health, including insightful works that focus on contemporary challenges, see Jane Dickson-Gilmore and Carol La Prairie's *Will the Circle Be Un-Broken?*, discussed in Chapter 3; Marrie Wadden, *Where the Pavement Ends: Canada's Aboriginal Recovery Movement and the Urgent Need for Reconciliation* (Vancouver: Douglas and McIntyre, 2008); Rupert Ross, *Returning to the Teachings: Exploring Aboriginal Justice* (Toronto: Penguin, 2006); Chris Walmsley, *Protecting Aboriginal Children* (Vancouver: UBC Press, 2005); Alvin Evans, *Chee Chee: A Study of Aboriginal Suicide* (Montreal/Kingston: McGill-Queen's University Press, 2004); Sophia Couzos and Richard Murray, *Aboriginal Primary Health Care: An Evidence-Based Approach*, 3rd ed. (Toronto: Oxford University Press, 2008); Fyre Jean Graveline, *Healing Wounded Hearts* (Halifax: Fernwood, 2004); Mary-Ellen Kelm, *Colonizing Bodies: Aboriginal Health and Healing in British Columbia, 1900-50* (Vancouver: UBC Press, 1999); Laurence Kirmayer and Gail Valaskakis, eds., *Healing Traditions: The Mental Health of Aboriginal Peoples in Canada* (Vancouver: UBC Press, 2008); Richard Thatcher, *Fighting Firewater Fictions: Moving beyond the Disease Model of Alcoholism in First Nations* (Toronto: University of Toronto Press, 2004); James Waldram, *Revenge of the Windigo: The Construction of the Mind and Mental Health of North American Aboriginal Peoples* (Toronto: University of Toronto Press, 2004); James Waldram, Ann Herring, and T. Kue Young, *Aboriginal Health in Canada: Historical, Cultural and Epidemiological Perspectives,* 2nd ed. (Toronto: University of Toronto Press, 2006); and Laurie Meijer Drees, *Healing Histories: Stories from Canada's Indian Hospitals* (Edmonton: University of Alberta Press, 2012).

On sport and leisure, see Michael Robidoux, *Stickhandling through the Margins: First Nations Hockey in Canada* (Toronto: University of Toronto Press, 2012), and

Janice Forsyth and Audrey R. Giles, eds., *Aboriginal Peoples and Sport in Canada: Historical Foundations and Contemporary Issues* (Vancouver: UBC Press, 2012).

On Aboriginal storytelling, literature, and art, see Gail Valaskakis, *Indian Country: Essays on Contemporary Native Culture* (Waterloo: Wilfrid Laurier University Press, 2005); Louis Bird, *The Spirit Lives in the Mind: Omushkego Stories, Lives, and Dreams* (Montreal/Kingston: McGill-Queen's University Press, 2007); Marie Battiste, ed., *Reclaiming Indigenous Voice and Vision* (Vancouver: UBC Press, 2000); Katherine Palmer Gordon, *We Are Born with the Songs Inside Us: Lives and Stories of First Nations People in British Columbia* (Madeira Park: Harbour Publishing, 2013); Sam McKegney, *Magic Weapons: Aboriginal Writers Remaking Community after Residential School* (Winnipeg: University of Manitoba Press, 2007); Stephanie McKenzie, *Before the Country: Native Renaissance, Canadian Mythology* (Toronto: University of Toronto Press, 2007); Laura Smyth Groening, *Listening to Old Woman Speak: Natives and Alternatives in Canadian Literature* (Montreal/Kingston: McGill-Queen's University Press, 2005); Karen Duffek, and Charlotte Townsend-Gault, eds., *Bill Reid and Beyond: Expanding on Modern Native Art* (Vancouver: Douglas and McIntyre, 2005); Aldona Jonaitis, *Art of the Northwest Coast* (Vancouver: Douglas and McIntyre, 2006); Charlotte Townsend-Gault, Jennifer Kramer, and Ki-ke-in, eds., *Native Art of the Northwest Coast: A History of Changing Ideas* (Vancouver: UBC Press, 2013); James D. Keyser and Michael A. Klassen, *Plains Indian Rock Art* (Vancouver/Washington: UBC Press/University of Washington Press, 2001); and Derek Norton and Nigel Reading, *Cape Dorset Sculpture* (Vancouver: Douglas and McIntyre, 2005).

Aboriginal contributions to media and music are outlined in Lorna Roth, *Something New in the Air: The Story of First Peoples Television Broadcasting in Canada* (Montreal/Kingston: McGill-Queen's University Press, 2005); Mary Jane Miller, *Outside Looking In: Viewing First Nations Peoples in Canadian Dramatic Television Series* (Montreal/Kingston: McGill-Queen's University Press, 2008); Helen Molnar and Michael Meadows, *Songlines and Satellites: Indigenous Communication in Australia, the South Pacific, and Canada* (Halifax: Fernwood, 2002); and Lyn Whidden, *Essential Song: Three Decades of Northern Cree Music* (Waterloo: Wilfrid Laurier University Press, 2007).

On Aboriginal religion and spirituality, see James B. Waldram, *The Way of the Pipe: Aboriginal Spirituality and Symbolic Healing in Canadian Prisons* (Peterborough, ON: Broadview, 1997); Jennifer S.H. Brown and Robert Brightman, *"The Orders of the Dreamed": George Nelson on Cree and Northern Ojibwa Religion and Myth, 1823* (Winnipeg: University of Manitoba Press, 1990); Ronald Niezen, Kim Burgess, Manley Begay, and Phyllis Fast, *Spirit Wars: Native North American Religions in the Age of Nation Building* (Berkeley: University of California Press, 2000); and Angela Robinson, *Ta'n Teli-ktlamsitasit (Ways of Believing): Mi'kmaw Religion in Eskasoni, Nova Scotia* (Toronto: Pearson Prentice Hall, 2005). For an overview, see Ken Coates, "Indigenous Traditions," Chapter 5 in *World Religions: Canadian Perspectives -- Western Traditions,* ed. Doris Jakobish (Toronto: Nelson 2014).

The experience of Aboriginal peoples in cities is explored in Bonita Lawrence, *"Real" Indians and Others: Mixed-Blood Urban Native Peoples and Indigenous Nationhood* (Vancouver: UBC Press, 2004); Jim Silver et al., *In Their Own Voices: Building*

*Urban Aboriginal Communities* (Halifax: Fernwood, 2006); Evelyn Peters and Chris Andersen, eds., *Indigenous in the City: Contemporary Identities and Cultural Innovation* (Vancouver: UBC Press, 2013); and Alan B. Anderson, ed., *Home in the City: Urban Aboriginal Housing and Living Conditions* (Toronto: University of Toronto Press, 2012).

Statistics on Aboriginal education come from Statistics Canada, 2011, "The Educational Attainment of Aboriginal Peoples in Canada," available online. See also Marlene Brant Castellano, Lynne Davis, and Louise Lahache, *Aboriginal Education: Fulfilling the Promise* (Vancouver: UBC Press, 2001); Blair Stonechild, *New Buffalo: The Struggle for Aboriginal Post-Secondary Education in Canada* (Winnipeg: UBC Press, 2006); and Jerry Paquette and Gérald Fallon, *First Nations Education Policy in Canada: Progress or Gridlock?* (Toronto: University of Toronto Press, 2010). See also Linda Goulet and Keith Goulet, *Teaching Each Other: Nehinuw Concepts and Indigenous Pedagogies* (Vancouver: UBC Press, 2014), and Lorenzo Cherubini, *Aboriginal Student Engagement and Achievement: Educational Practices and Cultural Sustainability* (Vancouver: UBC Press, 2014).

New approaches to research are explored in Shawn Wilson, *Research Is Ceremony: Indigenous Research Methods* (Halifax: Fernwood, 2008); Edward J. Hedican, *Applied Anthropology in Canada: Understanding Aboriginal Issues,* 2nd ed. (Toronto: University of Toronto Press, 2008); and Heather Devine, *The People Who Own Themselves: Aboriginal Ethnogenesis in a Canadian Family, 1660-1900* (Calgary: University of Calgary Press, 2004). See also Leslie Allison Brown and Susan Strega, eds., *Research as Resistance: Critical, Indigenous, and Anti-Oppressive Approaches* (Toronto: Canadian Scholars' Press, 2012); Anthony Hart, "Indigenous Worldviews, Knowledge, and Research: The Development of an Indigenous Research Paradigm," *Journal of Indigenous Voice in Social Work* 1, 1 (2010): 1-16; John Sutton Lutz and Barbara Neis, *Making and Moving Knowledge: Interdisciplinary and Community-Based Research in a World on the Edge* (Montreal/Kingston: McGill-Queen's University Press, 2013); Maggie Walker and Chris Andersen, *Indigenous Statistics: A Quantitative Research Methodology* (Walnut Creek, CA: Left Coast Press, 2013); and Brendan Hokowhitu, Nathalie Kermoal, Chris Andersen, Anna Petersen, Michael Reilly, Isabel Altamirano-Jiménez, and Poia Rewi, *Indigenous Identity and Resistance: Researching the Diversity of Knowledge* (Dunedin: Otago University Press, 2010).

## CHAPTER 7: BUSINESS AND ENTREPRENEURSHIP

On the broad contours of Aboriginal employment and government dependence, see Daniel Francis, *The Imaginary Indian: Images of the Indian in Canadian Culture* (Vancouver: Arsenal Pulp Press, 1992); John Lutz, *Makúk: A New History of Aboriginal-White Relations* (Vancouver: UBC Press, 2009); and Hugh Shewell, *"Enough to Keep Them Alive": Indian Welfare in Canada, 1873-1965* (Toronto: University of Toronto Press, 2004). Statistics on Aboriginal employment rates and income and welfare dependency come from Statistics Canada, Canada Yearbook 2011, 11-4-2-X, "Aboriginal Peoples"; Aboriginal Affairs and Northern Development Canada (AANDC), "Fact Sheet – 2011 National Household Survey Aboriginal Demographics, Educational Attainment and Labour Market Outcomes," available online; AANDC, "Aboriginal Income Disparity in Canada," available online;

Employment and Social Development Canada, "Aboriginal Labour Market Bulletin: Spring 2013," available online; and Daniel Wilson and David Macdonald, "The Income Gap between Aboriginal Peoples and the Rest of Canada," Canadian Centre for Policy Alternatives, 2010. Another study of value is Margaret Little, *If I Had a Hammer: Retraining That Really Works* (Vancouver: UBC Press, 2005).

Statistics on start-up rates and Aboriginal business owners are from Canadian Council for Aboriginal Business, *Promise and Prosperity: The Aboriginal Business Survey* (2011). There has been a great deal of scholarship on Aboriginal economic and business development. A good place to start is Stephen Cornell et al., *The State of Native Nations: Conditions under US Policies of Self-Determination* (New York: Oxford University Press, 2007). See also Alison Johnston, *Is the Sacred for Sale? Tourism and Indigenous Peoples* (Vancouver: UBC Press, 2005); Robert Mcpherson, *New Owners in Their Own Land: Minerals and Inuit Land Claims* (Calgary: University of Calgary Press, 2003); Paul Nadasdy, *Hunters and Bureaucrats: Power, Knowledge, and Aboriginal-State Relations in the Southwest Yukon* (Vancouver: UBC Press, 2003); Colin Scott, *Aboriginal Autonomy and Development in Northern Quebec and Labrador* (Vancouver: UBC Press, 2001); William Wonders, *Canada's Changing North* (Montreal/ Kingston: McGill-Queen's University Press, 2003); and Wanda Wuttunee, *Living Rhythms: Lessons in Aboriginal Economic Resilience and Vision* (Montreal/Kingston: McGill-Queen's University Press, 2004).

For studies that explore the line between Indigenous rights and economic development, see Jim Poling, *Smoke Signals: The Native Takeback of North America's Tobacco Industry* (Toronto: Dundurn Press, 2013); Anna Willow, *Strong Hearts, Native Lands: Anti-Clearcutting Activism at Grassy Narrow First Nation* (Winnipeg: University of Manitoba Press, 2012); Kenichi Matsui, *Native Peoples and War Rights: Irrigation, Dams, and the Law in Western Canada* (Montreal/Kingston: McGill-Queen's University Press, 2009); Hans Carlson, *Home Is the Hunter: The James Bay Cree and Their Land* (Vancouver: UBC Press, 2008); Thibault Martin and Steven M. Hoffman, eds., *Power Struggles: Hydro Development and First Nations in Manitoba and Quebec* (Winnipeg: University of Manitoba Press, 2008); and Peter Kulchyski, *The Red Indians: Aboriginal Resistance to Capitalism, Then and Now* (Winnipeg: Arbeiter Ring, 2007). For the evolution of the social economy in Aboriginal communities, see Lou Hammond Ketilson, Ian Macpherson, and University of Saskatchewan for the Study of Co-operatives, *A Report on Aboriginal Co-operatives in Canada: Current Situation and Potential for Growth* (Saskatoon: Centre for the Study of Co-operatives, University of Saskatchewan, 2001); Isobel M. Findlay, James Popham, Patrick Ince, and Sarah Takahashi, "Through the Eyes of Women: What a Co-operative Can Mean in Supporting Women during Confinement and Integration," Research Report, Centre for the Study of Co-operatives, University of Saskatchewan, 2013; Dwayne Pattison and Isobel M. Findlay, "Self-Determination in Action: The Entrepreneurship of the Northern Saskatchewan Trappers Association Co-operative," Research Report, Centre for the Study of Co-operatives, University of Saskatchewan, 2010; Lou Hammond Ketilson and Kimberly Brown, *Financing Aboriginal Enterprise Development: The Potential of Using Co-operative Models,* Occasional Paper, Centre for the Study of Co-operatives, University of Saskatchewan, 2009; and El Bachir Belhadji, *Socio-Economic Profile of Aboriginal Co-operatives in Canada* (Ottawa: Co-operatives Secretariat, 2001).

For discussions and debates on pipelines and resource development, see the series of reports by the Macdonald-Laurier Institute, including Ken Coates and Dwight Newman, *The End Is Not Nigh: Reason over Alarmism in Analysing the Tsilhqot'in Decision,* September 2014; Dwight Newman, *The Rule and Role of Law: The Duty to Consult – Aboriginal Communities and the Canadian Natural Resource Sector,* May 2014; Ken Coates and Greg Poelzer, *An Unfinished Nation: Completing the Devolution Revolution in Canada's North,* April 2014; Brian Lee Crowley and Ken Coates, *New Beginnings: How Canada's Natural Resource Wealth Could Re-shape Relations with Aboriginal People,* May 2013; Douglas Bland, *Canada and the First Nations: Cooperation or Conflict?,* May 2013; and Brian Lee Crowley and Ken Coates, *The Way Out: New Thinking about Aboriginal Engagement and Energy Infrastructure to the West Coast,* May 2013.

Casinos and gaming are discussed in Yale Belanger, *Gambling with the Future: The Evolution of Aboriginal Gaming in Canada* (Saskatoon: Purich Publishing, 2006); Yale Deron Belanger, ed., *First Nations Gaming in Canada* (Winnipeg: University of Manitoba Press, 2011) and "First Nations Gaming as a Self-Government Imperative: Ensuring the Health of First Nations Problem Gamblers," *International Journal of Canadian Studies* 41 (2010): 13-36. See also Robert B. Anderson, Léo-Paul Dana, and Teresa E. Dana, "Indigenous Land Rights, Entrepreneurship, and Economic Development in Canada: 'Opting-In' to the Global Economy," *Journal of World Business* 41, 1 (2006): 45-55. Opportunities for urban reserves are examined in Evelyn Peters, *Urban Reserves* (Vancouver: National Centre for First Nations Governance, 2007). See also Josh Brandon and Evelyn Peters, *Moving to the City: Housing and Aboriginal Migration to Winnipeg* (Winnipeg: Canadian Centre for Policy Alternatives, 2014); Evelyn Peters, "Aboriginal Peoples in Urban Areas," in *Urban Canada: Sociological Perspectives*, ed. Harry H. Hiller (Don Mills, ON: Oxford University Press, 2013), 188-211; Evelyn Peters and Chris Andersen, eds., *Indigenous in the City: Contemporary Identities and Cultural Innovation* (Vancouver: UBC Press, 2013); and Evelyn Peters, ed., *Urban Aboriginal Policy Making in Canadian Municipalities* (Kingston/Montreal: McGill-Queen's University Press, 2011).

## CHAPTER 8: GOVERNANCE AND CIVIC ENGAGEMENT

On the concept of social capital, see Robert D. Putnam, *Bowling Alone: The Collapse and Revival of American Community* (New York: Simon and Schuster, 2000). On women, community, and civic engagement, see Kim Anderson and Bonita Lawrence, *Strong Women Stories: Native Vision and Community Survival* (Toronto: Sumach Press, 2003); Grace Oullette, *The Fourth World: An Indigenous Perspective on Feminism and Aboriginal Women's Activism* (Halifax: Fernwood Publishing, 2002); and Carolyn Kenny and Tina Ngaroimata Fraser, *Living Indigenous Leadership: Native Narratives on Building Strong Communities* (Vancouver: UBC Press, 2012). See also Theresa Lynn Petray, "Protest 2.0: Online Interactions and Aboriginal Activists," *Media Culture Society* 33, 6 (2011): 923-40; Howard Ramos, "Opportunity for Whom? Political Opportunity and Critical Events in Canadian Aboriginal Mobilization, 1951–2000," *Social Forces* 87, 2 (2008): 795-823, and "What Causes Canadian Aboriginal Protest? Examining Resources, Opportunities and Identity,

1951-2000," *Canadian Journal of Sociology* 31, 2 (2006): 211-34; Joanne Barker, "Gender, Sovereignty, and the Discourse of Rights in Native Women's Activism," *Meridians: Feminism, Race, Transnationalism* 7, 1 (2006): 127-61; and Rima Wilkes, "The Protest Actions of Indigenous Peoples: A Canadian-U.S. Comparison of Social Movement Emergence," *American Behavioral Scientist* 50, 4 (2006): 510-25. On the Idle No More movement, see Ken Coates, *#Idle No More* (Regina: University of Regina Press, 2015).

Lorna Roth discusses Aboriginal people and media in *Something New in the Air: The Story of First Peoples Television Broadcasting in Canada* (Montreal/Kingston: McGill-Queen's University Press, 2005). See also Mary Jane Miller, *Outside Looking In: Viewing First Nations Peoples in Canadian Dramatic Television Series* (Montreal/Kingston: McGill-Queen's University Press, 2008), and Helen Molnar and Michael Meadows, *Songlines and Satellites: Indigenous Communication in Australia, the South Pacific, and Canada* (Halifax: Fernwood, 2002).

The following books and articles highlight success stories in the realms of self-government, self-administration, and co-management: Peter Kulchyski, *Like the Sound of a Drum: Aboriginal Cultural Politics in Denendeh and Nunavut* (Winnipeg: University of Manitoba Press, 2005); Dan Russell. *A People's Dream: Aboriginal Self-Government in Canada* (Vancouver: UBC Press, 2011); André Légaré, "Canada's Experiment with Aboriginal Self-Determination in Nunavut: From Vision to Illusion," *International Journal on Minority and Group Rights* 15 (2008): 335-67; and Paul Nadasdy, *Hunters and Bureaucrats: Power, Knowledge and Aboriginal-State Relations in the Southwest Yukon* (Vancouver: UBC Press, 2003). On successful land claims and agreements, see Christopher Alcantara, *Negotiating the Deal: Land Claims Agreements in Canada* (Toronto: University of Toronto Press, 2013) and John Harper, *He Moved a Mountain: The Life of Frank Calder and the Nisga'a Land Claims Accord* (Vancouver: Ronsdale Press, 2013).

Statistics on life expectancy and housing are from Statistics Canada. See online "Aboriginal Peoples in Canada in 2006: Inuit, Métis and First Nations, 2006 Census"; "Aboriginal Peoples in Canada: First Nations People, Métis and Inuit," National Household Survey, 2011, no. 99-011-X2011001; and "Life Expectancy," 39-645-X.

## CHAPTER 9: GLOBAL LESSONS

The global experience of Indigenous peoples is a large and complex subject. For an introduction to the comparative dimensions of this topic, see Ken S. Coates, *A Global History of Indigenous Peoples: Struggle and Survival* (London: Palgrave Macmillan, 2004). See also Julian Burger, *Report from the Frontier: The State of the World's Indigenous Peoples* (London: Zed, 1987); John H. Bodley, *Victims of Progress*, 6th ed. (Lanham: Rowman and Littlefield, 2014); and Jens Dahl, *Indigenous Space and Marginalized Peoples in the United Nations* (New York: Palgrave Macmillan, 2012). One of the best works of comparative contact studies is James Belich, *Replenishing the Earth: The Settler Revolution and the Rise of the Anglo-World* (Oxford: Oxford University Press, 2009).

There are many excellent books on the Māori of New Zealand. See, in particular, Claudi Orange, *The Treaty of Waitangi* (Auckland: Allen and Unwin, 1989). For an excellent introduction to Māori-Pākehā relations in New Zealand, see the impressive studies by James Belich: *Making Peoples: A History of the New Zealanders, from Polynesian Settlement to the End of the Nineteenth Century* (Honolulu: University of Hawaii Press, 1996), *Paradise Reforged: A History of the New Zealanders from the 1880s to the Year 2000* (Auckland: Penguin, 2002), and *The New Zealand Wars and the Victorian Interpretation of Racial Conflict* (Auckland: Auckland University Press, 1986). See also Vincent O'Malley and David Anderson Armstrong, *The Beating Heart: A Political and Socio-Economic History of Te Arawa* (Wellington: Huia, 2009); Vincent O'Malley, Bruce Stirling, and Wally Penetito, *The Treaty of Waitangi Companion: Māori and Pākehā from Tasman to Today* (Auckland: Auckland University Press, 2011); and Vincent O'Malley and Bryan Gilling, *The Treaty of Waitangi in New Zealand History* (Victoria: Treaty of Waitangi Research Unit, Victoria University, 2000). For an insider's view on Māori political re-emergence, see Ranginui Walker, *Ka Whawai Tonu Matou: Struggle without End* (Auckland: Penguin NZ, 1990).

There is a large scholarship on Australia's relations with Aboriginal peoples. See, in particular, the excellent work of Henry Reynolds: *The Other Side of the Frontier: Aboriginal Resistance to the European Invasion of Australia* (Ringwood: Penguin, 1981); *Frontier: Aborigines, Settlers, and Land* (Sydney: Allen and Unwin, 1987); *Dispossession: Black Australia and White Invaders* (Sydney: Allen and Unwin, 1989), *Aboriginal Sovereignty: Reflections on Race, State, and Nation* (St. Leonards: Allen and Unwin, 1996), *The Law of the Land* (Ringwood: Penguin, 2003); and *Fate of a Free People* (Ringwood: Penguin, 2004). For a provocative and critical perspective, see Keith Windschuttle, *The Fabrication of Aboriginal History*, Vol. 1, *Van Diemen's Land, 1803-1847* (Sydney: Macleay Press, 2002) and Vol. 3, *The Stolen Generations, 1881-2008* (Paddington: Macleay Press, 2009). See also Richard Broome, *Australian Aborigines: A History since 1788* (Sydney: Allen and Unwin, 2010) and Diane Austin-Broos, *A Different Inequality: The Politics of Debate about Remote Aboriginal Australia* (Sydney: Allen and Unwin, 2011).

There is less work available in English on the Sami of Scandinavia and the Indigenous peoples in Russia. Some useful works include Neil Kent, *The Sámi Peoples of the North: A Social and Cultural History* (London: Hurst, 2014); Eva Josefsen, *The Saami and the National Parliaments: Channels for Political Influence* (Geneva: Inter-Parliamentary Union, 2010); Alexia Block, *Red Ties and Residential Schools: Indigenous Siberians in a Post-Soviet State* (Philadelphia: University of Pennsylvania Press, 2003); John Zuker, *Peoples of the Tundra: Northern Siberians in the Post-Communist Transition* (Prospect Heights, IL: Waveland, 2002); and Anna Reid, *The Shamam's Coat: A Native History of Siberia* (New York: Walker and Company, 2002). For a useful comparative perspective, with strong northern European elements, see Günter Minnerup and Pia Solberg, eds., *First World, First Nations: Internal Colonialism and Indigenous Self-Determination in Northern Europe and Australia* (Brighton: Sussex Academic Press, 2011) and Henry Minde, *Indigenous Peoples: Self-Determination, Knowledge, and Indigeneity* (Chicago/Delft: University of Chicago Press/Eburon, 2008).

For some of the classic works on Native Americans in the United States, drawn from a huge field of popular and scholarly writing, see Dee Brown, *Bury My Heart at Wounded Knee* (New York: Holt, Rinehart, and Winston, 2007); Vine Deloria Jr., *Custer Died for Your Sins* (Norman: University of Oklahoma Press, 1988); Roxanne Dunbar-Ortiz, *An Indigenous Peoples' History of the United States* (Boston: Beacon, 2014); Charles C. Mann, *1491: New Revelations of the Americas before Columbus* (New York: Knopf, 2005) and *1493: Uncovering the New World Columbus Created* (New York: Knopf, 2011); Bill Bigelow, *Rethinking Columbus: The Next 500 Years* (Milwaukee, WI: Rethinking Schools, 1998); Alvin M. Josephy Jr., *Now That the Buffalo's Gone: A Study of Today's American Indians* (New York: Knopf, 1982) and *500 Nations: An Illustrated History of North American Indians* (New York: Gramercy Books, 2002). See, in particular, Francis Paul Prucha, *The Great Father: The United States Government and the American Indians* (Lincoln: University of Nebraska Press, 1986). For a theoretical approach to the subject of Indigenous-government relations, see Kevin Bruyneel, *The Third Space of Sovereignty: The Postcolonial Politics of U.S.-Indigenous Relations* (Minneapolis: University of Minnesota Press, 2007).

## CHAPTER 10: EQUALITY OF STATUS

On Canada's failure to address the recommendations of the Royal Commission, see Mary Ellen Turpel-Lafond and Jacob Desautels, "Summary of the Royal Commission on Aboriginal Peoples," http://library.lawsociety.sk.ca/inmagicgenie/documentfolder/AC1854.pdf; James P. Mulvale, "Justice and Human Rights for Aboriginal Peoples in Saskatchewan," in *Crime and Human Rights,* ed. Stephen Parmentier, Elmar G.M. Weitekamp, and Mathieu Deflem (London: Elsevier JAI, 2007), 215-38; and Peter Russell, "The Royal Commission on Aboriginal Peoples: An Exercise in Policy Education," in *Commissions of Inquiry and Policy Change: A Comparative Analysis,* ed. Gregory J. Inwood and Carolyn M. Johns (Toronto: University of Toronto Press, 2014), 154-71. For critiques of the Royal Commission, particularly its limited scope, see Chris Andersen and Claude Denis, "Urban Native Communities and the Nation: Before and After the Royal Commission on Aboriginal Peoples," *Canadian Review of Sociology and Anthropology* 40, 4 (2003): 373-90, and Kiera Ladner, "Negotiated Inferiority: The Royal Commission on Aboriginal People's Vision of a Renewed Relationship," *American Review of Canadian Studies* 31, 1 (2001): 241-64. In addition to Alan Cairns's discussion of the concept of citizens plus, see an informative discussion on the question of limited citizenship by David Mercer in "'Citizen Minus'? Indigenous Australians and the Citizenship Question," *Citizenship Studies* 7, 4 (2003): 421-45.

For studies that explore the Royal Commission's positive impact, see Deborah McGregor, "Aboriginal/Non-Aboriginal Relations and Sustainable Forest Management in Canada: The Influence of the Royal Commission on Aboriginal Peoples," *Journal of Environmental Management* 92, 2 (2011): 300-10, and Alexander McAuley, "Knowledge Building in an Aboriginal Context," *Canadian Journal of Learning and Technology* 35, 1 (2009), http://www.cjlt.ca/index.php/cjlt/article/view/514/244.

## CHAPTER 11: CITIZENSHIP AND A COMMONWEALTH

It is useful to examine the legal and administrative processes used by Aboriginal Affairs to determine membership. See the Government of Canada website, Aboriginal Affairs and Northern Development, "Registration, Membership and Status Cards." For a technical background, see Larry Gilbert, *Entitlement to Indian Status and Membership Codes in Canada* (Toronto: Carswell, 1996). For studies on this subject, see Assembly of First Nations/Indian and Northern Affairs, *First Nations Registration (Status) and Membership Research Report* (Ottawa: Indian and Northern Affairs, 2008); Federation of Saskatchewan Indian Nations, "First Nation Citizenship," available at www.afn.ca; Wendy Cornet, "Indian Status, Band Membership, First Nation Citizenship, Kinship, Gender, and Race: Reconsidering the Role of Federal Law," and Michelle Mann, "Indian Registration: Unrecognized and Unstated Paternity," in *Aboriginal Policy Research,* Vol. 5, *Moving Forward, Making a Difference,* ed. Jerry P. White, Susan Wingert, Dan Beavon, and Paul Maxim (Toronto: Thompson, 2007); and Ken Coates, "Being Aboriginal: The Cultural Politics of Identity, Membership and Belonging among First Nations in Canada," *Canadian Issues* 21 (Winter 1999): 23-41.

## CHAPTER 12: ABORIGINAL SELF-GOVERNMENT

On Aboriginal self-government and the Nisga'a agreement as a third order of government, see Dan Russell *A People's Dream: Aboriginal Self-Government in Canada* (Vancouver: UBC Press, 2000). For de Tocqueville's arguments regarding local government and democracy, see Richard Swedberg's *Tocqueville's Political Economy* (Princeton: Princeton University Press, 2009); Cheryl Welch, *The Cambridge Companion to Tocqueville* (Cambridge: Cambridge University Press, 2006); and James T. Schleifer, *The Chicago Companion to Tocqueville's Democracy in America* (Chicago: University of Chicago Press, 2012). For a critique of the constitutionalization of Aboriginal rights, see Thomas Flanagan, *First Nations? Second Thoughts* (Montreal/Kingston: McGill-Queen's University Press, 2008). To read more about variations in Aboriginal governance models, see Graham White, "Cultures in Collision: Traditional Knowledge and Euro-Canadian Governance Processes in Northern Land-Claims Boards," *Arctic* 59, 4 (2006): 401-14.

On off-reserve First Nations and the implications of the *Corbiere* decision on the rights of off-reserve Status Indians, see Ian Peach, *The Charter of Rights and Off-Reserve First Nations People: A Way to Fill the Public Policy Vacuum?* (Regina: Saskatchewan Institute of Public Policy, 2004). See also Sylvia Maracle, "The Eagle Has Landed: Native Women, Leadership, and Community Development," in *Gender and Women's Studies in Canada: Critical Terrain,* ed. Margaret Hobbs and Carla Rice (Toronto: Women's Press, 2013), 315-24. In addition to the Aboriginal and non-Aboriginal studies written on aspects of Aboriginal politics and reconciliation, see Yale Belanger, ed., *Aboriginal Self-Government in Canada: Current Trends and Issues,* 3rd ed. (Saskatoon: Purich Publishing, 2008). For a unique perspective on Aboriginal leadership, see Cora Voyageur, *Firekeepers of the Twenty-First Century: First Nations Women Chiefs* (Montreal/Kingston: McGill-Queen's University Press, 2008). See also Jennifer Henderson and Pauline Wakeham, eds., *Reconciling Canada: Critical Perspectives on the Culture of Redress* (Toronto: University of Toronto Press, 2012); Bonita Lawrence, *Fractured Homeland: Federal Recognition and Algonquin Identity in Ontario* (Vancouver: UBC Press: 2012); and Paul Depasquale, ed., *Natives and Settlers Now and Then: Historical Issues and Current Perspectives on Treaties and Land Claims In Canada* (Edmonton: University of Alberta Press: 2007).

For a useful community-based study, see Jo-Anne Fiske and Betty Patrick, *Cis dideen kat – When the Plumes Rise: The Way of the Lake Babine Nation* (Vancouver: UBC Press, 2000). Rick Ponting's *The Nisga'a Treaty: Polling Dynamics and Political Communication in Comparative Context* (Toronto: University of Toronto Press, 2007) is an important study of the internal dynamics of Aboriginal treaty making. On a more theoretical level, see Tim Schouls, *Shifting Boundaries: Aboriginal Identity, Pluralist Theory, and the Politics of Self-Government* (Vancouver: UBC Press, 2007). On the promise of Aboriginal autonomy, see Wayne Warry, *Unfinished Dreams: Community Healing and the Reality of Aboriginal Self-Government* (Toronto: University of Toronto Press: 1998) and John Whyte, ed., *Moving toward Justice: Legal Traditions and Aboriginal Justice* (Saskatoon: Purich Publishing, 2008). One of the best political studies is Peter Kulchyski's *Like the Sound of a Drum: Aboriginal Cultural Politics in Denendeh and Nunavut* (Winnipeg: University of Manitoba Press, 2005).

The quote "The government of Ontario has the power ..." comes from Jim Aldridge, "Self-Government: The Nisga'a Nation Approach," in British Columbia Treaty Commission, *Speaking Truth to Power III* (Vancouver: BC Treaty Commission, 2002).

## CHAPTER 13: COMMUNITY-BASED ECONOMIC WELL-BEING

For a crucial work in the field, see Stephen E. Cornell, *The Return of the Native: American Indian Political Resurgence* (New York: Oxford University Press, 1990). For a commentary on the Harvard Project's work with Aboriginal communities, see Stephen E. Cornell and Joseph P. Kalt, "Sovereignty and Nation-Building: The Development Challenge in Indian Country Today," *American Indian Culture and Research Journal* 22, 3 (1998): 187-214. See also Rachel Rose Starks, Jen McCormack, and Stephen E. Cornell, *Native Nations and U.S. Borders: Challenges to Indigenous Culture, Citizenship, and Security* (Tucson: Udall Center for Studies in Public Policy, University of Arizona, 2011); Stephen E. Cornell and Douglas Hartmann, *Ethnicity and Race: Making Identities in a Changing World* (Thousand Oaks, CA: Pine Forge Press, 2006); and Terry L. Anderson, Lee J. Alston, Bruce L. Benson, and Leonard Carlson, *Property Rights and Indian Economies* (Lanham, MD: Rowman and Littlefield, 1992). On the Arctic, see P. Whitney Lackenbauer, *The Canadian Rangers: A Living History* (Vancouver, UBC Press, 2013).

## CHAPTER 14: FINDING COMMON GROUND

For background data on government spending, see Ontario Ministry of Finance website, "2014 Ontario Budget," including Chart 1.15, "Program Spending Per Capita in 2012-2013." For historical data on government spending, see Statistics Canada's website and Mark Milke, "Ever Higher Government Spending on Canada's Aboriginals since 1947," by Centre for Aboriginal Policy Studies, December 2013. On the importance of property ownership to alleviating poverty, see Hernando de Soto, *The Mystery of Capital: Why Capitalism Triumphs in the West and Fails Everywhere Else* (New York: Basic, 2000). On the failure of "job and income" strategies, see the references to the work of Stephen Cornell in the preceding chapter. For a comprehensive statement on the emergence of developmental states, see Robert Wade, *Governing the Market: Economic Theory and the Role of Government in East Asian Industrialization* (Princeton: Princeton University Press, 2003).

# INDEX

Printed and bound in Canada by Friesens

Set in by Sero OT, Eames Century Modern,
and Baskerville by ApexCoVantage, LLC.

Copy editor: Matthew Kudelka

Proofreader: Helen Godolphin